Springer Proceedings in Business and Economics

Springer Proceedings in Business and Economics brings the most current research presented at conferences and workshops to a global readership. The series features volumes (in electronic and print formats) of selected contributions from conferences in all areas of economics, business, management, and finance. In addition to an overall evaluation by the publisher of the topical interest, scientific quality, and timeliness of each volume, each contribution is refereed to standards comparable to those of leading journals, resulting in authoritative contributions to the respective fields. Springer's production and distribution infrastructure ensures rapid publication and wide circulation of the latest developments in the most compelling and promising areas of research today.

The editorial development of volumes may be managed using Springer Nature's innovative EquinOCS, a proven online conference proceedings submission, management and review system. This system is designed to ensure an efficient timeline for your publication, making Springer Proceedings in Business and Economics the premier series to publish your workshop or conference volume.

This book series is indexed in SCOPUS.

Vikas Kumar · Evgeny Kuzmin · Wei-Bin Zhang ·
Yuliya Lavrikova
Editors

Consequences of Social Transformation for Economic Theory

Proceedings of the 2022 Euro-Asian Symposium on Economic Theory (EASET), Ekaterinburg, Russia

Springer

Editors
Vikas Kumar
Faculty of Business, Law and Social Sciences
Birmingham City University
Birmingham, UK

Wei-Bin Zhang
College of International Management
Ritsumeikan Asia Pacific University
Beppu, Oita, Japan

Evgeny Kuzmin
Department of Regional Industrial Policy and Economic Security
Institute of Economics
Ural Branch of the Russian Academy of Sciences
Ekaterinburg, Russia

Yuliya Lavrikova
Institute of Economics
Ural Branch of the Russian Academy of Sciences
Ekaterinburg, Russia

ISSN 2198-7246 ISSN 2198-7254 (electronic)
Springer Proceedings in Business and Economics
ISBN 978-3-031-27784-9 ISBN 978-3-031-27785-6 (eBook)
https://doi.org/10.1007/978-3-031-27785-6

This Springer imprint is published by the registered company Springer Nature Switzerland AG
The registered company address is: Gewerbestrasse 11, 6330 Cham, Switzerland

Contents

About the Editors

Dr. Vikas Kumar is an Associate Dean for Research, Innovation and Enterprise, Faculty of Business, Law and Social Sciences, Birmingham City University, Birmingham, UK. He serves on the editorial board of around six international journals including International Journal of Supply Chain and Operations Resilience, International Journal of Service, Economics, and Management and International Journal of Manufacturing Systems. Prof. Kumar's current research focus is on sustainable supply chain management and Supply Chain 4.0. His other research interests include supply chain improvement, short food supply chains, green supply chain, process modeling, innovation in SMEs, operations strategy and service supply chains.

Evgeny Kuzmin is a Researcher (Academic) of the Department of Regional Economic Policy and Economic Security of the Institute of Economics of the Ural Branch of the Russian Academy of Sciences. He is a reviewer of high impact international journals including Journal of Cleaner Production (Elsevier), Entrepreneurship and Sustainability Issues, etc. He has over 150 published scientific papers. Mr. Kuzmin has participated in the implementation of more than 10 research projects supported by grants from the Russian Foundation for Basic Research, the Russian Humanitarian Science Foundation, the Russian Science Foundation and the Ministry of Education and Science of Russia. His research interests are risk, uncertainty, economic crises, sustainability, public–private partnerships, investments, business planning, industrialization, industrial policy, industry markets, modeling, economic growth and development, entrepreneurship and business activity.

Dr. Wei-Bin Zhang teaches and does research at Ritsumeikan Asia Pacific University in Japan. Wei-Bin Zhang studied at the Peking University, Kyoto University and University of Umeå (Sweden), where he received his doctorate. Before coming to Ritsumeikan Asia Pacific University, he taught at the Beijing Normal University, Hong Kong University of Technology, Jönköping International Business School (Sweden), Swedish Institute for Futures Studies, Ocean University (China) and National University of Singapore. Wei-Bin Zhang is involved with 12 international academic journals editorial board members, including Journal of Financial Economic

About the Editors

Editorial: Consequences of Social Transformation for Economic Theory

Vikas Kumar, Yuliya Lavrikova, Evgeny Kuzmin, and Wei Bin Zhang

Abstract The chapter summarizes the best research from the 10th Euro-Asian Symposium on Economic Theory (EASET 2022) included in the book. The Editors evaluate the background and trends that have given impetus to the research. A brief overview of the contribution of each chapter is given, and the main conclusions of researchers in the relevant field are noted.

Keywords Economic theory · Social transformation

The modern world is characterised by uncertainty. The continuous transformation of socio-economic relations requires a permanent revision of fundamental concepts, which describe the functioning of systems, and practical approaches suitable for their regulation. Such a revision has become especially relevant considering the recent challenges.

V. Kumar
Faculty of Business, Law and Social Sciences, Birmingham City University, 15 Bartholomew Row, Birmingham B5 5JU, UK

Department of Management Studies, Graphic Era Deemed to be University, Bell Road, Clement Town, Dehradun, Uttarakhand, India

Y. Lavrikova
Institute of Economics of the Urals Branch of the Russian Academy of Sciences, 29 Moskovskaya St., 620014 Ekaterinburg, Russian Federation
e-mail: lavrikova.ug@uiec.ru

E. Kuzmin (✉)
Department of Regional Industrial Policy and Economic Security, Institute of Economics of the Urals Branch of the Russian Academy of Sciences, 29 Moskovskaya St., 620014 Ekaterinburg, Russian Federation
e-mail: kuzmin.ea@uiec.ru

W. B. Zhang
College of International Management (APM), Ritsumeikan Asia Pacific University, 1-1 Jumonjibaru, Beppu, Oita 874-8577, Japan
e-mail: wbz1@apu.ac.jp

V. Kumar et al. (eds.), *Consequences of Social Transformation for Economic Theory*, Springer Proceedings in Business and Economics,
https://doi.org/10.1007/978-3-031-27785-6_1

The global pandemic, technology development gaps, digitalisation and several other factors indicate new threats to sustainable development, especially to the sustainability of the economy. In particular, labour markets, which were not ready for the demand for new specialists, took a hit. In the context of growing inequality, population ageing, employment and education challenges, changes in consumer behaviour led to a distortion in the production structure. This clearly demonstrates that ensuring economic growth and overall sustainability should be discussed in relation to social determinants. Thus, examining the nature of social changes and their impact on the economic system is necessary. Analysis of social challenges allows adjusting the economic research methodology in order to determine transformation patterns and find effective ways to overcome crises.

The 10th Euro-Asian Symposium on Economic Theory (EASET 2022), which was held on June 29–30, 2022, at the Institute of Economics of the Ural Branch of the Russian Academy of Sciences (Ekaterinburg, Russia), discussed urgent issues of modern economic theory in conditions of instability and uncertainty. This year, the conference's key theme was assessing the viability of economic theories. EASET 2022 became a platform for its participants to present their vision of the ongoing socio-economic transformation and describe new patterns and trends. The discussion focused on the verification of assumptions and research hypotheses using the parameters of order and chaos.

This book presents the best scientific studies of the conference. What conclusions are the main conclusions?

- The economic sustainability of countries depends on several inherited and acquired determinants. Countries greatly differ regarding the amount and level of these determinants, while their composition can be unique and specific. The factors most contributing to economic sustainability are the industry and research and development (R&D) potential, production capacity reserves and the predominance of the large business segment with state participation. These factors can reduce the impact of economic shocks.
- The dynamic succession of economic recession and growth periods emphasises the need to revise models presented in the theory of cycles. The researchers pay particular attention to the business cycle models of Goodwin, Kalecki and Kaldor, a brief description of dynamic stochastic general equilibrium vector and autoregression models. Based on recurrence quantification analysis, recurrence plot and correlation index, a correlation structure was identified to assess the suitability of well-known business models in the current conditions. Such regular observations will be useful in expanding methods of monitoring and control in order to make appropriate managerial decisions.
- Economic growth models can be studied from different perspectives. Particular attention should be paid to the driving forces of the economy during crises. Sectoral analysis has highlighted the importance of sustainable manufacturing sectors in sustaining economic growth. During crises, representatives of such sectors strive for innovation and internationalisation. Moreover, they are characterised by the ability to adapt to customer needs.

- The relationship between social patterns, is another important aspect of economic growth models. Human capital is traditionally subject to detailed consideration. Education quality is also considered as an attribute of social influence on the economy. Many studies presented at the conference confirm that these factors affect the welfare of the population and, consequently, ensure countries' economic growth. Additionally, social patterns indirectly affect the population's life expectancy, happiness and quality of life.
- Social transformation clearly affects consumer behaviour. Collective decision-making plays an important role in regulating consumer preferences. Nowadays, social media trends often become dominant. Responsible consumption became a socially acceptable form of consumer demand in this situation. This is fundamentally changing the supply structure, accelerating the transition to a green economy, and posing certain sustainability threats. Since public incentives for green transition sometimes contradict economic efficiency arguments, it is necessary to create conditions for compromise.
- In regard to consumer equilibrium conditions, researchers came to the conclusion that utility is the fundamental criterion. Using this criterion, cardinal and ordinal approaches explain the balance of market demand and supply. Critical discussions combined these approaches, indicating that consumer equilibrium conditions in them cannot be different.
- Due to the gaps in the theory, the question of the target function of institutions and economic agents became relevant. An analysis of modern views on transaction costs clarified the nature of the institutional order. Institutions do not have the goal of minimising transaction costs: on the contrary, they are a catalyst for cost growth since the emergence of any institutional imperative leads to the rise of overall transaction costs. The resistance of economic agents against institutions comes up against an insurmountable minimum of transaction costs, determining the existence and functioning of a given institution or set of institutions. For actors striving to increase their own efficiency, it is only possible to reduce or minimise transaction costs when the improvement of the meta-production function is already limited.
- Separate case studies investigated the issues of economic security, open innovations and protection of property rights. In each case, applied problems became prerequisites for developing appropriate theoretical mechanisms to reduce or eliminate the existing barriers.
- A review of the conference papers indicates the difficulties in the further development of economic theory. The main obstacle is the lack of a conventional conclusion on various issues that have been discussed for many years. While there is a possibility of overcoming the crisis of the theory, the prospects are yet to be clearly determined. The solution is seen in synthesising the mainstream and political economy based on evolutionary genetics. To this end, fundamental research methods should be applied to develop basic categories and concepts. There is still hope that a consensus will be reached.
- The book includes the best papers from the 10th Euro-Asian Symposium on Economic Theory to introduce readers to some of the latest research in the field of

economic theory and its applied aspects. Despite the limited number of considered issues, the collection presents a general review of problem areas. The book will greatly interest to researchers, economists and financial experts, managers and entrepreneurs.

A Survey on Business Cycles: History, Theory and Empirical Findings

Giuseppe Orlando and Mario Sportelli

Abstract This work summarizes recent advances in modelling and econometrics for alternative directions in macroeconomics and cycle theories. Starting from the definition of a cycle and continuing with a historical overview, some basic nonlinear models of the business cycle are introduced. Furthermore, some dynamic stochastic models of general equilibrium (DSGE) and autoregressive models are considered. Advances are then provided in recent applications to economics such as recurrence quantification analysis and numerical tools borrowed from other scientific fields such as physics and engineering. The aim is to embolden interdisciplinary research in the direction of the study of business cycles and related control techniques to broaden the tools available to policymakers.

Keywords Business cycles · Nonlinearities in economics · DSGE models · RQA

JEL Classification C61 · E32 · E37

1 Introduction

The purpose of this paper is to embolden interdisciplinary research in the direction of the study of business cycles and related control techniques to broaden the tools available to policymakers. To do this we provide an overview of the evolution of complex dynamic theory in macroeconomics and then, to conclude, we present a concise treatment of advances in recent applications to economics such as recurrence quantification analysis and numerical tools borrowed from other scientific fields such as physics and engineering.

G. Orlando (✉)
Department of Economics and Finance, HSE University, 16 Soyuza Pechatnikov Street, St Petersburg 190121, Russia
e-mail: giuseppe.orlando@uniba.it

G. Orlando · M. Sportelli
Department of Mathematics, University of Bari, Via E. Orabona 4, 70125 Bari, Italy
e-mail: mario.sportelli@uniba.it

V. Kumar et al. (eds.), *Consequences of Social Transformation for Economic Theory*, Springer Proceedings in Business and Economics,
https://doi.org/10.1007/978-3-031-27785-6_2

With regard to the meaning of "dynamics", it is worthwhile to recall the different views on it. John Stuart Mill (1848), and later Hicks Hicks (1946), meant that "economic dynamics refers to that part of economic theory in which all quantities must be dated". Jevons (1879), followed by Wicksell (1898) and Keynes (1936), similarly to physical mechanics, by "statics" intended the relations of forces at equilibrium, versus the changes in movements towards equilibrium represented by the "dynamics". Those views were rejected by Kuznets (1930) who argued that "statics" concerns the conditions of equilibrium while "dynamics" relates to the changes leading towards equilibrium. An interesting account on the meaning of "statics" and "dynamics" in macroeconomics from a historical perspective is in Rivot and Trautwein (2020).

In the present work, by "economic dynamics" we refer to the definition given by Day (1994): dynamics in economics deals with the systematic study of changes in micro and macro-economic variables. Specifically, since we are focusing on business cycles, other aspects of economic dynamics are neglected.

The paper is organized as follows: Sect. 2 introduces the topic of nonlinear dynamics in economics which encompasses the definition of business cycles, a historical overview of the research, some well known models on business cycles such as the ones by Goodwin, Kalecky and Kaldor and, finally, a brief description of dynamic stochastic general equilibrium (DSGE) vector and autoregressions models. Section 3 describes Recurrence Quantification Analysis (RQA) which highlights the correlation structure of the observed phenomenon along with the Recurrence Plot (RP) and the RQE Correlation Index (RQCI). Section 4 describes an original setup of a Kaldor-Kalecki model on the business cycle displaying common features with real-world data. Section 5 concludes.

2 Background and Literature

Business Cycles

In the dynamics of the economic system, the alternation between recession and expansion is universally known as the business cycle. A recession consists of a decline in economic activity throughout the economy, lasting at least two quarters, and affecting employment, real GDP, real income, consumption, etc. A recession ends when the economy reaches its minimum and corresponds to the period between the minimum and the peak reached during the previous expansion. Such expansion is the norm and most recessions are short and were rare in recent periods.

When studying stock market crises in conjunction with credit and housing market, Claessens et al. (2021) adopted this classical definition and, employing Harding and Pagan (2002) algorithm, found that when "credit downturns coincide with equity price busts, their duration does not become significantly longer, but these downturns are more severe than others. If credit downturns are accompanied by financial crises, they are much longer, deeper, and more violent than other downturns (though these

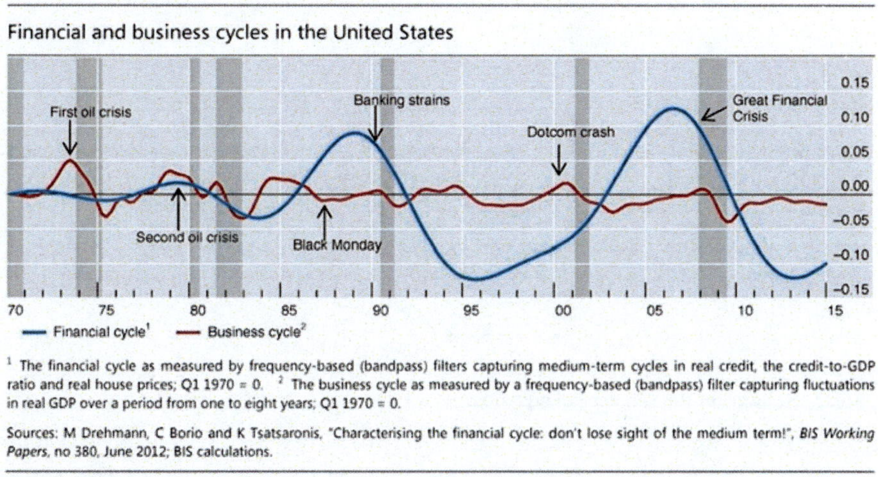

Fig. 1 BIS 85th annual report 2015

differences are not statistically significant)". Figure 1 shows how often economic and financial crises are not synchronized and that the latter is much stronger than the former.

Historical Overview

The study of the business cycle has always been at the core of classical and neoclassical inquiries in economics. However, in the past, economists did not employ mathematical formalizations to explain the ups and downs in economic activity (see, Sherman, 2014; Rosser, 2013). This implied that "logical inconsistencies could not always be avoided" (Lorenz, 1993).

Only after the Keynesian revolution Nicholas Kaldor, Michal Kalecki and Roy Harrod understood that Keynes's multiplier and Clark's (1917) acceleration principle were adequate tools to explain the business cycle. It was their mathematical approach to the business cycle that progressively made it possible to overcome the old theories.

However, it quickly became clear that their models were inadequate to describe the persistence of business cycles because they used linear differences or differential equations that were capable of generating only damped or undamped oscillations. Consequently, the main original purpose, which was the description of persistently oscillating behavior, could not be achieved.

In 1933, one of the first issues of Econometrica published a short note by the French mathematician Philip Le Corbeiller where he suggested the use of non-linear functions to describe cycles (Le Corbeiller, 1933). Referring to the van der Pol equation (e.g., see Ginoux & Letellier, 2012), Le Corbeiller hoped that economists

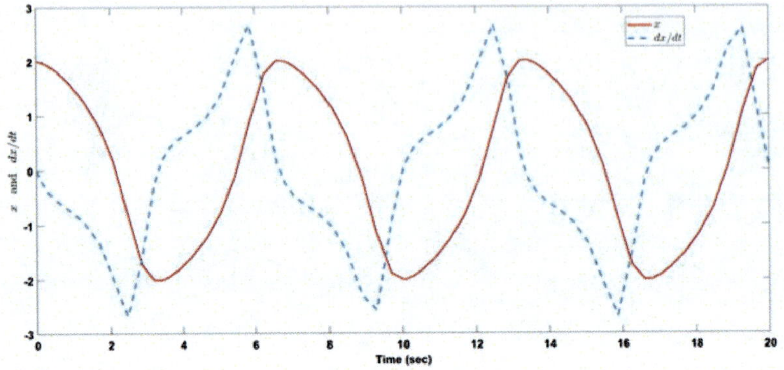

Fig. 2 Solution of the van der Pol equation, $\mu = 1$

would start using it in nonlinear models to describe business cycles. This because that equation produces cycles endogenously (see Fig. 2). However, neither Frisch nor Tinbergen and Schumpeter, the founders of the Econometric Society and its journal, gave credit to Le Corbeiller's arguments. This probably happened because Frisch, as argued by Slutzky (1937), was convinced that economic models should be stable, while cycles were generated and sustained by exogenous shocks.

Only at the beginning of the 1940s, thanks to the meeting with Le Corbeiller at Harvard University, did Richard Goodwin understand the great relevance and potential applications of nonlinear dynamics to Economics. In 1951, Goodwin published an article in Econometrica entitled "The nonlinear accelerator and persistence of business cycles" (Goodwin, 1951) showing that the interaction between accelerator and multiplier yielded a Lienard type equation (Liénard, 1928).

Since that equation can generate stable limit cycles, the persistence of oscillations seemed to well describe the fluctuations of the economic system. Although Goodwin's nonlinear accelerator model did not get much attention among contemporary scholars, it had the merit of opening Economics to the mathematical theory of dynamical systems (see, Orlando & Taglialatela, 2021b). Therefore, it represents a kind of watershed between the old and the new dynamic theory in economics.

In the 1970s, studies on deterministic chaos proliferated in pure and applied mathematics, especially after the paper by Li and Yorke (1975), where the complicated behaviour of iterated maps was investigated. In fact, in their work, Li and Yorke reconsidered a special case of the more general result previously obtained by Sharkovskij (1964), where the family of one-dimensional maps $x_{t+1} = \mathrm{F}(x_t)$ displays chaotic motions when the map has a period-3 cycle.

In 1976, the work by Li and Yorke was successfully publicized by Robert May in a paper published in Nature (May, 1976, 2004), where the Malthus hypothesis of exponential population growth was replaced by the Verhulst (1847) logistic equation $\lambda_{t+1} = \lambda_t(\alpha - \beta\lambda_t)$. . For a wide list of models using a one-dimensional map, see (Lorenz, 1993; Orlando et al., 2021a). For a specific example on the logistic map, see (Orlando & Taglialatela, 2021a; Orlando et al., 2021b).

The emergence of chaos in a one-dimensional map had great success in economics (see, Yoshida, 2021). Through a difference equation like a logistic map, a plethora of contributions appeared in the field of overlapping generation models and optimal economic growth. While the emergence of chaos may seem relatively simple in discrete time models, in contrast, a chaotic movement is very difficult to detect when time is continuous. In this case, chaos appears only when the system is described by at least three nonlinear differential equations. This is because trajectories of two-dimensional systems cannot intersect themselves and therefore only a simple dynamic motion is possible (i.e., limit cycles).

During the first half of the 1980s, economic models only featured discrete-time dynamics. In 1991, a survey of chaotic dynamics and economics by Brock and Dechert (1991) in the volume "Handbook of Mathematical Economics" mentioned as continuous-time models only the Lorenz (1963) geometric butterfly object and the Mackey and Glass (1977) attractor. Both have nothing to do with economics (for example, the MacKey–Glass attractor investigates the hematologic disorder in leukemic patients).

Only in the second half of the 1980s and in the 1990s, models generating chaotic motions in continuous time emerged in economics. For example, Chiarella and Flaschel (1996) and Chiarella et al. (2013), studied macroeconomic models of monetary growth in the Tobin and Keynes-Wicksell tradition. Their purpose was to build a framework where the non-market-clearing approach to macroeconomics led to integrated models of disequilibrium growth. Further examples are the contribution by Goodwin (1990), which is an extension of his predator–prey model, where the Rössler (1977) Rössler (1976); Letellier and Rossler (2006) attractor (which originates in chemical kinetics) is applied to account for aperiodic cycles; the non-linear version of the Metzler (1941) inventory cycle model suggested by Lorenz (1992); the formalization of Harrod's dynamics by Sportelli (2000); Piscitelli and Sportelli (2004).

In summary, there is a long debate on chaos and non-linear dynamics in economics, and even the use of these concepts has been questioned. Although stochastic modeling has proven effective, the theoretical implication is that reality is made up of exogenous randomness. The opposite view of the chaos theory is that reality is deterministic and nonlinearities are endogenous.

To the criticism that chaos theory would explain little in terms of real economics, Orlando and Della Rossa (2019) carried out an empirical test on a chaotic model specification of the Harrod's open economy showing the agreement between theoretical predictions and actual data. Similarly, Araujo and Moreira (2021) tested a Goodwin's model with capacity utilization to the US economy. Furthermore, Orlando and Zimatore (2020a) proved that reality can be represented by a chaotic model as well as a stochastic model. can do. In the same work, it was shown that a chaotic model can reproduce an extreme event such as a black swan. Further evidence can be found in (Orlando & Bufalo, 2022; Orlando, 2022; Orlando et al., 2022; Lampart et al., 2022).

Some Basic Nonlinear Business Cycle Model

In recent decades, a growing number of economists agree with the non-linear approach to the business cycle, because it better describes the complexity of the real economy. Therefore, in this section, we present an overview of three seminal models, which still act as a reference for new and more advanced theoretical works.

Wage Share-Employment Dynamics (Goodwin Model)

A relevant contribution developed by Goodwin in the late 1960s (Goodwin, 1982) was intended to describe how the Marxian class struggle could cause persistent swings in the growth rate of the economic system. That work is an economic translation of the predator–prey model originally developed by Lotka (1925) and Volterra (1931) for the study of the antagonistic growth of two populations (Anisiu, 2014; Orlando & Sportelli, 2021).

Goodwin considered an economy consisting of workers and capitalists. Workers spend all their income on consumption, while capitalists save and invest all their profits. Given the labour productivity Y/L = $a_0 \exp^{\alpha t}$ ($0 < \alpha =$ constant), the labour supply N = N_0exp{βt} (0 < β = constant) and the capital/output ratio K/Y = σ (σ = constant), Goodwin set v = the employment rate and u = the labor income share and assumed that the real wage rate ($\dot{w}$/w = −γ+) changes according to a linear Phillips curve.

The logarithmic differentiation of v and u and the necessary rearrangement yields

$$\begin{cases} \frac{\dot{v}}{v} = \left[\frac{1}{\sigma} - (\alpha + \beta)\right] - \frac{1}{\sigma}u \\ \frac{\dot{u}}{u} = (\gamma - \alpha) - \rho v \end{cases} \tag{1}$$

By setting $1/\sigma > \alpha + \beta$ the system has two equilibrium points: the origin, which is a saddle point (every trajectory approaching the equilibrium is always pushed away from it) and (v∗, u∗), which is a center of infinitely many closed orbits. The specific closed orbit the system is in depends on the initial conditions.

In this model (which is a rare example of an integrable system of nonlinear differential equations) the employment rate v serves as the prey, while the wage bill share acts as the predator. When there is no employment, the wage bill tends to zero. When the wage bill tends to zero, the employment rate increases because there are no relevant labor costs (see Figs. 3 and 4).

As mentioned by Semmler (1986) this model explains cyclical growth and was applied by Goodwin to explain the Marxian idea of the industrial reserve labor army and its role in the capitalist economy. Goodwin has the merit of representing a growing economy, while most other non-linear oscillation models refer only to a stationary economy. Moreover, Goodwin's predator–prey model "does not really model business cycles but rather long cycles. On the other hand, for a theory of long cycles, the dynamical interaction of other important variables (such as waves

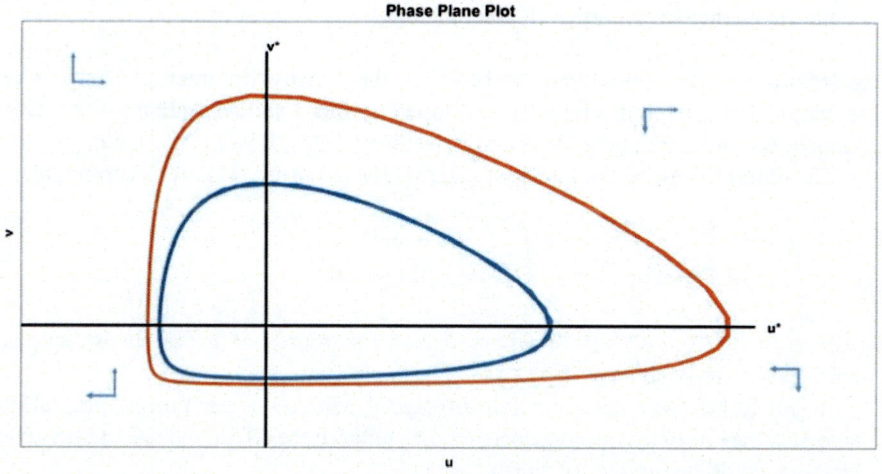

Fig. 3 Ordinate v, abscissa u. In the northwest region (low labor, high employment, share in production) the economy moves north-east (employment increases as well as the share of workers). Once the u$*$ line is crossed, the dynamics start moving southwest

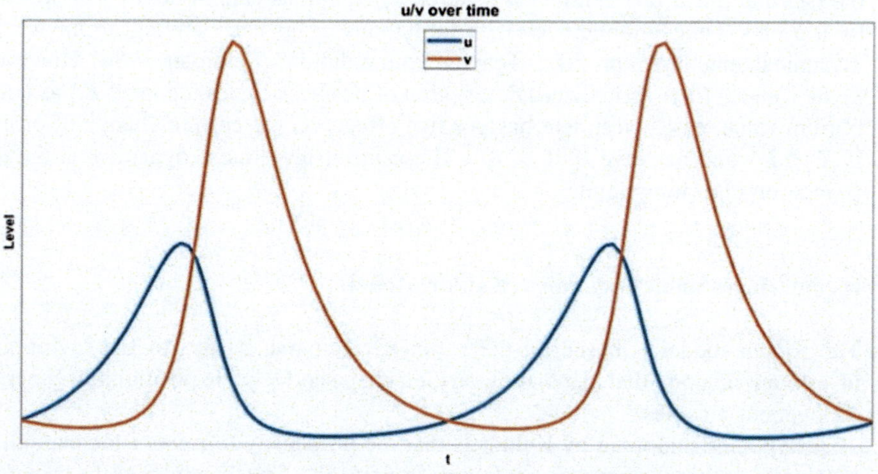

Fig. 4 Ordinate v and u, abscissa t (time). Oscillation of v and u over time

of innovations, changes of capital/output ratio, relative prices and interest rates) are unfortunately neglected" (Semmler, 1986).

As a demonstration of the long-lasting interest in the scientific debate opened by Goodwin, there is a number of recent generalizations and extensions of his model such as Fanti (2003), Yoshida and Asada (2007), Sportelli and De Cesare (2019), Haddad et al. (2020), etc. For a test to the USA economy, see (Araujo & Moreira, 2021) and for a review, see (Gonze & Ruoff, 2021).

Profit-Investment Dynamics (Kalecki Model)

Kalecki (1971) describes cycles as based on the dynamic interaction of profits and accumulation of capital originally developed by Marx and McLellan (2008). Other comparable approaches can be found in Veblen (1904), Lowe (2017), etc.

The aforementioned dynamics of capital (K) and profit (Π) are described by

$$\begin{cases} \dot{K} = \alpha\Pi \\ \dot{\Pi} = -\beta\Pi - \gamma K \end{cases} \tag{2}$$

with $\dot{K} = (I - \delta K) \gtrless 0$ where I and δK represent gross investment and depreciation, respectively.

In this model "the net increment of capital equipment per unit of time affects adversely the rate of investment decision, i.e., without the effect, the rate of investment decision would be higher" (Kalecki, 1971).

Thus, the second equation in (2) has a negative sign. The interaction between Π and $\dot{\Pi}$ implies that whilst profits derive from past investments (of profits), the accumulation of capital leads to $\dot{\Pi} < 0$ at some point. This model "depicts only a stationary economy where the capital stock remains constant in the long run. This and the fact that linear differential (or difference) equations cannot be used to produce limit cycles (i.e. economic cycle) are limitations of his early attempt to model the dynamic interaction of profits and capital accumulation" (Semmler, 1986). However, in the Kalecki (non-formalized) description of business cycles, denoted K^* as equilibrium value, past investment has positive effects on the current change of profits if $K < K^*$ and negative if $K > K^*$. These profit-investment dynamics allow the generation of turning points.

Income-Investment Dynamics (Kaldor Model)

The Kaldor model is based on the geometrical characteristics of the saving and investment function that, depending on their shape and relative positioning, generate endogenously cycles.

A hypothesis adopted by Kaldor is that the propensity to save of the capitalists (S^p) is higher than the propensity of wage earners (S^w). The dynamics of the economy are described by the following equations:

$$\begin{cases} \dot{Y}_t = \alpha(I_t - S_t) \\ \dot{K}_t = I_t - \delta K_t, \end{cases} \tag{3}$$

where the subscripts denote the macroeconomic variables income (Y), investment (I), saving (S) and capital (K) at time t. In the Eqs. (3), α is the rate at which the output responds to the excess investment I-S and δ represents the capital depreciation rate K.

Furthermore, Kaldor assumes that

$$\begin{cases} I_Y > 0, \ I_K < 0, \\ S_Y > 0, \ S_K > 0. \end{cases} \tag{4}$$

A stable equilibrium is the only income level where savings and investment are equal. When S and I are linear, there is only one equilibrium and it is stable or unstable. In the first case the model shows greater stability than what appears to be present in reality (Fig. 5), in the second case the equilibrium is unstable and the resulting income is infinite or zero (Fig. 6).

To explain the dynamics of I and S, Kaldor assumed that $I = I(Y, K)$ and $S = S(Y, K)$ are nonlinear functions of income and capital.

Kaldor's inspiration was to conceive a structure in which nonlinear functions move dynamically. Figure 7 illustrates that the curves $I(Y)$ and $S(Y)$ cross at three

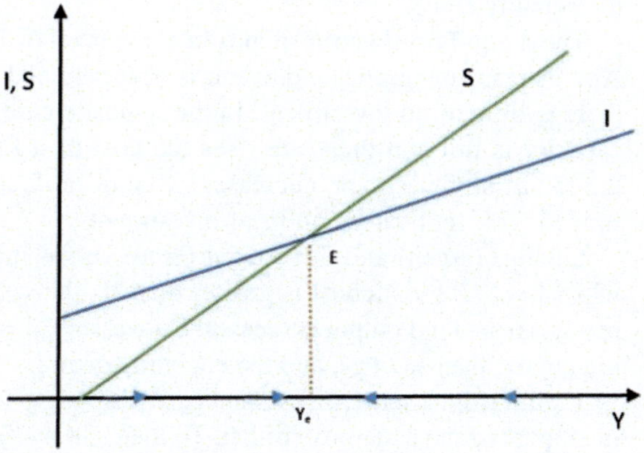

Fig. 5 Ordinate S and Y, abscissa t (time)

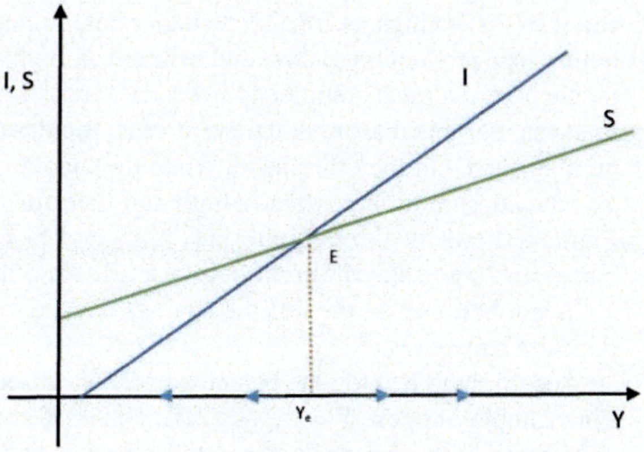

Fig. 6 Savings (green) and investment (blue) versus income (abscissa). Stable equilibrium

Fig. 7 Savings (green) and investment (blue) versus income (abscissa). Unstable equilibrium

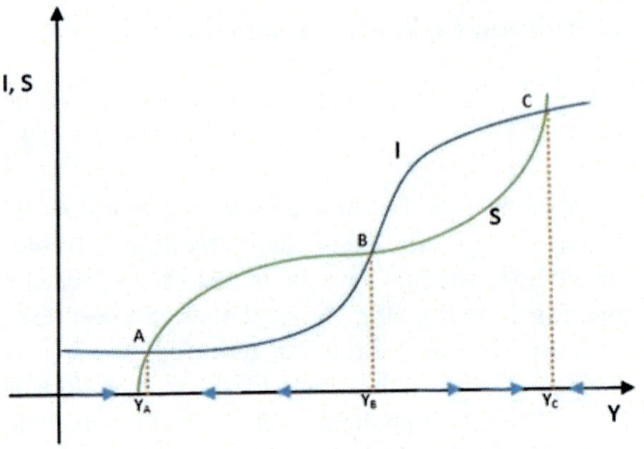

points A, B and C. These points correspond to three different equilibria defined by the equality $I = S$.

The A equilibrium corresponds to a low level of Y_A production and overcapacity. Any increase in aggregate demand is absorbed and, consequently, in this situation, there is little or no investment. In the opposite case, when $Y = Y_C$, the production capacity is full and therefore rises the cost of a further unit of capital. However, the return on investment decreases as more profitable activities have already been funded. This motivates nonlinear investments.

Savings (green) and investment (blue) versus income (abscissa). Equilibrium is when $I = S$. If the income is greater than Y_B the savings are greater than the investments, so the total output decreases. Conversely, income is less than Y_B, investments are greater than savings, and the economy grows.

Equilibrium is when investment equals savings. To the right of Y_B, the high investment pushed the economy further. To the right of Y_B, on the other hand, savings are greater than investments and the economy gradually declines.

The equilibrium exists for the level of income corresponding to the investment equal to the savings as for the savings rates, it can be assumed that they are high both when production is low and when it is high. The cause is that for $Y = Y_A$, the income is almost completely used and families have presumably exhausted their finances. For this reason, in the event of an increase in income, savings are likely to be reinstated. On the other hand, when the income is high and corresponds to $Y = Y_C$, the consumption is already high and therefore the additional income is saved. Figure 8 shows the three equilibria (Y_A, Y_B and Y_C) between investment and savings corresponding to the different output level. Note that while Y_A and Y_C are stable, Y_B is not because on the left the savings exceed investment while on the right the opposite happens.

According to Kaldor, the business cycle is caused by the accumulation of capital. For example, suppose $Y = Y_C$ and I depend on K such that $\frac{dI}{dK} < 0$. This implies that on the one hand, the stock of capital increases and on the other hand the marginal productivity of capital decreases as does the investment curve. For high levels of

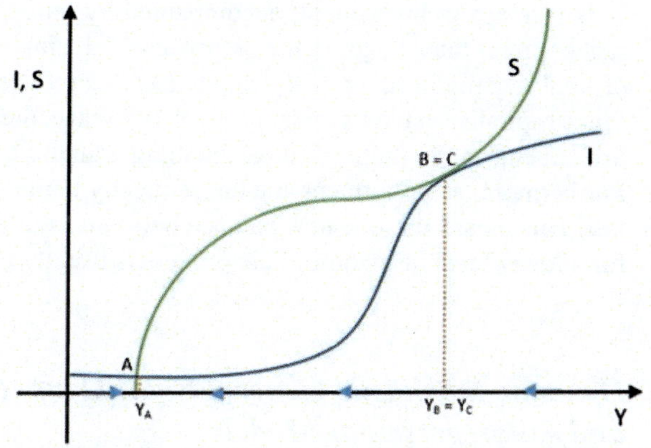

Fig. 8 Dynamic analysis of investments and savings

output, prices decrease with a positive effect on savings. This produces $\frac{dS}{dK} > 0$, which means that the savings curve shifts up.

This implies that on the one hand, the stock of capital increases and on the other hand the marginal productivity of capital decreases as does the investment curve. For high levels of output, prices decrease with a positive effect on savings.

The effect of this process is to move Y_C down and Y_B up (see Fig. 8), until the curves meet at the tangent point. On the left, the next equilibrium point is for $Y = Y_A$ which represents a severe economic downturn.

As regards the equilibrium point $Y_B = Y_C$ it can be observed that it is stable since, on the left, when $S < I$, the economy increases and on the right, when $S > I$, the output shrinks.

Due to the decline in productivity, the investment shifts downwards and the consequent reduction in price shifts savings upwards.

The special characteristics of the cyclical process just described are self-generation and dynamic adjustments of macroeconomic variables. In case the income is high, opposing dynamics keep it under control, producing a downward movement. The opposite thing happens when the income is low. In particular, the dynamics that elastically bring income down or up correspond to the shift of the two investment and savings curves and accumulation towards the reduction of capital. These events occur during the cycle and are embedded in the dynamics of the model. In terms of fiscal policy, the implication of Kaldor's model concerns the observation that the different distribution of income between capitalists and workers has effects on investment and saving. Income distribution can serve to bring the economy back into equilibrium. This aspect differentiates Kaldor's thinking from that of other contemporary economists dealing with cycle theory such as Harrod. While for Kaldor the system dynamically self-regulates and the distribution mechanism can help achieve a higher equilibrium, for Harrod a change in the investment curve triggers a cumulative process of decline (or growth) in income and production without counterweight. Finally, inflation in the Kaldor model plays an important role. In fact, when there is greater use of factors, investments generally grow and are greater than savings.

This increase in investment, accompanied by induced growth in demand, leads to higher prices than wages in the presence of full employment. This changes the share of total income in favor of the capitalists and reduces that in favor of the workers. Since capitalists have a greater propensity to save, the saving will increase more than investment, to the point of re-establishing equality between saving and investment. Furthermore, as investment and consequently demand fall, wage prices will tend to fall. This means that the new balance between saving and investing will be restored for a lower level of income. This process is usually called the "Kaldor Effect".

Dynamic Stochastic General Equilibrium (DSGE) Vector and Autoregressions Models

As a tool for analyzing how in general the entire economy evolves, stochastically and in equilibrium, dynamic stochastic general equilibrium (DSGE) models are used. Their linearized version can be expressed in form of linear vector autoregressions (VARs).

DSGE models stem from the idea of providing microeconomics foundations to econometric models. The process starts with the equilibrium conditions of a nonlinear DSGE model and it is followed by a linearization around the non-stochastic steady state. Then, the log-linearized state transition equation is found in terms of a vector of observable variables represented by a VAR whose parameters are suitably calibrated. DSGE models have been adopted by many central banks for policy analysis and forecasting: the IMF (GEM), Norges Bank (NEMO), Bank of Canada (ToTEM), the European Commission (QUEST III), European CentralBank (NAWM), Sveriges Riksbank (RAMSES), Bank of England (BEQM), the US Federal Reserve (SIGMA).

While the whole framework has provided new insights and helped in identifying the consequence of the change of a given variable (the so-called impulse response analysis), several issues need to be addressed: (a) The mapping from the DSGE to the VAR model (Giacomini, 2013), (b) The wrong microfoundations (Stiglitz, 2018), (c) The lack of regime dependent VAR specification (Mittnik & Semmler, 2012).

On the latter, Mittnik and Semmler (2012) show that a fiscal multiplier that varies according to the state of the business cycle can be modeled with a two-regime VAR. In particular, for the U.S.A. the "expansion multiplier is much higher in a regime of a low economic activity than in a regime of high activity" Mittnik and Semmler (2012). Moreover, they prove that it is size-dependent. So, multi-regime models can capture different states of business cycles and are policy-relevant. Figure 9 provides an example of a DSGE-VAR model.

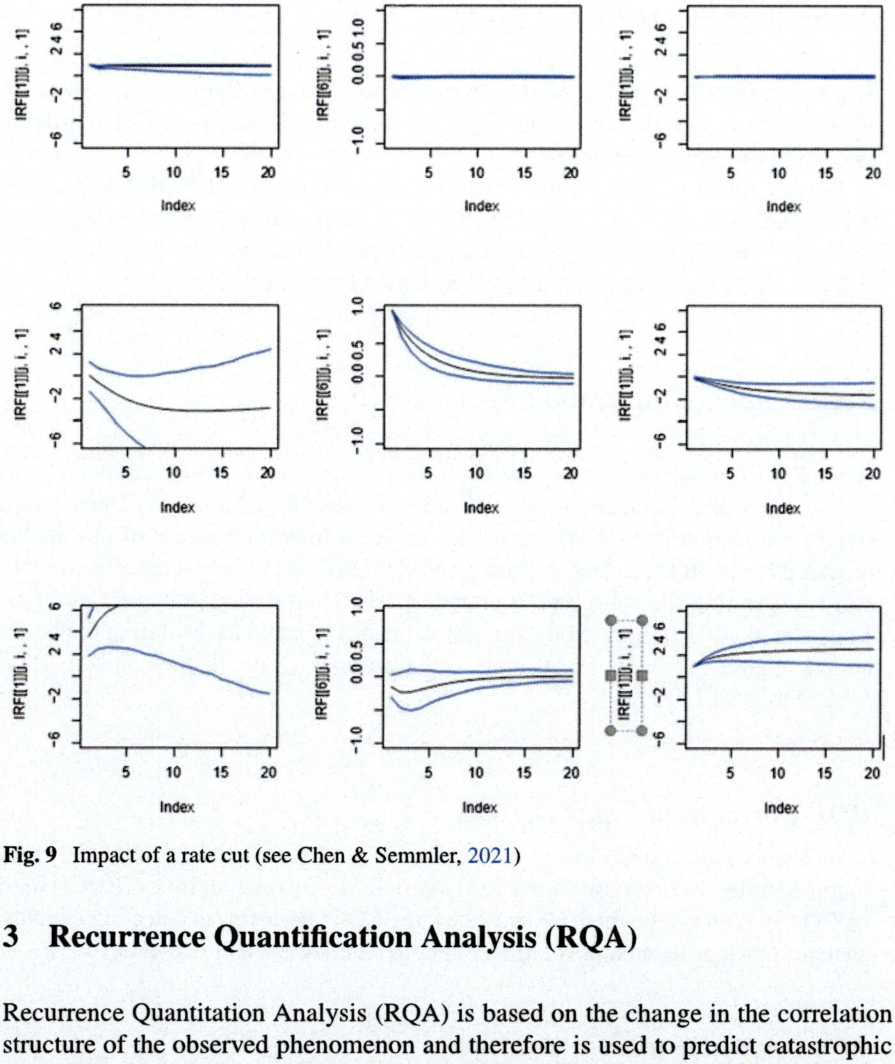

Fig. 9 Impact of a rate cut (see Chen & Semmler, 2021)

3 Recurrence Quantification Analysis (RQA)

Recurrence Quantitation Analysis (RQA) is based on the change in the correlation structure of the observed phenomenon and therefore is used to predict catastrophic changes in various systems: from geophysics (Zimatore et al., 2017) and physiology (Zimatore et al., 2011) to economy (Crowley, 2008; Orlando & Zimatore, 2021). For a brief overview, see (Orlando et al., 2021e).

Among the first applications to economics we can mention the study by Gorban et al. (2010) which demonstrates how, in the UK stock market, correlation (i.e. determinism) increases during a crisis and decreases when the market recovers. More recently, Orlando and Zimatore (2017, 2021) found that RQA and statistical techniques applied to real-world time series highlight potential indicators of structural changes in economic time series that are harbingers of downfall.

Recurrence Plot (RP)

The Recurrence Plot (RP) is also called the Distance Matrix (DM) as it is denoted as R^{u}_{ij} the distance between the vectors $\mathbf{x}_i$ and $\mathbf{x}_j$ based on Phase Space Reconstruction as defined by Eckmann et al. (1987).

For example, Fig. 10 at the top shows the historical series of US GDP % and at the bottom the relative RP. In correspondence with the grey areas that denote periods of economic recession in the USA economy, it is possible to observe the anticipations of the transitions in turbulent phases represented by vertical lines.

Recurrence Quantification Epoch (RQE)

When RQA is performed on windows/sub-intervals, rather than not on the whole time series, it is called Recurrence Quantification Epoch (RQE) analysis. Determinism (DET) and laminarity (LAM) are among the most important pieces of information provided by the RQA, in fact, A Bastos and Caiado (2011) found a reduction in DET and LAM during the sub-prime mortgage crisis. Fabretti and Ausloos (2005) and Kousik et al. (2010) reported the highest value of DET and LAM during the bullish period. Figure 11 shows an example of Recurrence Quantification Epoch (RQE) applied to USA GDP %.

RQE Correlation Index (RQCI)

In this section, we first introduce a newly built RQE Correlation Index (RQCI) based on RQA measures and, then, we show how the RQCI performs in detecting structural changes (such as mean and volatility) in both simulations and real data.

RQE Correlation Index on Test Data

As explained in (Orlando & Zimatore, 2017, 2018), it is possible to define the so-called *RQE correlation index* (RQECI) composed of the correlations of the recurrence quantification measures of the recurrence such as the aforementioned DET and LAM obtained by performing the RQE several times over a given time series.

To test if the RQECI can detect changes in a time series, we take $\varepsilon \sim \mathcal{N}(\mu, \sigma^2)$ normally distributed and simulate two signals, one not perturbed and the other perturbed (both in average and in variance) as shown in Fig. 12.

Although the RQECI on the original time series shows nothing of note (see Fig. 13), the RQECI on the perturbed time series detects 9 out of 10 changes in mean and variance (see Fig. 14).

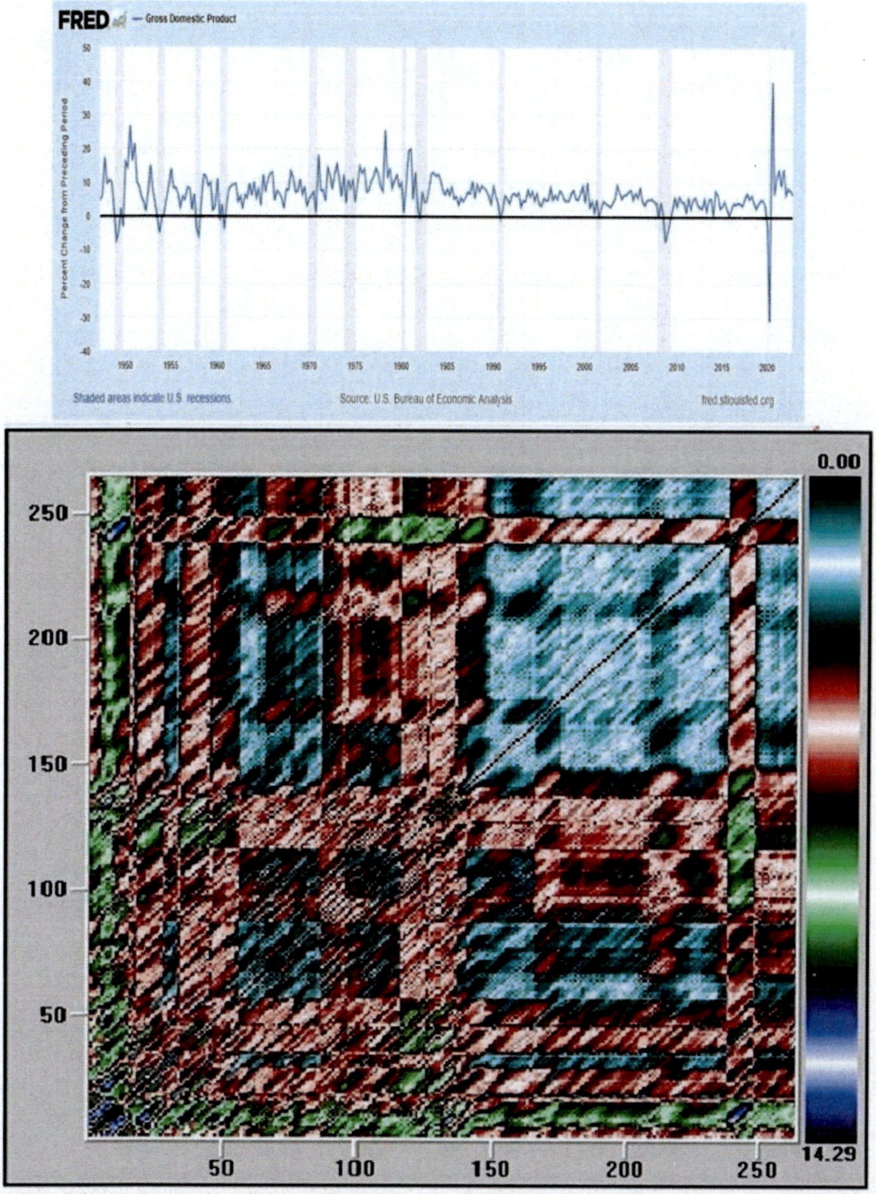

Fig. 10 Percent change of USA GDP-A191RP1Q027SBEA (above) versus the its RP (below). *Source* St. Louis Fed, Orlando and Zimatore (2017, 2021)

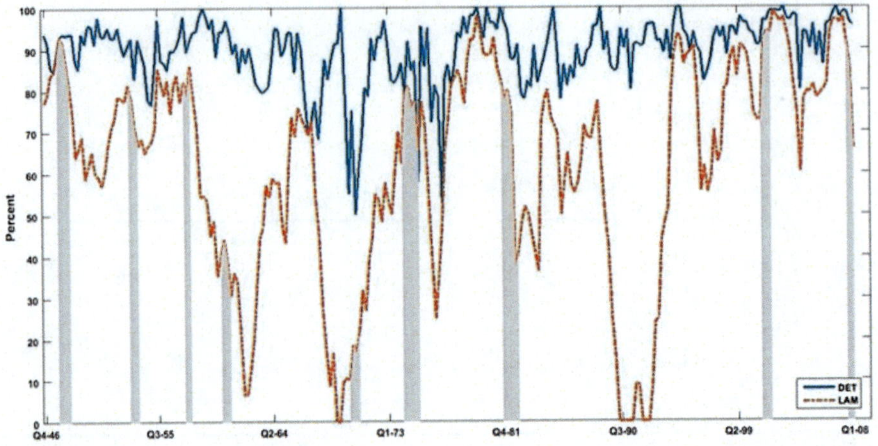

Fig. 11 RQE (i.e., dynamic RQA) with respect to laminarity (LAM) and determinism (DET) applied to the same time series as Fig. 10

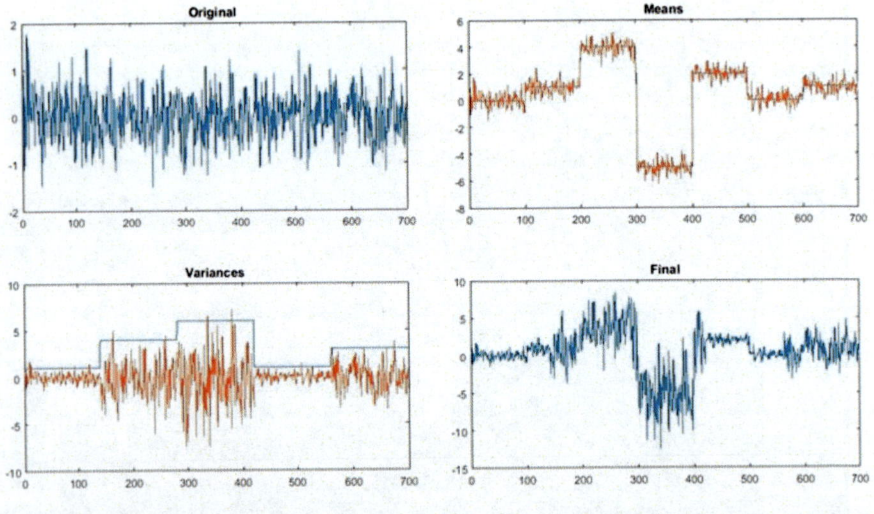

Fig. 12 Clockwise from top left: original non perturbed signal, shifts in mean, changes in variance and resulting final perturbed signal

RQE Correlation Index on Real Data

As shown in the previous paragraph, the RQECI can detect regimes' changes that are difficult to see at a glance. Therefore, the additional potential use of the index is as an early indicator in economics for recessions and market crashes, in seismology for earthquakes, etc. To show an application to economics, we have retrieved from the OECD database the USA GDP OECD (2016) and then we have run an RQE

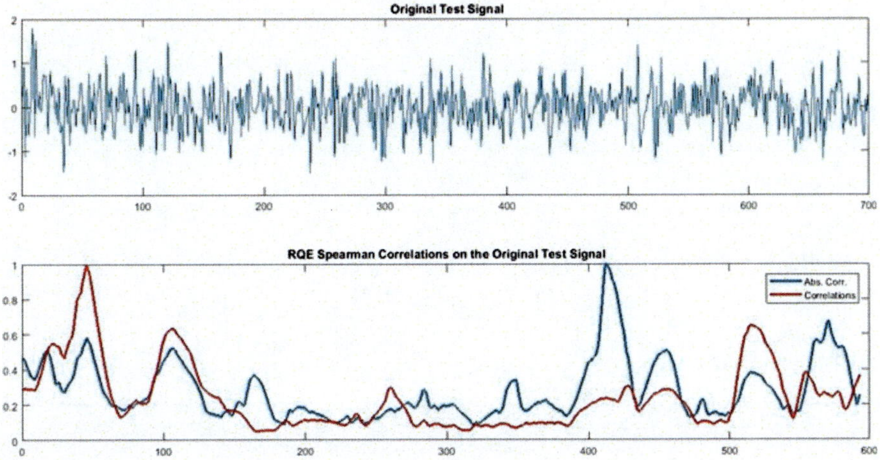

Fig. 13 Original test signal (above) and RQCI correlations (below)

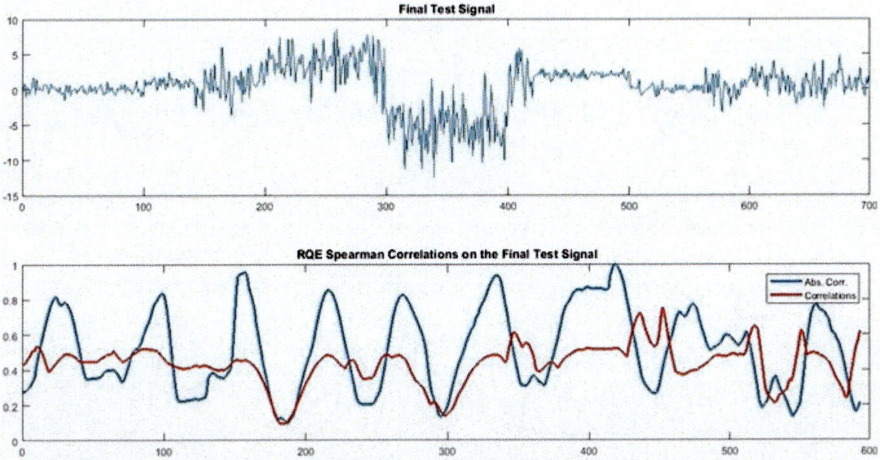

Fig. 14 Perturbed test signal (above) and RQCI correlations (below)

on the data. In the following graphs, we show first the set of RQE indicators on USA (quarterly) GDP changes as taken from OECD database Fig. 15 and second the Spearman correlation indices next to the USA GDP changes Fig. 16. Finally, by considering the correlation among RQE measures (see Fig. 11), business cycles of 5–7 years were found (which is consistent with existing literature, e.g. Prescott (1986) defines business cycles as 12–32 quarter cycles).

RQCI is performed either by considering the absolute values of the correlations (blue) or the simple Spearman correlation (red). The difference in abscissa between the top and bottom graphs is due to the windowing mechanism.

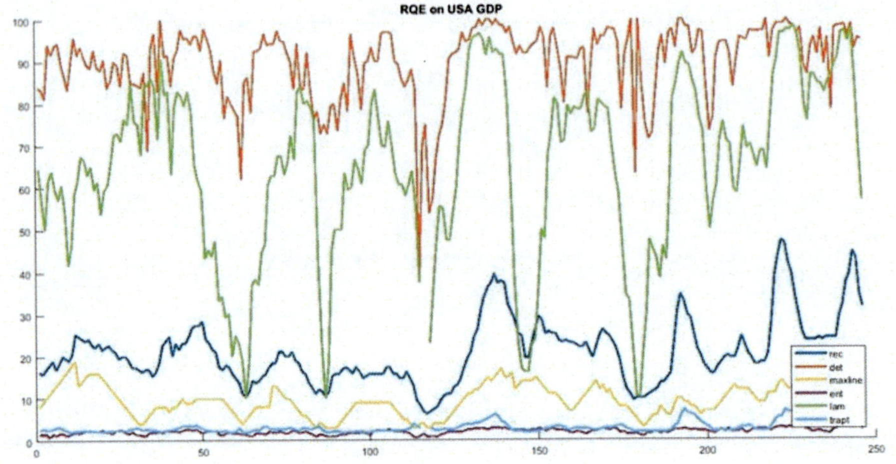

Fig. 15 RQE indicators on USA (quarterly) GDP as retrieved from OECD database ("USA QGDP TOT PC_CHGPP Q")

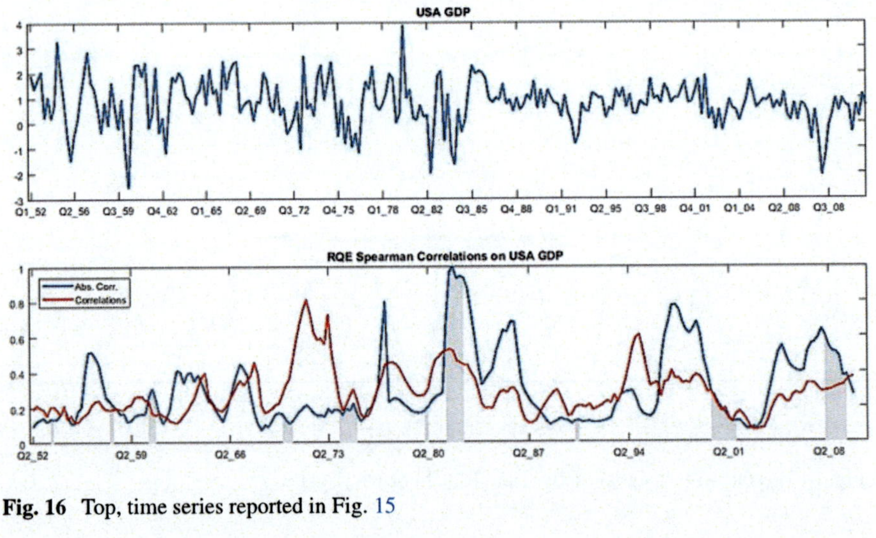

Fig. 16 Top, time series reported in Fig. 15

RQCI is performed either by considering the absolute values of the correlations (blue) or the simple Spearman correlation (red). The difference in abscissa between the top and bottom graphs is due to the windowing mechanism.

Bottom, RQECI versus recession periods (in grey). RQCI is performed either by considering the absolute values of the correlations (blue) or the simple Spearman correlation (red). A change in the RQECI is often linked to a recession. The difference in abscissa between the top and bottom graphs is due to the windowing mechanism.

4 An Original Set-Up of a Kaldor-Kalecki Model

This section describes an original setup of a Kaldor-Kalecki model on the business cycle that not only adheres to theoretical specifications but, also, displays common features with real-world data.

Forewords

As mentioned, the Kaldor business cycle model was a major departure from the traditional Keynesian concept of a multiplier accelerator to explain the main reasons for cycles in the economy.

Below, we propose a sketch of a Kaldorian-type model exhibiting chaotic dynamics by adding a delay mechanism à la Kalecki. Following Kaldor, investment and savings functions are set to be nonlinear, regular and not decreasing when income and capital grow.

One of the main objectives of the model proposed by Orlando (2016, 2018) is to study the chaotic dynamics generated not by the use of the usual arcotagent function but by a variant of the hyperbolic function.

The discretized Kaldor model is

$$\begin{cases} Y_{t+1} - Y_t = \alpha(I_t - S_t) = \alpha[I_t - (Y_t - C_t)] \\ K_{t+1} - K_t = I_t - \delta K_t \end{cases} \tag{5}$$

where $I = I(Y, K)$ and $S = S(Y, K)$ are non-linear functions of income and capital and α, δ are some parameters describing the speed of adjustment between investment and saving and the depreciation of capital, respectively (for further details, see Orlando, 2016, 2018).

Graphs: Simulations and Strange Attractor

Figures 17 and 18 show the model in Eq. (5) behavior where the only difference is a perturbation on the initial condition. These simulations show the irregular behavior of the variables over time and the sensitive dependence on the initial conditions.

Figure 19 displays a strange attractor for the considered model in Eq. (5). Note that a strange attractor is defined as an attracting set that has a fractal dimension and zero measure in the embedding phase space (see, Adachi, 1993; Orlando et al., 2021d).

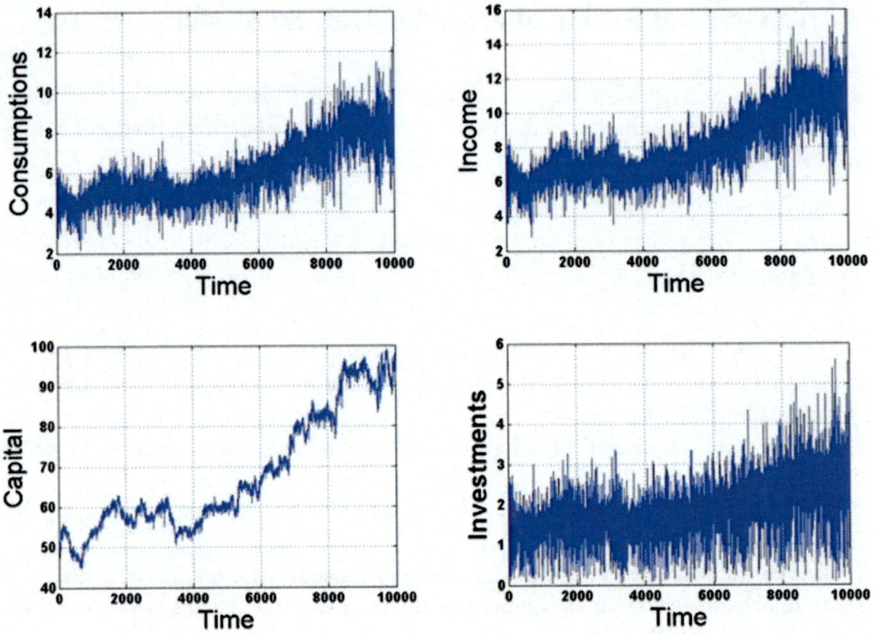

Fig. 17 Simulation of a growing economy

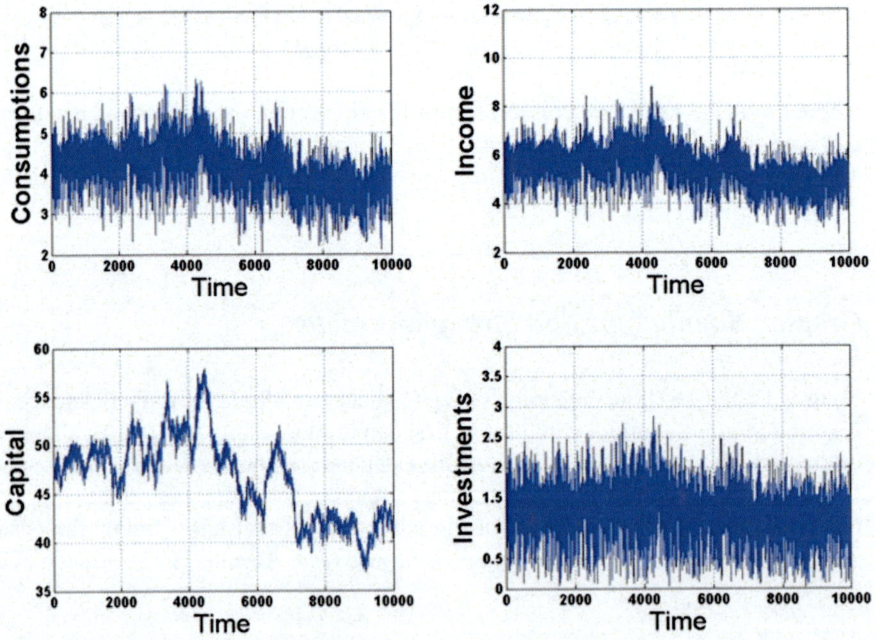

Fig. 18 Simulation of a declining economy

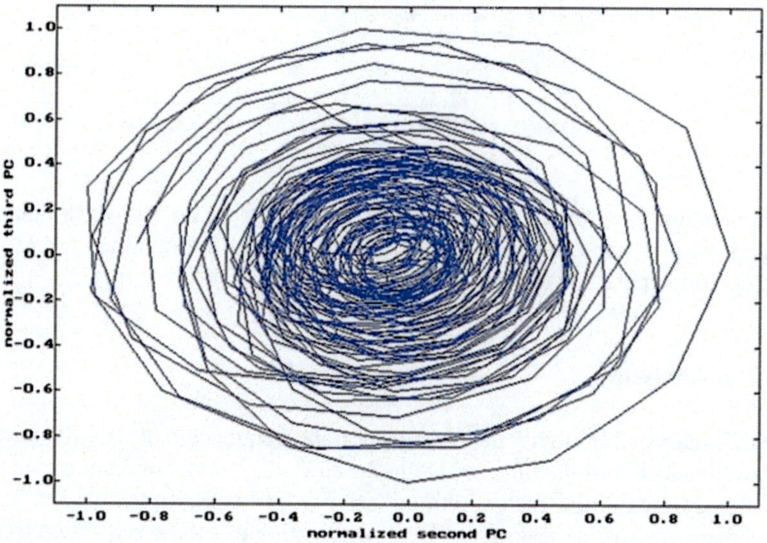

Fig. 19 Strange attractor for the system (3) obtained with RRChaos

Numerical Analysis

To better understand the nature of the system, we use some additional tools such as Lyapunov exponents, Kolmogorov entropy, spectral analysis, correlation integral and embedding dimension.

Lyapunov Exponents

Lyapunov exponents indicate the speed with which the neighbouring trajectories of a dynamic system diverge. Since dissipativity is one of the characteristics of a chaotic system, the system is said to be chaotic if its maximum Lyapunov exponent is positive (see, Orlando et al., 2021c). For the system in Eq. 3 the calculated Lyapunov exponents range from a minimum of 5.511 to a maximum of 19.64 across the four macroeconomic variables.

Correlation Integral

In Table 1 it can be observed that the correlation integral does not increase with the embedding dimension confirming that the system behaves in a stochastic way even if we know that it is deterministic by construction.

Table 1 Correlation integral versus embedding dimension

Embedding dimension (average)							
Variable	2	3	4	6	6	7	8
C	0.302	0.260	0.231	0.211	0.197	0.186	0.178

Correlation integral and embedding dimension of *C*. As shown the correlation integral is quite stable for $m = 2,..., 8$. Similar results are obtained for *K*, *I* and *Y* (see, Orlando et al., 2021a).

Spectral Analysis

Spectral analysis highlights the most important frequencies of a signal with peaks (for an advanced introduction, see Della Rossa et al., 2021). For example, in the case of the sine function the peak is unique (see Fig. 20) while in the case of a random signal there are several peaks (see Fig. 21) indicating that there is no main frequency. Thus, we can observe that the presence of different frequency peaks suggests that irregular orbits (chaos) can be identified in the model.

By applying the spectral analysis to the time series generated by the proposed model, similarly to the random signal, we can observe that the presence of multiple frequency peaks suggests the presence of chaos (see Fig. 22).

RP on Both Simulated and Real-World Data

The RP is particularly interesting also because it shows patterns that are not evident to other means of analysis. In particular, simulations can produce a time series of any length. This is especially useful to show fractal structures that (if existing in real data) are difficult to assess with certainty. Figure 23 shows the RP for both a simulation (for which fractal recurrence can be seen) of K and real capital stock. While real data span for a limited time, simulations are virtually unlimited.

Notice that the different scale between the two sub-figures displayed in Fig. 23 is because the simulation has 10,000 points versus 62 of the real-world time series. For this reason, Fig. 23b can be seen as a zoomed frame of Fig. 23a.

The Kaldor-Kalesky business cycle model described by the system (3) has been further investigated by Orlando and Zimatore (2020a, 2020b). In there, simulated data are further analyzed with nonlinear techniques such as recurrence quantification analysis, the Poincaré graph and related quantifiers. Through a comparison with real-world data, the analysis conducted provides evidence on the fractal dimension and entropy for both real data and the ones produced by the simulations. This demonstrates that the dynamics of the real and simulated economic cycle have similar characteristics and that the model can be a useful tool for simulating reality.

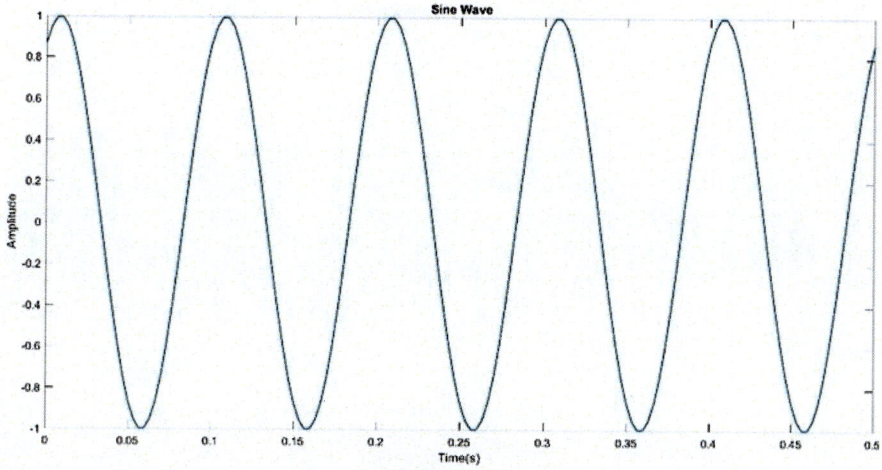

(a) Sine wave

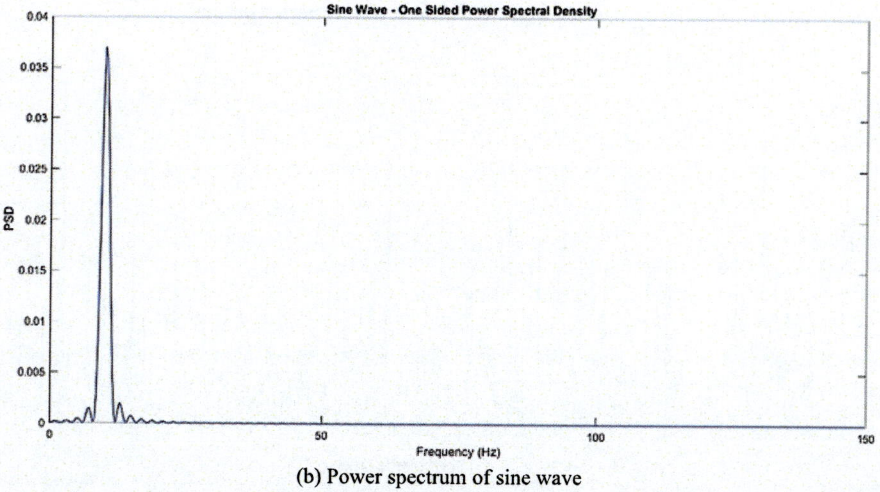

(b) Power spectrum of sine wave

Fig. 20 A sine wave signal and its power spectrum

5 Conclusion and Future Research

As mentioned by Goodwin "economists will be led, as natural scientists have been led, to seek in nonlinearities an explanation of the maintenance of oscillation". For this reason, we have studied business cycles as generated endogenously by nonlinear modeling and we have shown its chaotic behavior.

The contribution of the present work is to provide a synthesis of recent advances in modeling and econometrics for alternative directions in macroeconomics and cycle theories. This was achieved by introducing business cycles and continuing with a historical overview. Subsequently, some basic non-linear models of the business

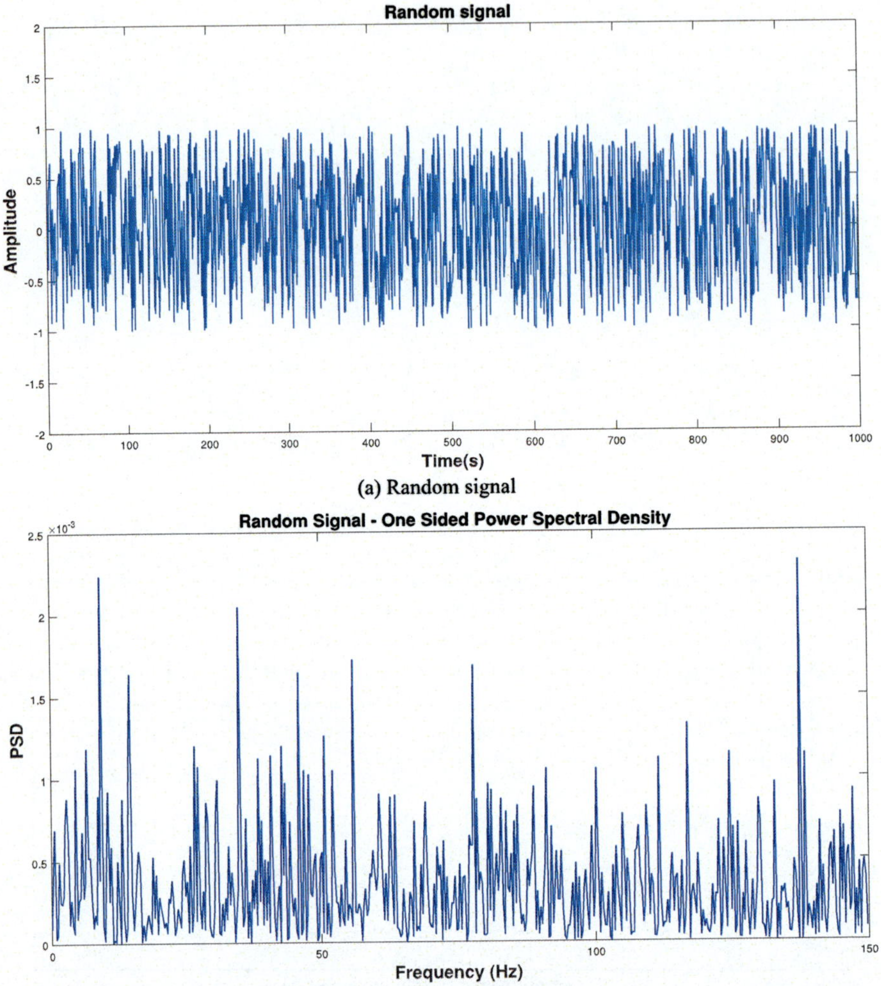

(a) Random signal

(b) Power spectrum of random signal

Fig. 21 A random signal and its power spectrum

cycle were introduced, as well as dynamic stochastic models of general equilibrium (DSGE) and autoregression models. Interdisciplinary advances such as the analysis of the quantification of recurrences and numerical tools borrowed from physics and engineering were provided along with their implementation in economics. These techniques were applied to a theoretical model to show how they can in practice help highlight common features between simulations and the real world that could be exploited by policymakers. In this regard, in terms of future research, we highlight the need to address the policy implications that a regulator or the government might set to achieve their goals. Interdisciplinary research applying chaos control theory

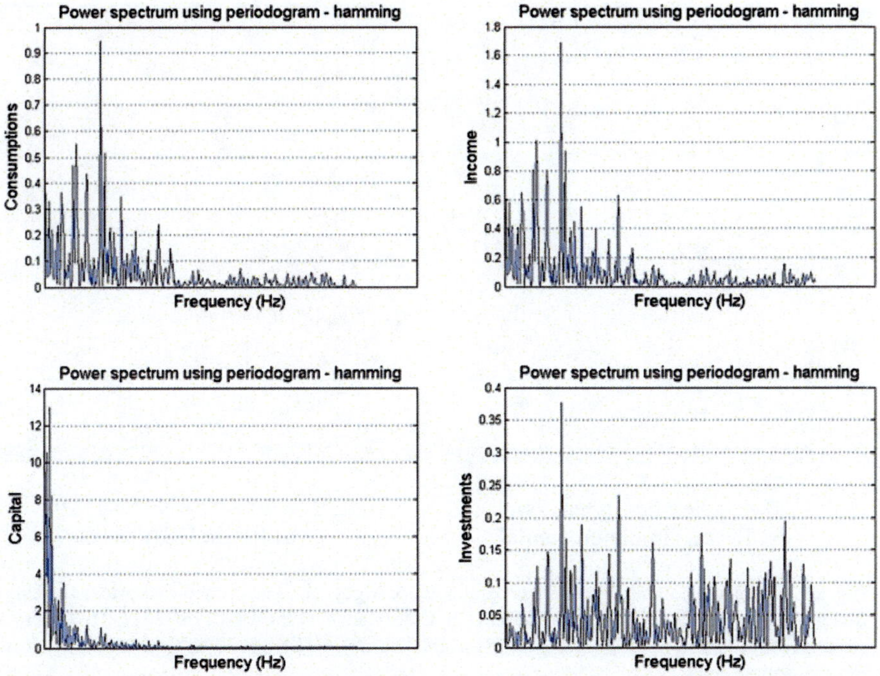

Fig. 22 Power spectrum with Hamming window

in economics (e.g., Stoop (2021)) can be of some help. Among the limitations of the present work is the lack of discussion of recent advances in weather forecasting using techniques such as ensembles (see, for example, (Taillardat et al., 2016; Buizza, 2018; Jouan et al., 2022). In fact, the aforementioned techniques could be usefully adopted to calibrate and predict nonlinear economic systems (e.g., Orlando et al. 2022).

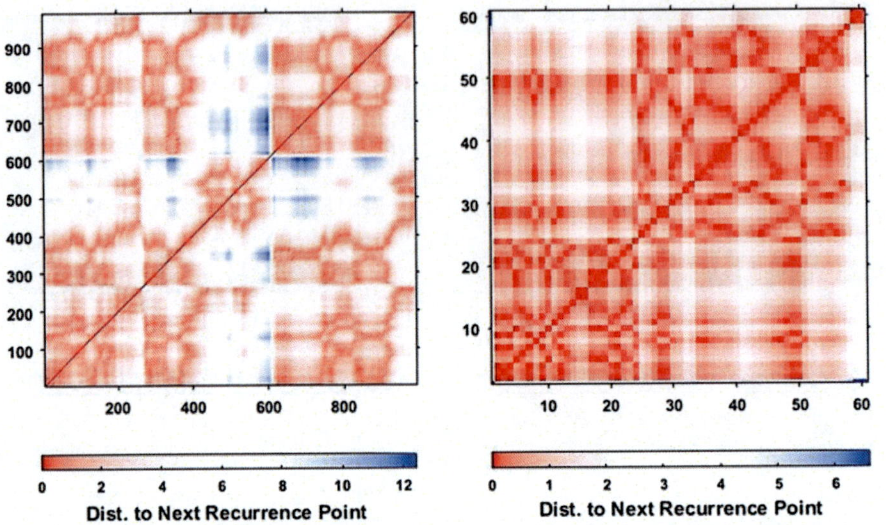

(a) RP on simulated capital (b) RP on USA capital

Fig. 23 Simulated capital (left) versus capital stock (right) at constant national prices for United States—Series ID: RKNANPUSA666NRUG. Date Range: 1950-01-01 to 2011-01-01. Fractal structures in simulations look similar to RP on real data. *Source* University of Groningen, University of California, Davis

References

Adachi, M. (1993). *Embeddings and immersions*. American Mathematical Society.

Anisiu, M.-C. (2014). Lotka, Volterra and their model. *Didáctica Mathematica, 32*, 9–17.

Araujo, R. A., & Moreira, H. N. (2021). Testing a Goodwin's model with capacity utilization to the US economy. In G. Orlando, A. Pisarchik, & R. Stoop (Eds.), *Nonlinearities in economics* (pp. 295–313). Springer.

Bastos, J., & Caiado, J. (2011). Recurrence quantification analysis of global stock. *Physica A-Statistical Mechanics and Its Applications, 390.*

Brock, W. A., & Dechert, W. D. (1991). Non-linear dynamical systems: Instability and chaos in economics. In W. Hildenbrand & H. Sonnenschein (Eds.), *Handbook of mathematical economics* (vol. 4, pp. 2209–2235).

Buizza, R. (2018). Ensemble forecasting and the need for calibration. *Statistical postprocessing of ensemble forecasts* (pp. 15–48). Elsevier.

Chen, P., & Semmler, W. (2021). Financial stress, regime switching and macrodynamics. In G. Orlando, A. N. Pisarchik, & R. Stoop (Eds.), *Nonlinearities in economics: An interdisciplinary approach to economic dynamics, growth and cycles* (pp. 315–335). Springer International Publishing.

Chiarella, C., Flaschel, P., Groh, G., & Semmler, W. (2013). *Disequilibrium, growth and labor market dynamics: Macro perspectives*. Springer Science & Business Media.

Chiarella, C., & Flaschel, P. (1996). Real and monetary cycles in models of Keynes-Wicksell type. *Journal of Economic Behavior & Organization, 30*(3), 327–351.

Claessens, S., Kose, M. A., & Terrones, M. E. (2021). Financial cycles: What? How? When? *NBER International Seminar on Macroeconomics.*

Crowley, P. M. (2008). Analyzing convergence and synchronicity of business and growth cycles in the euro area using cross recurrence plots. *The European Physical Journal Special Topics, 164*(1), 67–84.

Day, R. H. (1994). *Complex economic dynamics: An introduction to macroeconomic dynamics* (vol. 2). MIT Press.

Eckmann, J.-P., Kamphorst, S. O., & Ruelle, D. (1987). Recurrence plots of dynamical systems. *EPL (Europhysics Letters), 4*(9), 973.

Fabretti, A., & Ausloos, M. (2005). Recurrence plot and recurrence quantification analysis techniques for detecting a critical regime. examples from financial market indices. *International Journal of Modern Physics C, 16*(05), 671–706.

Fanti, L. (2003). Labour contract length, stabilisation and the growth cycle. *Rivista internazionale di scienze sociali*, pp. 1000–1024.

Giacomini, R. (2013). The relationship between DSGE and VAR models. *VAR models in macroeconomics–new developments and applications: Essays in honor of Christopher A. Sims.*

Ginoux, J.-M., & Letellier, C. (2012). Van der Pol and the history of relaxation oscillations: Toward the emergence of a concept. *Chaos: An Interdisciplinary Journal of Nonlinear Science, 22*(2), 023120.

Gonze, D., & Ruoff, P. (2021). The Goodwin oscillator and its legacy. *Acta Biotheoretica, 69*(4), 857–874.

Goodwin, R. M. (1982). A growth cycle. *essays in economic dynamics* (pp. 165–170). Palgrave Macmillan.

Goodwin, R. M. (1951). The nonlinear accelerator and the persistence of business cycles. *Econometrica: Journal of the Econometric Society*, 1–17.

Gorban, A. N., Smirnova, E. V., & Tyukina, T. A. (2010). Correlations, risk and crisis: From physiology to finance. *Physica A: Statistical Mechanics and Its Applications, 389*(16), 3193–3217.

Haddad, E. A., Cotarelli, N., Simonato, T. C., Vale, V. A., & Visentin, J. C. (2020). The grand tour: Keynes and Goodwin go to Greece. *Economic Structures, 9*(1), 1–21.

Harding, D., & Pagan, A. (2002). Dissecting the cycle: A methodological investigation. *Journal of Monetary Economics, 49*(2), 365–381.

Hicks, J. R. (1946). *Value and capital: An inquiry into some fundamental principles of economic theory.* Clarendon Press.

Jevons, W. S. (1879). *The theory of political economy.* Macmillan and Company.

Jouan, G., Cuzol, A., Monbet, V., & Monnier, G. (2022). Gaussian mixture models for clustering and calibration of ensemble weather forecasts. *Discrete and Continuous Dynamical Systems - S.* https://doi.org/10.3934/dcdss.2022037

Kalecki, M. (1971). *Selected essays on the dynamics of the capitalist economy 1933–1970.* Cambridge University Press.

Keynes, J. M. (1936). *1973, the general theory of employment, interest, and money* (vol. 7). Macmillan for the Royal Economic Society.

Kousik, G., Basabi, B., & Chowdhury, A. R. (2010). Using recurrence plot analysis to distinguish between endogenous and exogenous stock market crashes. *Physica a: Statistical Mechanics and Its Applications, 389*(9), 1874–1882.

Kuznets, S. (1930). Static and dynamic economics. *The American Economic Review, 20*(3), 426–441.

Lampart, M., Lampartová, A., & Orlando, G. (2022). On extensive dynamics of a Cournot heterogeneous model with optimal response. *Chaos: An Interdisciplinary Journal of Nonlinear Science, 32*(2), 023124.

Le Corbeiller, P. (1933). Les systèmes autoentretenus et les oscillations de relaxation. *Econometrica: Journal of the Econometric Society, 1*, 328–332.

Letellier, C., & Rossler, O. E. (2006). Rossler attractor. *Scholarpedia, 1*(10), 1721.

Li, T., & Yorke, J. A. (1975). Period three implies chaos. *American Mathematical Monthly, 82*, 985–992.

Liénard, A. (1928). Etude des oscillations entretenues. *Revue Générale De L'électricité, 26*, 901–912.

Lorenz, E. N. (1963). Deterministic nonperiodic flow. *Journal of Atmospheric Sciences, 20*, 130–141.

Lorenz, H.-W. (1992). Complex dynamics in low-dimensional continuous-time business cycle models: The Šil nikov case. *System Dynamics Review, 8*(3), 233–250.

Lorenz, H. W. (1993). *Nonlinear dynamical economics and chaotic motion*. Springer Verlag.

Lowe, A. (2017). *On economic knowledge: Toward a science of political economics*. Routledge.

Mackey, M. C., & Glass, L. (1977). Oscillation and chaos in physiological control systems. *Science, 197*(4300), 287–289.

Marx, K., & McLellan, D. (2008). *Capital: An abridged edition*. Oxford University Press.

May, R. M. (1976). Simple mathematical models with very complicated dynamics. *Nature, 261*(5560), 459–467.

May, R. M. (2004). *Simple mathematical models with very complicated dynamics*. In: B. R. Hunt, T. Y. Li, J. A. Kennedy & H. E. Nusse (Eds.), *The theory of chaotic attractors*. Springer. https://doi.org/10.1007/978-0-387-21830-4_7

Metzler, L. A. (1941). The nature and stability of inventory cycles on JSTOR. *Review of Economics and Statistics, 23*(3), 113–129.

Mill, J. S. (1848). *Principles of political economy with some of their applications to social philosophy*. John W. Parker.

Mittnik, S., & Semmler, W. (2012). Regime dependence of the fiscal multiplier. *Journal of Economic Behavior & Organization, 83*(3), 502–522.

OECD. (2016). Quarterly GDP (indicator). https://doi.org/10.1787/b86d1fc8-en

Orlando, G. (2016). A discrete mathematical model for chaotic dynamics in economics: Kaldor's model on business cycle. *Mathematics and Computers in Simulation, 125*, 83–98.

Orlando, G. (2022). Simulating heterogeneous corporate dynamics via the Rulkov map. *Structural Change and Economic Dynamics, 61*, 32–42.

Orlando, G., & Bufalo, M. (2022). Modelling bursts and chaos regularization in credit risk with a deterministic nonlinear model. *Finance Research Letters, 47*, 102599.

Orlando, G., & Della Rossa, F. (2019). An empirical test on Harrod's open economy dynamics. *Mathematics, 7*(6), 524.

Orlando, G., & Sportelli, M. (2021). Growth and cycles as a struggle: Lotka-Volterra, Goodwin and Phillips. In G. Orlando, A. Pisarchik, & R. Stoop (Eds.), *Nonlinearities in economics* (pp. 191–208). Springer.

Orlando, G., & Taglialatela, G. (2021a). An example of nonlinear dynamical system: The logistic map. In G. Orlando, A. Pisarchik, & R. Stoop (Eds.), *Nonlinearities in economics* (pp. 39–50). Springer.

Orlando, G., & Taglialatela, G. (2021b). Dynamical systems. In G. Orlando, A. N. Pisarchik, & R. Stoop (Eds.), *Nonlinearities in economics: An interdisciplinary approach to economic dynamics, growth and cycles* (pp. 13–37). Springer International Publishing.

Orlando, G., & Zimatore, G. (2017). RQA correlations on real business cycles time series. *Proceedings of the Conference on Perspectives in Nonlinear Dynamics, 2016*(1), 35–41.

Orlando, G., & Zimatore, G. (2018). Recurrence quantification analysis of business cycles. *Chaos, Solitons & Fractals, 110*, 82–94.

Orlando, G., & Zimatore, G. (2020b). Recurrence quantification analysis on a Kaldorian business cycle model. *Nonlinear Dynamics, 100*(1), 785–801.

Orlando, G., & Zimatore, G. (2021). Recurrence quantification analysis of business cycles. In G. Orlando, A. Pisarchik, & R. Stoop (Eds.), *Nonlinearities in economics* (pp. 269–282). Springer.

Orlando, G., Pisarchik, A. N., & Stoop, R. (Eds.). (2021a). *Nonlinearities in economics: An interdisciplinary approach to economic dynamics, growth and cycles*. Springer International Publishing.

Orlando, G., Stoop, R., & Taglialatela, G. (2021b). Bifurcations. In G. Orlando, A. Pisarchik, & R. Stoop (Eds.), *Nonlinearities in economics* (pp. 51–72). Springer.

Orlando, G., Stoop, R., & Taglialatela, G. (2021c). Chaos. In G. Orlando, A. Pisarchik, & R. Stoop (Eds.), *Nonlinearities in economics* (pp. 87–103). Springer.

Orlando, G., Stoop, R., & Taglialatela, G. (2021d). Embedding dimension and mutual information. In G. Orlando, A. Pisarchik, & R. Stoop (Eds.), *Nonlinearities in economics* (pp. 105–108). Springer.

Orlando, G., Zimatore, G., & Giuliani, A. (2021e). Recurrence quantification analysis: Theory and applications. In G. Orlando, A. Pisarchik, & R. Stoop (Eds.), *Nonlinearities in economics* (pp. 141–150). Springer.

Orlando, G., Bufalo, M., & Stoop, R. (2022). Financial markets' deterministic aspects modeled by a low-dimensional equation. *Science and Reports, 12*(1693), 1–13.

Orlando, G., & Zimatore, G. (2020a). Business cycle modeling between financial crises and black swans: Ornstein–Uhlenbeck stochastic process vs Kaldor deterministic chaotic model. *Chaos: An Interdisciplinary Journal of Nonlinear Science, 30*(8), 083129.

Orlando, G. (2018). *Chaotic business cycles within a Kaldor-Kalecki framework*. In: Pham, V. T., Vaidyanathan, S., Volos, C., Kapitaniak, T. (eds.). Nonlinear dynamical systems with self-excited and hidden attractors. Studies in systems, decision and control, vol. 133. Springer. https://doi.org/10.1007/978-3-319-71243-7_6

Piscitelli, L., & Sportelli, M. C. (2004). A simple growth-cycle model displaying "Sil'nikov Chaos." *Economic complexity* (Vol. 14, pp. 3–30). Emerald Group Publishing Limited.

Prescott, E. C. (1986). Theory ahead of business-cycle measurement. In *Carnegie-Rochester conference series on public policy* (vol. 25, pp. 11–44). Elsevier.

Rivot, S., & Trautwein, H.-M. (2020). Macroeconomic statics and dynamics in a historical perspective. *European Journal of the History of Economic Thought, 27*(4), 471–475.

Della Rossa, F., Guerrero, J., Orlando, G., & Taglialatela, G. (2021). Applied spectral analysis. In G. Orlando, A. Pisarchik, & R. Stoop (Eds.), *Nonlinearities in economics* (pp. 123–139). Springer.

Rosser, J. B., Jr. (2013). *A conceptual history of economic dynamics*. Madison University.

Rössler, O. E. (1976). An equation for continuous chaos. *Physics Letters A, 57*(5), 397–398.

Semmler, W. (1986). On nonlinear theories of economic cycles and the persistence of business cycles. *Mathematical Social Sciences, 12*(1), 47–76.

Sharkovskij, A. (1964). Co-existence of cycles of a continuous map of the line into itself. *Ukranian Math. Z., 16*, 61–71.

Sherman, H. J. (2014). *The business cycle: Growth and crisis under capitalism*. Princeton University Press.

Slutzky, E. (1937). The summation of random causes as the source of cyclic processes. *Econometrica: Journal of the Econometric Society, 5*(2), 105–146.

Sportelli, M. C. (2000). Dynamic complexity in a Keynesian growth-cycle model involving Harrod's instability. *Zeitschr. f. Nationalökonomie., 71*(2), 167–198.

Sportelli, M., & De Cesare, L. (2019). Fiscal policy delays and the classical growth cycle. *Applied Mathematics and Computation, 354*, 9–31.

Stiglitz, J. E. (2018). Where modern macroeconomics went wrong. *Oxford Review of Economic Policy, 34*(1–2), 70–106.

Stoop, R. (2021). *Signal processing*. In G. Orlando, A. N. Pisarchik & R. Stoop (Eds.), Nonlinearities in economics. Dynamic modeling and econometrics in economics and finance (vol. 29). Springer. https://doi.org/10.1007/978-3-030-70982-2_8

Taillardat, M., Mestre, O., Zamo, M., & Naveau, P. (2016). Calibrated ensemble forecasts using quantile regression forests and ensemble model output statistics. *Monthly Weather Review, 144*(6), 2375–2393.

Veblen, T. (1904). *The theory of business enterprise*. Charles Scribner's Sons.

Verhulst, P. (1847). Deuxième mémoire sur la loi d'accroissement de la population. *Mémoires De L'académie Royale Des Sciences, Des Lettres Et Des Beaux-Arts De Belgique, 20*, 1–32.

Wang, K., Steyn-Ross, M. L., Steyn-Ross, D. A., Wilson, M. T., Sleigh, J. W., & Shiraishi, Y. (2014). Simulations of pattern dynamics for reaction-diffusion systems via simulink. *BMC Systems Biology, 8*(1), 1–21.

Wicksell, K. (1898). *Geldzins und Güterpreise. Eine Untersuchung über die den Tauschwert des Geldes bestimmenden Ursachen. Gustav Fischer, Jena, as quoted in Laidler, D. (1991), The golden age of the quantity theory*. Princeton University Press.

Yoshida, H., & Asada, T. (2007). Dynamic analysis of policy lag in a Keynes-Goodwin model: Stability, instability, cycles and chaos. *Journal of Economic Behavior & Organization, 62*(3), 441–469.

Yoshida, H. (2021). From local bifurcations to global dynamics: Hopf systems from the applied perspective. In G. Orlando, A. N. Pisarchik, & R. Stoop (Eds.), *Nonlinearities in economics. Dynamic modeling and econometrics in economics and finance* (vol. 29). Springer. https://doi.org/10.1007/978-3-030-70982-2_5

Zimatore, G., Fetoni, A. R., Paludetti, G., Cavagnaro, M., Podda, M. V., & Troiani, D. (2011). Post-processing analysis of transient-evoked otoacoustic emissions to detect 4 khz-notch hearing impairment–a pilot study. *Medical Science Monitor: International Medical Journal of Experimental and Clinical Research, 17*(6), MT41.

Zimatore, G., Garilli, G., Poscolieri, M., Rafanelli, C., Terenzio Gizzi, F., & Lazzari, M. (2017). The remarkable coherence between two Italian far away recording stations points to a role of acoustic emissions from crustal rocks for earthquake analysis. *Chaos: An Interdisciplinary Journal of Nonlinear Science, 27*(4), 043101.

Implementation of the Evolutionary-Genetic Methodology in the Mechanisms of Synthesis of Economic Theory

Olga Brizhak, Svetlana Gladkaya, and Evgeny Martishin

Abstract The article reveals the evolutionary-genetic mechanism of the modern systemic synthesis of a number of economic theory areas, including conservative and liberal approaches, mainstream and political economy, orthodoxy and unorthodox economic theory, institutionalism and evolutionary economics, etc. The tools of the research methodology are evolutionary-genetic mechanisms, the logical-semiotic nature of economic genes and the genotype of the system, genotypic concepts and their frames, other gene categories, as well as a block-modular approach. The primary module of the economic genotype forms the "hereditary program" of the secondary module—economic concepts, logical judgments and conclusions, decision-making, as well as the main stages of the economic system evolution and economic teachings. Classical political economy forms the evolutionary foundation of modern economic theory system logics. The concepts of the value paradigm are a prerequisite for the functioning of subsequent paradigms. The secondary module is based on a logical-structural approach. The second system block is formed with the help of economic genetic mechanisms of morphogenesis, replication, transcription and translation. Stochastic factor analysis methods are used. Conservatism and liberalism are manifested in modern Keynesian and classical approaches. Theories of motivation have their genetic basis descriptors-categories. The genetic unity of economic theory directions is substantiated due to the identity of its original subject, the relations between the main spheres of economic theory.

O. Brizhak (✉)
Financial University Under the Government of the Russian Federation, 49 Leningradsky Prospekt, 125993 Moscow, Russian Federation
e-mail: brizhak71@mail.ru

S. Gladkaya
Southern Federal University, 105/42 Bolshaya Sadovaya Str, 344006 Rostov-On-Don, Russian Federation
e-mail: s-hutomer@yandex.ru

E. Martishin
South Russian State Polytechnic University, 132 Enlightenment Str, 346428 Novocherkassk, Russian Federation
e-mail: martishin@bk.ru

V. Kumar et al. (eds.), *Consequences of Social Transformation for Economic Theory*, Springer Proceedings in Business and Economics,
https://doi.org/10.1007/978-3-031-27785-6_3

Keywords Synthesis in economic theory · Evolutionary genetics
JEL Classification B10 · B41 · B52

1 Introduction

Evolutionary-genetic methodology contributes to the identification of patterns of divergence and convergence processes in the economic system, including its theories, reveals the mechanisms for the loss of previous methodological tools and the acquisition of new ones, accumulates vast experience in knowing evolutionary and genetic processes by various sciences. Evolutionary genetics in economic science as a synthetic unorthodox direction has significant heuristic potential in the development of institutional engineering, the design of the dynamics of complex self-organizing systems. Evolutionary genetics reveals the mechanisms of systemic genesis in the sense of formation and subsequent development with succession mechanisms. Therefore, it contributes to the synthesis of a number of areas in economic science—the mainstream and political economy, orthodoxy and unorthodox economic theory, institutional and evolutionary economics, new neoclassical and neo-Keynesian approaches, etc. An interdisciplinary and intra-disciplinary synthetic approach solves many problems not available to highly specialized cognition.

A successful synthesis (consensus of various theories) of economics was the Keynesian-neoclassical synthesis of the 1940s–1960s (J. Hicks, P. Samuelson, J. Tobin, F. Modigliani, etc.), which was destroyed in the 1970s in favor of neoclassics and transformed into a "new neoclassical theory" and a "new neo-Keynesian theory". These directions formed the "new neoclassical synthesis" of the 1990 and the modern mainstream. Nevertheless, the new synthesis could not solve the problems of forecasting cycles set by practice, as well as fully take into account historical, socio-cultural, institutional specifics, etc. The content of monetary policy and inflation, competition, pricing, wages and employment, closing the gap between micro- and macroeconomics, etc. In parallel were actualized the problems of the "dispute between the two Cambridge's". All this, according to many authors, points to the crisis of modern economic theory and the need for a new consensus, a "new" neoclassical synthesis and other named areas of economic science (Kirdina-Chandler, 2021; De Vroey and Duarte, 2013; Blacke and Wojcik, 2008; Grodsky, 2005; Burov, 2021; Blaug, 2002; Kollander 2010).

The evolutionary-genetic approach becomes the conceptual basis of modern system synthesis for these areas of scientific economic theories. Genology by nature—a systemic unity, an organic whole. Vernadsky wrote, "One can trace how one came from the other, and for all long centuries there was something common that remained unchanged. This general and unchanging is a scientific *method of searching*, there is a *scientific attitude* towards the surrounding" (Vernadsky, 1997).

Modern synthesis is the genetic systemic unity of conceptual paradigms of these directions. The methodology and theory of synthesis of the noted directions are important. This article reflects the results of the study, the purpose of which was to show the mechanisms of continuity in the development of economic theory, the synthesis of mainstream and classical political economy, other areas of economic theory, and the potential for practical use of the justified approach.

2 Literature Review

In modern literature on the problem under consideration, there is a convergence of number concepts of economic science areas. In the relationship of political economy and general economic theory, "there are essentially neither methodological nor theoretical grounds for their separation, both in their subject matter and composition" (Cherkovets et al., 2011). Institutionalism points to the need "not so much to develop institutionalism as such, as to synthesize certain elements of institutionalist, Marxist and post-Keynesian analysis" (Hodgson, 2003).

Kleiner wrote about the trends towards convergence of neoclassical, institutional and evolutionary theories (Kleiner, 2010), neo-institutional and post-Keynesian approaches are synthesized (Skorobagatov, 2006), the "methodological convergence" of the main trends in macroeconomics is noted (Woolford, 2010).

Samuelson's 'synthesis' consists in the reconciliation of the labor theory of value and the theory of marginal utility... Samuelson writes that most economists in the West are "trying, through effective monetary and fiscal policy, to connect Smith and Marshall's classical microeconomics with the modern macroeconomics of income level determination, combining everything healthy in both approaches" (Chereshnev et al., 2011). In the synthesis aspect, educational literature is developed (Buzgalin et al., 2019).

There are also opposite approaches to the modern synthesis of classical political economy. It is noted "a long process of emergence and development of political economic analysis and an equally long process of its extinction or, better to say, development into a more general social science" (Voeikov, 2008; 2009). Frolov writes, "The main reason for the crisis of the evolutionary economy is the exhaustion of the metaphorical potential of Darwinism (neo–Darwinism). Darwin's theory of evolution from the very beginning was and still remains the paradigmatic basis of all studies of evolutionary economists" (Frolov, 2020).

Darwinism is not the only paradigmatic basis of evolutionary economics. In economic evolutionism, there are:

(1) theories where the main role in the mechanisms of economic evolution is assigned to the processes of adaptability, selection, environment, hence the impossibility of long-term forecasting of the economy. "People ... achieve the results they need without any goal set from the outside" (Buchanan, 1994);
(2) concepts of orientation, determinism, finalism, programming of economic evolution, etc. The system "is still the result of a reasonable design (Eggertsson, 2011). Both given worldview approaches to development have existed since antiquity, when Empidocles marked the first lines of the doctrine of struggle and

selection, and Socrates, Plato and Aristotle laid the foundation for the concept of expediency and targeted development.

Scientists also criticize the modern theory of economic evolution for the pluralism of interpretations. "The evolutionary economy still does not have not only a common methodological framework and a coordinated research program, but also a coherent system of regulatory recommendations" (Frolov, 2020). At the same time, even in modern biology, one can count more than a dozen concepts of evolution. These are—symbiogenesis, not Darwin evolution, dynamics of gene networks, block-modular type of evolution, coevolution theories, others; "evolution from below—"from micro- to macro-formations, "evolution from above"—from global biosphere, biogeocenoses, ecosystems to transformation 'down' to components of the system. There are theories in which evolution is interpreted as the formation of a new, an increase in diversity, the unity of continuity and discontinuity, the accumulative process of the emergence of a new and old, self-organization, self-regulation retentions, etc. Modern economic science considers evolution from the standpoint of cybernetics methodology, game theory, communications, information transfer mechanisms, etc. Evolution is defined as "the spread of hereditary changes (mutations) to many organisms (populations)," this is—a stochastic programmed process, a kind of a population with a medium strategic games, etc. In the epigenetic concept, evolution is not associated with a change in genotypes, but on the contrary, evolution determines the change in genotypes. Many naturalists actually proceed from the synthesis of various concepts of evolutionism, avoiding 'extremes' and adhering to the consensus of basic views (synthetic theory of evolution, others). Commonality in the patterns of nature and society developments implies unified methodological research approaches. The coevolution strategy allows, "To bridge the gap between the evolutionist approach to nature and the evolutionist approach to humans, to outline the synthesis paths between evolutionism in biology and evolutionism in sociocultural sciences" (Liseev, 2004). The above review of the literature on the topic shows the relevance of the goals set by us in the article.

3 Material and Methods

As a methodological tool for evolutionary genetic research, first, the *economic genotype* (EG) is distinguished—a set of economic genes that determine the economic system. Interpretations of economic genes and genotype are presented in the literature (Mayevsky, 2005; Danilov, 2021; Riechmann, 1999), where economic genes are interpreted as semantic communications, memory images, mimes—stereotypes of behavior transmitted to generations, routines—norms, patterns of behavior transmitted in time, etc.

Our article justifies the *logical-semiotic nature* of economic genes and genotype. Semiotics is an interdisciplinary theory; it integrates the natural and human sciences, studies the patterns of information transmission through sign structures, and contributes to the transition to synthetic knowledge. You can build a 'chain' of formation of the sign structures we use in the genotype. This is a—*economic object* (denotate, spheres of production-exchange-distribution-consumption (Pr-O-R-Po) and relations between them) → denoting a *word* (sign, designate) → a *term* (a special word with significant functions (representative, communicative (informational), cognitive, symbolic, etc.). The terms are classified and systematized, i.e. organized, based on the meanings of the logical valence relationship of the Pr-Po, O-P phases, thus transforming into genotypic concepts.

Genotypic concepts are divided into primary direct mechanisms—a 'hard core' and an indirect 'protective belt'—descriptors—key structures that ensure the inheritance of denotative spheres. Direct and mediated mechanisms constitute category economic genes. Categories—more general characteristics of an object, they collect, store, transmit collective knowledge, 'deploy' and inherit the economic information of concepts. At the same time, concepts form frames—a semiotic field, a functional-semantic frame, a scenario, a model of conceptual activity, a space of organization and actions of concept mechanisms.

The study also uses a block-modular methodology that involves grouping processes with the allocation of control flow diagrams. The consistency of modules and their components lies at the base of block-modular, since modules are relatively autonomous in the functioning and evolution of an object. The EG consists of two modules: the primary—essential 'timeless' module containing the main hereditary sign information about the economic system and the secondary module—the genotypic matrix (GM) of the economic system formed by the primary module. GM is built on a *logical-structural approach*, in which the elements of the matrix are connected into a single structure through logical interactions.

In modern conditions, the need arises for the widespread use of stochastic factor analysis methods, which make it possible to take into account the influence of probabilistic and indefinite factors combinations, in contrast to tightly regulated methods of deterministic analysis. This is a correlation-regression analysis, elasticity used in our study in justifying a number of concepts, etc. The source of empirical data was statistical collections: 'Russia in Numbers' for 2010–2021.

4 Results

With the help of these methodological tools, we highlight the concepts of EG:

First. The concept of *reproduction* of Pr-Po spheres carried out through category descriptors–needs-goals-means-other elements-results (values) related to the 'double thread' of Pr-Po. All components of the concept are connected and implemented through a causal narrative and subordination discourse (hierarchy of the cohesion of semantic meanings of elements). Data from the relationship of gene categories and spheres of the reproducible concept confirm the results of using statistical methods.

Production Model—Requirements. Productive indicator (Y) 'production'—gross benefit, explaining indicator (X) 'needs,' satisfaction of needs—consumer spending of households. Statistical analysis results: Change X explains 98.13% of variability Y, correlation coefficient 0.991, elasticity coefficient 1.316. Thus, X significantly affects Y.

The reproducible concept forms mainly *conservative* forms of EG with the dominance of public institutions over economic entities (enterprises, households) (Brizhak et al., 2020). The company provides the process of reproduction by resources, consumers, institutions, etc. There are a number of theories of conservative stimulation (coercion) of the growth of Pr-Po spheres. The conservative approach primarily uses the identification of needs and the identification of motives of economic actors. This is the—theory of the 'hierarchy of needs' of A. Maslow, the acquired needs of D. McClelland, the two-factor (medium and content of work) theory of F. Herzberg, the concept of needs of K. Alderfer using Maslow's theory, 'theory X,' etc. These theories focus on the analysis of factors underlying motivation, but weakly analyze the motivation process itself. The advantage of using a conservative approach is attention to the essential side of the reproduction process, a comprehensive consideration of economic dynamics, and an emphasis on the role of structural shifts in the reproduction process. Disadvantages include excessive emphasis on the sphere of material production, etc. Theories consider a rather narrow range of factors that motivate the behavior of an economic subject (Ermolenko et al., 2019). Some theories do not always apply in the practical activities of enterprises. Ultimately, the content of the motives of the concepts of the conservative approach becomes descriptors-categories-needs-goals-means-others, elements-results (values) related to Pr-Po spheres.

Conservatism was explored in 'old' institutionalism—T. Veblen, J. Commons, W. Mitchell. New Keynesianism applies a conservative model of management.

Second. *An equilibrium* concept that ensures balance (socio-economic unity, balance, equality and justice) in the O-R spheres through category descriptors−social division of labor (sector structure), public division of owners of factors of production, relevant socio-economic groups and institutions. Relations between economic entities in the implementation of the O-R spheres imply an institutional narrative of functional relationship (communication) and discourse—coordination (harmonization, exchange of information) of subjects of these spheres in the unity of which an institutional equilibrium is formed between the subjects of these category descriptors.

Equilibrium concept model. A study of the equality in income per capita of the 20% of the poorest in Russia (Y) and the impact on them of sector wages (X). Results: Wages in mining and manufacturing, construction and trade have the greatest impact on Y in the Russian Federation. The impact of wages in industry as a whole, agriculture, services is insignificant or negative.

The equilibrium concept forms *liberal* EG, mechanisms aimed at the predominance of individual economic entities over public institutions. The liberal nature of motives, stimuli−procedural theories of motivation, S. Adams's theory of justice, Porter and Lawler's theory of the ratio of costs and results, 'Y theory,' etc. In the concept of V. Vroom, the main motive is the expected result of work, the promise of remuneration, supported by confidence in the veracity of such a promise, increases employee satisfaction. Economic functionalism is a form of 'critical positivism'. Algorithms of behavior become institutions. Motivation is an integral element of both market and state institutions. The main provisions of structuralism theory's and functional economics are combined, which contributes to the formation of motivation concepts based on a structural–functional approach. Structural functionalism represents society as an organism with the functions of its parts (Leverett & Lyon, 1920).

Neo-institutional theory is based on the principle of methodological individualism. The new classic uses the provisions of the liberal model of management.

Third. The concept of *harmonization* and *optimization* as the emergent unity of these concepts and spheres Pr-Po, O-R, as well as narrative discourses with a periodic change in the dominance of their concepts. Superposition allows conservative and liberal models, motives and incentives of management to be simultaneously in opposite states and to obtain effective results. A comprehensive theory of motivation for economic activity is being developed. Nevertheless, there is no single synthetic theory of motivation based on conservative and liberal approaches. There are no uniform approaches to developing effective methods of motivation management in domestic science. Motivation theories have to be considered mainly as hypotheses that need to be tested in the course of a practical study of the behavior of economic subjects. It is the complex application of the provisions of various theories of motivation based on category descriptors that gives the most complete idea of the structure of the motives of economic entities, allowing genotypic concepts to be realized.

Moreover, it is impossible to create a unified system of institutions formations that encourages economic actors to act equally in similar situations in different societies. Thus, the aggregate of institutions that motivates saving and investing is effective and contributes to the increase in wealth, and institutions that stimulate current consumption and do not provide confidence in the future, reduce the rate of savings, slow down economic growth, lead to poverty and therefore are ineffective. What follows is the need to increase the savings rate due to the improvement of the efficiency of institutions, which cannot be carried out without certain intervention or reform of the spheres of public life. Thus, there is a synthesis of genotypic concepts and their category genes, conservative (Keynesian) and liberal (classical) models of management.

The authors of this article conducted a survey to identify labor motives from the standpoint of conservatism and liberalism. More than 70 respondents took part in the survey, including owners of enterprises, heads of companies and organizations, managers, employees and students of Rostov-on-Don, Novocherkassk, and Moscow. The motives of consumer behavior, the production process and the sphere of labor relations were revealed. Fifty-two percent of respondents named liberal motivation as dominant in these areas. Forty-eight percent of respondents named conservative factors as the dominant motives for the highlighted areas of consumer behavior, the production process and labor relations. The survey data correspond to the substantiated theoretical approach.

A number of the state functions in the Keynesian approach—ensuring security, lawmaking, the production of public goods, etc., are conservative, subordinated (hierarchical), while institutional vertical relations in a strong civil society with developed private rights and freedoms coexist with horizontal, network, coordination institutional relations and organizational structures. The main social obligations are shifted from the state to private and market structures. The free competition market expresses liberal (classical) relations, at the same time, in this market; sellers have already been set prices to which they are subordinate. Both conservatives and liberals have much in common, advocating for private property, equality of norms and rules for economic entities, etc.

Conservatism and liberalism are manifested in the 'realist' and 'nominalist' conceptual institutional approaches of the economic system studies. In a *realistic (conservative-Keynesian)* direction, universal interconnection, uniform norms and rules are understood as dominating over individual economic entities that determine their functioning and development externally. In the *nominalist (liberal-classical)* direction, uniform system norms and rules, their interconnection—the result of the active participation of economic entities in the economic processes regulation. The EG system represents the unity of opposing models of realism and nominalism (conservatism and liberalism).

The contradiction of conservatism and liberalism is resolved by a periodic change in the stadiality and cyclicity of economic evolution. Conservatism and liberalism are realized in long cycles. The transition from one conservative long cycle to another and further to their emergent unity begins after the final cycle and the systemic crisis. Without dwelling in detail on the entire history of cycles and crises, we note, briefly, the sequence of cycles with the Great Depression. The systemic crisis of the final cycle from 1920–1921 to 1929–1933 characterizes the transition from the long cycle of the liberal economic model (from the 1880s) to the stage of conservative state regulation (Keynesian model of economics). 1958–1975—the final cycle is already characterized by the transition from the long cycle of the conservative model of state regulation to the liberal model of economics. The final cycle (1998–2007) and the 2007–2009 systemic crisis—it is connected with the transformation of the liberal (market) economy into a unity of conservative and liberal economic models. The area of liberalization is narrowing, as evidenced by the predominantly conservative policy of the US administration and other countries. There is a superposition (overlap) of the ways of conservatism and liberalism. Competition and the action of specific interests of different countries are intensifying, in contrast to the liberal model, which serves as the basis for the mechanisms of integration processes and supranational institutions (Martishin, 2020).

At the same time, EG *mutations* are possible—essential inherited genotypic changes that negatively (or positively) affect the effectiveness of systems.

Conceptualization theory methodologically occupies a 'middle' position in the evolution of the mechanisms of realism and nominalism. In the mechanisms of synthesis of mainstream, political economy, unorthodox economic theory, etc., realism initially identifies a priori the general, universals of the named directions of economic theory, which proceed from their internal unity and identity. Conceptualism implements the commonality of theoretical economic trends in epistemological models of their research. Nominalism is a single embodiment of the general in the independent existence of economic science directions.

Evolution—the accumulative process of the emergence of a new and preservation, the self-retention of the old, the ability to contain the constancy of the internal environment. Let us highlight factors and mechanisms aimed at stabilization, sustainable self-support and self-regulation of evolutionary and economic processes.

Firstly, the ability to resist aggressive external socio-economic and historical environment. The evolutionary mechanisms of the world economic system act as the socio-economic environment of country models, although one should take into account the internal environment, for example, of economic entities to changing socio-economic conditions. An important role here is given to the economic mechanisms of divergence and convergence.

Secondly, the ability to restore the identified modified fundamental concepts. The main socio-economic mechanisms of interaction with the environment, as studies show (Korel, 2005); ensure the reproduction of the historical type of production factors and the system of economic relations. Lost socio-economic balances and balance—homeostasis are restored; optimization (harmonization) processes are preserved, which is manifested in directed development (homeoresis—the ability of the system to stabilize the growth process and return to the specified economic genetic program in cases of deviation from it under the influence of external factors).

Robert King Merton pointed out the inconsistency and conflict of the institution. The interpretive approach is characterized by liberalism—the active position of the subjects, when the socio-economic situation can be interpreted as subjectively unacceptable and maladaptive. The interpretive direction developed in the works of Ch. H. Cooley, J. G. Meade, G. Bloomer, L. Ross, R. Nisbetta, etc. The complex normative and interpretive concept of interaction with the environment, as a synthesis of the above approaches, proceeds from the process of transformation, interpretation by the subject of the objective social world, the image of the world in the subject and the subject in this world, setting the meanings and direction of optimal adaptation.

Thirdly, the minimal interaction with the environment demonstrates the concepts of directed evolution, development programming, determinism and finalism of economic evolution, general laws of development. The goals and meanings of historical development are interconnected, the meanings of history imply its orientation and movement towards the goal. This area includes the concepts of K. Yaspers, A. Alferov, B. Gubman, the 'world-systemic' analysis of F. Brodel, I. Wallerstein, others. For example, in the theory of equifinality—through the goals of various country economic systems, the world process comes to a single goal, a single ending, an outcome; in some finalist concepts, a given program replaces the goal. Development management is implemented through strategic forecasting and planning, while it is important not to unambiguously or probabilistically anticipate development scenarios, but to establish, first, a logical sequence of economic events. Strategic management involves the implementation of the goals of socio-economic development and priorities (preferences) of socio-economic policy. Such goals at macro and micro levels are the content of genotypic concepts—the mechanisms of reproduction, equilibrium, harmonization and optimization of the content of the evolutionary system contents.

The economic evolutionary-genetic mechanisms discussed above indicate numerous factors and complex relationships that determine country models of genotypes and their implementation in economic development. The previously established conceptual 'timeless' level of EG can be defined as a system of 'primary' economic categories-genes, including those taking into account the phenotypic features of country models. 'Primary' economic genes with their carriers—genotypic concepts (primary EG block) are transformed into a level of long-term economic processes with modification of categories-genes into forms of economic concepts, logical judgments and conclusions (secondary block)—systems of 'secondary' economic genes already taking into account the national characteristics of the economic genotype.

Let us show this in a subsequent analysis.

GM is the second systemic economic block, built based on EG with the help of economic genetic mechanisms of morphogenesis, replication, transcription and translation. *Replication* is the process of doubling the EG with replica synchronization. The development of the social division of labor, the emergence of new industries and spheres, new products, hence new economic entities Pr or Po, O and R, new economic relations between these entities generate new genotypic structures. At the same time, the reproductive concept with dominant spheres of production forms a cost theoretical paradigm. The cost is determined by the socially necessary costs of resources that consumers reimburse to producers for their further normal functioning and development. Cost-based theories, with all their diversity, can be "combined into one theory based on the principles of the reproductive approach" (Bodrikov, 2009). The paradigm of utility is based on the balance of individual and social spheres of economic activity; utility is the degree of satisfaction of social needs by individual goods. The third alternative-cost paradigm incorporates the two preceding ones and, in the unity of costs and utility, determines the conditions of the optimum Pr-Po, O-R.

Self-copying of the genotype concepts of economic activity is associated with the process of genetic material *transcriptions*, the translation of economic information, economic values from costs to results, from producer to consumer and vice versa. Genotypic information is transcribed (rewritten) into the GM language, a secondary module of economic genes is formed—first, economic concepts, logical judgments and conclusions, decision-making through which intermediate and final economic results, 'chains' of social wealth are synthesized. Economic categories are transformed in GM into logical forms of concepts, judgments, and conclusions. There are concepts in the narrow sense, as components of a judgment and concepts in the broad sense "as a system of knowledge", including judgments and conclusions. GM is based on the logic of economic processes presented initially in classical political economy, being completed with concepts, logical judgments and conclusions of the theories of marginalism and neoclassicism, as well as modern synthesis. There is a topological modeling of economic concepts, which reveals a two−way relationship: the influence of logic on the structure of concepts and vice versa—the structure of concepts determines the horizontal and vertical connections of GM. Genotypic processes also determine the logic of economic theory developments.

There are three main stages in the evolution of economic teachings: (a) Classical political economy based on the cost paradigm of dominant spheres of Pr-Po (A. Smith, D. Ricardo, J. Miles, K. Marx, etc.); (b) The theory of marginalism and Neoclassicism based on the utility paradigm of dominant spheres of O-R (K. Menger, W. Jevons, E. Boehm-Bawerk, L. Walras, J. Clark, A. Marshall, etc.); c) Emergent unity of the named concepts (spheres of Pr-O-R-Po)—the main directions of modern economic theory 'new Keynesianism' (J. Akerlof, J. Stiglitz, N. Mankiw, O. Blanchard, D. Romer, etc.), 'new classical theory' (J. Muth, R. Barro, E, Prescott, F. Kidland, etc.) transformed into 'new neo-Keynesian theory' (J. Gali, M. Gertler, N. Kiyotaki, M. Woodford, Gr. Mankiw) and 'new neoclassical theory' (M. Friedman, R. Lucas, T. Sargent, etc.).

The utility paradigm does not 'destroy' the value paradigm, but complements and restricts its actions. *The principle of complementarity* has a universal, general character, reflects the facets and stages of development of a single integral human activity. E. Bernstein, M. Tugan-Baranovsky, A. Marshall, P. Struve, V. Dmitriev, and others also pointed out the harmonious complement of value and utility theories. The theory of marginal utility complements the theory of value in the sense that both theories represent essential knowledge about economic processes from the standpoint of the spheres of Pr-Po, O-R.

Due to the limited scope of the article, the Appendix describes in more detail the first level of GM on the convergence of concepts, logical judgments and conclusions of various areas of modern economic theory, including classical political economy.

At the given first level of GM, the qualitative characteristics of public wealth are distinguished: commodity wealth (value), use value, exchange value; economic benefits (utility), total and marginal utility; budget constraint (opportunity cost), indifference curves, optimum consumer choice). Quantitative characteristics: quantity and magnitude of value, quantitative value relations; quantities of supply and demand, their equilibrium; individual demand (effects), market demand and elasticity, consumer surplus. A measure of social wealth in the form of money: money as a measure of value, means of circulation and preservation of value; the magnitude of the demand for money and the supply of money, their equilibrium; partial demand for cash balances (effects), total demand for cash balances and monetary aggregates, the optimum of cash reserves.

Consumption value (1.2.1.2) in interaction with value (1.2.2.2) form the function of money as a means of circulation (1.2.3.2). The GM has a level structure, where each concept can be detailed and expanded in the aspect of EG levels. For example, *consumer value* takes forms: *consumer value as such*—the real embodiment of goods costs; *the public consumption* cost is included in the exchange and distribution relationship between the producer and the consumer; by means *of consumer value* as a relationship of economic entities, the commodity acquires the property of exchange value.

The formation by categories of the primary EG module of the secondary concepts GM module can be shown by the example of consumption cost and utility. The quality of goods—the consumer value of the value paradigm of classical political economy is formed by the norms and rules (technological and institutional) of the Pr-Po spheres, as well as the needs, goals, means, values and results. The quality of goods is influenced by market relations, in particular, the quality-price ratio, the activities of the state in the person of numerous norms and standards, organizations and areas of quality management.

Utility—a paradigm concept reflects the equilibrium mechanisms of the system. Market mechanisms aim to balance and equalize the marginal utility of the goods exchanged. Utility theory was used in public policy (Fabians, others) to achieve socio-economic justice in state and municipal reform. The economic equilibrium is focused on the development of the sector structure, other genes-categories of EG. Thus, the equilibrium mechanism is implemented by the market, the state, institutions, to a certain extent the activities of enterprises and households as producers and consumers.

The primary EG module, genes and genotypic concepts are deployed logically, as has been shown, in the content of GM, but also historically in stages, steps and cycles of economic evolution, setting the direction of development to economic systems (Martishin, 2020) and economic theories. At the same time, 'multilevel' ('multilayer', 'fan') stages and steps of the evolutionary process are revealed. All this is the first property of GM.

Second property of GM. In GM, there is a *frequency* of formation of economic values, their logical forms in accordance with the logic of economic paradigms. Every third group of the logical form represents unity with the two preceding ones. For example, the optimal consumer choice (1.9.1.9)—the unity of the budget constraint (1.7.1.7) and indifference curves (1.8.1.8).

Third property of GM. There are '*horizontal*' relationships and interactions of economic processes. The increase in value is created, first, 'horizontally'.

Fourth property of GM. At the fourth level, GM GDP, national income, personal disposable income horizontally is directly determined by the mechanisms for generating income in the markets of factors of production and the redistribution of income. There are '*vertical*' GM relationships that form the immediate revenues of the results of the system.

From the standpoint of logic, the movement of economic values is carried out from the *first level*– the categories of *being* social wealth, the formation of goods and money of the system to the next *second* level of the *essence* categories of the economic system. The transformation of money into capital and its results, the technological basis, the processes of accumulation and reproduction of capital constitute the content of this matrix's level. At the same time, the unity of being direct forms of the first level and the essence of capital of the second level forms the *forms of* capitals *manifestation* and circulation (the *third* level of GM). In addition, respectively, the second and third levels constitute a chain of economic elements that form the *fourth level of the economic system results.*

5 Conclusion

There is a genetic unity of the considered directions of economic theory, due to the identity of its original subject, the relations between the spheres of Pr-Po, O-R and their unity. The logical-semiotic nature of economic genes, genotype, and genotypic matrix is determined, which is an increment of the scientific novelty of the study, as well as the subsequent provisions of the conclusion. Genotypic concepts of—reproduction, equilibrium, harmonization and optimization, the mechanisms of their inheritance determine theoretical system paradigms—cost, utility, alternative-cost and their synthesis. Inheritance mechanisms constitute the main content and theories of motivation of the main areas of economic activity (Pr-O-R-Po). Methodological approaches to identifying evolutionary mechanisms aimed at stabilization, sustainable self-support and self-regulation of socio-economic processes are determined.

Genotypic mechanisms allow conservative (Keynesian, 'realistic') and liberal (classical, nominalist) economic models to be simultaneously in opposite EG states and obtain effective results. The new 'neoclassical synthesis' is based on EG mechanisms. The contradiction of these models is resolved by a periodic change in the stadiality and cyclicity of the economic evolution of the selected models.

The primary EG module forms the 'hereditary program' of the secondary GM economic gene module. GM is built on the basis of EG using the economic genetic mechanisms of morphogenesis, replication, transcription and translation. Topological modeling of economic concepts takes place. Hence, classical political economy, forming the evolutionary foundation, sets the logical structure of the modern system of economic theory, and the cost paradigm—the prerequisite for the functioning of subsequent paradigms. The synthesis of orthodoxy and unorthodox economic theory (represented by evolutionary genetics), as well as the synthesis of institutional and evolutionary economics, proceeds from genology (the initial unity of directions), generic and species commonality.

Acknowledgements The article was prepared with the financial support of the Russian Foundation for Basic Research (RFBR), project No. 20-010-00323-A.

Appendix

The first level of GM on the integration of various areas of modern economic theory, including classical political economy.

1.1.1.1—commodity wealth (value); 1.2.1.2—consumption cost; 1.3.1.3—exchange value; 1.4.1.4—economic benefits (utility); 1.5.1.5—general and 1.6.1.6—marginal utility; 1.7.1.7—budget limit (alternative cost); 1.8.1.8—indifference curves; 1.9.1.9—optimum consumer choice;

1.1.2.1—quantity and 1.2.2.2—value; 1.3.2.3—quantitative value ratios; 1.4.2.4—demand values and 1.5.2.5—supply; 1.6.2.6—their balance; 1.7.2.7—individual demand (effects); 1.8.2.8—market demand and elasticity; 1.9.2.9—consumer surplus;

1.1.3.1—money as a measure of value; 1.2.3.2—means of circulation and 1.3.3.3—preservation of value; 1.4.3.4—money demand and 1.5.3.5—money supply; 1.6.3.6—balance of money supply and demand; 1.7.3.7—partial demand for cash balances (effects); 1.8.3.8—total demand for cash balances and cash units; 1.9.3.9—optimum cash reserves

2.1.1.1—capital; 2.2.1.2—capitalist property; 2.3.1.3—capitalist production process; 2.4.1.4—production function; 2.5.1.5—general and 2.6.1.6—limit products; 2.7.1.7—isocosts; 2.8.1.8—isoquents; 2.9.1.9—optimum production selection;

2.1.2.1—capitalist costs; 2.2.2.2—capital value; 2.3.2.3—surplus value; 2.4.2.4—the amount of demand and revenues of the company; 2.5.2.5—its costs and the company's offer; 2.6.2.6—balance of supply and demand of the company; 2.7.2.7—individual proposal (effects); 2.8.2.8—market offer; 2.9.2.9—excess manufacturer;

2.1.3.1—material and technical base of capitalism; 2.2.3.2—capital accumulation; 2.3.3.3—initial capital accumulation; 2.4.3.4—consumer and investment demand; 2.5.3.5—balance of income and expenses; 2.6.3.6—equilibrium extension and multiplier; 2.7.3.7—effects of government expenditures and taxes; 2.8.3.8—balance of the state budget; 2.9.3.9—automatic stabilizers

References

Arkhipov, A. Yu., Martishin, E. M., & Zotova, T. A. (2020). Evolutionary and genetic mechanisms of economic growth and development. *Journal of Institutional Studies, 12*(2), 6–24.

Blacke, P., & Wojcik, C. (2008). Credit booms, monetary integration and the new neoclassical synthesis. *Journal of Banking and Finance, 32*(3), 458–470.

Blaug, M. (2002). *Disturbing processes in modern economic theory. What economists actually do? On the question of the so-called "crisis" of economics*. IMEMO RAS.

Bodrikov, M. (2009). Classical theories of value: The modern sound of unsolved problems. *Questions of Economics, 7*, 102.

Brizhak, O., Klochko, E., & Adamenko, A. (2020). Neoindustrial paradigm of Russian Corporations integration into the economy system under the conditions of transition to the sixth technological order. *Lecture Notes in Networks and Systems, 111*, 619–626.

Buchanan, J. (1994). Constitution of Economic politicians. *Economic Issues, 6*, 106

Burov, M. P. (2021). *"Covid" crisis and Russia's adaptation to the new realities of post-crisis development*.

Buzgalin, A. V., Kolganov, A. I., & Barashkova, O. V. (2019). *Classical Political Economy: Modern Marxist direction. Basic level. Advanced level.*

Chereshnev, V. A., Tatarkin, A. I., & Glazyev, S. Yu. (2011). *Forecasting the socio-economic development of the region*. UIEC.

Cherkovets, V. N. (2011). *Capital and economics: Issues of methodology, theory, teaching*. TEIS.

Danilov, A. N. (2021). Culture as a genome of civilizational development. *Questions of Philosophy, 3*, 215–222.

De Vroey, M., & Duarte, P. G. (2013). In search of lost time: Neoclassical synthesis. *The B. E. Journal of Macroeconomics, 13*(1), 114–126.

Ermolenko, A. A., Brizhak, O. V., & Digtyar, O. Yu. (2019). New forms of relations arising in the capital flow. In *Marxand Modernity. A Political and Economic Analysis of Social Systems Management* (pp. 299–320). Charlotte.

Eggertsson, T. (2011). Znaniya i teoriya institutsional'nykh izmeneniy. *Voprosy ekonomiki – Issues of Economics, 7*, 4–16

Frolov, D. P. (2020). Evolutionary economy at its peak and in crisis: The prospect of a new paradigm. *Journal of Institutional Studies, 12*(1), 019–037. https://doi.org/10.17835/2076-6297.2020.12.1.019-037

Grodsky, V. S. (2005). *Modern directions of economic theory: problems of interaction and synthesis: abstract of the dissertation.* Thesis Doctor of Economics: 08.00.01. Samara. SFEU.

Hodgson, J. (2003). *Economic theory and institutions: Manifesto of modern institutional economic theory.* Business.

Kirdina-Chandler, S. G. (2021). Paradoxes of synthesis in economic theory. *Terra Economicus, 19*(3). https://doi.org/10.18522/2073-6606-2021-19-3-37-52

Kleiner, G. B. (2010). Growth through Integration (about the international conference 'institutional economics: Development, teaching, applications'). *Journal of the New Economic Association, 5*, 90.

Kollander, D., et al. (2010). Financial crisis and failures of modern economics. *Questions of Economics, 6*, 259–265.

Korel, L. V. (2005). *Sociology of adaptations: Questions of theory, methodology and methodology.* Science.

Leverett, S., & Lyon, A. (1920). Functional approach to social-economic data. *Journal of Political Economy, 28*(7), 529–564.

Liseev, I. K. (2001). The emergence of a new paradigm in biological research. *Philosophy of Science and Technology, 7*(1), 106–123.

Martishin, E. M. (2020). Identification of cyclicity in the world economy. *Issues of the New Economy, 3–4*(55–56), 4–11.

Mayevsky, V. I. (2005). *Evolutionary macroeconomic theory. Introduction to institutional economics.* Science.

Nelson, R. R. (2018). *Modern evolutionary economics: An overview Cambridge.* Cambridge University Press.

Riechmann, Th. (1999). Learning and behavioral stability. An economic interpretation of genetic algorithms. *Journal of Evolutionary Economics, 9*(2), 225–242.

Skorobagatov, A. (2006). Institutions as a factor of order and as a source of chaos: Neo-institutional-post-Keynesian analysis. *Questions of Economics, 8*, 102–118. https://doi.org/10.32609/0042-8736-2006-8-102-118

Vernadsky, V. I. (1997). *About science.* Dubna Press.

Voeykov, M. I. (2008). On the question of the end of classical political economy. *Bulletin of the Institute of Economics of the Russian Academy of Sciences, 4*, 94–128.

Voeykov, M. I. (2009). Once again on the subject of political economy and its boundaries (response to opponents). *Bulletin of the Institute of Economics of the Russian Academy of Sciences, 2*, 109.

Woolford, M. (2010). Convergence of views in macroeconomics: Elements of a new synthesis. *Economic Issues, 10*, 26.

Synthesis of Mainstream and Political Economy as an Emerge from the Economic Theory Crisis

Maria E. Konovalova, Turakul R. Rizokulov, Nadezhda Yu. Blinichkina, Ravshan A. Karimov, and Olga Yu. Kuzmina

Abstract The prospects for the further development of economic theory are not fully defined due to the crisis in its main course and the lack of a consensus on promising directions of development in the scientific community. The main discussion is growing around the question of the necessity to synthesize the concepts of the mainstream with the foundations of political economy. It is necessary to determine the reasons for the rejection of synthesis and the conditions under which such a synthesis will be possible to resolve the dilemma. It can be argued that such a synthesis is possible in principle, taking into account the fact that the foundations of modern economic theory are laid within the framework of political economy. Evolutionary and dialectical methods make it possible to determine that the main condition for synthesis is the necessity to apply the fundamental research methods for the development of mainstream concepts. Considering the general state of the modern mainstream, a change in the methodological apparatus can contribute to recover from the crisis, and synthesis with political economy seems to be the most optimal way to solve the growing problems.

Keywords Mainstream · Mainstream crisis · Evolution of economic thought

JEL Classification A1

M. E. Konovalova · O. Yu. Kuzmina
Samara State University of Economics, 141 Soviet Army Str, 443090 Samara, Russian Federation
e-mail: mkonoval@mail.ru

O. Yu. Kuzmina
e-mail: pisakina83@yandex.ru

T. R. Rizokulov · N. Yu. Blinichkina (✉) · R. A. Karimov
Tajik State University of Law, Business and Politics, 17 Microdistrict, Building 1, 735700 Khujand, Tajikistan
e-mail: n.blinichkina@mail.ru

T. R. Rizokulov
e-mail: t_rizokulov@mail.ru

R. A. Karimov
e-mail: karimovravshan@mail.ru

V. Kumar et al. (eds.), *Consequences of Social Transformation for Economic Theory*, Springer Proceedings in Business and Economics,
https://doi.org/10.1007/978-3-031-27785-6_4

1 Introduction

Any science cannot remain static. Philosophy of science states that "even a cursory comparison of modern science and the science of previous eras reveals striking changes. A scientist of the classical era would hardly have accepted the ideas and methods of quantum mechanical description, since he considered it unacceptable to include references to the observer and means of observation in the theoretical description and explanation" (Stepin, 2006).

This statement is especially relevant for such a science as economic theory due to the fact that its object is a society which changes every second. The development of science involves the interaction of different ideas. Often such ideas can be completely opposite. The best result of such an interaction is a new idea that has arisen as a result of the synthesis of previous. But also, a complete rejection of one of the previous ideas in view of the confirmation of its unviability can be a possible result. Sometimes the result of such interaction can be extremely negative and the crisis in science begins under its influence.

These principles of development are characteristic of economic theory, as well as of any other social science. In the process of its development the mainstream of modern economic theory has significantly moved away from its foundation—political economy. In this context, the mainstream is understood as a set of economic theories and models that underlie modern economic research and determine the main content of economic science in the current period. Political economy refers to a paradigm in economics, the basis of which was laid within the framework of the theories of Adam Smith and David Ricardo, and which served as the basis for market economy research.

The number of internal problems in the economic mainstream is growing with the growth of number of the new ideas. Moreover, some authors note that "representatives of the mainstream have completely abandoned the study of the realities of economic life and are only engaged in solving mathematical puzzles that are interesting only to themselves" (Bazhenov & Maltsev, 2018). Other studies note that although supporters of the no-crisis position argue that there is only a crisis of individual economic doctrines, and not of economic science as a whole, this will not change the fact that the mainstream is not able to "respond to modern social economic challenges of the time" due to the lack of theoretical and methodological principles that allow "an objective analysis of modern socio-economic problems" (Bochko, 2012). Even such opponents of the mainstream version of the crisis as Vernon Smith note that certain models of modern economic science are not fully adequate for understanding the world (Remic, 2019).

However, the issues of the growing crisis in the mainstream remains debatable and there are researchers who refute the existence of the crisis in mainstream and scientists who consider the crisis in mainstream a proven fact (Bochko, 2012; Fligstin & Vogel, 2021; Grishchenko, Tkachev, Ostapenko, & Tunyov, 2021; Nekipelov, 2019; Sukharev, 2013; Zaostrovtsev, 2013).

At the same time, both of them recognize the impossibility of applying the existing theoretical and methodological principles for an objective assessment of contemporary problems. On this background, there is an active discussion in the scientific community on the possibility of combining political economy and concepts of the modern economic mainstream (Biryukov, 2020; Egorov, 2021; Harvey, 2020; Kirdina-Chandler, 2021; Kirdina-Chandler & Mayevsky, 2020).

2 Literature Review

Based on the formulation of the question, it is obvious that there are two diametrically opposed approaches to the possibility of synthesis of political economy and the mainstream at present. The first approach categorically denies the very possibility of such a union. Adherents of such a position justify it by the estrangement of the concepts of political economy from the humanistic ideas of modernity and the multidisciplinary approach. This position is taken mainly by representatives of Western economic thought. Of particular note are Kenneth Arrow, Vernon Smith, Graham Looms, Frank Hahn, Harvey David among them (Bochko, 2012; Harvey, 2020; Hodgson, 2008; Kvasov, 2020; Upravitelev, 2020). Adherents of this concept especially insist that the mainstream is developing quite dynamically and there is no crisis in economic science. They highlight the shortcomings of individual economic doctrines, while representatives of a different approach consider these to be manifestations of the crisis. As an argument, they cite the fact that scientists have been talking about the crisis for more than a century, but in reality this does not hinder the development of economic science. In particular, Kenneth Arrow, who developed his own equilibrium model, noted that crises arise as a result of the system's deviation from the equilibrium position, and did not take into account the emergence of non-economic factors that could lead to a crisis (Maskin, 2019).

Representatives of the second approach insist that such a synthesis is necessary for the renewal and development of economic science. They justify their position by the crisis state of the mainstream and its distance from the real economy, by the tendency to study minor private issues within the framework of mathematical models. Adherents of this position are Bochko (2012), Belskaya and Chuvakina (2010), Hodgson (2008), Khumaryan and Zhikharevich (2021), Kuligin (2014), Martyanov and Fishman (2020). Upravitelev (2020). To some extent, the adherents of this approach are concerned about the condition of modern economic science and its ability to adequately respond to the challenges of reality. There is a harsh criticism of the applied mainstream methodology in some works of Western researchers and the need for discussion in this area is noted there (Drakopoulos, 2014).

Thus, summarizing what has been said, it can be argued that the approach of a particular researcher to the question of the possibility of synthesis of the mainstream and political economy depends to a large extent on his position regarding the presence of a crisis in the mainstream.

3 Materials and Methods

It is necessary to go beyond the standard economic debate about the object and method of research within the mainstream and political economy to answer the question of the interaction of these two approaches and look at the issue from the standpoint of philosophy and, in particular, dialectics. What is the difference between these approaches? What is their fundamental contradiction? What is it based on? And, finally, under what conditions can this contradiction be eliminated?

Research of the problem of synthesis of the mainstream and political economy should be aimed at obtaining answers to these questions based on the application of dialectical, historical methods and system analysis.

4 Discussion

At some moment economic science has accumulated enough fundamental ideas on a variety of issues of economic activity. It was necessary that these ideas be overgrown with practical research and developed into full-fledged theories. It took time. Therefore, fundamental research was temporarily suspended and the general principles and methods of classical political economy were discarded in order to make it possible to examine particular objects of research. After some time, mainstream came into conflict with the previously used methodology. However, in our opinion, the dialectical law of mutual transition of quantitative and qualitative changes is applicable here in the following context. The synthesis of political economy and the mainstream is inevitable at the stage of transition from quantity to quality but these approaches of economic theory can be opposed to each other at the stage of accumulation of quantity.

If we take into account the presence of certain signs of a crisis in the mainstream in the current period, it can be argued that the time for fundamental changes has come. The basis of such changes can be the integration of the principles and methods of political economy with the key ideas of the mainstream. Such an association can serve as the necessary impetus for the emergence of new ideas and approaches within the mainstream. In addition, the use of a different research methodology will allow us to look at existing problems from a different point of view and, at least, will contribute to finding new approaches to solving them.

In practice, the synthesis of the mainstream and political economy will make it possible to solve economic problems more accurately and fully in the context of dynamic changes caused by the features of the conduct of economic activities by modern states and by such processes as globalization and digital transformation.

The modern mainstream has significant differences from political economy (Table 1). There are differences not only in methods and approaches to solving economic problems. The existing differences are much deeper and significant. Over time, the object and subject of study of economic science have changed. The reason for this

Table 1 Correspondence of the main parameters of the mainstream and political economy

	Mainstream (modern stage)	Political economy
Object	Decision-making process	Socium
Subject	Behavior of business entities in the decision-making process	Socio-economic phenomena
Methods	Math modeling	Analysis, synthesis, systematization, abstraction, induction, deduction
Key points	Rational behavior of the subject; equilibrium state of the world	Industrial relations; productive forces
Particular qualities	Specifics	Fundamentality
Study methods	Abstraction	Empiricism
Postulates	Social justice	Unity of moral and economic principles
Disadvantages	The contradiction between social utility and the abstract nature of constructions	Lack of theories to explain market failures

was that at the turn of the nineteenth and twentieth centuries economists came to the conclusion that the previous object of study within the framework of economic theory had been sufficiently studied. They believed that it was not possible to say something new about it taking into account the available research results.

At first glance, the divergence in the approaches presented in Table 1 is irresistible. However, a more detailed analysis shows that the object of study in the modern mainstream is a special case or element of the object of study of political economy since the decision-making process in the economic system is part of the life of society. Similarly, the subject of mainstream studies is a reduced subject of studies used by representatives of political economy. Thus, the assertion of critics of the modern mainstream about the reduced focus of its research and the tendency to study particular cases in isolation from all economic activity as a whole is confirmed.

First of all, an analysis of the need for a synthesis of the mainstream and political economy requires an unambiguous answer to the question of the presence of a crisis in the mainstream because there is no need for any radical changes in the absence of a crisis.

The main argument given by researchers in support of the version of the existence of a crisis is that economic science is not able to predict the crises of modernity and deal with them (Bochko, 2012; Grishchenko, Tkachev, Ostapenko, & Tunyov, 2021; Nekipelov, 2019; Zaostrovtsev, 2013). Also, some studies note the need to revise the methodological apparatus of modern economic science due to its inefficiency (Kiełczewski, 2020). It is difficult to argue this argument. This is confirmed by the lack of substantiated arguments of the opponents of the theory of the existence of a crisis.

Further analysis of the data presented in Table 1 allows us to make some conclusions about the causes of the crisis that began in the mainstream.

First, the development of modern mainstream concepts began during a relatively stable period of economic development. Economic crises were not a common occurrence and did not have such serious consequences for the whole world at that time, since the development of globalization processes was at the very beginning. Practical economics did not set such major goals to the economic community and did not serve as a challenge.

Secondly, the further development of the mainstream against the background of more and more frequent failures of the state should have forced scientists to think about the following. If all the theories put forward on the basis of any base do not work, it should be concluded that there are problems in the base itself.

To date, this question is being asked more and more often, that's why studies on the prospects for the synthesis of the mainstream with a variety of oppositional directions are appearing.

In our opinion, such a synthesis may not be effective enough, since other modern economic concepts are also not able fully to answer the questions on the agenda. In addition, the presence of significant contradictions will not allow such a synthesis to be carried out effectively with a high probability. The reasoning is that the very fact of the existence of concepts different from the concepts of the mainstream suggests the existence of contradictions which could not be overcome in the process of forming these concepts.

Certainly, if any of these concepts is revised in detail and if the existing contradiction is eliminated as a result, then such a concept may eventually become an element of the mainstream. However, here we are talking more about joining the mainstream without any significant changes in it, and not about synthesis, which involves cardinal changes and obtaining a new format that includes certain features of all the original elements.

In this context, it should be noted that political economy remains the foundation of all modern economic concepts including the concepts emerging within the mainstream. It is impossible to deny this provision, since political economy in its essence is the base in the science of the market economy. Until humanity creates a new model of economic relations and begins to actively apply it in practice, the features of the development of economic science will force researchers to return to the roots periodically, if only to rethink the existing ideas.

Schematically, this position can be depicted as follows (Fig. 1).

This scheme clearly shows the action of one of the basic laws of dialectics—the law of mutual transition of quantitative and qualitative changes. Obviously, economic science in its development will gradually move away from political economy, which serves as a kind of core for it, since any development involves a certain change in the base.

Philosophy teaches us that any development is impossible without crises that take on a variety of forms. A crisis is a natural phenomenon that occurs at a time when fundamental changes are required. The process of development of science is characterized by a crisis of thought, when new ideas do not find a basis in the formed basis or are rejected by the scientific community, which tends to conservatism in most cases. The search for a new direction begins in these cases. However, any

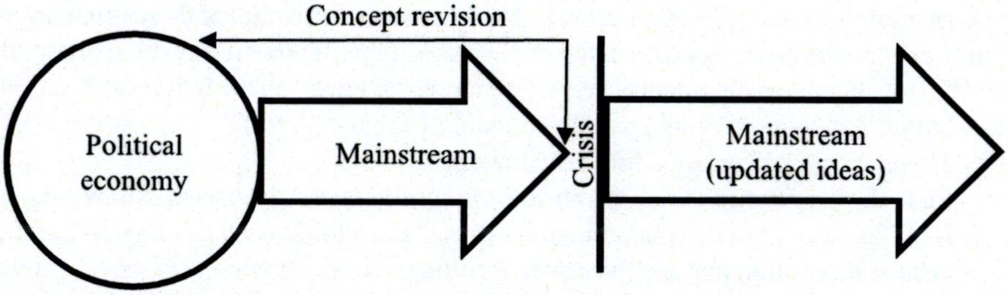

Fig. 1 Features of the development of the mainstream in economic science

new idea builds on existing ones, no matter how innovative it is. The crisis forces researchers to go at least one step back in search of the mistake that caused it. A new development vector allowing further moving forward must be found in the course of such a rethinking.

The foregoing allows us to state that rethinking certain provisions of political economy within the framework of the concepts of the mainstream and (if it is necessary) combining the individual components of these areas of economic science is an urgent need today (Table 2).

The systematization carried out in Table 2 once again confirms the possibility of solving the problems existing in economic science through the application of the basic principles and methods of political economy within the mainstream concepts. Moreover, an analysis of the elements of Table 1 leads to the conclusion that there are no significant objective obstacles to such a synthesis. Consequently, such a synthesis is not only possible objectively but is also necessary today.

This raises the question: What can actually serve as an obstacle to such a synthesis?

In our opinion, the problem of synthesis of the mainstream and political economy based, first of all, on the fact that the representatives of the mainstream themselves categorically deny the possibility of applying the foundations of political economy

Table 2 Ways to overcome the crisis in the mainstream based on synthesis with political economy

An unsolved problem in the mainstream	A possible solution through political economy	Expected result
Loss of prediction function	Expansion of the object of study in conjunction with a change in the methodology used	Emergence of working predictive models
Lagging behind rapid changes in economic activity	Combining abstraction with empiricism in the process of research	Reducing the number of crises by reducing the number of state failures
Prevalence of the descriptive function in the analysis	Expansion of the methodological apparatus	Improving the effectiveness of ongoing research
Refusal to study individual subjects of research	Return to the fundamental approach	The emergence of new ideas due to the shift of research centers

(Bazhenov & Maltsev, 2018; Kretov, 2016). Moreover, the denial of these foundations may explain the growing crisis in the mainstream. In particular, it is noted in the study of Kretov that the mainstream is becoming more and more "an artificial construction" and more and more moving away from reality (Kretov, 2016).

There are several reasons for this situation.

First, the propensity of the scientific community towards conservatism was noted above. The paradox of this phenomenon lies in the fact that each individual researcher strives for innovation and demonstrates a willingness to generate new ideas. On this background each individual scientist and the scientific community as a whole is not ready to abandon immediately those postulates that were universally recognized, considered to be substantiated in detail and, moreover, received practical confirmation in a certain situation.

Such skepticism is quite justified, since it does not allow scientists to accept any new concepts at once without their detailed understanding and verification. However, the currently widespread conviction of the inability of the political economy to ensure the effective functioning of the modern economic system inhibits the perception and acceptance of its elements within the mainstream.

The second more objective reason for the current situation follows from what has been said. It is the real inability of political economy to detect and prevent market failures. This circumstance can really become a negative factor in the process of synthesizing the analyzed approaches. However, synthesis does not mean at all that all elements of the original models should be present in the final model. On the contrary, it is required to apply only such an element that most fully meets the requirements of the time. Thus, the identified obstacle can be overcome with certain efforts on the part of the scientific community.

Thirdly, the existing concepts of the mainstream substantiate the regularity and necessity of the most predatory manifestations of capitalism. As a consequence, the owners of the world's largest capitals are interested in keeping the concepts supporting their activities unchanged. Synthesis with political economy is capable of giving impetus to the strengthening of socialist doctrines and the weakening of the position of modern capitalists. Since a significant part of the research is financed by private foundations, it is obvious that the topics of research are formed taking into account the interests of the holders of such funds, and the formulation of the question may change depending on these interests.

Thus, the underlying reasons preventing the synthesis of political economy and the mainstream are largely subjective. Therefore, it can be argued that at present there are no real objective obstacles to such a synthesis.

Another significant question needs to be answered to complete the analysis: What situation can develop in economic science if the synthesis of the mainstream and political economy does not take place?

In order to answer this question, it is necessary to return to the main reason for the current crisis of the mainstream—its inability to offer adequate development models in conditions of economic instability.

The impossibility of significant changes within the mainstream through synthesis with other modern economic concepts and approaches has already been noted above.

Consequently, significant changes in the concept of the mainstream should not be expected in the near future in the face of the impossibility of synthesis with political economy. The situation can develop as follows under this assumption.

Stage 1—the ongoing stagnation in science and the growth of internal contradictions due to the impossibility of solving problems within the framework of the existing methodological apparatus. This stage will have negative consequences for the development of economic activity, since there are no effective measures to deal with economic crises.

Stage 2—chaos as a result of the emergence of many new trends in economic science. Such a situation is likely due to the fact that the impossibility of returning to the past and the lack of effective results in the present will push researchers to look for alternatives and generate completely new ideas. In practice, this can result in an increase in cases of both government failures and market failures since it is impossible to verify the effectiveness of the proposed model without testing in practice and the practical testing of many new ideas will naturally lead to an increase in the number of errors in the system.

Stage 3—two possible versions of events. The first option assumes a return to the basics culminating in the synthesis of the mainstream and political economy taking into account the law of negation of negation. The second scenario may lead to the formation of a new core in economic science and the creation of a new business model different from the market economy. In this case, the discussion about the need for a synthesis of the mainstream and political economy will not make sense, since the content of the mainstream will completely change.

Thus, the synthesis of the mainstream and political economy seems to be the most likely and natural result of the development of economic science while maintaining a market economy as the main form of management even in the conditions of refusal of synthesis at this stage.

Returning to the analysis of the differences between the mainstream and political economy, we note that the main difference between these scientific currents lies in the methodology in spite of some differences in the object and subject of study. However, it is necessary to change the approach to scientific research in order to overcome the crisis due to the need to introduce qualitative changes in modern economic concepts. General methods of study rather than private methods of the modern mainstream are most suitable for any research at the initial stage if it is necessary to identify general patterns as it should be done today. There are many new processes and problems in the modern world requiring study from the very foundations. The application of fundamental methods of research by political economy and return to such a generalized object of research as socium can become a way out of the existing impasse.

The following can be singled out among the positive results of the synthesis of the mainstream and political economy:

1. The formation of a new methodological apparatus based on unification will create conditions for the development of new types of economic models that have a greater practical focus.

2. Modification of the object and subject of research will allow scientists to take a different look at the most significant issues and increase the probability of finding the optimal solution.
3. The prospect of forming new concepts appears based on the synthesis of existing ideas with traditional approaches of political economy.
4. There is a possibility of the formation of a new more viable paradigm in economic theory in the future.

However, there is a considerable possibility of some negative results, which boil down to the following:

1. If the synthesis is successful, there is little chance of turning the basic provisions of political economy into dogmas that should not be questioned.
2. There is a possibility of an increase in the number of market failures, since neither political economy nor the mainstream has found a way to counteract them.
3. There may be a tendency to deviate from the course of state support for the economy, since the mainstream has not found a way to avoid the failures of the state, while political economy tends to be completely liberal.

At the same time, researchers should not seriously fear the negative consequences of the synthesis of the mainstream and political economy. The probability of their occurrence is extremely small. Furthermore, today the mainstream crisis has much more negative consequences that have a negative impact directly on the economic system.

In our opinion, the priority task for the near future in economic science is building a working model that describes the features of macroeconomic development. Such a model is necessary for more accurate forecasting and the formation of a strategy for the actions of economic entities at the macro level.

The temptation of the transition to a liberal economic model is much lower in these conditions since the main goal in the end is exactly the search for the optimal form of state intervention in the economy. This provision further reduces the likelihood of a real impact of the identified consequences of the synthesis of the mainstream and political economy on economic science and on the practice of economic activity.

5 Conclusion

The question should be asked not about a principal possibility of synthesis between political economy and the mainstream, but about the conditions under which such a synthesis will take place. In our opinion, the most significant of these conditions are the following:

1. Significant qualitative changes in economic activity and in the life of society, when existing concepts are unable to describe the observed phenomena and ongoing processes. Under these conditions, not only a fundamental change in approaches is required, but also a rethinking of the established foundations.

2. Completion of the process of accumulating the quantity of studies within the framework of the current paradigm and the necessity of introducing qualitative changes in science. This phenomenon is accompanied by a crisis of economic thought resulting from the fact that researchers are unable to draw new conclusions and conduct new research based on theories that turn out to be ineffective in a rapidly changing economic situation.
3. The need to solve fundamental problems which is a natural consequence of the need to adapt economic concepts to new economic conditions. This provision is most clearly manifested in practice during crises of the economic system first of all transformational crises.
4. A change in the methodological apparatus and a return to the research methodology used in the framework of political economy. Such changes are characteristic of a situation when it is required to solve the most general problems and conduct research on fundamental problems.

It should also be noted that the synthesis of political economy and the mainstream does not mean an unconditional return to the principles of political economy at all. Obviously, the synthesis involves the adaptation of the ideas of the classics to the concept of the mainstream of the twenty-first century on the basis of repeated practical confirmation of such ideas. In addition, synthesis means the possible rejection of any concepts underlying the modern paradigm as a result of practical confirmation of its fallacy, first of all, in connection with the changes that have taken place both in economic activity and in society itself.

At the same time, the synthesis of the mainstream and political economy at the current stage is not only possible, but also vital for the formation of a fundamental idea that will give a new impetus to the development of mainstream concepts. In case of full-scale success, these concepts will form the basis of a new paradigm describing economic processes in a society oriented towards social justice. Such a paradigm will be able to explain the patterns of development of the economic system including the context of changes in the economic structure and will enable the governments of states to develop an optimal program to reduce the risk of a crisis.

Thus, we have been able to solve one of the most significant problems facing the economic community today by combining two fundamental questions of modern economic science—the question of the possibility of synthesis of the mainstream and political economy and the question of the presence of a crisis in the mainstream.

References

Bazhenov, G., & Maltsev, A. (2018). Modern heterodox directions of economic theory in the context of mainstream transformation. *Society and Economy, 1*, 5–21.

Belskaya, G. S., & Chuvakina, V. S. (2010). Does "mainstream" adequately reflect the Russian economy. *Bulletin of Tomsk State University, 1*(9), 5–9.

Biryukov, V. V. (2020). Post-institutionalism: Formation features through a change in the research paradigm. *Russian Journal of Social Sciences and Humanities, 14*(3), 158–164. https://doi.org/10.17238/issn1998-5320.2020.14.3.19

Bochko, V. S. (2012). Crisis of the mainstream of modern economic theory: Content and consequences. *Journal of the Ural State University of Economics, 2*(40), 5–15.

Drakopoulos, S. (2014). Mainstream aversion to economic methodology and the scientific ideal of physics. *MPRA Paper, 57222*, 2–23.

Egorov, D. G. (2021). How many paradigms are there in economics, and can it become a science with one paradigm. *Social Sciences and Modernity, 5*, 129–142.

Fligstin, N., & Vogel, S. (2021). Political economy after neoliberalism. *Journal of Economic Sociology, 22*(4), 35–48.

Grishchenko, V. O., Tkachev, V. N., Ostapenko, V. M., & Tunyov, V. D. (2021). Modern monetary theory (MMT): New paradigm or a set of recommendations for macroeconomic policy? *Economic Policy, 16, 3*, 8–43. https://doi.org/10.18288/1994-5124-2021-3-8-43

Harvey, D. (2020). The condition of postmodernity. An enquiry into the origins of cultural change. *Journal of Economic Sociology, 21*(2), 62–75.

Hodgson, J. (2008). Evolutionary and institutional economics as the new mainstream? *Economic Bulletin of Rostov State University, 6*(2), 8–21.

Khumaryan, D. G., & Zhikharevich, D. M. (2021). To reassemble capitalism: Economic sociology and its "political unconscious" on "political economy after neoliberalism" by Neil Fligstein and Steven Vogel. *Journal of Economic Sociology, 22(4)*, 149–158. https://doi.org/10.17323/1726-3247-2021-4-149-158

Kiełczewski, D. (2020). Mainstream economics versus heterodox economics – between dispute and dialogue. *Optimum Economic Studies, 2*(100), 121–131. https://doi.org/10.15290/oes.2020.02.100.09

Kirdina-Chandler, S. G. (2021). Paradoxes of synthesis in economics. *Terra Economicus, 19*(3), 37–52. https://doi.org/10.18522/2073-6606-2021-19-3-37-52

Kirdina-Chandler, S. G., & Mayevsky, V. I. (2020). Evolution of heterodox mesoeconomics. *Terra Economicus, 18*(3), 30–52. https://doi.org/10.18522/2073-6606-2020-18-3-30-52

Kretov, S. I. (2016). The sixth technological order, cybernetic epistemology, political economy and mainstream. *Bulletin of Chelyabinsk State University, 6*(388), 7–18.

Kuligin, V. D. (2014). Adam Smith's invisible hand. *Bulletin of the University, 2*, 142–148.

Kvasov, A. S. (2020). In search of a new paradigm (analytical review). *Scientific and practical journal "Bulletin of the University of the Russian Academy of Education", 3*, 69–77. https://doi.org/10.24411/2072-5833-2020-10030

Martyanov, V. S., & Fishman, L. G. (2020). After the coronavirus: From an optimized old to a new world? *Free Thought, 3*(1681), 9–28.

Maskin, E. (2019). The Economics of Kenneth J. arrow: a selective review. *Annual Review of Economics, 11*, 1–26. https://doi.org/10.1146/annurev-economics-080218-030323

Nekipelov, A. D. (2019). Crisis in economic science—nature and ways to overcome. *Bulletin of the Russian Academy of Sciences, 89*(1), 24–37.

Remic, B. (2019). Review of Vernon L. Smith & Bart J. Wilson's Humanomics: Moral sentiments and the wealth of nations for the Twenty-First Century. *Erasmus Journal for Philosophy and Economics, 12*, 118–134. https://doi.org/10.23941/ejpe.v20i2.456

Stepin, V. S. (2006). *Philosophy of Science. General problems: A textbook for graduate students and applicants for the degree of candidate of sciences*. Gardariki.

Sukharev, O. S. (2013). The problem of periodization of technological development in evolutionary analysis. *Economic Analysis: Theory and Practice, 23*(326), 2–17.

Upravitelev, A. A. (2020). Behavioral economics: Path to the mainstream through classical economics. *Russian Journal of Economic Theory, 17(2)*, 509–513. https://doi.org/10.31063/2073-6517/2020.17-2.23

Zaostrovtsev, A. P. (2013). Douglas North: An escape from the neoclassical mainstream. *Social Sciences and Modernity, 4*, 140–150.

Dynamic Interaction Between Human Capital Accumulation and Economic Growth

Aysel Guliyeva, Marina V. Faminskaya, and Elena V. Potekhina

Abstract Our contribution focuses on the dynamic interaction between human capital accumulation and economic growth. In order to do so, it applies the toolkit of the classic economic theory and scrutinizes the provisions of the human capital formation and other key variables on economic growth. In addition, it evaluates the impact of education and other key variables on the economic growth of countries that have varying human development indicators. In order to adequately examine the impact of human capital accumulation on the GDP per capita increase, the link between the human capital accumulation and income inequality needs to be developed. The theoretical foundation allows us to estimate the effect of human capital accumulation and other variables on per capita GDP growth, drawing on an enhanced version of a neoclassical growth model. Our results call for the enhanced regulation of the human capital that needs to be fostered and supported by the decision-makers such as governmental officials responsible for the labor market policies and regulation of schooling, training as well as education that plays an important role in shaping up high-quality human capital and sustaining its quality and standards for the benefits it can bring for the society and economy.

Keywords Human capital · Economic growth · Economic theory

JEL Classification J01 · J24 · O38

1 Introduction

Regulating the accumulation of human capital could serve as the new engine of economic growth, and foster its development over the long run. Human capital

A. Guliyeva (✉)
International Economy Department, Azerbaijan State University of Economics, 6 Istiglaliyyat Str., AZ 1001 Baku, Azerbaijan
e-mail: aguliyeva@unec.edu.az

M. V. Faminskaya · E. V. Potekhina
Russian State Social University, 4/1 Wilhelm Pik Str., 129226 Moscow, Russian Federation

V. Kumar et al. (eds.), *Consequences of Social Transformation for Economic Theory*, Springer Proceedings in Business and Economics,
https://doi.org/10.1007/978-3-031-27785-6_5

influences economic growth and can contribute to economic development through expanding knowledge and skills among the population (Qamruzzaman et al., 2021). Human capital indirectly contributes to economic growth by stimulating physical capital accumulation and improving levels of technical innovation. Among other things, the evidence indicates that economic growths response to the accumulation of physical capital, institutional development, the accumulation of human capital, and total factor productivity vary somewhat among countries groups (Zhao & Zhou, 2021).

In several economic theory-related studies, a number of education variables are introduced (e.g., the proportion of adults who have a high school education or less, the mean years of schooling), more commonly as control variables in order to capture the human capital developments (Humpert, 2013; Strielkowski & Weyskrabova, 2014). While agreement exists about the presence of a positive economic return on education, measured in terms of earnings levels, the theoretical predictions about the unequal effects of changes in educational attainment are not straightforward (Gruzina et al., 2021; Ogundari & Awokuse, 2018). The basic logic is that changes in technology in the economy drive the demand for highly educated workers, and that the aggregate inequality impact depends, by and large, on the extent to which higher educational attainment is elastic relative to this increased demand. Workers with higher education or better skills typically earn higher wages, which, in turn, boosts economic growth via extra consumption spending (Bordea et al., 2017). Both consumption spending and corporate investment contribute to not just higher economic growth, but they play an important role in determining workers levels of education and advancement (Klofsten et al., 2019). As a result of business investment, it often happens that businesses are more productive while GDP grows because business investment is the main ingredient in growth (Li et al., 2022). Whether employees stay with tech companies or launch a new one, initial investments in human capital ultimately drive economic growth. While investments in human capital generally produce greater growth, this does not necessarily mean that jobs are open to newly-educated workers (Čábelková et al., 2015; Horváthová et al., 2022). Changes in skill composition and pay structures within labor markets are a major component of evidence (Card et al., 2018). The mutual relationship between economic growth and human capital development is likely an important clue for sustainable economic growth. Knowledge confers economic value, as an educated labor force may result in higher productivity. Some governments have recognized that knowledge that individuals acquire from education helps to grow an economy and promote economic growth. The view that more educated workforces may lead to greater income inequality in developed economies as well as emerging economies is also made by Capozza and Divella (2019). In terms of magnitude increases in mean education levels during 1980–2008 more than compensated for the effect of de-equalization caused by other factors. Capital investments, which involve a significant expenditure of money or capital, are designed to increase the productivity and profits of firms in the long run. The supply side cannot account for continued human capital expansion, since that implies self-limiting reductions in rates of return below alternative investments (Boikos et al., 2022). Leisure and innovation in the growth of horizontally-oriented research and development.

2 Human Capital Investment

Indivisibility in human capital investment prevents poor agents accumulating skills positively affects technological progress (Chirwa & Odhiambo, 2018). For example, human capital and technological innovations on the life expectancy in BRICS countries. Few empirical studies identify the major drivers of BRICS health outcomes, such as healthcare expenditures; healthcare systems; health financing as well as GDP and none of these studies have investigated the effect of human capital investments and technological innovations on the BRICS health outcomes (Mohanty & Sethi, 2019). Results of some economic studies also revealed that increased investment in human capital and technical innovations had a positive effect on health, while decreased investments in human capital and technical innovations generally had negative effects on the long-term health of populations (Jahanger et al., 2022). The researchers found that positive shocks in the investment of human capital and technology innovation contribute to an increase in life expectancy, whereas negative shocks in human capital investment and technological innovation contribute to a decrease in life expectancy (Liu et al., 2022). Human capital investments (education, and technology innovation) also have the potential to influence people's health, although via indirect channels, that is, through environmental factors. Positive investments in education are a major source of the development of human capital in any country. Human capital investments are the critical mechanism for transmitting inequality to growth. High-quality education and equitable access to education are not just important goals on their own, they are critical enablers for almost all other goals (ElMassah & Mohieldin, 2020). A corrupted environment is unfriendly to technological change, and it erodes firms' incentives to invest in innovation and R&D. Corrupt countries also tend to invest less in education, which has implications for the quality of the human resources available, in the public sector as well as in the private sector (Mocetti & Orlando, 2019). More productive technologies, in turn, demand more complex qualifications and entail higher training costs. As discussed earlier, slowing growth of productivity and rising inequality are linked by the adverse effects of these dual challenges to the occupational opportunities of and the human capital accumulation of lower-income households (Indrawati & Kuncoro, 2021). Some researchers in their numerous studies and reports found that the most significant impacts are related to ecosystem health, human health, and resource exhaustion. This trend is evident in charts showing human population numbers, economic growth, and ecological indicators. Sustainable economic growth needs to be achieved and preserved at all costs provided that the economic growth is the priority of the governments.

At a macroeconomic level, labor mismatch increases unemployment and decreases GDP growth by the loss of human capital and resulting lower productivity (Liu, 2022). There are competing views about whether improvements in technical efficiency and innovation would allow for the full decoupling of economic growth from environmental degradation. Under such logic, market-based solutions to environmental crises (ecological economics, ecological economics, green economics) are dismissed as technological fixes which fail to address the structural failings of the present linear economic system (Razzaq et al., 2021). One branch of the economic theory, ecological economics, studies a field of scholarly study aimed at solving problems in the economics of humans and natural ecosystems. Biodiversity loss is principally caused by habitat loss and fragmentation caused by the appropriation of land by humans for development, forestry, and agriculture, with the gradual conversion of natural capital into man-made capital (Spash, 2020). On the other side of the specter of the economic theory are the economic historians who may be able to provide compelling accounts of current effects from changes of the distant past, but social scientists are less capable of predicting the effects of present changes to human systems in equal measure into the future (Clifton et al., 2020). Such cases must be collected, in order that they may be studied in systematic ways, and to generate testable hypotheses as to which kinds of innovations are likely to gain social traction to have lasting, increasing effects on the global environment, such as those resulting from the technology of the carbon-fluorocarbons, or the Brazilian development strategies used in the Amazon basin (Pereira et al., 2019). This fast growth has come about because scientific and technical developments are having an economic effect—in particular, increasing irrigation lands, industrial and electricity sector growth, and intense dam building, all over the continent (Romanova & Kuzmin, 2021). Informality also limited state's ability to raise taxes, and thus resources, which could have been used to foster inclusive and sustainable growth, for instance, by state investments in infrastructure and education, and by developing labor market programs (Čábelková & Strielkowski, 2013).

3 Human Capital Accumulation and Modern Technologies

Jobs which are not experiencing a fast shift in growth are nevertheless seeing rapid changes in technology adoption, requiring workers in these fields to acquire new skills (Deming & Noray, 2020). Individuals with higher levels of skills are better at taking advantage of new technologies in order to adjust to the changing nature of the job. Changes in the nature of work are somehow most obvious in advanced economies, where technologies are widely available and labor markets have started to emerge from higher levels of formalization.

The changing nature of work requires skillsets that enhance workers adaptability, making it easier for them to move easily from job to job (Anner et al., 2019). As jobs develop with a higher pace of change across sectors, locations, tasks, and skills requirements, many workers will require help in adjusting. Implications for job demands needed to cope with changes in job characteristics include technology knowledge, an openness to change and technology, skills to manage time and tasks, and further career and occupational growth (Chernyak-Hai & Rabenu, 2018). Even within a given profession, the effects of technology on skills needed for job performance are changing—but not always in the directions that one would expect. What is happening depends, in part, on whether the new technologies are automating and replacing workers on existing tasks faster than they are creating new demand for labor (Acemoglu & Restrepo, 2019).

The new technologies alter the nature of the labor market and its main essence. Novel technologies make some outdated jobs to cease to exist while, in the same time, they are creating new jobs in the fields not known to anyone before, as well as they create some new ways of earning income. Technology has also made it easier for jobs to be created by working online, or joining what is called the gig economy. Technology has consistently powered economic growth, improved standards of living, and opened avenues for new, better kinds of jobs (Graham et al., 2017). Technological advances are changing how we work, diminishing demand for certain types of jobs while expanding demand for others. The evidence is clear that technological changes are decreasing the demand for mechanized routine jobs, while increasing both demand for, and the pay for, highly technical, analytical jobs. Those workers who have high skills and qualifications would surely gain from the technological changes while the workers with lower skills (e.g., those engaged in manual and low-paid jobs) are likely to lose. Even though the workers with low skills employed in tech jobs would have the potential for greater gains in production and productivity, they could face pressure on wages given a potentially larger supply of similar low-skill workers, unless the demand for those occupations grows faster than the supply of workers (Lee & Clarke, 2019). There is a different group of jobs that might be more desirable, but those jobs are not available because they require higher levels of skills or education than workers are getting. It might be impossible to train workers in the skills of the future, for a variety of reasons, including the fact that no jobs would exist for them to be trained in, or the jobs would shift too rapidly. By the time training programs are widespread, the skills needed will not be needed anymore.

Having frequent training programs also will create a routine assessment of employees, skills, and processes. Training and development may stimulate company analytics and planning; this requires employers to look at existing talent and evaluate internal growth and development opportunities, instead of through hiring (Litau, 2019, 2020; Niederman, 2021). An assessment of the skills and capabilities currently in a group will allow managers to strategically plan targeted training programs, taking into account any potential skills gaps of their workers and to prepare special training programs targeted at the needs of these workers. It is becoming clear that employees should be analyzed and also recognized for their particular skills, technical fluency, and learning approaches. Role expectations and opportunities to develop are dependent on the way that occupation and technology are interrelated, particularly in working with automated systems (Makarius et al., 2020).

The identified research gaps must be addressed in order to ensure that employees are supported, on an evidence-based basis, in dealing with emerging technologies in their workplaces sustainably, taking responsibility for their performance and well-being, and seeking out and using opportunities to develop professionally and professionally. While efforts at making these changes are promising, employers, employees, educators, and policymakers must ensure more people are able to take advantage of these opportunities, and that technologies enhance how all of us work (Koman et al., 2022; Majid, 2020). Education systems have not kept up with the new alternations and changes on the labor market which makes many employers to complain about the lack of employees with the required skills. Skills and education required for higher-paying jobs ahead are still increasing, while jobs such as home health aides require less education, pay less, and offer fewer opportunities for professional growth (Dill & Hodges, 2019). While it is well-known that technology has been displaced by lower-skilled, blue-collar workers, higher-skilled jobs are for the most part protected, as jobs requiring greater education and more sophisticated cognitive skills such as analytics, problem-solving, and decision-making are far less codifiable (Ormerod, 2021).

By analyzing qualifications requirements with respect to the rate of job displacement and wage growth, it is suggested that automation of workplace tasks is replacing routine, lower-skill tasks, and thereby preferring individuals who are capable of performing complex, higher-skilled jobs due to their educational background and cognitive skills. Some researchers find employment is significantly higher for jobs requiring average or high skills gained either through specific education, work experience, and training at work), considerable knowledge of interpersonal, cross-cultural and managerial skills, as well as some analytical thinking and computing skills (Almazova et al., 2020). Many people in fact think and proclaim whenever asked that a typical college education at an institution helps to develop non-replicable, non-online skills, thus building the skillsets of people for whom the education services are too expensive, but that they expected that job-specific training would be handled on-the-job by employers and through new approaches. As pay falls for tasks that can be done by machines more and more, some employees might cut their time at work or searching for other possibilities such as unemployment benefits or spending more time with their families or friends, that can be comparably more appealing (Waring et al., 2020). Greater interplay will boost productivity, but it calls for approaches that might include embracing novel technologies and techniques as well as alternative renumeration models and novel approaches to building and nourishing in-house human capital. Overall, it is estimated that the technology changes replacing routine jobs created over 23 million jobs in Europe between 1999 and 2016, which is nearly half the total growth of jobs in that period (Grigoli et al., 2020). Novel technologies represented by the ICT and artificial intelligence-based technologies would surely have a wide impact on the labor markets literally all around the world. As a result, the worldwide labor market is likely to shift and yield profound changes. Thence, steps need to be made to react to these changes and to solve these new issues promptly and quickly.

4 Equilibrium Dynamics Productivity Growth

The equilibrium dynamics may be characterized by a combined evolution of the growth rate in output, schooling costs, and income distribution (Chugunov et al., 2021). Some researchers tackle this task through the elaborate development of a general equilibrium model aimed at analyzing the marginal and joint effects that different macroeconomic, schooling, and social insurance policies have on employment and unemployment dynamics at skill levels (Jaimovich et al., 2021). There are many studies that quantify the aggregate impact of the firing costs in a model of firm dynamics in which firm-level productivity is determined by innovation. One can refer with this regard to the well-known and popular (albeit quite simpler) Schumpeterian model of growth to explain why rising R&D productivity increases both top income shares and social mobility (Akcigit & Nicholas, 2019). More closely related to our analyses in this paper, some economists find positive relationships between both top 10% income shares and the growth rate across the United States (Basu, 2019). Other studies tend to contribute to the economic literature by showing that innovation-led growth is the source of the inequality at the top. Sustained economic growth requires technical changes that improve marginal capital productivity. At any given level of capital per worker, the mean and marginal productivity of capital rises as technology advances (Zhou et al., 2020). The revolution in information technology thus turns the productive function up, increasing the tilt of it at each level of capital per worker. At the new level of productivity and at the old level of real wages, firms are making enough profits either to lure new firms in or to motivate existing firms to increase their output. As a consequence, technological advance increases the resources firms must invest to expand production, while it also provides an incentive for continued investment. Because the markups are larger in sectors that employ the new technologies, the total revenue flows in relative terms away from workers to entrepreneurs every time the share of the output of a line with the new technologies increases. The former increases the inequality at the top, while entrant-driven creative destruction decreases it.

Another important point of view also comes from the works of the Austrian economist Joseph Schumpeter that was just presented and discussed above in this section. In a Schumpeterian model, instead, new innovation (entrants) increases the mark-ups of a relevant industry, while, absent new innovation, the mark-ups are partially destroyed through copying. While all innovations decrease wage shares; productive innovations raise the wage level, while defensive innovations lower it 10. Finally, an entrepreneurs share of income is not affected by previous periods intensity of innovation, so temporary increases in innovation lead to a temporary rise in entrepreneurs income share (Schreyer & Zinni, 2021). The departures from lower-productivity firms contributed one-quarter of the growth in productivity, while 17% was contributed by reallocations of jobs and output from lower-productivity firms to higher-productivity firms. Data from many countries around the world, for instance, indicate that more than two-thirds of productivity growth occurred within firms (similar to Walmart's examples in the United States) (Setzler & Tintelnot, 2021).

In addition, the past decade has seen important progress toward decreasing inequality in Latin America, but this progress is threatened by sluggish productivity growth and weak structural changes. In this very important but also very turbulent region, as in many other places around the globe, governments and business owners realize that the investments in human capital and education provides significant positive outcomes in terms of economic gains. They also attempt to influence on this trend and to foster education and formation of human capital which would yield significant benefits both for the entrepreneurs and the economy as a whole. Recent changes in Latin America (most notably such countries as Brazil or Colombia) make researches to think that the change of economic perspectives is occurring.

5 Conclusion

All in all, our results demonstrate that there is a clear dynamic interaction between human capital accumulation and economic growth. With regard to that finding, it becomes apparent that regulating the accumulation of human capital is an action that should be pursued by the governments seeking economic advancements for their economies.

There is also the apparent connection between the build-up of human capital and the future of work, looking closely at why governments should invest in human capital, and why they frequently fail to do so; presents a new project on the world bank on human capital, including establishing a global reference point; and presents cross-country comparisons of economies around the world. An overview of findings from literature linking early life health with school performance is followed by discussion of studies on the effects of health care provision in early life and public health policies on children's human capital accumulation. As we demonstrated in our paper, several studies have examined how the presence of particular health conditions during early childhood influences the human capital accumulation of later in life. A substantial amount of empirical work suggests that negative conditions (such as poor diet, disease, in-utero alcohol exposure, iodine deficiency, severe trauma, or ill maternal health, as well as psychological distress) in early childhood—the period between conception and five years old—have lasting adverse effects on human capital accumulation and economic outcomes, and adult health. The hypothesis that the origins of health and human capital accumulation during early life are referred to as fetal source suggests that the origins of many chronic, degenerative adult health problems (such as type 2 diabetes and cardiovascular disease) are attributed to prenatal conditions, particularly poor nutrition). In one line of work, researchers used an indirect measure of health during pregnancy and examined the effect it had on educational attainment later in life. A comprehensive reference rate measures productivity in the next generation of workers, compared with the reference rates for completed education and complete health. The new benchmark measures how much of a person's capital can expect to have at the age of 18, given the risks of mediocre education and ill-health prevalent in the country where they are born. Over time, new labor force participants with the status quo in education and health will displace incumbent labor force participants, until finally all the future labor force has an expected number of years with the schools and levels of health adapted in the global reference case. In a companion paper we extended our model to examine the effects of informality on human capital accumulation as workers work, given any education they received prior to entering the labor force. In our view, informality is the manifestation of imperfections in the structure and functioning of institutions that govern firm and worker behavior on the job market.

Our basic finding is that a dysfunctional labor market is, de facto, an anti-educational policy, since it reduces returns to schooling, hence, the incentives to invest in schools. Governments may be unaware that the institutions regulating their labor markets are reducing returns on significant investments in schools. In all of these countries, governments are making big investments in schools with the expectation that these investments will boost wages and speed up growth. It is possible that improving the operation of labor markets is a powerful vehicle for increasing investment in schools. For instance, when workers are participating in competitive, well-functioning labor markets, they are motivated to gain more human capital, since more education and skills pay higher wages. This recipe for economic growth—investing in worker productivity, through investments in human capital and technology, as well as increased physical capital—also applies to other economies. A healthy environment for GDP per capita and labor productivity growth involves human capital deepening, physical capital deepening, and technology gains operating within a market-oriented economy with supportive public policies. Although investments in physical capital are important to labor productivity growth and GDP per capita, building human capital is at least as important. A more important reason for building the output per capita function is to understand the contributions of both human capital and physical capital. The conventional approach uses the aggregate production function to assess how much of the growth of economic output per capita can be explained by increases in both.

References

Acemoglu, D., & Restrepo, P. (2019). Automation and new tasks: How technology displaces and reinstates labor. *Journal of Economic Perspectives, 33*(2), 3–30. https://doi.org/10.1257/jep.33.2.3

Akcigit, U., & Nicholas, T. (2019). History, microdata, and endogenous growth. *Annual Review of Economics, 11*, 615–633. https://doi.org/10.1146/annurev-economics-080218-030204

Almazova, N., Krylova, E., Rubtsova, A., & Odinokaya, M. (2020). Challenges and opportunities for Russian higher education amid COVID-19: Teachers' perspective. *Education Sciences, 10*(12), 368. https://doi.org/10.3390/educsci10120368

Anner, M., Pons-Vignon, N., & Rani, U. (2019). For a future of work with dignity: A critique of the World Bank Development Report, the changing nature of work. *Global Labour Journal, 10*(1), 2–19. https://doi.org/10.15173/glj.v10i1.3796

Basu, S. (2019). Are price-cost markups rising in the United States? A discussion of the evidence. *Journal of Economic Perspectives, 33*(3), 3–22. https://doi.org/10.1257/jep.33.3.3

Boikos, S., Bucci, A., & Stengos, T. (2022). Leisure and innovation in horizontal R&D-based growth. *Economic Modelling, 107*, 105730. https://doi.org/10.1016/j.econmod.2021.105730

Bordea, E., Manea, M., & Pelligrini, A. (2017). Unemployment and coping with stress, anxiety, and depression. *Czech Journal of Social Sciences, Business and Economics, 6*(2), 6–14. https://doi.org/10.24984/cjssbe.2017.6.2.1

Čábelková, I., & Strielkowski, W. (2013). Is the level of taxation a product of culture? A cultural economics approach. *Society and Economy, 35*(4), 513–529. https://doi.org/10.1556/SocEc.2013.0007

Čábelková, I., Abrhám, J., & Strielkowski, W. (2015). Factors influencing job satisfaction in post-transition economies: The case of the Czech Republic. *International Journal of Occupational Safety and Ergonomics, 21*(4), 448–456. https://doi.org/10.1080/10803548.2015.1073007

Capozza, C., & Divella, M. (2019). Human capital and firms' innovation: Evidence from emerging economies. *Economics of Innovation and New Technology, 28*(7), 741–757. https://doi.org/10.1080/10438599.2018.1557426

Card, D., Cardoso, A. R., Heining, J., & Kline, P. (2018). Firms and labor market inequality: Evidence and some theory. *Journal of Labor Economics, 36*(S1), S13–S70. https://doi.org/10.1086/694153

Chernyak-Hai, L., & Rabenu, E. (2018). The new era workplace relationships: Is social exchange theory still relevant? *Industrial and Organizational Psychology, 11*(3), 456–481. https://doi.org/10.1017/iop.2018.5

Chirwa, T.G., & Odhiambo, N.M. (2018). Exogenous and endogenous growth models: A critical review. *Comparative Economic Research. Central and Eastern Europe, 21*(4), 63–84. https://doi.org/10.2478/cer-2018-0027

Chugunov, I., Pasichnyi, M., Koroviy, V., Kaneva, T., & Nikitishin, A. (2021). Fiscal and monetary policy of economic development. *European Journal of Sustainable Development, 10*(1), 42. https://doi.org/10.14207/ejsd.2021.v10n1p42

Clifton, J., Glasmeier, A., & Gray, M. (2020). When machines think for us: The consequences for work and place. *Cambridge Journal of Regions, Economy and Society, 13*(1), 3–23. https://doi.org/10.1093/cjres/rsaa004

Deming, D. J., & Noray, K. (2020). Earnings dynamics, changing job skills, and STEM careers. *The Quarterly Journal of Economics, 135*(4), 1965–2005. https://doi.org/10.1093/qje/qjaa021

Dill, J., & Hodges, M. J. (2019). Is healthcare the new manufacturing? Industry, gender, and "good jobs" for low-and middle-skill workers. *Social Science Research, 84*, 102350. https://doi.org/10.1016/j.ssresearch.2019.102350

ElMassah, S., & Mohieldin, M. (2020). Digital transformation and localizing the sustainable development goals (SDGs). *Ecological Economics, 169*, 106490. https://doi.org/10.1016/j.ecolecon.2019.106490

Graham, M., Hjorth, I., & Lehdonvirta, V. (2017). Digital labour and development: Impacts of global digital labour platforms and the gig economy on worker livelihoods. *Transfer: European Review of Labour and Research, 23*(2), 135–162. https://doi.org/10.1177/1024258916687250

Grigoli, F., Koczan, Z., & Topalova, P. (2020). Automation and labor force participation in advanced economies: Macro and micro evidence. *European Economic Review, 126*, 103443. https://doi.org/10.1016/j.euroecorev.2020.103443

Gruzina, Y., Firsova, I., & Strielkowski, W. (2021). Dynamics of human capital development in economic development cycles. *Economies, 9*(2), 67. https://doi.org/10.3390/economies9020067

Horváthová, A., Hrnčiar, M., & Rievajová, E. (2022). Changes in the skills of the workforce for future development of the labor market in the Slovak Republic. *Entrepreneurship and Sustainability Issues, 9*(4), 212–224. https://doi.org/10.9770/jesi.2022.9.4(11)

Humpert, S. (2013). A note on the immigrant-native gap in earnings. *International Economics Letters, 2*(4), 41–48. https://doi.org/10.24984/iel.2013.2.4.4

Indrawati, S. M., & Kuncoro, A. (2021). Improving competitiveness through vocational and higher education: Indonesia's vision for human capital development in 2019–2024. *Bulletin of Indonesian Economic Studies, 57*(1), 29–59. https://doi.org/10.1080/00074918.2021.1909692

Jahanger, A., Usman, M., Murshed, M., Mahmood, H., & Balsalobre-Lorente, D. (2022). The linkages between natural resources, human capital, globalization, economic growth, financial development, and ecological footprint: The moderating role of technological innovations. *Resources Policy, 76*, 102569. https://doi.org/10.1016/j.resourpol.2022.102569

Jaimovich, N., Saporta-Eksten, I., Siu, H., & Yedid-Levi, Y. (2021). The macroeconomics of automation: Data, theory, and policy analysis. *Journal of Monetary Economics, 122*, 1–16. https://doi.org/10.1016/j.jmoneco.2021.06.004

Klofsten, M., Fayolle, A., Guerrero, M., Mian, S., Urbano, D., & Wright, M. (2019). The entrepreneurial university as driver for economic growth and social change-key strategic challenges. *Technological Forecasting and Social Change, 141*, 149–158. https://doi.org/10.1016/j.techfore.2018.12.004

Koman, G., Tumová, D., Jankal, R., & Mičiak, M. (2022). Business-making supported via the application of big data to achieve economic sustainability. *Entrepreneurship and Sustainability Issues, 9*(4), 336–358. https://doi.org/10.9770/jesi.2022.9.4(18)

Lee, N., & Clarke, S. (2019). Do low-skilled workers gain from high-tech employment growth? High-technology multipliers, employment and wages in Britain. *Research Policy, 48*(9), 103803. https://doi.org/10.1016/j.respol.2019.05.012

Li, T., Li, X., & Liao, G. (2022). Business cycles and energy intensity. Evidence from emerging economies. *Borsa Istanbul Review, 22*(3), 560–570. https://doi.org/10.1016/j.bir.2021.07.005

Litau, E. Y. (2019). Concept of entrepreneurship anti-ideology. *Entrepreneurship and Sustainability Issues, 7*(2), 1308–1318. https://doi.org/10.9770/jesi.2019.7.2(35)

Litau, E. Y. (2020). Scoring method as applied to innovation project evaluation for startup support. *Entrepreneurship and Sustainability Issues, 7*(4), 2978–2990. https://doi.org/10.9770/jesi.2020.7.4(27)

Liu, A. Y. (2022). The minimum wage and occupational mobility. *International Economic Review, 63*(2), 917–945. https://doi.org/10.1111/iere.12552

Liu, Y., Sohail, M. T., Khan, A., & Majeed, M. T. (2022). Environmental benefit of clean energy consumption: Can BRICS economies achieve environmental sustainability through human capital? *Environmental Science and Pollution Research, 29*(5), 6766–6776. https://doi.org/10.1007/s11356-021-16167-5

Majid, M. A. (2020). Renewable energy for sustainable development in India: Current status, future prospects, challenges, employment, and investment opportunities. *Energy, Sustainability and Society, 10*(1), 1–36. https://doi.org/10.1186/s13705-019-0232-1

Makarius, E. E., Mukherjee, D., Fox, J. D., & Fox, A. K. (2020). Rising with the machines: A sociotechnical framework for bringing artificial intelligence into the organization. *Journal of Business Research, 120*, 262–273. https://doi.org/10.1016/j.jbusres.2020.07.045

Mocetti, S., & Orlando, T. (2019). Corruption, workforce selection and mismatch in the public sector. *European Journal of Political Economy, 60*, 101809. https://doi.org/10.1016/j.ejpoleco.2019.07.007

Mohanty, S., & Sethi, N. (2019). Outward FDI, human capital and economic growth in BRICS countries: An empirical insight. *Transnational Corporations Review, 11*(3), 235–249. https://doi.org/10.1080/19186444.2019.1657347

Niederman, F. (2021). Project management: Openings for disruption from AI and advanced analytics. *Information Technology & People, 34*(6), 1570–1599. https://doi.org/10.1108/ITP-09-2020-0639

Ogundari, K., & Awokuse, T. (2018). Human capital contribution to economic growth in Sub-Saharan Africa: Does health status matter more than education? *Economic Analysis and Policy, 58*, 131–140. https://doi.org/10.1016/j.eap.2018.02.001

Ormerod, R. (2021). The fitness and survival of the OR profession in the age of artificial intelligence. *Journal of the Operational Research Society, 72*(1), 4–22. https://doi.org/10.1080/01605682.2019.1650619

Pereira, E. J. D. A. L., Ferreira, P. J. S., de Santana Ribeiro, L. C., Carvalho, T. S., & de Barros Pereira, H. B. (2019). Policy in Brazil (2016–2019) threaten conservation of the Amazon rainforest. *Environmental Science & Policy, 100*, 8–12. https://doi.org/10.1016/j.envsci.2019.06.001

Qamruzzaman, M., Jianguo, W., Jahan, S., & Yingjun, Z. (2021). Financial innovation, human capital development, and economic growth of selected South Asian countries: An application of ARDL approach. *International Journal of Finance & Economics, 26*(3), 4032–4053. https://doi.org/10.1002/ijfe.2003

Razzaq, A., Wang, Y., Chupradit, S., Suksatan, W., & Shahzad, F. (2021). Asymmetric inter-linkages between green technology innovation and consumption-based carbon emissions in BRICS countries using quantile-on-quantile framework. *Technology in Society, 66*, 101656. https://doi.org/10.1016/j.techsoc.2021.101656

Romanova, O. A., & Kuzmin, E. (2021). Industrial policy: A new reality in the context of digital transformation of the economy. *Lecture Notes in Information Systems and Organisation, 44*, 13–23. https://doi.org/10.1007/978-3-030-73261-5_2

Schreyer, P., & Zinni, M. B. (2021). Productivity measurement, R&D assets, and mark-ups in OECD countries. *Review of Income and Wealth, 67*(4), 787–809. https://doi.org/10.1111/roiw.12492

Setzler, B., & Tintelnot, F. (2021). The effects of foreign multinationals on workers and firms in the United States. *The Quarterly Journal of Economics, 136*(3), 1943–1991. https://doi.org/10.1093/qje/qjab015

Spash, C. L. (2020). A tale of three paradigms: Realising the revolutionary potential of ecological economics. *Ecological Economics, 169*, 106518. https://doi.org/10.1016/j.ecolecon.2019.106518

Strielkowski, W., & Weyskrabova, B. (2014). Ukrainian labour migration and remittances in the Czech Republic. *Tijdschrift voor economische en sociale geografie, 105*(1), 30–45. https://doi.org/10.1111/tesg.12052

Waring, J., Lindvall, C., & Umeton, R. (2020). Automated machine learning: Review of the state-of-the-art and opportunities for healthcare. *Artificial Intelligence in Medicine, 104*, 101822. https://doi.org/10.1016/j.artmed.2020.101822

Zhao, J., & Zhou, N. (2021). Impact of human health on economic growth under the constraint of environment pollution. *Technological Forecasting and Social Change, 169*, 120828. https://doi.org/10.1016/j.techfore.2021.120828

Zhou, X., Song, M., & Cui, L. (2020). Driving force for China's economic development under Industry 4.0 and circular economy: Technological innovation or structural change? *Journal of Cleaner Production, 271*, 122680. https://doi.org/10.1016/j.jclepro.2020.122680

Economic Resilience Determinants Under Shocks of Different Origins

Victoria Akberdina

Abstract During crisis, scientists' attention is focused on the shock effect on economic dynamics. The shock may be catastrophic for one country and painless for another. Scientific studies of crises postulate the thesis about the resilience, i.e. the capability of economic systems to recover from negative impacts. The paper examines the shocks of various nature in the beginning of the twentieth century, their impact on the economic dynamics of countries. The author comes to the conclusion about the existence of the "multi-crisis" phenomenon, i.e. a compound of financial, trade, political and pandemic crises. The paper presents a theoretical review of "economic resilience" and describes two groups of resilient determinants—innate and acquired determinants. The author applied the decomposition method to macroeconomic indicators (GRP and unemployment dynamics) and assessed the resilience of developed countries and Russia. The study proves that when shocks of different nature are combined, each country has its own unique combination of resilient determinants.

Keywords Economic resilience · Shocks · Economic systems · Economic dynamics
JEL Classification E20 · E32 · H12

1 Introduction

Historical experience clearly shows that any scale economic system can be inflexible and unstable due to economic and financial shocks. External shocks have a disastrous effect on some countries, while being invisible to other ones. The global economic crisis in 2020 caused by COVID-19 has clearly demonstrated how vulnerable communities, states and continents are to shocks of a non-economic nature.

When a sharp endogenous shock occurs, countries and regions pay great attention and spend a lot of money to mitigate the consequences. However, preventive actions

V. Akberdina (✉)
Institute of Economics of the Ural Branch of the Russian Academy of Sciences, 29 Moskovskaya Str., 620014 Ekaterinburg, Russian Federation
e-mail: akberdina.vv@uiec.ru

V. Kumar et al. (eds.), *Consequences of Social Transformation for Economic Theory*, Springer Proceedings in Business and Economics,
https://doi.org/10.1007/978-3-031-27785-6_6

and predictive analytics could not only reduce direct losses, but also significantly cut the anti-crisis budget. Preventive steps aim at the adaptability of the economy (effective structure of the economy and employment, diversification of industry, flexible government policy and institutions), avoid potential losses and strengthen resilience—the most important feature of the economic system in a crisis period. Interest in resilience has been rising rapidly during the last 20 years, as feedback to increasing disquietude about potential shocks that check the limits of overcoming countries' capacities.

The purpose of the paper is to identify the resilient determinants of developed countries and the Russian economy due to different crises for the period of 2000–2020. The paper raises *the following research questions*: (1) which countries have achieved resilient outcomes during and after the crisis? (2) is it possible to identify the country's features and determinants associated with resilient outcomes? (3) have some countries been able to use the crisis as an opportunity for further development? The answers to these questions offer cases for monitoring resilience and a starting point for effective policy decisions in the future. Also, it will allow adding the theoretical foundations of resistance with new determinants, highlighted by the example of three successive crises in Russia.

2 Theoretical Framework

Shocks are an integral part of economic dynamics. In macroeconomics, shocks are caused by non-price determinants that shift supply and demand curves and lead to a new equilibrium (Brinca et al., 2020; Rio-Chanona et al., 2020). In cyclic theory, shocks are understood as independent impulses of wave dynamics that trigger cause-and-effect dependencies and provide the cyclical development of the economic system (Bongers & Díaz-Roldán, 2019; Yuan et al., 2018). The nature of shocks leading to economic crises can be quite diverse. These can be natural disasters and technogenic catastrophe, global economic changes and political decisions, rapid technological changes, and much more. The year of 2020 was marked by a new kind of global crisis caused by a pandemic (Yu et al., 2021).

The description of resistance is based on the "system view" of our conceptual framework. Economic shocks can be both one-time (for example, a natural disaster) and slow (for example, technological changes and the large Kondratiev cycles caused by them). Any economic system—national economy, sub-region, industry or company—should give feedback on the shock. And the measure of resilience is determined by how quickly the economic system will come out of recession, fully recover and continue to grow.

The term "resilience" is quite close to the terms "stability", "resistance", "durability" and "strength". However, a more exact emphasis is associated with the translation from Latin *resilire*, which means to leap back—"elasticity", "flexibility".

Initially, the term resilience appeared in economic studies as a cross-disciplinary term (Reid & Botterill, 2013). The first mentions of resilience are related with the estimation of the economic consequences of technogenic catastrophe and natural disasters. Environmentalists were the first to give a useful and broad definition of resilience associated with the "survival" of the systems (Rose & Liao, 2005; West & Lenge, 1994).

Thus, ecologists defined resilience as a system characteristic associated with the absorption of any changes (Holling, 1973). Halling called this system's feature as "buffer capacity". Perrings (2001) and other environmental economists shifted the attention from "any changes" particularly to "shocks and stress". The term of a "buffer capacity" best corresponds to the term of resilience in the economy. This is not just about a decline in economic activity, but rather about a real decline compared to a potential one. Adger (2000) was one of the first to extend the ecological definition of resilience to society as a whole.

A new round of interest in the concept of economic resilience emerged after the global financial crisis of 2008 (Didier et al., 2012; Jain & Jordan, 2009; Rose & Krausmann, 2013). For the first time, researchers started talking about the determinants of the resilience of the global and regional economies, implying the ability of the economic system to quickly return to its original position in response to a structural or systemic failure (Didier et al., 2012; Jüttner & Maklan, 2011). Many researchers have focused on measuring economic resilience using traditionally economic indicators—gross domestic product and unemployment rate (Bristow & Healy, 2017; Reid & Botterill, 2013).

There are some studies devoted to research of regional resilience. Some authors interpret regions as individual countries. For example, the resilience of European countries was studied both in the context of the 2008 financial crisis and in the context of the pandemic crisis (Brada et al., 2021; Davis, 2011). Another part of the researchers focused on the study of the internal regions of one country (Courvisanos et al., 2016; Hu et al., 2022). There are also studies of the urban economic resilience (Vanolo, 2015).

The COVID-19 pandemic has become *a new trigger* for economic resilience research (Hu et al., 2022; Pierri & Timmer, 2020; Rahmadana & Sagala, 2020; Zhai & Yue, 2022). Many studies suggest that the nature of COVID-19 extremely differs from global financial crisis (Brada et al., 2021; Sensier & Devine, 2020). This special context of the crisis should be taken seriously. Many researchers have noted that economic resilience in the conditions of COVID-19, unlike the 2008 financial crisis, is formed not only by economic structural determinants, but also under the influence of state institutions in terms of economic constraints and recovery measures.

Whatever the nature of the crisis, researchers always pay considerable attention to social risks. Thus, some studies concern the consequences of the crisis for the health and social security sector (Trump & Linkov, 2020), the specifics of social crises in economically disadvantaged regions (Crețan et al., 2017), the impact of social partnership and culture on crisis mitigation (Drakaki & Tzionas, 2017; Vanolo, 2015), as well as research of investment crises affecting depopulation in mono-industry regions (Vesalon & Creţan, 2013) and others.

We can say that *there are two approaches to economic resistance.* The first approach is technical, or equilibrium. Also in the literature, it is called an "engineering" approach. This approach is associated with the return of the system to initial equilibrium point (by analogy with the elasticity of materials). With this approach, the "strength" of the shock plays a significant role. The second one is an ecosystem (or evolutionary) approach. In the context of this approach, resilience means constant adaptation and improvement in response to changes.

We see that everywhere there is an emphasis on the internal characteristic of the economic system to "bend" and recover from the shock due to structural adaptation. Let's give our own definition. *Economic resilience is the ability of the economic system to fully recover after the shocks of various origins due to internal features:*

(1) *"innate" determinants* of the economic system (for example, the established evolutionary path, the structure of the economy, the peculiarities of the labor market, the ability of enterprises to replace the initial resources with those that turned out to be scarce, etc.);
(2) *"acquired" (adaptive) determinants* of the economic system—the ability of the economy to smooth out the consequences of the crisis through additional efforts (these may include state policy, national innovation system, affordable financing, etc.).

Next, we will consider these factors of economic resilience on the example of Russia and a number of developed countries.

3 Data and Methods

The paper uses the recent crisis experience of countries as a unique natural experiment to provide identification for measuring resilience at the country level. To study the resilience determinants in crises of various origins, we will use data from the International Monetary Fund on GDP and unemployment for the period of 2000–2020 in five countries—Great Britain, Germany, France, the USA and Russia. We do not analyze data for 2021–2022 due to the lack of sufficient data. The main research method is the decomposition method of macroeconomic indicators' visualization.

4 Results and Discussion

Figure 1 shows a graph of GDP growth in analyzed countries. Let's consider the main turning points of economic dynamics. During this period, the world economy faced two crises—the global financial crisis of 2008 and the crisis of 2020 caused by the coronavirus pandemic. For Russia, there was one more individual crisis during this period—the sanctional crisis (2014–2020). Thus, with regard to Russia, we can talk about multi-crisis—an overlapping financial, pandemic and trade crises.

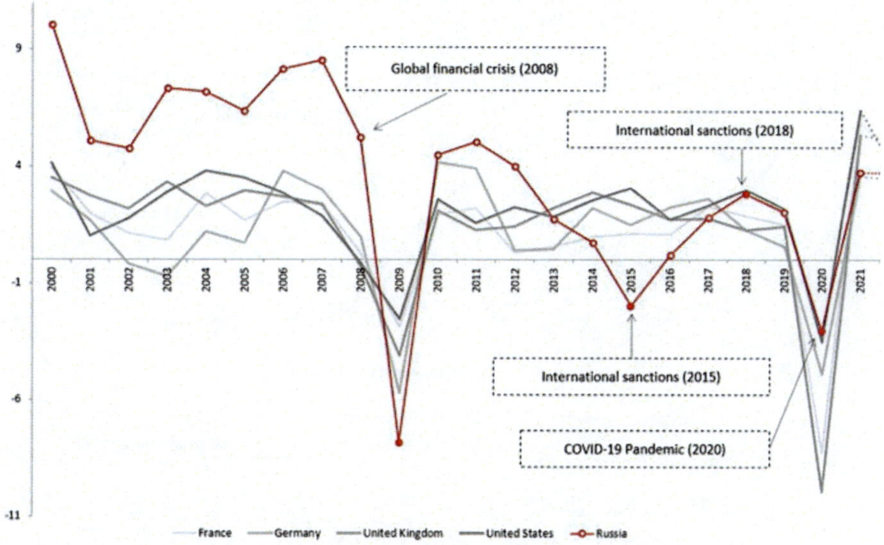

Fig. 1 Gross domestic product, growth rate (percent)

The first shock of the twenty-first century is the global financial crisis of 2008. This crisis evolved from the financial crisis in the United States. In 2009, the world GDP for the first time since the 1940s turned out to be negative. In Russia, the financial crisis was related to high creditworthiness of the private sector.

We can see that the decline of the Russian economy was more significant than in other countries in question. The banking crisis, the fall in stock indices and the decline in export prices at the end of 2008 led to a sharp decline in industrial production and growth of unemployment.

At the same time, it should be noted that the Russian labor market was more flexible than in the USA (Fig. 2). In response to the shock in 2009, unemployment in Russia increased to 8.2%, while in the United States—to 9.2%. But the GDP decline rate in Russia over the same period was 7.8%, and in the United States—2.5%.

The decline continued in 2009. At the end of 2008, the first anti-crisis mechanisms related to solving the most difficult problem began to operate: it was the strengthening of financial system. The main directions of the state anti-crisis policy are presented in Table 1. As early as in 2010, the Russian economy completely recovered from such a sharp drop, the Russian stock market became the leader of growth in the world.

The second shock was purely individual for Russia. These were the international economic sanctions. The United States and a number of other countries applied sanctions against Russia in 2014. The first package of sanctions was a "symbolic act". The first wave of sanctions in 2014 did not have a significant impact on the Russian economy. The restrictions of 2015 were more significant, as they affected specific organizations and banks, and sanctions were also imposed on the import of technologies and weapons. The expected effect of this package of sanctions was

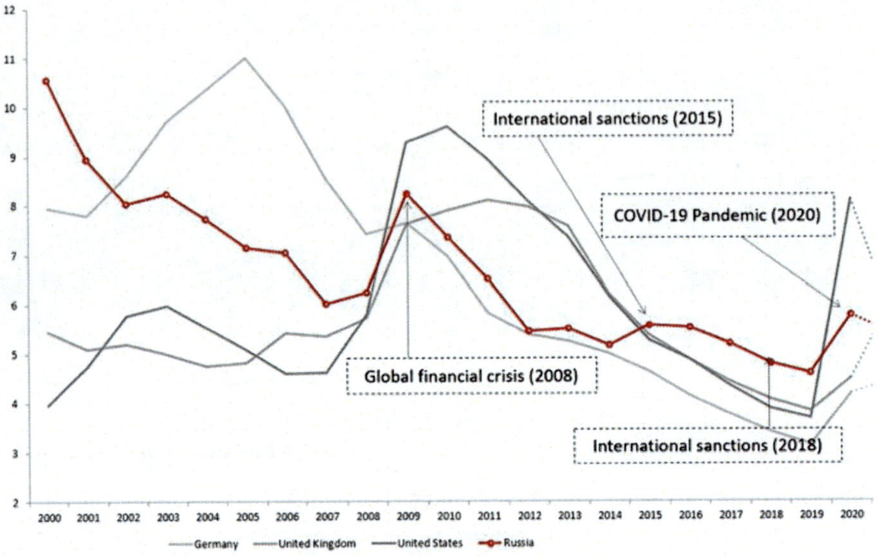

Fig. 2 Unemployment rate (percent of total labor force)

predicted as quite high, leading to a sharp deficit of the federal budget. A little later, the Credit Rating Analytical Agency estimated that the sanctions had a weak impact on Russian banks and companies. We see this by a slight decrease in GDP in 2015. In 2016, Russia reached zero growth rate, and in 2017, a steady recovery growth began.

Sanctions have created in Russia opportunities for the development of high-tech industry. The restrictions proved to be a powerful impetus for import substitution and localization of new production facilities in the country. In addition, in response to the sanctions, Russia in 2014 restricted the food products import from the countries that joined the sanctions. This has led to a serious strengthening of Russia's food independence. It is important to note that the sanctions did not lead to an increase in unemployment (Fig. 2). From 2015 to 2019, the unemployment rate in Russia steadily declined, largely due to the policy of import substitution.

The third shock is the economic crisis caused by the pandemic. Figure 1 shows that in Russia its impact is slightly more significant than the sanctions, but significantly less (more than 2 times) than the crisis of 2008–2009. If we compare the decline in the economy in 2020 with previous crises, the decline in Russia's GDP in 2020 (−3.1%) was slightly worse than the result of the 2015 crisis (−2.0%), but noticeably better than the 2009 crisis (−7.8%).

Moreover, we see that the decline of the Russian economy is significantly less than that of the world's leading countries. Although the Russian economy shrank by 3% in 2020, its dynamics was one of the best among the 15 countries with the largest GDP. According to official data, only China coped with the pandemic better than Russia. For the first time, Russia survived the economic crisis better than the world

Table 1 Resilient determinants of the Russian economy

Shock	Effect of the crisis	Government policy	Resilient determinants
Global financial crisis (2008)	The private sector crisis caused by its high creditworthiness in the context of the deterioration of foreign trade conditions and capital outflow	Monetary and fiscal policy instruments aimed at paying off the external debt of large banks and corporations, increasing liquidity and restructuring banks. The anti-crisis budget amounted to 3% of GDP	Availability of reserves
International sanctions (2015–2020)	Initially, there was a decrease in the outflow of foreign investment, the freezing of investment projects, and a decline in GDP. Subsequently, the change of trading partners, the growth of production due to import substitution, the growth of research and development funding	State programs for import substitution and localization of production in Russia. A large-scale export support program. Access of industrial enterprises to cheap financing. The anti-crisis budget amounted to 2.2% of GDP	Huge potential of the industry and R&D sector. Significant reserves for industrial development (greenfield and brownfield)
COVID-19 pandemic (2020)	An unprecedented shutdown of business activity, a collapse in oil prices and a drop in export demand. The pandemic crisis has led to a drop in GDP, a record decline in real disposable income, rising unemployment, and a drag on consumption and investment	Tools for selective support of industries, state support for system-forming enterprises, support for employment and income, exemption from payments and control and audit checks. The anti-crisis budget amounted to 1–1.5% of GDP	The dominance of large businesses with state participation Localization of value chains within the country

as a whole: the fall in Russia's GDP was 3.1% against the 3.5%-drop in global GDP. At the same time, the unemployment rate in Russia has increased, but not as sharply as, for example, in the United States. While unemployment in Russia between 2019 and 2020 increased from 4.6 to 5.7%, in the United States it soared from 3.6 to 8.1% (Fig. 2).

5 Conclusion

We have analyzed what kind of crises the country's economy may face. Using the example of Russia, we have shown the phenomenon of multi-crisis for a fairly short period of time.

During the global financial crisis of 2008, the Russian economy showed such "innate" determinants as significant federal reserves and capital mobility between the financial and industrial sectors, as well as "adaptive" determinants related with the anti-crisis government policy. The resilient determinants of the Russian economy during the sanctions period were the huge potential of industry and the R&D sector, significant reserves production capacity (greenfield and brownfield), what ensured the success of the import substitution policy. And finally, during the 2020 pandemic, Russia coped with the economic crisis much better than the world's leading countries, thanks to the high share of large businesses with government participation and the localization of value chains within the country.

In conclusion, we can identify niche segments for further studies of economic resilience. Such relevant research niches include measurement of the resilience threshold level and its sensitivity analysis, as well as an assessment of regional resilience.

Acknowledgements The research was carried out at the expense of the grant of the Russian Science Foundation No. 22-28-01674, https://rscf.ru/project/22-28-01674/.

References

Adger, W. N. (2000). Social and ecological resilience: Are they related? *Progress in Human Geography, 24*(3), 347–364. https://doi.org/10.1191/030913200701540465

Bongers, A., & Díaz-Roldán, C. (2019). Stabilization policies and technological shocks: Towards a sustainable economic growth path. *Sustainability, 11*(1), 205. https://doi.org/10.3390/su11010205

Brada, J. C., Gajewski, P., & Kutan, A. M. (2021). Economic resiliency and recovery, lessons from the financial crisis for the COVID-19 pandemic: A regional perspective from Central and Eastern Europe. *International Review of Financial Analysis, 74*, 101658. https://doi.org/10.1016/j.irfa.2021.101658

Brinca, P., Duarte, J. B., & Faria-e-Castro, M. (2020). Measuring sectoral supply and demand shocks during COVID-19. *Covid Economics, 20*, 147–171. https://doi.org/10.20955/wp.2020.011

Bristow, G., & Healy, A. (2017). Innovation and regional economic resilience: An exploratory analysis. *The Annals of Regional Science, 60*(2), 1–20. https://doi.org/10.1007/s00168-017-0841-6

Courvisanos, J., Jain, A., & Mardaneh, K. K. (2016). Economic resilience of regions under crises: A study of the Australian economy. *Journal Regional Studies, Theme Issue: Resilience Revisited, 50*(4), 629–643. https://doi.org/10.1080/00343404.2015.1034669

Crețan, R., Guran-Nica, L., Platon, D., & Turnock, D. (2017). Foreign direct investment and social risk in Romania: Progress in less-favoured areas. In *Foreign direct investment and regional development in East Central Europe and the Former Soviet Union* (pp. 305–348). Routledge. https://doi.org/10.4324/9781351158121-15

Davies, S. (2011). Regional resilience in the 2008–2010 downturn: Comparative evidence from European countries. *Cambridge Journal of Regions Economy and Society, 4*(3), 369–382. https://doi.org/10.1093/cjres/rsr019

Didier, T., Hevia, C., & Schmukler, S. L. (2012). How resilient and countercyclical were emerging economies during the global financial crisis? *Journal of International Money and Finance, 31*(8), 2052–2077. https://doi.org/10.1016/j.jimonfin.2012.05.007

Drakaki, M., & Tzionas, P. (2017). Community-based social partnerships in crisis resilience: A case example in Greece. *Disaster Prevention and Management, 26*(2), 203–216. https://doi.org/10.1108/DPM-09-2016-0190

Holling, C. (1973). Resiliency and stability of ecological systems. *Annual Review of Ecological Systems, 4*, 1–24. http://www.jstor.org/stable/2096802

Hu, X., Li, L., & Dong, K. (2022). What matters for regional economic resilience amid COVID-19? Evidence from cities in Northeast China. *Cities, 120*, 103440. https://doi.org/10.1016/j.cities.2021.103440

Jain, A., & Jordan, C. (2009). Diversity and resilience: Lessons from the financial crisis. *UNSWLJ, 32*, 416. http://hdl.handle.net/11343/30152

Jüttner, U., & Maklan, S. (2011). Supply chain resilience in the global financial crisis: An empirical study. *Supply Chain Management: An International Journal, 16*(4), 246–259. https://doi.org/10.1108/13598541111139062

Martin, R. (2012). Regional economic resilience, hysteresis and recessionary shocks. *Journal of Economic Geography, 12*(1), 1–32. https://doi.org/10.1093/jeg/lbr019

Notteboom, T., Pallis, T., & Rodrigue, J. P. (2021). Disruptions and resilience in global container shipping and ports: The COVID-19 pandemic versus the 2008–2009 financial crisis. *Maritime Economics & Logistics, 23*(2), 179–210. https://doi.org/10.1057/s41278-020-00180-5

Perrings, C. (2001). Resilience and sustainability. In H. Folmer, H. L. Gabel, S. Gerking & A. Rose (Eds.), *Frontiers of environmental economics*. Edward Elgar. https://doi.org/10.4337/9781843767091.00021

Pierri, N., & Timmer, Y. (2020). IT shields: Technology adoption and economic resilience during the COVID-19 pandemic. *Available at SSRN 3721520*. http://hdl.handle.net/10419/229538

Rahmadana, M. F., & Sagala, G. H. (2020). Economic resilience dataset in facing physical distancing during COVID-19 global pandemic. *Data in Brief, 32*, 106069. https://doi.org/10.1016/j.dib.2020.106069

Reid, R., & Botterill, L. C. (2013). The multiple meanings of 'resilience': An overview of the literature. *Australian Journal of Public Administration, 72*(1), 31–40. https://doi.org/10.1111/1467-8500.12009

Rio-Chanona, R. M., Mealy, P., Pichler, A., Lafond, F., & Farmer, J. D. (2020). Supply and demand shocks in the COVID-19 pandemic: An industry and occupation perspective. *Oxford Review of Economic Policy, 36*(Supplement_1), S94–S137. https://doi.org/10.1093/oxrep/graa033

Nicoleta Toader Risteiu, N. T., Creţan, R., & O'Brien, T. (2022). Contesting post-communist economic development: Gold extraction, local community, and rural decline in Romania. *Eurasian Geography and Economics, 63*(4), 491–513. https://doi.org/10.1080/15387216.2021.1913205

Rose, A. Z., & Krausmann, E. (2013). An economic framework for the development of a resilience index for business recovery. *International Journal of Disaster Risk Reduction, 5*, 73–83. https://doi.org/10.1016/j.ijdrr.2013.08.003

Rose, A., & Liao, S. (2005). Modeling regional economic resilience to disasters: A computable general equilibrium analysis of water service disruptions. *Journal of Regional Science, 45*(1), 75–112. https://doi.org/10.1111/j.0022-4146.2005.00365.x

Sensier, M., & Devine, F. (2020). Understanding regional economic performance and resilience in the UK: Trends since the global financial crisis. *National Institute Economic Review, 253*, R18–R28. https://doi.org/10.1017/nie.2020.27

Sensier, M., Bristow, G., & Healy, A. (2016). Measuring regional economic resilience across Europe: Operationalizing a complex concept. *Spatial Economic Analysis, 11*(2), 128–151. https://doi.org/10.1080/17421772.2016.1129435

Simmie, J., & Martin, R. (2010). The economic resilience of regions: Towards an evolutionary approach. *Cambridge Journal of Regions, Economy and Society, 3*, 27–43. https://doi.org/10.1093/cjres/rsp029

Trump, B. D., & Linkov, I. (2020). Risk and resilience in the time of the COVID-19 crisis. *Environment Systems and Decisions, 40*(2), 171–173. https://doi.org/10.1007/s10669-020-09781-0

Vanolo, A. (2015). The Fordist city and the creative city: Evolution and resilience in Turin, Italy. *City, Culture and Society, 6*(3), 69–74. https://doi.org/10.1016/j.ccs.2015.01.003

Vesalon, L., & Creţan, R. (2013). Mono-industrialism and the struggle for alternative development: The case of the Roşia Montană gold-mining project. *Tijdschrift Voor Economische En Sociale Geografie (journal of Economic and Human Geography), 104*(5), 539–555. https://doi.org/10.1111/tesg.12035

West, C., & Lenge, D. (1994). Modeling the regional impact of natural disaster and recovery. *International Regional Science Review, 17*, 121–150. https://doi.org/10.1177/016001769401700201

Yu, Z., Razzaq, A., Rehman, A., et al. (2021). Disruption in global supply chain and socio-economic shocks: A lesson from COVID-19 for sustainable production and consumption. *Operations Management Research, 15*, 233–248. https://doi.org/10.1007/s12063-021-00179-y

Yuan, W., Lai, S., & Hu, H. (2018). Optimal consumption analysis for a stochastic growth model with technological shocks. *Applied Stochastic Models in Business and Industry, 34*(5), 746–755. https://doi.org/10.1002/asmb.2384

Zhai, W., & Yue, H. (2022). Economic resilience during COVID-19: An insight from permanent business closures. *Environment and Planning a: Economy and Space, 54*(2), 219–221. https://doi.org/10.1177/0308518X211055181

The Significance of Higher Education Adaptation Reforms for Russia's Economic Growth

Daria Amelicheva, Elizaveta Semenova, and Elena Kalabina

Abstract Currently, the educational sector, considered the basis for the country's development in the post-industrial era, is facing global challenges: the importance of higher education is declining, the dependence between education level and wage level is weakening, and traditional formats are losing popularity. Reforming the system of higher education institutions is an urgent problem, and the solution to it may lead to large-scale changes in higher education with a positive effect on all stakeholders. The purpose of the study is to determine the role of higher education in the growth of the country's GDP, reveal factors decreasing the value of Russian higher education, analyze the trends characterizing the development of education, as well as peculiarities of education perception in different countries, and develop proposals for reforming the structure of education in Russia to increase its compliance with the requirements of the external environment. The research implies a complex analysis of the interconnection between higher education and the employers' expectations of the young employees' qualifications, including the analysis of Big Data on the employers' requirements for the employees' collected in Russia in 2020–2021. The article identifies the most significant recruitment factors and, based on them, proposes a system, which is a combination of the most successful practices of adaptation measures for the education sector to correspond to the needs of the labor market.

Keywords Higher education institutions · Candidate evaluation · Higher education reform · Requirements to employees · Hiring factors

JEL Classification J11 · J23 · J24

D. Amelicheva (✉) · E. Semenova · E. Kalabina
Ural Federal University named after the first President of Russia B.N. Yeltsin, 19 Mira Str, 620002 Ekaterinburg, Russia
e-mail: amelicheva.daria@gmail.com

E. Kalabina
Ural State University of Economics, 62 8 Marta Str, 620144 Ekaterinburg, Russia

V. Kumar et al. (eds.), *Consequences of Social Transformation for Economic Theory*, Springer Proceedings in Business and Economics,
https://doi.org/10.1007/978-3-031-27785-6_7

1 Introduction

The education sector, traditionally perceived as a sphere that is little affected by external factors, is currently facing global challenges. Limited personal communications during the COVID-19 pandemic actively stimulated digitalization, and generational change, accompanied by other factors, led to a decrease in the value of higher education as a tool for successful employment and career development. The pace of labor market development continues to grow, provoking new structural shifts in requirements for candidates—especially for university graduates. At the same time, traditional higher education is increasingly moving away from meeting employers' requests for practical skills and knowledge of graduates. Therefore, the new challenges for the education emerge, which can no longer be solved by narrow local reforms.

Additionally, national and regional specifics affect the education sector and strongly influence the correlation between the quality of education and the career perspectives of young specialists. Therefore, the issue raised above gains special characteristics and manifests itself to varying degrees in different regions of the world. Some geographical areas illustrate the opposite tendency to a rise in education value perceived by both employers and employees, while others portray other negative and positive ways of education affecting young employees' lives. However, the power of higher education and its potential to have an impact on national economies, labor markets, and quality of life is undeniable, even though it may vary depending on the preferred attitude towards it in certain regions of the world.

2 Literature Review

Relationship Between Education and Economic Growth

In the current economic conditions, educational services have become the most compelling factor since in today's labor market it is not an employee that is in demand but his qualifications, knowledge, and skills. It follows from this that education directly affects the formation of GDP, as it affects the quality of human capital and, as a result, the amount of income it generates. In general, education can be considered one of the main factors of economic growth and technological progress.

Education is an object of promising investments, since its condition and efficiency determine economic and production potential, defense capability, and living standards of citizens.

The influence of the educational factor on economic performance has become one of the central issues of recent economic research, largely due to the wide emergence of the theory of human capital, which studies the role of human resources in the production process. With the advent of this theory, investment in education and the accumulation of human capital have been recognized as core determinants of economic development in the long term (Teixeira, 2014).

The theoretical substantiation of economic growth and education correlation was developed in the studies of many prominent economists of the twentieth century (A. Greiner, N. Mankiw, D. Romer, and others), who confirmed a positive correlation between human capital, economic growth, gross domestic product (GDP per capita), domestic innovation, competitiveness, and sustainable technological development (Bouhajeb et al., 2018).

This topic seems to be especially relevant in the post-industrial economy, where services production prevails over commodity production, while the significance of science and the role of theoretical knowledge increase. Therefore, the successful and sustainable development of the economy is impossible without the development of education. In addition, in connection with the new trend of the post-industrial society—the reindustrialization of the economy—there is a need to update the energy, transport, information and telecommunications systems, healthcare, and environmental protection. The efficacy of the relevant measures depends on the quality of educational capital.

General Review on the Higher Education Trends

The main problem that higher education is facing in the modern world is its depreciation, which triggers the emergence of new challenges for the labor market and the national economy. This tendency is particularly prominent in Russia and CIS (Akaev et al., 2022). Such problems as difficulties in adequately assessing the knowledge, skills, and abilities of university graduates (Akaev et al., 2022), the need for businesses to adjust recruitment requirements or organize additional training for employees, and the students' necessity to combine studies with practically oriented activities (Alexandrova et al., 2022), appear, to a certain extent adding chaos to the relationships of subjects interested in the actualization of higher education. Contrary to the growing demand in the labor market for young ambitious specialists with practical skills in such areas as IT, marketing, management, design, science, and many more, the connection between educational programs and employees' requirements is weakening, which leads to a decrease in the effectiveness of education and generally questions its necessity for confirmation of the professionalism level (Backes-Gellner et al., 2021). Due to the fact that higher education institutions do not meet the needs of the labor market, alternative ways of getting an education, such as online courses, start gaining popularity (Neugebauer & Daniel, 2022). The root of this trend lies in the fundamental change in the perception of young specialists' competencies—modern employees understand that university education is not oriented toward providing practical skills, whereas online courses imply practical focus. As a result, the whole education sector is facing a lack of stability and an increase in the population's uncertainty about the importance of higher education, which is stimulated by examples of famous and successful individuals, who choose blogging or freelancing as their professional path (Sobotka, 2021).

The problems of higher education are the main topic of many scientific articles, which indicates an increase in attention to the subject and the actual spread of educational shortcomings. Researchers have repeatedly addressed the perspectives of solving educational problems by reforming the higher education curricula in one way or another, linking the need for changes with various factors—from the mass and accessibility of digital technologies (Claudia, 2019; Grosemans & De Cuyper, 2021; Grosemans et al., 2017) to changes in the life values and orientations of the younger generation (Konstantinovskiy, 2014).

Higher Education Issues Around the World

Moreover, numerous scientists tend to address the peculiarities of education and career path correlation in certain regions of the world. For instance, Alexandrova and Glukhov (2021) highlight that the Russian labor market is undergoing a shift from employers' assessing young specialists by their education to paying more attention to additional activities that students had been involved in during the educational process. For example, employers tend to evaluate candidates' skills based on their scientific activity, participation in events and their organization, internship, contests, etc. Belfield and Bailey (2019), on the contrary, suggest that higher education in the USA is becoming more valuable for the labor market, which is a long-lasting tendency that can be proven by the evidence of direct dependence on the level of income and the quality of young specialists' higher education. This trend is strongly related to the tight relationship between the fast development of the American labor market, which requires a wide variety of competencies from university graduates, and the status of its higher education institutions, that are trying to update their curricula in the course of time. Referring to the European case, Obiols-Homs and Sánchez-Marcos (2018), as well as Ţiţan et al. (2014) indicate a phenomenon of 'overeducation' that exists in the European labor market, which is connected with the lack of positions offered for specialists with high-quality multi-layered education that fit their level of competencies. As a result, a considerable number of young employees appear obliged to perform less complicated and demanding tasks than they could according to their education-related job function. However, despite the growing interest in the research topic, the issues of further development of higher education facilities have not been sufficiently considered since existing articles, as a rule, review the problem to a greater extent than they offer solutions.

This article aims to develop measures to improve the efficiency of higher education institutions and their adaptability to modern trends and challenges of the external environment, as well as to identify the most significant characteristics of graduate applicants for the employer, taking into account the high turbulence of the market. Moreover, the article is intended to compare issues related to the education sector in different regions of the world in order to identify the main directions of correcting the negative externalities of higher education development in Russia in accordance with the international experience and existing best practices.

3 Methods

The research methodology is based on a comprehensive analysis of the higher education role in the labor market and the specifics of the correlation between educational programs and labor market demands in different regions of the world. Solving theoretical and empirical research problems implied general scientific methods, including systematization and generalization, description and analysis of data, comparison, critical analysis, and formalization. As part of the study, information on relevant requests from employers was collected at the hugest Russian recruiting websites using Big data technologies. Recommendation development included the analysis and critical evaluation of both classical concepts of higher education and modern ones used in the top 100 best universities of the world according to the international rating association QS Rankings. The authors believe that the study results are objective and reflect the general trends in the development of higher education in the research field.

4 Results

Currently, the unswerving higher education status is being questioned by interested parties. To be more exact, studies of recruiting companies over the past few years have highlighted a decrease in vacancies requiring a candidate to complete higher education as such or in any specialty. According to the hugest Russian recruitment portals—Head Hunter and Super Job, only 30% of vacancies contained requirements for the higher education of applicants, while 58% of vacancies did not include educational demands in 2020 (Global Online Recruitment Platform Market Research Report to 2027, 2022).

Several studies show that more than 60% of young people (among Europeans and Russians) do not include obtaining a higher education diploma among the factors of career success, while the key to success is considered to be a willingness to devote a proportionately significant part of their life to work and having work experience in the field of interest (Table 1) (Fakhrutdinova et al., 2015).

According to Deloitte, Generation Z, which is now expected to leave school and enter universities, is not planning to follow traditional paths perceived as ways to success (Deloitte, 2019). Statistics covering Russia and Europe show that only 43% of school graduates plan to become university applicants (Barhate & Dirani, 2022). In other words, the perception of higher education has changed significantly, which has led to a decrease in young individuals' perception of higher education as a priority for building a career. Moreover, the specificity of Generation Z—their aspiration of personal comport and fulfillment of ambitions along with the value of freedom

Table 1 Graduates' competitive advantages from the perspective of higher education institutions students. Gender specificities, %

Competitive advantages of applicants from the perspective of students	Men	Women
Luck	10.4	9
Appearance	1.6	3.9
Gender	3.8	1.8
Age	13.2	14.4
Connections	10.9	8.5
Willingness to continuously improve knowledge and skills	28.7	40.8
Willingness to work hard	41.7	41.3
Work experience	55.5	54.8
Good education	28.7	37.8

and childish behavior (Barhate & Dirani, 2022)—affect their career expectations and willingness to devote themselves to certain jobs, which results in personnel shortages and triggers employers' changing their requirements for vacancies and offered working conditions.

Meanwhile, claiming that higher education has lost its meaning is inappropriate, since it is still the most significant factor in hiring—especially for the vacancies that imply intellectual work and have the potential for long-term career development. Nowadays, the diploma of higher education, first of all, testifies to the graduates' ability to master large amounts of information, their responsibility, the general level of knowledge, and social circle, which in any case is necessary when applying for positions implying intellectual work in conditions of the variability of the external environment (Oswald-Egg & Renold, 2021). Moreover, in the countries with a high-quality education that suits the demands of the labor market employers trust young specialists' diplomas and presume that education provides them with certain relevant skills and knowledge.

However, currently, in Russia, employers do not rely on the fact that the applicant has received higher education since this fact is no more relevant—instead, they are more inclined to trust the university brand image, which primarily concerns the status of metropolitan universities and some intensively developing regional ones (Alexandrova & Glukhov, 2021). The same situation happens in Europe where the private sector seems to prefer male graduates from old and well-established universities (Berggren, 2011). Such a shift in the benchmark is due to the fact that universities that occupy high positions in the rankings, as a rule, have access to more efficient funding, which means that the teaching staff of such higher education institutions is more qualified and motivated than in others (Industry Competitiveness: Digitalization, Management, and Integration, 2021). Therefore, the young specialists' diplomas mainly serve as symbols of the institutions where they studied, which primarily allows employers to assess the university level of development, not the candidates', which can be assumed as a misinterpretation of the actual level of knowledge of university graduates.

Students' Motivation to Combine Work and Study

Since the presence of a diploma of higher education in most cases is not a sufficient condition for deciding on accepting a candidate for a position (however, it is most often necessary) (Kobets et al., 2021), students face the necessity to acquire additional skills, abilities, and knowledge while studying at the university. The phenomenon of students combining study and work is currently so widespread in certain regions—for instance, Russia—that it can be called massive: more than half of Bachelors and specialty students and 84% of Master candidates somehow gain work experience during their studies (Oswald-Egg & Renold, 2021). This factor illustrates the volatility level of the education curricula in Russia, since the most efficient activities for students to gain competitive advantages exclude the studying process as a concept, meaning that the usefulness of higher education is decreasing drastically, while students have to continue following this path and get an extra load in order to become demanded specialists. Such a surrealistic pattern is not healthy and should be reviewed by the state, businesses, and students themselves so that a new system, satisfies the interests of all the interested parties with the minimal possible level of harm to any of them.

Among the factors motivating students to combine study and work that are illustrated in Fig. 1, the reasons associated with the need or desire to improve their financial situation and the desire to gain work experience prevail. At the same time, networking (building connections with people who are potentially able to help in building a career) remains the least popular reason for combining study and work (Kolesnikova et al., 2015)—these results refer to the Russian higher education sector. At the same time, for the U.S. students, the most significant factor that motivates them to work while studying is the opportunity to start building a career in a certain company earlier than finishing the university or institute (Cociu et al., 2019). The difference between these two perspectives is obvious—students of the analyzed countries have different, almost polar, expectations of their careers and plans for the future. While Russian students seem to be preparing for hard competition in candidate selection processes after finishing university and are focused on the opportunities of gaining wide experience during the first few years at work to continue their career further in more appealing companies, Americans tend to be more oriented to long-term strategic planning of their personal development with the use of higher education and other opportunities.

One more important fact about Russian students is that the majority of those who combine study and work presumably have a higher level of abilities and initial knowledge compared to the total mass of students. Therefore, it seems possible to talk about the close relationship of a high level of intellectual potential, thanks to which such applicants enter prestigious universities by passing the state exams for high scores, as well as the possibilities of combining education and scientific activity with the prospect for combining it with work harmless for the studying process (Vogel, 2015). This may seem controversial due to the discrepancy between the traditional perception of the education process as time-consuming and demanding,

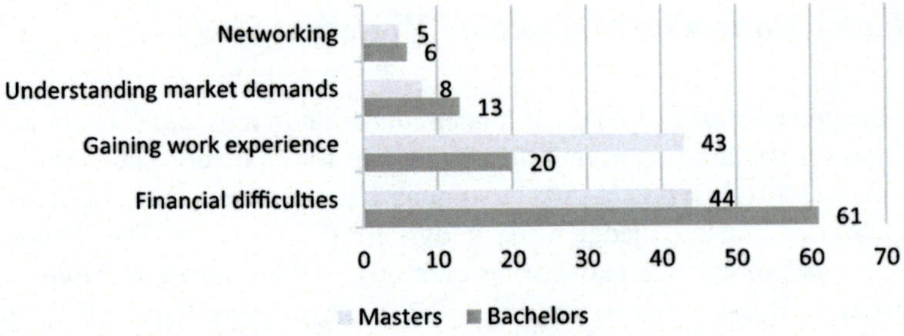

Fig. 1 The reasons for students' reconciling studies with work, %

and the patterns of successful students' behavior, which illustrate that these students do not devote their free from studies time to gain extra knowledge related to their education program.

Employers Stimulating Changes in Higher Education

Employers, in turn, also actively stimulate the process of reorientation of students from studies in the direction of early learning of work experience. According to Duta et al. (2020) research, the most indicative qualities of applicants that set them apart from other graduates are relevant experience and skills. Moreover, the candidates, who manage to obtain such privileges by finishing their universities, are valued more than others (Duta et al., 2020). Advanced employers are increasingly paying attention to the availability of additional education for candidates, which indicates a high level of internal motivation of the applicant and his adequate perception of the demands of the labor market for ambitious, result-oriented specialists (Cleary et al., 2017). With the traditional requirement for higher education for almost any intellect-labored vacancies, students face the necessity to balance their practical experience and formal education process.

An equally significant reason for the decline in the quality of higher education was its mass character and literal commitment, which has become a trend in Russia and Europe in recent decades, forcing employers to reconsider their values when hiring, and applicants to be critical of the opportunities provided by universities (Enders, 2010). Currently, candidate evaluation involves paying significant attention to the extracurricular activities of the applicant. More specifically, employers focus more on the work experience of the potential candidate, the main reason for which is that they cannot be sure of a diploma as a guarantor of the applicant's required competencies, knowledge, and skills (Kuznetsova et al., 2019), which forces them to invent new assessment technologies and adapt their recruiting system.

Markers of student proactivity are also scientific activities, participation in contests, competitions, public events, conferences, and case championships, since the student's involvement in such activities along with successful studies characterizes them as a responsible person who never misses opportunities for their personal and professional development and competently allocate time. Moreover, extracurricular activities are highly effective to acquire and develop soft skills, which are greatly valued by most employers (Fakhretdinova et al., 2021). Flexible skills, including communication, leadership, emotional intellect, ability to adapt and gain knowledge in short periods of time, are the most in-demand skills when applying for a job, especially for young specialists without working experience (Fakhretdinova et al., 2021). The researchers explained the popularity of soft skills by their versatility: they are required for almost any working position, and they largely determine the demand for young professionals in the labor market since they allow employers to trust the new employee's ability to become a part of the company shortly, learn to act in accordance with the company's interests and develop professional skills.

Governmental Approach to Reforming Higher Education

Due to the decline in the perceived value of higher education both on the part of Russian students and employers, this social institution is currently acutely aware of the need for a radical transformation, which would imply structural changes, reform of interaction between participants within the educational process, the semantic content of training programs, as well as the forced increase in flexibility of the educational curricula as a whole and its parts separately. Employment policies should address the need to apply micro- and macroeconomic policies], seeking new, unconventional ideas and policies in order to help create the necessary volume of high-quality employment to meet current adverse conditions (Serrano et al., 2022) The main reason for the need to reorient the higher education institutions is the increasing role of intellectual capital, which is becoming a decisive factor in the modernization of the economy (Cezara & Șarai, 2022), an adequate response of business and the state to the challenges of global competition (Sobotka, 2021), and the stimulation of scientific progress (Claudia, 2019).

Based on international experience and current trends, the authors suggest the following directions for improving the effectiveness of higher schools and, as a result, restoring their significance for all parties involved in the process:

1. Education personalization.
2. Educational process non-linearity and flexibility.
3. Educational, research, and innovation activities synergy.
4. Focus on entrepreneurship.
5. Dual education system ("university—business") rooting.

Each of the suggested educational development areas is overviewed in more detail below.

Education Personalization

Personalization is the process of adapting the educational process to the individual characteristics of students. In addition to allowing students to choose educational modules according to an individual learning trajectory, this process includes a qualitative change in the communication model for teachers and students from authoritarian-subordinate relations in favor of a mentoring format. The presumed effect is an increase in the attractiveness of universities for applicants, which will also be ensured by the rejection of outdated standards that limited the possibility of mastering disciplines "at the junction" of different sciences, which are especially in demand in modern professions. Interaction with mentors—tutors—will contribute to improving the assimilation of the material by students and become a competitive advantage of universities in comparison with alternative formats of education—in particular, online platforms. The effectiveness of the implementation of this model—its impact on the employment of university graduates and their career success—is confirmed by the British boarding university system (Matei et al., 2016). Other examples of such an approach to the organization of education are reflected in the American education sector, where universities provide their students with an opportunity to choose courses and modules that they consider significant for their future careers or interesting for their personal development. Implementing a similar order would require resources and time, but the results are expected to be a breakthrough in students' attitudes towards education and in methods of recruitment.

Educational Process Non-linearity and Flexibility

In the current Russian education sector, it is necessary to abandon the formed linear-cliched system ("kindergarten—school—university") and provide the younger generation with an opportunity to choose a professional path consciously. Modern trends in Generation Z lifestyle show that the main focus of the young specialists is avoiding traditional paths in order to form unique trajectories of personal development that would not depend on the customary rules and life stages. Students are trying to build new patterns that would provide them with an opportunity to choose for themselves and be fully independent.

Scandinavian countries have already made some advances in this direction, proving the practical effectiveness of the proposed measure. Thus, the rejection of following the Bologna system in favor of non-linear advancement of the flexible educational process, allowed young professionals to understand their interests better and build the process of obtaining professional knowledge more efficiently. Steps in this direction are already being undertaken by the state, and, if implemented properly, they would benefit all the interested parties. Employers would get their demands satisfied from the perspective of them hiring interested in their profession young specialists, students would be more self-fulfilled and conscious, and the state would achieve the desired economic stimulation.

The Synergy of Educational, Research, and Innovation Activities

One more direction implies that universities should simultaneously implement three missions: education, research, and innovation, aimed at the commercialization of knowledge. From a conservative social institution, in the modern world, the university becomes the central link in the development of the innovative economy and the social sphere—a scientific, educational, and innovative center, that produces the socio-economic development of a particular region and the country as a whole, as well as global processes (Ţiţan et al., 2014). These criteria are the main ones for University 3.0, while at the same time, innovative activity and commercialization of knowledge are considered no less important than education and science (Backes-Gellner et al., 2021). That is why in the knowledge-based economy, such universities become instruments of economic growth and exist in close connection with business and government. Such effects can be provided by stimulating scientific activity among students of all specializations by, for instance, offering scholarships and developing the grants system for implementing projects offered and designed by students. In addition to the increase in students' level of ambitions fulfillment, such measures would boost innovation development, which is a vital point in any developing country's strategic policy.

Focus on Entrepreneurship

The model of an entrepreneurial university should include the following principles: entrepreneurship as a discipline, entrepreneurship as a method of teaching, and entrepreneurship as a partnership with business. The entrepreneurial approach in training is expressed in choosing the most appropriate method and technology to achieve the planned result, taking into account the characteristics of the target audience (Krotov et al., 2014). Teachers should have the freedom to choose teaching methods and technologies. At the same time, it is necessary to introduce control over the relevance of the information given to students—for example, by resorting to an independent assessment of existing courses by leading experts from relevant industries. It is also necessary to develop an infrastructure to support student entrepreneurship—for example, by creating university studios for student technological entrepreneurship, business incubators, accelerators, entrepreneurship support centers, and stimulating the completion of theses in the form of startups. The idea of the university in the minds of schoolchildren, applicants, and their parents, as well as employers, can thus be modernized.

Therefore, by commercializing not only the approach to gaining knowledge but also the main behavioral economic patterns of students, higher education institutions may stimulate their flexibility development due to the realization of fresh business ideas that are produced by young students. Young specialists, while gaining knowledge at university, would then be able to see the results of their studying process faster, plan their life more thoroughly, achieve a higher level of financial literacy, value the education process and perceive personal development in the chosen area more seriously. Thus, the new generation of career starters would be making more balanced decisions, hence positively influencing the labor market, economic processes, innovation development, and the improvement of their life level, which would also cause positive shifts in the country's national course.

Rooting of the Dual Education System

Partnership with business should develop in all areas of activity and various forms—both traditional for the university (organization of industrial practice, involvement of practitioners in teaching), and through consulting projects, participation in professional communities, expert activities, development of business incubators. The variety of offered activities is vital due to the significance of the opportunity to choose, which is prevailing over numerous other factors for Generation Z, which is expected to affect the labor market strongly during the upcoming years. In other words, a wide range of opportunities to participate in business-related activities should surround students and constantly offer them chances to test their skills, which would contribute to the general alteration of the students' state of mind from focusing on the negative aspects, fears and lack of self-assurance in the profession choice to the willingness to gain benefits from the offered knowledge and skills.

'Close cooperation with businesses would also help to overcome the existing gaps between the actual demand of employers for the competencies of young specialists and the educational program of universities' (Duta et al., 2020). The duality of the education at all stages of training will help not only to adapt courses to market demands but also to acquire an additional competitive advantage for universities in the form of providing employment opportunities in partner companies. Businesses, in turn, will be able to reduce the costs of finding high-quality young personnel who trust the knowledge of graduates. 'The positive effects of such system were already proved in European universities' (Serrano et al., 2015).

Change in the Financing System

Undoubtedly, one of the key aspects that catalyze the depreciation process of higher education is its massification. One of the most significant income items of any higher education institution is profit from contract students. At the same time, except for several high-ranking universities in Russia, in many higher schools, there is no competition for paid places; it is enough for applicants to pass final exams for passing scores in order to start getting higher education. The amount of non-budgetary funds employed directly correlates with the amount of incoming financial resources, which, in the context of insufficient funding from the state (according to the State Duma Committee, universities lack about 1.7 billion rubles for the maintenance of premises and utility bills (Education that we may lose, n.d.)), play a significant role both in solving the issue of raising the wages, prestige and social status of scientific and pedagogical workers of universities and in supporting the viability of Russian higher education in the face of global competition. On the one hand, this increases the accessibility of higher education, one of the strategic goals of Russia's development in 2000–2010 (TASS, n.d.) in the eyes of employers. Therefore, the need to increase the role of the state in funding higher education institutions seems to be reinforced by the capability of the state in supporting the education sector, which also correlates with the main provisions of the Russian Constitution.

The authors believe that in this situation it is necessary to resume work on the normative per capita financing. Various mechanisms for the development of the calculation base are given in the works of Rozina and Zueva (2015, 2017). We will not delve into their features, only noting that these researchers not only developed tools for the calculation methodology but also proved the effectiveness of normative financing of higher education. However, the implementation of their calculation creates a detailed model that connects factors, which differ from each other greatly in the context of their origin and tendencies they are affected by. Moreover, the model considers the impact that the subjective, immeasurable factors have on the mentioned financing system.

State nominal financial obligations system (SNFO) would be a solution to the current problems of education financing and development, since it could contribute to improving the level of higher education significance. This system implies introducing state obligations as a method of stimulation of per capita funding implementation, and aims to provide the successful shift in the higher education financing system.

SNFO system was meant to be materialized via voucher system, according to which every student would get a financially secure voucher (The results of an experiment on financing individual institutions of higher professional education using GIFO in 2003, 2004). These personal "entrance sheets" were aimed to be financially supported by the points received by student during the Unified State Examination and reinforced through the state funding. More specifically, the higher education institution chosen by each student would get financial support from the state according to the USE points these students had gained. Among additional effects of the system's implementation, SNFO would also stimulate the higher education institutions' development owing to the reallocation of the monetary flows obtained by the universities. Due to the expected growing amount of students with vouchers in prestigious universities, these institutions would get more opportunities for developing the facilities, infrastructure, and studying process, which, accompanied by the introduction of healthy competition between the students, would provide the basis for the fair education, supporting the most talented and bright students.

The resumption of using this system can improve the current situation. Using differentiated funding will increase the competitive struggle of higher education institutions for strong graduates. In this situation, universities will not have to fill places with able-to-pay students. As a result, focus of educational institutions will shift from the general amount of students to the quality of their knowledge. Correspondingly, it could be expected that the level of knowledge of higher education graduates will increase, and the importance of higher education in the eyes of employers will grow.

These changes will help higher education transform from a rather conservative and limited in functions social institution into a central link in the development of an innovative economy and social sphere, to become a scientific, educational and innovative center that produces the socio-economic development of a particular region, country as a whole, as well as global processes.

5 Discussion

The suggested measures that should be undertaken to reform the Russian higher education sector mainly aim to rebuild the image of higher education institutions in the eyes of students, employers, and other interested parties. Qualified changes in the education sector require the analysis of the international experience and cases of implementing and maintaining successful education, which include such elements as personalization, building a solid connection between the educational institutions and business, and regulating their communication processes by the state. Renovation of the finance system, with its adaptation to the modern higher education sector demands, taking into account the initial purposes of the SNFO system, which was not implemented properly in the past, would cause a great positive shift in the process of applying to universities, creating a healthy competitive environment for contract students. Hence, the renewed higher education institutions would be able to make a significant contribution to the Russian economy and general development by increasing the importance of higher education and strengthening its practical imposition.

6 Conclusion

Thus, the decline in the authority of universities forces labor market participants to significantly transform patterns of behavior due to distrust of the quality of knowledge, skills, and abilities obtained within the academic educational process—both on the part of students and employers. From the employer's perspective, a diploma currently serves as a marker of the level of general development and applicant's outlook rather than testifies to his competencies, and, unfortunately, does not provide a university graduate with competitive advantages. In this regard, ambitious students aimed at building a successful career resort to active participation in extracurricular activities, which leads to paying much less attention to obtaining knowledge as the main element of the educational process, resulting in the quality of knowledge decrease. The aggravation of the situation and the lack of measures to reduce the essential gap between employers' requirements for graduates and training programs may cause a complex devaluation of higher education as the key to successful employment and career building. On a greater scale, this may negatively affect the state's economic development and Russia's economic indicators.

References

Akaev, A., Petryakov, A., Jorg, R. S., & Ungvari, L. (2022). Education system and labor market in the context of digital transformation. In A. Rudskoi, A. Akaev & T. Devezas (Eds.). *Digital transformation and the world economy. Studies on entrepreneurship, structural change and industrial dynamics.* Cham: Springer. https://doi.org/10.1007/978-3-030-89832-8_7

Alexandrova, G. N., & Glukhov, G. V. (2021). Role of additional education in the context of labor market volatility. In S. I. Ashmarina, & V. V. Mantulenko (Eds.), *Digital Economy and the New Labor Market: Jobs, Competences and Innovative HR Technologies IPM 2020. Lecture Notes in Networks and Systems* (vol. 161). Cham: Springer. https://doi.org/10.1007/978-3-030-60926-9_1

Alexandrova, G. N., Gagarinskii, A. V., & Gagarinskaia, G. P. (2022). digital education can help decrease labor market imbalance. In S. I. Ashmarina, & V. V. Mantulenko (Eds.), *Digital Technologies in the New Socio-Economic Reality. ISCDTE 2021. Lecture Notes in Networks and Systems* (vol. 304). Cham: Springer. https://doi.org/10.1007/978-3-030-83175-2_94

Backes-Gellner, U., Herz, H., Kosfeld, M., & Oswald, Y. (2021). Do preferences and biases predict life outcomes? Evidence from education and labor market entry decisions. *European Economic Review, 134*, 103709. https://doi.org/10.1016/j.euroecorev.2021.103709

Barhate, B., & Dirani, K. M. (2022). Career aspirations of generation Z: A systematic literature review. *European Journal of Training and Development, 46*(1/2), 139–157. https://doi.org/10.1108/ejtd-07-2020-0124

Belfield, C. R., & Bailey, T. R. (2019). The labor market value of higher education: Now and in the future. In M. Paulsen & L Perna (Eds.), *Higher education: Handbook of theory and research* (p. 34). Cham: Springer. https://doi.org/10.1007/978-3-030-03457-3_9

Berggren, C. (2011). Transition of higher education graduates to the labour market: Are employment procedures more meritocratic in the public sector? *Journal of Higher Education Policy and Management, 33*(2), 91–100. https://doi.org/10.1080/1360080X.2011.550031

Bouhajeb, M., Mefteh, H., & Ben Ammar, R. (2018). Higher education and economic growth: The importance of innovation. *Atlantic Review of Economics (ARoEc), 1*(2).

Cezara, A., & Şarai, N. (2022). Professional and transversal skills and lifelong learning systems in the context of social challenges. *Annals of Constantin Brancusi Economy Series, 1*, 75–82.

Claudia, M.-P.M. (2019). The new challenges of the labor market. *Annals of Constantin Brancusi Economy Series, 6*, 183–188.

Cleary, J. L., Kerrigan, M. R., & Van Noy, M. (2017). Towards a new understanding of labor market alignment. *Higher education: Handbook of theory and research* (p. *32*). Cham: Springer. https://doi.org/10.1007/978-3-319-48983-4_12

Cociu, V.-C., Postavaru, N., Costoiu, M., Dobrescu, T. G., & Silvestru, C. I. (2019). Competences between labor market and higher education through ESCO. *Informatica Economica, 23*(4), 89–100. https://doi.org/10.12948/issn14531305/23.4.2019.08

Deloitte. (2019). *Understanding generation Z in the workplace.* Deloitte United States. https://www2.deloitte.com/us/en/pages/consumer-business/articles/understanding-generation-z-in-the-workplace.html

Duta, A., Wielgoszewska, B., & Iannelli, C. (2020). Different degrees of career success: Social origin and graduates' education and labour market trajectories. *Advances in Life Course Research, 47*, 100376. https://doi.org/10.1016/j.alcr.2020.100376

Education that we may lose. (n.d.). www.emomi.com. Retrieved June 13, 2022, from http://www.emomi.com/download/sadovnichiy/putin.htm

Enders, J. (2010). Higher education and the labor market. *International Encyclopedia of Education*, 365–369. https://doi.org/10.1016/b978-0-08-044894-7.00827-7

Fakhretdinova, G. N., Osipov, P., & Dulalaeva, L. P. (2021). Extracurricular activities as an important tool in developing soft skills. *Educating Engineers for Future Industrial Revolutions* 480–487. https://doi.org/10.1007/978-3-030-68201-9_47

Fakhrutdinova, E. V., Fakhrutdinova, A. V., Yagudin, R. H., & Vishnjakov, N. I. (2015). The needs of the Russian federation labor market in the workforce with different levels of education. *Procedia—Social and Behavioral Sciences, 191*, 2515–2518. https://doi.org/10.1016/j.sbspro.2015.04.593

Global Online Recruitment Platform Market Research Report to 2027–*Featuring DHI Group, Indeed and Jobvite Among Others—ResearchAndMarkets.com* (2022). morningstar.com. https://www.morningstar.com/news/business-wire/20220510006270/global-online-recruitment-platform-market-research-report-to-2027-featuring-dhi-group-indeed-and-jobvite-among-others-researchandmarketscom

Grosemans, I., & De Cuyper, N. (2021). Career competencies in the transition from higher education to the labor market: Examining developmental trajectories. *Journal of Vocational Behavior, 128*, 103602. https://doi.org/10.1016/j.jvb.2021.103602

Grosemans, I., Coertjens, L., & Kyndt, E. (2017). Exploring learning and fit in the transition from higher education to the labour market: A systematic review. *Educational Research Review, 21*, 67–84. https://doi.org/10.1016/j.edurev.2017.03.001

Industry Competitiveness: Digitalization, Management, and Integration. (2021). In A. V. Bogoviz & J. V. Ragulina (Eds.). *Lecture Notes in Networks and Systems*. Springer International Publishing. https://doi.org/10.1007/978-3-030-80485-5

Kobets, V., Yatsenko, V., & Buiak, L. (2021). Bridging business analysts competence gaps: Labor market needs versus education standards. In *ICTERI 2020 Communications in Computer and Information Science* (vol. 1308). Cham: Springer. https://doi.org/10.1007/978-3-030-77592-6_2

Kolesnikova, J., Kamasheva, A., & Fakhrutdinova, A. (2015). Higher education demands of the labor market. *Procedia—Social and Behavioral Sciences, 191*, 1183–1186. https://doi.org/10.1016/j.sbspro.2015.04.446

Konstantinovskiy, D. L. (2014). Education, labor market, and social behavior of youth. *Sociological Journal, 0*(3), 55–69. https://doi.org/10.19181/socjour.2014.3.512

Krotov, S. V., Shulgin, D. B., & Terliga, N. G. (2014). Predprinematelskaya model razvitia federalnogo universiteta. *Innovations, 8*(190), 42–50.

Kuznetsova, O. N., Maksimov, V. Y., Narozhnaya, G. A., Tkachenko, A. E., & Toiskin, V. S. (2019). Approaches to quality of education that conform to the needs of labor market in information society. In E. Popkova & V. Ostrovskaya (Eds.), *Perspectives on the use of new information and communication technology (ICT) in the modern economy. ISC 2017. Advances in intelligent systems and computing* (p. 726). Springer, Cham. https://doi.org/10.1007/978-3-319-90835-9_128

Matei, A., Rotaru, F. G., & Cristache, S. E. (2016). Assessment methods in developing skills within the university education process for its direct beneficiaries/students and users of Tes services. *Competitiveness of Agro—Food & Environmental Economy*, 168–175.

Neugebauer, M., & Daniel, A. (2022). Higher education non-completion, employers, and labor market integration: Experimental evidence. *Social Science Research, 105*, 102696. https://doi.org/10.1016/j.ssresearch.2022.102696

Obiols-Homs, F., & Sánchez-Marcos, V. (2018). Education outcomes and the labor market. *Labour Economics, 54*, 14–28. https://doi.org/10.1016/j.labeco.2018.06.001

Oswald-Egg, M. E., & Renold, U. (2021). No experience, no employment: The effect of vocational education and training work experience on labour market outcomes after higher education. *Economics of Education Review, 80*, 102065. https://doi.org/10.1016/j.econedurev.2020.102065

Rozina, N. M., & Zuev, V. M. (2015). Per capita financing of higher education: Concepts and realities. *Bulletin of the Financial University, 3*, 122–135.

Rozina, N. M., & Zuev, V. M. (2017). On the normative funding of higher education: Current state and development trends. *Bulletin of the Financial University, 2*(21), 132–144.

Serrano, G., Llamazares, F., & Javier Otamendi, F. (2015). Measurement and sustainability of the qualifications frameworks in the European higher education area through an employment survey on access to the labour market. *Sustainability (switzerland), 7*(10), 13777–13812. https://doi.org/10.3390/su71013777

Sobotka, B. (2021). Labour market changes and challenges for education in the VUCA era. *Journal of Modern Science, 46*(1), 191–208. https://doi.org/10.13166/jms/138662

TASS. (n.d.). N.tass.ru. Retrieved June 13, 2022, from https://n.tass.ru/obschestvo/3822679

Teixeira, P. N. (2014). Gary Becker's early work on human capital—Collaborations and distinctiveness. *IZA Journal of Labor Economics, 3(12)*. https://doi.org/10.1186/s40172-014-0012-2

The results of an experiment on financing individual institutions of higher professional education using GIFO in 2003. (2004). In T. V. Abankina (Eds). Russian State Library. https://search.rsl.ru/ru/record/01002811541

Ţiţan, E., Burciu, A., Manea, D., & Ardelean, A. (2014). From traditional to digital: The labour market demands and education expectations in an EU context. *Procedia Economics and Finance, 10*, 269–274. https://doi.org/10.1016/s2212-5671(14)00302-5

Vogel, P. (2015). Addressing the gap between the education system and the labor market. In *Generation jobless?* Palgrave Macmillan, London. https://doi.org/10.1057/9781137375940_5

Impact of the Duration of Compulsory Education on Economic Growth and Welfare

Alla V. Molchanova and Aida Guliyeva

Abstract The human capital model from the basic economic theory considers schooling to be an investment in human capital, and thus the change to mandatory schooling forces the low-educated group to become more productive, raising its wages, with no effect on schooling decisions for others. This paper focuses on the important issue of economic theory approach to education and studies how the duration of compulsory education affects the economic growth and welfare. The economic theory predicts that by investing in education and supporting schooling, governments of developing and less developed countries can improve their labor force and enhance their economic growth and welfare. Our results show that educational policies can become the important tool for the developing countries for catching up with their wealthier counterparts. Therefore, public education policies such as the prolongation of compulsory education should be installed by the governments in less developed countries for improving the quality of their human capital and thence increasing the productivity and innovativeness of their economies. Thus, based on the findings from the economic theory, it would be beneficial for the policymakers in such countries to promote this approach for the sake and benefit of their economic growth and welfare.

Keywords Economic growth · Compulsory education · Welfare · Economic theory

JEL Classification I25 · I30 · J01 · O38

A. V. Molchanova
Moscow Psychologic-Social University, 9A 4th Roshinsky Proezd, 115191 Moscow, Russian Federation

A. Guliyeva (✉)
Faculty of Digital Economy, Azerbaijan State University of Economics, 6 Istiglaliyyat Str., AZ1001 Baku, Azerbaijan
e-mail: a.guliyeva@unec.edu.az

V. Kumar et al. (eds.), *Consequences of Social Transformation for Economic Theory*, Springer Proceedings in Business and Economics,
https://doi.org/10.1007/978-3-031-27785-6_8

1 Introduction

The majority of economists has long believed that investments in education, or human capital, are a major source of economic growth (Khan et al., 2020). As a result, many countries have provided funds to promote K-12 (a system of publicly-supported school grades from kindergarten prior to college) education in order to boost economic output (Habib et al., 2019). In most general terms, any given country does not need to provide a vast network of colleges or universities in order to reap the benefits of education. Instead, it can provide basic literacy programs and still see improvements in the economy.

Nowadays, more children and adolescents all around the world are enrolled in preschool, primary, and secondary education than in the past. To increase the lifespans of individuals, governments must seek to enhance higher education, as well as to curb the numbers of young adults who leave school and become unemployed (Ryan & Lőrinc, 2018). The recommendation for the improvement can be that most countries should focus on improving the social education for the young by implementing free education programs and other means, in an effort to efficiently increase the health status of the population, at the same time as attempting to increase mandatory spending. Countries have to find ways how to guarantee, by legislation and employment programs, that all of their citizens can obtain education and training that will elevate workers, businesses, and the entire economy. Prenatal and early childhood health care programs, which incorporate both education and health care, are therefore essential for realizing that potential (Ashford et al., 2020). A number of educational development pathways may be effective in varying ways to promote growth and alleviate poverty.

Some time ago, government officials and development partners in various countries around the world affirmed the importance of education for development for economic development, and more generally to the betterment of human lives and jointly declared education for all a goal (Shi et al., 2019). Because growth, development, and poverty reduction are all about the knowledge and skills people gain, not how many years they sit in class, we should shift our call to action from education for all to learning for all. This is because quality needs to be the goal of education investments, and learning outcomes are a critical measure of quality (Datzberger, 2018). Whatever education's contribution to growth in the past, investments in human capital are likely to grow in importance relative to investments in other forms of capital as we move toward a postindustrial, knowledge-based economy (Gruzina et al., 2021). The direct impact is magnified because a portion of the increased revenue generated from higher growth is reinvested into both physical and human capital. The economy's productivity increases when its educated workforce increases, because workers with higher skills are better able to do tasks more effectively. A country's economy becomes more productive as the share of educated workers increases because educated workers can more effectively complete tasks requiring literacy and critical thinking. Countries where large percentages of the population go to and complete high school experience faster economic growth compared to countries where fewer workers are educated (even though even this issue can be somewhat effectively solved through immigration (Strielkowski & Weyskrabova, 2014)).

Over the past couple of decades, there has been a greater focus on theories about how education can influence economic growth, and these works have implications for how we can model the effects of increasing levels of educational attainment. There is a general consensus that government investments in education result in economic growth. Yet advocates for early education have recently stressed the economic benefits of early education programs, and they have had difficulty winning support for such investments in the short run given the longer-term nature of the benefits for the economy (Babatunde, 2018). As concerns have grown over the efficacy of existing schools, policymakers have challenged the centrality and function of governments in allocating education resources, and they have turned toward markets or market-related mechanisms. K-12 schooling has traditionally been allocated by the government, on the federal, state, and local levels, while postsecondary education has been allocated through some combination of markets and the government (Rosinger et al., 2022). Educational expenditures may be undertaken by private individuals as well as by governments via public expenditures. The decision of how education at various levels of education should be allocated is, in essence, an economic decision of how best to allocate scarce resources in order to maximize the production of (i.e., educational) output. Even if society might gain more from a well-educated individual, the individual making an educational decision might not view these benefits as their own (Ainscow, 2020). This existence of societal benefits that come with a primary education is probably the main reason governments typically made schooling compulsory at the primary and secondary levels (Nureev et al., 2020).

As such, while the earnings of a worker might be lower in the short run for the purpose of education, in the future, the wages are likely to be higher, after training has been completed. The higher wages are because there is a smaller supply of workers who are capable of working in these industries, and the required education and training are costly (Bonacini et al., 2021). In some works of the economists there are models in which growth is seen as endogenous, so the immediate effect of increasing the 10% amount of education that individuals receive can be as much as 7 or 8%, and increasing the investment rate in education can lead to permanent increases in growth rates (Von Wachter, 2020). There appears to be some relationships among different measures of education (level of education completed—tertiary, number of non-employment—school years, school—tertiary years) and life expectancy at birth across countries in the sample. In addition, educational outcomes adult education level-tertiary, school life expectancy-tertiary, and not in employment, education, or training (NEET) rates might also affect such parameters as the life expectancy at birth.

2 Compulsory Education, Economic Growth, and Welfare

Generally, it is admitted that the length of the compulsory education might have some positive effect on the economic growth and welfare The results mentioned in some academic studies indicate that one additional year of mandatory education increases total years in schooling from 0.6 to 0.8 years (Elsayed, 2019). This was confirmed by examining the different changes to compulsory schooling laws over the post-second world war period across 12 European countries, in which, on average, the changes to compulsory schooling entailed 0.3–0.4 years of additional education for individuals on the lower end of the distribution, whereas it decreased to 0.1 years for the remainder of the population. In particular, it comes out that the expansion increases the gap between the educational attainment of male and female students by between 0.3 and 0.48 years (Lee & Lee, 2016). The expected effect of changing mandatory schooling is, in large part, to raise levels of education for those who are more likely to drop out early. When that is a larger cohort, and if compliance is robust, then this would raise the average levels of schooling across the population as well (McGee et al., 2021).

In the spirit of this study of behavioral economics in education, mandatory schooling laws function as a vehicle for setting and changing students' expectations. As such, many countries allocate funds to K-12 education to promote better economic outcomes. A country does not need to provide a vast network of colleges or universities in order to reap the benefits of education (Fallon & Poole, 2014). Instead, it can provide basic literacy programs and still see improvements in the economy. A country's economy becomes more productive when its share of educated workers increases, because educated workers are better able to perform tasks requiring literacy and critical thinking. They are also good in observing the rules such as paying taxes (Čábelková & Strielkowski, 2013).

In general, any economy's productivity increases as the number of educated workers increases because educated workers can more efficiently perform tasks. Countries where large proportions of the population go to and complete college experience faster economic growth compared to countries where workers are less educated. The contribution of education to labor productivity growth has been estimated by various studies at 13–30% of the overall growth (Singh & Kumar, 2021). Furthermore, the neoclassical or exogenous studies on growth described earlier suggest that the direct effect of increasing the number of workers with education by 10% will only increase GDP by around 4 or 5% (Osiobe, 2019). Over the past couple of decades, there has been a lot of focus on theories about how education can influence economic growth, and that work has implications for how we can model the effects of increasing education. The direct impact is magnified by the fact that a portion of the increased revenue generated from increased growth is reinvested into both physical and human capital (Ahmed et al., 2020). Eventually, the years of schooling that those students receive increases, and this has two effects. Under these assumptions, some researchers estimate the average increase in education for all children because of a preschool program would be 0.36 years (Delalibera &

Ferreira, 2019). At first, it is important to estimate the impact of the particular policy intervention on schooling on education attainment, then to analyze the impact of this added schooling on economic growth compared with projected path of growth absent the policy. There appear to be some relationships among different measures of education (adult educational attainment—tertiary, NEET (not in employment, life expectancy—tertiary) and life expectancy at birth across many. Some researchers investigated whether the educational outcomes adult education level-tertiary, school life expectancy-tertiary, and NEET (not in employment, education, or training) rates affect life expectancy at birth. The conclusion is that tertiary education is the most important factor of all levels of education in improving the country's economic strength and level of health (Niño-Amézquita et al., 2017; Wang & Wang, 2020). Countries which place a greater emphasis on higher education and school enrolment can result in more public health awareness, which may manifest itself through better vaccination rates for children. To extend the lifespan of individuals, governments should seek to increase higher levels of education, as well as to curb the rate at which young adults leave school and become unemployed (the already mentioned NEET rate). Thence, economists recommend that most countries improve the social education for the young by implementing free education programs and other means, in an effort to efficiently increase the health status of the population, at the same time as attempting to increase mandatory spending (Lee et al., 2022). In order to do so countries must guarantee, by legislation and employment programs, that all of their citizens can obtain education and training that will elevate workers, businesses, and the entire economy. In general, countries have improved their health status and education over time, as well as reduced their infant mortality rates. The OECDs education program is in continuous development, with information that is constantly growing.

Another interesting example is the state of California. As required under the laws of California, state authorities make annual recommendations that give the State Superintendent of Public Instruction (SSPI) guidance on potential actions that could support schools to increase student participation and decrease the dropout rate within a state's public education system. In 1974, the legislature passed California Education Code, which was intended to strengthen the implementation of mandatory school laws and to divert students who had problems with attendance or conduct at school from the juvenile justice system until all available resources were exhausted (Meyer & Keenan, 2018). California's compulsory education laws require all persons aged six through eighteen years of age to attend school, with exceptions for students who have completed high school or passed the California High School Proficiency Examination (CHSPE) and obtained parental authorization.

3 Education Policy for Developing Countries

Due to many issues like the digitalization or the effects of COVID-19 pandemic, education is declining in both developed and developing countries, and may not be recovering rapidly. Relying on online instruction from developing communities is not a sustainable way to keep children pursuing their education. We saw that in action in Afghanistan, where concern developed an educational program that relies on communities. In Latin America, where schools were completely closed for over a year, the education ministries launched resources and trainings for teachers that showed them how to implement evidence-based practices, including giving students' feedback. In Argentina, in some ways, education ministries are coordinating education responses. In many municipalities of Argentina, it is good to see efforts from one side, but limited results, unfortunately (Coolican et al., 2020). In Brazil, in most municipalities, there was one and half years of closed schools due to the very severe impacts of COVID-19 pandemic and the unavailability of vaccines (Malta Campos & Vieira, 2021).

Today, it is a great opportunity to see that timeframe for going back to school, for education being transformed to be different. More children and teens are now in preschool, elementary, and secondary school than at any time before. There has been a convergence of students attending primary schools, and far more younger children now attend schools in developing countries. When it comes to the average levels of educational achievement—how much children learned, and how much time they spent in school—there is still a wide gap. The educational levels of the adult labor force, typically measured in terms of the average years spent in school, are almost twice as high in developing countries as they are among developed peers (Jayachandran, 2021).

The developed world continues to enjoy in the twenty-first century the same average levels of schooling achieved by many Western countries by the first decades of the twentieth century. It is important to note here that a number of lower-income countries experienced very little increase in educational attainment, coupled with very little increase in income. Countries where large shares of the population are attending school and graduating from college experience faster economic growth compared to countries where the number of workers who are less educated is smaller (Han & Lee, 2020).

Let us consider productivity growth, generally considered a major factor in GDP growth, while it is also determined by a country's level of population education. A country's economy becomes more productive when its share of educated workers increases, since educated workers are able to perform tasks requiring literacy and critical thinking more effectively. The education and training of a country's labor force is an important determinant of how a country's economy performs. Countries must make sure, through legislation and employment programs, all their citizens are accessing education and training that can elevate workers, businesses, and the entire economy (Malik, 2018). For students throughout the developing world to make it to school and back to safety, governments will have to put the availability of education at the forefront of their priorities. Students in the developing world experience longer absences from school, and have more difficulty making up lost ground when they finally do get back. At current rates of advancement, students in developing countries would need to spend much more time to catch up with today's students learning levels in science than their colleagues in the developed countries. Rich countries have enjoyed higher levels of education for a very long time, but the poorest countries are just now making up for lost time.

Over the last decade, there has been significant progress in increasing access to education and in achieving higher rates of school enrolment across levels. Over the last 20–30 years, researchers in education, economics, and international development have built up substantial bodies of evidence showing strategies that are effective in increasing school enrollment and school-going (Pleaner et al., 2022). In a field moving forward at breakneck speed, innovative solutions to educational problems are popping up all around. Countries around the world are wondering how best to invest in education restoration, and billions of dollars are already being invested in schools. As a result, many countries are providing money to K-12 schools in order to boost economic output. A country does not need to provide a vast network of colleges or universities in order to reap the benefits of education; it can provide basic literacy programs and still see improvements in the economy.

Many countries are placing more emphasis on developing education systems that produce workers who are capable of working in emerging industries, such as science and technology. In addition, many countries have difficulty using resources efficiently, and it is quite common for increases in educational expenditures to fail to lead to increased training and improved human capital (Olopade et al., 2019).

Spending a higher share of GDP on education does not necessarily guarantee a higher-educated country's population. The latter perspective—that is, that education may increase productivity—is at the heart of the belief that building schools in poor countries will contribute to rising productivity, and hence to convergent incomes. One needs to think, specifically, of policies that are built around the premise that building schools in poor countries may be one way of helping the economy to pick up. While remote schooling is never going to be enough for all students it seems like a good fit for developing countries. Not as much in parts of Eastern Europe, Latin America is highly unequal, and Brazil was one of the most unequal countries for education before COVID-19 (Garcia et al., 2020). But other places such as Africa also suffer from the same issues. For instance, in Mali, the average number of years in school per 25-year-old was hardly three years, making Mali the least educated nation among those on the continent (Toulmin, 2020). In an examination of 15 countries across Sub-Saharan Africa, researchers at the World Bank and International Centre for Research on Women found educated women tended to have fewer children and give birth later in life (Yaya et al., 2019). Many young people in developing countries who are not able to get a good education are lacking basic skills, as well as higher-level skills, to succeed in their jobs and lives (Čábelková et al., 2015; Litau, 2018). Yet, for many children and adolescents in More Today, school does not result in learning and that was before COVID-19 closed schools around the world and upended learning, creating the pressing need for education to be reinvented. In many developing countries, education systems were already facing learning crises, with COVID-19 pandemic forcing massive disruptions.

4 Compulsory Education and Government Policy

It appears, however, that using the variable interest entity (VIE) framework, which is required to redress reforms, might have to be gradually eliminated within the mandatory education sector (Mathooko & Ogutu, 2015). This can be shown on the example of China and its educational system: although these education sector measures were likely to have been part of policy efforts to focus educational activity on China's mainstream non-profit public education system and reduce the financial pressures and other burdens on parents associated with private tutoring businesses, it does appear that the use of VIE structures, as required to be rectified under the tutoring education sector opinions, may need to be phased out in the compulsory education sector (Sun et al., 2021). Some investors are concerned that a particular prohibition against using VIE Structures for activities related to non-curricular activities related to tutoring could indicate an overall step toward Mainland Chinese authorities to clamp down on VIE structures for other sectors in which foreign ownership is restricted or prohibited.

In the United States, local authorities are no longer be allowed to authorize new off-campus training facilities for students who are not part of compulsory education. This orientation mirrors historical development in the role of the Federal Government in education as a sort of contingency response system, as a means to bridge gaps in state and local education support where there are pressing nationwide needs (Enriquez et al., 2019). K-12 education has traditionally been allocated by government, federally, at the State, and local levels, while postsecondary education has been allocated through some combination of markets and the Government. Yet, even today, education policy takes precedence over spending in infancy, with most government investments during infancy funneled through compulsory school systems in developed welfare states and elsewhere. This existence of the societal benefits that accrue to primary education is probably the main reason governments typically have made schools compulsory at both primary and secondary levels (Elliott & Lewis, 2018). Not only can educational systems be more integrated throughout life's journey, there are a number of public policies worth greater government investment that could sustain children's education, especially if well integrated. For countries seeking to enhance social and economic progress, and currently banking on school systems, a comprehensive, life-course-based approach children's policies and education is not just desirable, it is essential. Education and learning must benefit from the complementarity of a comprehensive social policy framework, strengthening home-school partnerships, so as to ensure all government expenditures are responsive to life course development, with optimal investments in children's education following optimal investments in pre-school, to the benefit of children, schools, and society. Relatively successful economies can invest heavily in their population's education, as measured by duration and levels of schooling and training, but this can at least partly be the consequence, not cause, of economic success (Lee & Clarke, 2019). Not the least among the benefits to interjecting competition will be making schoolteachers pay responsive to market forces. The preservation of public schools would, in turn, however, need to be justified on grounds different from the ones we have so far addressed. The system thus obtained would, in its broadest outline, follow the arrangements adopted by the United States in the aftermath of the Second World War for funding veterans' education, except that fund would, it is assumed, be drawn from the states, rather than the federal government. The retention of state schools themselves would, however, have to be justified on grounds other than those we have so far considered (Hammack & Smith, 2018). The provision under which the Government continues to run certain schools, parents choosing to enroll their children in alternative schools would pay an amount equivalent to the estimated costs of raising the child at the Government School, provided at least this amount is spent on the education of their children in approved schools. Government has adequately funded universal education for citizenship, but has been led by that process also to administer the majority of schools providing that education. Education costs may be undertaken by private individuals as well as governments, via public spending. The Federal share for K-12 education is approximately 8%, including funds from not just the Department of Education (ED) but other U.S. Federal agencies, such as the Department of Health and Human Services Head Start Program and the Department of Agriculture's School Lunch Program (Friedersdorf, 2020). The expected effect of the changes to mandatory schooling is, in general, to increase educational attainment among those who are more likely to drop out early. In case when that is a larger cohort and compliance is stronger, then that would raise the average levels of schooling across the population.

5 Education and Accumulation of Human Capital

Education helps to generate human capital and this capital influences economic growth. In addition, it can help to grow the economy by expanding its human knowledge and skills. Such insights are crucial and necessary to the developing economies for conducting empirical research into the linkages among financial development, human capital, and economic growth (Sima et al., 2020). It is also apparent that human capital and financial development enhance the growth rate of economic development of emerging economies (Humpert, 2013). This recipe for economic growth—investing in labor productivity, accompanied by investments in human capital and technology, as well as increases in physical capital—applies to all economies worldwide. Although investments in physical capital are important to increases in labor productivity and GDP per capita, building human capital is at least as important. A more important reason for building the output per capita function is to understand the contributions of both human capital and physical capital. The conventional approach uses the aggregate production function to assess how much of the growth of economic output per capita can be explained by increases in both physical and human capital (Gardiner et al., 2020). The inputs are average levels of human capital per capita, average levels of physical capital per capita, and levels of technology per person. To make an easy parallel with a standard Solow-Swan framework for growth, constant rates of human capital investment will necessarily result in more human capital per worker, should growth of the workforce be slower (Mose, 2021). While investments in human capital generally produce higher growth, this does not necessarily imply that jobs are made available for newly-educated workers. Increased investments in human capital may also occur on the tight end, with higher spending on each year's schooling, with variations in class sizes, supplemental equipment, number of hours per day of schooling, or quality of teachers, as well as pay rates. If one sets the output elasticities to human capital to the base value of 0.33, slower population growth leads to higher consumption per equivalent adult, for any elasticity used to measure quantity-quality tradeoffs. Kim et al. (2020) find that while longer-run growth is driven by changes in the quality of the product at an independent scale, hence showing no linearity, human capital is a longer-run effect of the rate of economic growth. Some researchers also claimed that when capital returns are greater than economic growth rates, a likely outcome is concentrated capital ownership leading to increased inequality (Cerra et al., 2021). Given the probable evolution of global populations, and the rather low expectations that many people have about the growth rate per capita in economic output, there might be the possibility of the rate of return to capital being greater than the economic growth rate leading to increasing wealth concentration and greater inequality seems justified. The danger in slower economic growth is that the concentration of capital which results will serve to return to 20th-century patrimonial capitalism, where one made one's fortune more efficiently through marriage to the heir of a large fortune rather than through working hard to develop one's talents in service to productive careers (Peterson, 2017). It has also been claimed that the demographic expansion caused by higher levels of birthrates, as is frequently the case in lower-income countries, may diminish overall prosperity, as opposed to growth caused by falling death rates, which is usually thought to have a more benign effect on savings and economic growth. There is growing evidence that countries cannot attain sustained, inclusive economic growth without strengthening their human capital, do not have workforces prepared to take up more high-skilled jobs of the future, and do not compete effectively in the global economy. Despite the unprecedented gains in human development in the last 25 years, significant challenges still exist, particularly for developing countries. Finance ministers' annual meetings of the World Bank Group underscored the importance of human capital for job-creation and economic transformation agendas of countries in various stages of development. The Human Capital project supports scaling-up such policy and institutional reform support, as well as working on a number of tools and products that can assist countries to meet their goals, such as human capital government spending and institutional overhauls, as well as case studies that highlight country-level successes and innovations (Hunter & Shaffer, 2022). The involvement adds to the World Bank Group's longstanding engagement with countries on sectors contributing to human development. While both indices emphasize human capabilities as critical for a nation's development, the human capital indices also reinforce the economic case for investing in human capital. Both consumption expenditures and corporate investments lead to more economic growth, and they play an important role in determining workers levels of education and development. A healthy climate for economic growth while physical and human capital improvement and better technologies are important, just as important for a nations welfare is the climate, or the system, within which those inputs are grown. A healthy climate for GDP per capita growth and labor productivity includes a combination of human capital deepening, physical capital deepening, and technology gains operating within a market-oriented economy with supportive public policies. Moreover, it induces improvements in human capital, physical capital, and technology, operating in a market-oriented environment with supportive public policies and institutions. The interaction term value also suggests that the impact of the financial development increases growth which indicates that the interaction terms of human capital and financial development have a positive and significant impact on economic growth.

6 Conclusion

In summary, it becomes apparent that education is the single most important element of all levels of education in order for a country to increase its economic strength and its level of health. Our findings suggest that the duration of compulsory education indeed has positive effects on economic growth and welfare which can be used by the governments for mitigating their educational and economic policies for increasing welfare.

It also becomes clear that education can have the impact on wages and the state of the labor market. The higher wages are because there is a smaller supply of workers capable of working in these industries, and the required education and training are costly. Because education and training take time to finish, changes in the demand for certain types of workers have varying effects over the long and short terms.

Education creates and maintains human capital and therefore becomes an important means for its support. It also helps to prevent the adverse effects of the economic downturns such as the brain drain or the migration of the most skilled workers abroad with an aim of joining foreign labor markets.

It can be therefore concluded that lower levels in tertiary education have an adverse effect on the health status of the country with regard to the number of premature deaths. Countries with greater attention to higher education and school enrolment can impart greater health consciousness to their populations.

References

Ahmed, T., Chandran, V. G. R., Klobas, J. E., Liñán, F., & Kokkalis, P. (2020). Entrepreneurship education programmes: How learning, inspiration and resources affect intentions for new venture creation in a developing economy. *The International Journal of Management Education, 18*(1), 100327. https://doi.org/10.1016/j.ijme.2019.100327

Ainscow, M. (2020). Promoting inclusion and equity in education: Lessons from international experiences. *Nordic Journal of Studies in Educational Policy, 6*(1), 7–16. https://doi.org/10.1080/20020317.2020.1729587

Ashford, N. A., Hall, R. P., Arango-Quiroga, J., Metaxas, K. A., & Showalter, A. L. (2020). Addressing inequality: The first step beyond COVID-19 and towards sustainability. *Sustainability, 12*(13), 5404. https://doi.org/10.3390/su12135404

Babatunde, S. A. (2018). Government spending on infrastructure and economic growth in Nigeria. *Economic Research-Ekonomska Istraživanja, 31*(1), 997–1014. https://doi.org/10.1080/1331677X.2018.1436453

Bonacini, L., Gallo, G., & Scicchitano, S. (2021). Working from home and income inequality: Risks of a "new normal" with COVID-19. *Journal of Population Economics, 34*(1), 303–360. https://doi.org/10.1007/s00148-020-00800-7

Čábelková, I., Abrhám, J., & Strielkowski, W. (2015). Factors influencing job satisfaction in post-transition economies: The case of the Czech Republic. *International Journal of Occupational Safety and Ergonomics, 21*(4), 448–456. https://doi.org/10.1080/10803548.2015.1073007

Čábelková, I., & Strielkowski, W. (2013). Is the level of taxation a product of culture? A cultural economics approach. *Society and Economy, 35*(4), 513–529. https://doi.org/10.1556/SocEc.2013.0007

Cerra, V., Lama, R., & Loayza, N. V. (2021). Links between growth, inequality, and poverty. *International Monetary Fund, 68*, 1–54. https://doi.org/10.1093/oso/9780192846938.003.0002

Coolican, M., Borras, J. C., & Strong, M. (2020). Argentina and the COVID-19: Lessons learned from education and technical colleges in Buenos Aires Province. *Journal of Education for Teaching, 46*(4), 484–496. https://doi.org/10.1080/02607476.2020.1802204

Datzberger, S. (2018). Why education is not helping the poor. Findings from Uganda. *World Development, 110*, 124–139. https://doi.org/10.1016/j.worlddev.2018.05.022

Delalibera, B. R., & Ferreira, P. C. (2019). Early childhood education and economic growth. *Journal of Economic Dynamics and Control, 98*, 82–104. https://doi.org/10.1016/j.jedc.2018.10.002

Elliott, W., & Lewis, M. (2018). *Making education work for the poor: The potential of children's savings accounts.* Oxford University Press.

Elsayed, M. A. (2019). Keeping kids in school: The long-term effects of extending compulsory education. *Education Finance and Policy, 14*(2), 242–271. https://doi.org/10.1162/edfp_a_00254

Enriquez, L. E., Hernandez, M. M., Millán, D., & Vera, D. V. (2019). Mediating illegality: Federal, state, and institutional policies in the educational experiences of undocumented college students. *Law & Social Inquiry, 44*(3), 679–703. https://doi.org/10.1017/lsi.2018.16

Fallon, G., & Poole, W. (2014). The emergence of a market-driven funding mechanism in K-12 education in British Columbia: Creeping privatization and the eclipse of equity. *Journal of Education Policy, 29*(3), 302–322. https://doi.org/10.1080/02680939.2013.820354

Friedersdorf, L. E. (2020). Developing the workforce of the future: How the national nanotechnology initiative has supported nanoscale science and engineering education in the United States. *IEEE Nanotechnology Magazine, 14*(4), 13–20. https://doi.org/10.1109/MNANO.2020.2994799

Garcia, P. J., Alarcón, A., Bayer, A., Buss, P., Guerra, G., Ribeiro, H., & Atun, R. (2020). COVID-19 response in Latin America. *The American Journal of Tropical Medicine and Hygiene, 103*(5), 1765. https://doi.org/10.4269/ajtmh.20-0765

Gardiner, B., Fingleton, B., & Martin, R. (2020). Regional disparities in labour productivity and the role of capital stock. *National Institute Economic Review, 253*, R29–R43. https://doi.org/10.1017/nie.2020.28

Gruzina, Y., Firsova, I., & Strielkowski, W. (2021). Dynamics of human capital development in economic development cycles. *Economies, 9*(2), 67. https://doi.org/10.3390/economies9020067

Habib, M., Abbas, J., & Noman, R. (2019). Are human capital, intellectual property rights, and research and development expenditures really important for total factor productivity? An empirical analysis. *International Journal of Social Economics, 46*(6), 756–774. https://doi.org/10.1108/IJSE-09-2018-0472

Hammack, D. C., & Smith, S. R. (2018). Foundations in the United States: Dimensions for international comparison. *American Behavioral Scientist, 62*(12), 1603–1638. https://doi.org/10.1177/0002764218775159

Han, J. S., & Lee, J. W. (2020). Demographic change, human capital, and economic growth in Korea. *Japan and the World Economy, 53*, 100984. https://doi.org/10.1016/j.japwor.2019.100984

Humpert, S. (2013). A note on the immigrant-native gap in earnings. *International Economics Letters, 2*(4), 28–41. https://doi.org/10.24984/iel.2013.2.4.4

Hunter, B. M., & Shaffer, J. D. (2022). Human capital, risk and the World Bank's reintermediation in global development. *Third World Quarterly, 43*(1), 35–54. https://doi.org/10.1080/01436597.2021.1953980

Jayachandran, S. (2021). Social norms as a barrier to women's employment in developing countries. *IMF Economic Review, 69*(3), 576–595. https://doi.org/10.1057/s41308-021-00140-w

Khan, Z., Hussain, M., Shahbaz, M., Yang, S., & Jiao, Z. (2020). Natural resource abundance, technological innovation, and human capital nexus with financial development: A case study of China. *Resources Policy, 65*, 101585. https://doi.org/10.1016/j.resourpol.2020.101585

Kim, D. H., Chen, T. C., & Lin, S. C. (2020). Does oil drive income inequality? New panel evidence. *Structural Change and Economic Dynamics, 55*, 137–152. https://doi.org/10.1016/j.strueco.2020.08.002

Lee, D., Rundle-Thiele, S., Wut, T. M., & Li, G. (2022). Increasing seasonal influenza vaccination among university students: A systematic review of programs using a social marketing perspective. *International Journal of Environmental Research and Public Health, 19*(12), 7138. https://doi.org/10.3390/ijerph19127138

Lee, J. W., & Lee, H. (2016). Human capital in the long run. *Journal of Development Economics, 122*, 147–169. https://doi.org/10.1016/j.jdeveco.2016.05.006

Lee, N., & Clarke, S. (2019). Do low-skilled workers gain from high-tech employment growth? High-technology multipliers, employment and wages in Britain. *Research Policy, 48*(9), 103803. https://doi.org/10.1016/j.respol.2019.05.012

Litau, E. Y. (2018). Cognitive science as a pivot of teaching financial disciplines. In *Proceedings of the 31st International Business Information Management Association Conference, IBIMA 2018: Innovation Management and Education Excellence through Vision 2020* (pp. 72–80).

Malik, R. S. (2018). Educational challenges in 21st century and sustainable development. *Journal of Sustainable Development Education and Research, 2*(1), 9–20. https://doi.org/10.17509/jsder.v2i1.12266

Malta Campos, M., & Vieira, L. F. (2021). COVID-19 and early childhood in Brazil: Impacts on children's well-being, education and care. *European Early Childhood Education Research Journal, 29*(1), 125–140. https://doi.org/10.1080/1350293X.2021.1872671

Mathooko, F. M., & Ogutu, M. (2015). Porter's five competitive forces framework and other factors that influence the choice of response strategies adopted by public universities in Kenya. *International Journal of Educational Management, 29*(3), 334–354. https://doi.org/10.1108/IJEM-12-2013-0187

McGee, R. S., Homburger, J. R., Williams, H. E., Bergstrom, C. T., & Zhou, A. Y. (2021). Model-driven mitigation measures for reopening schools during the COVID-19 pandemic. *Proceedings of the National Academy of Sciences, 118*(39), e2108909118. https://doi.org/10.1073/pnas.2108909118

Meyer, E. J., & Keenan, H. (2018). Can policies help schools affirm gender diversity? A policy archaeology of transgender-inclusive policies in California schools. *Gender and Education, 30*(6), 736–753. https://doi.org/10.1080/09540253.2018.1483490

Mose, N. (2021). Determinants of regional economic growth in Kenya. *African Journal of Business Management, 15*(1), 1–12. https://doi.org/10.5897/AJBM2020.9118

Niño-Amézquita, J., Dubrovsky, V., & Jankurová, A. (2017). Innovations and competitiveness in regional development: A comparison of Latin America, Europe, and China. *Czech Journal of Social Sciences, Business and Economics, 6*(1), 28–36. https://doi.org/10.24984/cjssbe.2017.6.1.4

Nureev, R., Volchik, V., & Strielkowski, W. (2020). Neoliberal reforms in higher education and the import of institutions. *Social Sciences, 9*(5), 79. https://doi.org/10.3390/socsci9050079

Olopade, B. C., Okodua, H., Oladosun, M., & Asaleye, A. J. (2019). Human capital and poverty reduction in OPEC member-countries. *Heliyon, 5*(8), e02279. https://doi.org/10.1016/j.heliyon.2019.e02279

Osiobe, E. U. (2019). A literature review of human capital and economic growth. *Business and Economic Research, 9*(4), 179–196. https://doi.org/10.5296/ber.v9i4.15624

Peterson, E. W. F. (2017). The role of population in economic growth. *SAGE Open, 7*(4), 2158244017736094. https://doi.org/10.1177/2158244017736094

Pleaner, M., Kutywayo, A., Beksinska, M., Mabetha, K., Naidoo, N., & Mullick, S. (2022). Knowledge, uptake and patterns of contraception use among in-school adolescents in three South African townships: Baseline findings from the Girls Achieve Power (GAP Year) Trial. *Gates Open Research, 6*(67), 67. https://doi.org/10.12688/gatesopenres.13636.1

Rosinger, K., Kelchen, R., Baker, D. J., Ortagus, J., & Lingo, M. D. (2022). State higher education funding during COVID-19: Lessons from prior recessions and implications for equity. *AERA Open, 8*, 23328584221091276. https://doi.org/10.1177/23328584221091277

Ryan, L., & Lőrinc, M. (2018). Perceptions, prejudices and possibilities: Young people narrating apprenticeship experiences. *British Journal of Sociology of Education, 39*(6), 762–777. https://doi.org/10.1080/01425692.2017.1417821

Shi, L., Han, L., Yang, F., & Gao, L. (2019). The evolution of sustainable development theory: Types, goals, and research prospects. *Sustainability, 11*(24), 7158. https://doi.org/10.3390/su11247158

Sima, V., Gheorghe, I. G., Subić, J., & Nancu, D. (2020). Influences of the industry 4.0 revolution on the human capital development and consumer behavior: A systematic review. *Sustainability, 12*(10), 4035. https://doi.org/10.3390/su12104035

Singh, A. K., & Kumar, S. (2021). Assessing the performance and factors affecting industrial development in Indian states: An empirical analysis. *Journal of Social Economics Research, 8*(2), 135–154. https://doi.org/10.18488/journal.35.2021.82.135.154

Strielkowski, W., & Weyskrabova, B. (2014). Ukrainian labour migration and remittances in the Czech Republic. *Tijdschrift voor economische en sociale geografie, 105*(1), 30–45. https://doi.org/10.1111/tesg.12052

Sun, S., Goldberg, S. B., Lin, D., Qiao, S., & Operario, D. (2021). Psychiatric symptoms, risk, and protective factors among university students in quarantine during the COVID-19 pandemic in China. *Globalization and Health, 17*(1), 1–14. https://doi.org/10.1186/s12992-021-00663-x

Toulmin, C. (2020). *Land, investment, and migration: Thirty-five years of village life in Mali.* Oxford University Press.

Von Wachter, T. (2020). The persistent effects of initial labor market conditions for young adults and their sources. *Journal of Economic Perspectives, 34*(4), 168–194. https://doi.org/10.1257/jep.34.4.168

Wang, J., & Wang, Z. (2020). Strengths, weaknesses, opportunities and threats (SWOT) analysis of China's prevention and control strategy for the COVID-19 epidemic. *International Journal of Environmental Research and Public Health, 17*(7), 223. https://doi.org/10.3390/ijerph17072235

Yaya, S., Odusina, E. K., & Bishwajit, G. (2019). Prevalence of child marriage and its impact on fertility outcomes in 34 sub-Saharan African countries. *BMC International Health and Human Rights, 19*(1), 1–11. https://doi.org/10.1186/s12914-019-0219-1

Efficiency of Institutions and Economic Agents from Transaction Costs Perspective

Evgeny A. Kuzmin and Arina V. Suvorova

Abstract Transaction costs are among the fundamental parameters of economic relations. Nevertheless, there is a controversy over the understanding of transaction costs when establishing the efficiency of institutions and economic agents. Having performed a critical analysis of contemporary views, we substantiate a number of assumptions that clarify the nature of the institutional order. The research results show that institutions not only do not have the goal to minimize transaction costs, but, on the contrary, they serve a catalyst for their growth, since the emergence of any institutional normative imperative (which is also a new institution) leads to an increase in overall transaction costs. At the same time, the functioning of the market and competitive interactions between economic agents are detected precisely by the presence of transaction costs, while the transaction costs incurred by the actors cause a change in the level of uncertainty and complexity of this interaction. The veiled 'struggle' of economic agents against institution in any of its forms faces an insurmountable (ceteris paribus) minimum of transaction costs, which determines the existence and functioning of a given institution or a complex of institutions. The confrontation between the criteria for the efficiency of institutions and economic agents creates conditions for finding a balance between complexity and uncertainty in the economic mechanism.

Keywords Transaction costs · Institutions · Economic agents · Uncertainty · Complexity · Economic efficiency

JEL Classification L14 · D02 · E02 · D80

E. A. Kuzmin (✉) · A. V. Suvorova
Institute of Economics of the Ural Branch of the Russian Academy of Sciences, 29 Moskovskaya Str., 620014 Ekaterinburg, Russian Federation
e-mail: kuzmin.ea@uiec.ru

A. V. Suvorova
e-mail: suvorova.av@uiec.ru

V. Kumar et al. (eds.), *Consequences of Social Transformation for Economic Theory*, Springer Proceedings in Business and Economics,
https://doi.org/10.1007/978-3-031-27785-6_9

1 Introduction

The role of transaction costs in institutional methodology is hard to overestimate. Acting, at first glance, only as a measure of expenditures associated with business contracts' implementation, transaction costs have gone far beyond the scope of only a parameter characteristic. Their dynamics has become an indicator of uncertainty and risk, the complexity of interaction, and the viscosity of the economic environment. The seemingly trivial scientific objective of determining the efficiency of institutions and economic agents made it possible to rethink the significance of transaction costs. All debates over this topic, one way or another, come down to the search for target functions that describe the work of institutions and economic agents. A new vision of these processes is possible through the prism of transaction costs and the current study will be built in this vein.

The prevailing approaches to understanding transaction costs and their role for business entities are based on the works of a plethora of theorists who formed the basis of the institutional scientific field. Even though the ideas about the nature of transaction costs in the research literature vary greatly, their authors have reached a consensus on some fundamental provisions. Therefore, we will discuss the issue of the efficiency of institutions and economic agents in the context of a critical analysis of modern views.

Thus, the present study aims to establish the significance of transaction costs in characterizing the efficiency and target functions of institutions and economic agents operating in the institutional space. To attain the stated purpose, the following objectives are to be achieved: to clarify the nature and essence of transaction costs; to substantiate institutions' targets and identify the role of transaction costs in them; to establish the relationship between the efficiency of economic agents and the non-production costs they incur; to reconsider the approach to measuring and observing transaction costs in the economy.

2 Transaction Costs: The Essence and Peculiarities

Prior to the works by Coase (1937), Marschak (1950) and Commons (1931), ideas about costs related to the implementation of commodity and resource exchange transactions arose on a regular basis. However, the very concept of transaction in the context of economics was introduced by Commons (1931), who characterized it as "the alienation and acquisition, between individuals, of the rights of property and liberty created by society" (p. 652). Later, numerous alternative definitions of the term were proposed. One of them is a rather valid interpretation by Fischer (1999), who states that every transfer of goods, services, and property rights, which takes place between individuals and legal entities, is a transaction.

As for the substance of transaction costs, Efimova et al. (2008) highlight that the exchange of assets, always associated with the transfer of property rights to them, implies additional costs for all the parties involved. This means that the functioning of the market and the emergence of competitive interactions are determined by the presence of transaction costs, which, in turn, result from the costs that accompany production processes and are of value for exchange operations (the exchange mechanism is activated due to the difference between the value of the good for consumers and the volume of production costs).

Speaking about exchange operations as a source of transaction costs, a whole range of works is of special interest that focus on providing the scientific rationale for the transformation of a product's value influenced by the specificity of the product exchange organization. A striking example of such a work is Carl Menger's study on the phenomenon of 'economic sacrifices' (Menger, 2007) that subjects are forced to bear in the interests of commodity exchange. Among the examples of these economic sacrifices are costs associated with assets transportation, temporary losses, etc. At the same time, Menger also drew attention to the fact that in the absence of such costs, exchange transactions acquired the features of non-economic (indifferent) ones.

Taken broadly, transaction costs can be interpreted as "costs that accompany the relationships between economic agents" (Kuzminov et al., 2006, p. 203). In particular, in his quite capacious interpretation Kenneth Arrow (Arrow, 1969, p. 48) draws attention to such a function of transaction costs as "keeping the economic system on track" (as Kushlin puts it, "exploitation of the economic system" (Kushlin, 2000, p. 13)). Thus, according to the adherents of the broad approach to the essence of transaction costs, they serve as an attribute of open economic systems with many actors operating in them that are forced to bear such costs to maintain their relationships and keep these interactions. Despite the fact that Kuzminov et al. (2006) were very critical of Arrow's definition noting its practical uselessness, it should be recognized that it contains a deep conceptual meaning: Arrow's interpretation allows dealing with transaction costs in all their diversity (based on their relations to the phenomenon of exchange) without focusing on the specificities of their typology. Here, it is worth noting that the systematization of transaction costs, which is of undoubted interest in the theoretical aspect, in practice can only complicate the process of modeling economic activity and establishing conditions for its optimization (although examples of such classifications have become widespread in the scientific literature, such as Milgrom and Roberts (1999), Eggertsson (2001)) due to the impossibility to accurately measure each type of transaction costs (it is only necessary to assess the cost value when analyzing their structure and proposing specific tactical solutions). The problem of observability and measuring of transaction costs was identified by Wallis and North (1986), who, while assessing the transaction sectors shares in the structure of the product manufactured, noted that "the most difficult conceptual problem is created by those transaction costs that arise within the firm" (p. 100). A similar thesis can be found in works by Malahov (1996), who argues that "a significant part of transaction costs is intangible, invisible" (p. 93).

Another important feature of transaction costs emphasized by Niehans (1987) is their inseparable connection with the market economy. This correlates with the ideas of Coase, who argued that under communism, the costs incurred in making a deal would equal zero (Wang, 2003). However, it should be noted that the costs associated with the exchange and interaction of at least two economic entities are inherent in any economic system, regardless of whether it is planned or market one. At that, the contribution of transaction costs to the total amount of costs that agents are forced to bear within systems of different types will be different. This is largely due to transaction costs conditioned by the market aspect of uncertainty: in the market environment, exchange operations often require significant investments due to attempts by economic counterparties to reduce information asymmetry (which is insignificant in a planned system and does not require large-scale resources to ensure its leveling). The emergence of the asymmetry is associated with the uncertainty of the contract size and technological uncertainty (Walker & Weber, 1983), and with the inability to distinguish between consumer types (Kangoh, 1989). Moreover, "uncertainty is a core assumption in transaction costs theory" (Slater & Spencer, 2000, p. 61), and transaction costs are an inherent property of uncertainty (Arkhipov & Bolshakova, 2009).

It is obvious that amid information asymmetry inherent in the market characterized by high uncertainty and entropy, economic agents are ready to bear the costs incurred in obtaining price data, searching for potential suppliers and consumers, etc., in other words, to spend available resources on carrying transaction costs, searching for mechanisms and tools to overcome risks (the strategy of reducing the level of uncertainty is also scrutinized by Aubin et al. (2001). At the same time, such characteristics as the uniqueness of the assets used and their complexity determine the logical connection between risk and uncertainty, on the one hand, and transaction costs, on the other. For example, if the subject of exchange transactions is unique assets, the demand and supply of which are limited by their specificity, then there are significant problems with finding counterparties, as well as considerable risks of price manipulations (due to the lack of alternatives, price can be both artificially boosted and dropped), and intermediary-initiated competitive pressure. This threatens a successful outcome of the transaction and ultimately results in the refusal of the economic agent to use assets of this type in its exchange transactions. In this case, the significance of transaction costs increases dramatically: their growth is associated with an increase in the level of uncertainty. Such a relationship is noted by Kovalenko et al. (2010) who argue that "for a manufacturing firm, transaction costs caused by uncertainty are very high, and the impossibility of timely delivery of specialized assets entails the danger of production shutdown". However, the converse is also true: transaction costs incurred by the actors cause a change in the level of uncertainty.

3 Transaction Costs and Institutions

Minimization of transaction costs is believed to be the criterion for assessing the efficiency of individual institutions and the entire institutional environment. However, this explains neither absolute nor relative growth of the transaction sector. Wang (2003) seeks to resolve this controversy by arguing that "the rise of the transaction sector is exactly to serve that purpose", but "apparent discrepancy between the aggregated transaction sector and transaction costs at the micro level forces us to rethink the validity of the transaction sector as a measurement of transaction costs".

The economic mechanism institutions do not aim to minimize transaction costs, but, on the contrary, act as catalysts for their growth, since the functioning of such institutions is subject to the idea and conception of transaction costs: on the one hand, the emergence of institutions generates transaction costs; on the other hand, transaction costs are a necessary resource for them to exist. Self-renunciation of institutions from transaction costs that are so important to them simply cannot fit into the existing paradigm of institutional economics. In this context, it is worth emphasizing that the veiled 'struggle' of economic agents against institution in any of its forms runs into an insuperable (ceteris paribus) minimum of transaction costs, which are, in a certain sense, normal. The intention of actors to enhance their own efficiency leads to the fact that the only means to do this is to reduce or minimize transaction costs, when opportunities for further improvement of the meta-production function are limited.

In this case, an institution is a very conditional likeness to an economic agent, or, in other words, a 'quasi-economic' agent. Obviously, it is erroneous to equate an institution with a certain business entity amorphous in theory, but real in practice, as indicated by differences in their nature: according to North (1992), institutions cannot be seen, felt, touched and even measured; institutions are constructs created by human mind. However, hypothetically if an institution is a conditional likeness to an economic agent, at least in an abstract interaction, it is possible to identify new features of institutions' target function.

The very mechanism of interaction between them is clear and understandable, "when the former determine the 'rules of the game', and the latter are the 'players'" (North, 1997, p. 6). But in the interaction between institutions and economic agents (organizations), there are competition and, in some way, confrontation emerging. The desire to bend the 'rules of the game' (those that hinder economic exchange) is nothing more than an attempt to minimize transaction costs, which is what any economic agent is striving for. However, the options to legally circumvent statutory formal and long-standing informal rules and norms encounter institutional restrictions, where in order to maintain stability and controllability of the economic mechanism, there exist not only the disposition of agents' economic behavior, but also sanctions.

The interrelated nature of costs and institutions, as well as actors in the institutional environment, implies rather clear and distinct provisions of the target function of institutions, which by no means boils down to "minimization of transaction costs" or even their "optimization within the normal range" (Frolov, 2011). Apparently, the target function of institutions does not need to contain such formulations of 'signs of efficiency': the functioning of institutions is determined by the role they play as a guarantor of the stability of organizational-economic systems, establishing the operation order of economic mechanisms and the norms and rules of socio-economic processes, and thereby minimizing the uncertainty of the conditions under which business entities are forced to carry out their activities.

The uncertainty in the organizational-economic system cannot increase endlessly. There is its objective limit, as is the limit of certainty. Reaching some invisible critical level of uncertainty can lead to the fact that the system will get itself into self-destruction and enforced self-transformation, which results in the construction of a new institutional order, or, in other words, the transition to a new evolutionary level. This partly explains the evolution not only of artificial systems, including organizational-economic ones, but also of natural systems, such as the biological evolution.

As for the efficiency of the functioning of institutions, we believe it cannot be assessed through the characteristics of the transaction costs dynamics. It is more expedient to apply such an assumption not to institutions, but directly to economic agents, but with a significant caveat that the size of transaction costs does not reflect either efficiency or success or any other sign of economic rationality and maximization of positive performance.

It should be considered that both the formulation and the solution of the question about the efficiency of the existing institutional environment should take into account the regularity of its increase due to the growth of transaction costs associated with institutional benefits; however, if the volume of other expenditures for an economic agent or organizational-economic system persists, the similar increase in costs will have the opposite effect, i.e., its efficiency will decrease. Therefore, it is reasonable to delimit the issue of efficiency for two parties: first, for institutions, and second, for the actors of the organizational-economic system.

Although attempts to confuse these essentially different questions based on the assumption that the efficiency of institutions depends on the efficiency of economic agents are erroneous, a number of researchers seem to proceed from this very point. Imagine that it is correct to assume that the institution should minimize transaction costs to the level necessary to maintain the institution itself, which results in the formation of one of institutions' functions in minimizing transaction costs (Rudenkov, 2010), then it will be difficult to explain the growth in transaction costs and the transaction sector in developed countries that is observed these days. Based on this knowingly false hypothesis, we can claim that throughout their existence the institutions of developed countries have continuously been losing their efficiency. This objectively proves the falsity and economic absurdity of such an assumption. The dubiousness of the hypothesis is also confirmed by Litvintseva (2003), who admits that "it is difficult to recognize the minimization of transaction costs as a universal criterion for the efficiency of institutions. This is only one of the means to achieve socio-economic goals" (p. 304).

Kuzminov et al., (2005, 2006) highlight the ambiguous perception of the usefulness that an institution can (should) have. They see institution as a structure within which transaction costs are minimized and evaluate it based on this criterion, but the problem is that an institution is able to ensure local minimization of transaction costs and at the same time create global inefficiency. Hence, the thesis about the impossibility to assess the efficiency of institutions using the dynamics of transaction costs is confirmed not only by the theoretical justification of the hypothesis's validity, but also by the fundamental provisions.

Maevsky (2001) also touches upon the direct relationship between the efficiency of economic institutions and the increase in transaction costs. While agreeing that transaction costs increase in the evolutionary dynamics, one should take into account that this rapid growth is due to the increasing complexity of socio-economic processes, the lingering uncertainty of their implementation results, and the growing likelihood of the accompanying threats being carried out. Moiseev (1998) aptly described the current interaction trends in society. He showed that the enhancing complexity of a system was accompanied by the exponential increase in the difficulties with coordinating the functioning of its elements. This means that the tendency to loss of stability and the risk of it going beyond the border of homeostasis are increasing. Thus, it is transaction costs that are the indicative measure of the manifestation of 'difficulties in coordination' and are aimed at reducing the entropy caused by them. At the same time, the absolute values of uncertainty are also rising with an increase in both the number of alternatives and the number of outcomes. As a result, attempts by economic agents to reduce entropy run into opposition from the very organizational-economic system and allow, at best, keeping it within a certain range of acceptable stable self-organization. The thesis about the possibility of measuring the efficiency of institutions by assessing the parameters of economic agents' transaction costs dynamics seems to be false (which has been repeatedly emphasized earlier). The purpose of the functioning of institutions cannot be reduced to regulating the cost of transactions; rather, it is related to the formation of the 'rules of the game', both formal and informal norms, and, hence, to the "organization of interaction" (North, 1990) between economic entities and improving the predictability of socio-economic complexes. "Institutions reduce uncertainty by providing a structure to everyday life" (North, 1990, p. 3): "These uncertainties arise as a consequence of both the complexity of the problems to be solved and the problem-solving software (…) possessed by the individual. There is nothing in the above statement that implies that the institutions are efficient" (North, 1990, p. 25). Therefore, the efficiency of institutions should be measured not by assessing the size of the reduction in transaction costs, but by identifying the impact that these institutions have on the degree of uncertainty in the economy and by determining the degree of stability and effectiveness of the norms they create.

4 Transaction Costs and Economic Agents

Production does not simply reflect the activity of an economic agent, but represents its mono-purpose function, where all the main and secondary processes are aimed at fulfilling a single task, that is the creation of economic benefits in response to a formed need. Then production costs, if decomposed, are the sum of the main activity costs, i.e., transformation costs (productive costs of an economic agent) and the costs of ancillary activities, in other words, unproductive costs.

The transformation of initial unproductive costs into partly transaction costs occurs only when these costs have a special purpose, which distinguishes the transaction function from other functions in the economic mechanism, i.e., ensuring and consolidating economic exchange. This is confirmed by North (1990), who stated that "institutions affect the performance of the economy by their effect on the costs of exchange and production. Together with the technology employed, they determine the transaction and transformation (production) costs that make up total costs" (pp. 5–6). In this case, "transformation costs are the costs associated with transforming inputs into outputs, the costs of performing the transformation function" (Wallis & North, 1986, p. 97).

Only material resources are not enough for this transformation to take place, it is necessary to give them an integrated form of utility. At that, the desire of an economic entity to maximize its own benefits pushes it to acquire not only resources at minimal cost, but operational transactional benefits. In this context, Wallis and North (1986) note that "to perform either the transaction or transformation function requires the use of inputs. When we speak of transaction costs we mean the economic value of the inputs used in performing the transaction function".

Thus, within the framework of the neoclassical tradition Douglass North unambiguously describes the difference between transformation costs and transaction costs, while introducing a property of value and utility into the process of differentiation. Kuzminov and Yudkevich (2002, p. 48) uphold this tradition and stress that transformation costs are those that accompany the process of physical change of material, which results in a product possessing a certain value. The moment this value emerges, apparently, is one of the sacred secrets of the economic mechanism. On the one hand, value is subjective, and, therefore, arises not as a given, but as a product of the subject's needs and interests, which only visibly (tangibly) develop within the same trend, while constantly changing, evolving together with the institutional environment and the economic system. On the other hand, according to North, value is introduced at the initial stage with the resources used in the transformation process.

Presumably this is why Kuzminov and Yudkevich (2002, p. 48) state that "transformation costs can be called 'production costs' only conditionally, because significant production costs include both transformation and transaction costs. Nevertheless, for the sake of distinction, we will call them this way, using the term 'production costs' when referring to transformation rather than integral costs".

Based on this thesis, we can state that transformation costs are initial costs (Ostrom, 1990) encouraging economic agents to related (non-core) operations. In this regard, the assumption by Solo (2000) is of special interest, who proposed the idea that transformation costs are a function of the 'distance' between processes. Considering the interconnected chain of processes, the transition from one level to the next one can be thought of as a micro goal of continuous activity, so transformation costs are simply the costs to achieve this goal. According to Solo, transformation costs are the costs incurred in creating operations. In an attempt to calculate the cost of transformation, the cost of changes and the magnitude of the change, it is necessary to take into account this 'distance' between higher and lower processes.

Having clarified a number of ideas about transformation costs, move on to explaining the principle of efficiency for an economic agent in various perceptions of these costs.

First of all, it should be noted that the conditions for efficient functioning of an economic entity are as ambiguous as the conditions for the efficiency of the institutions themselves. Therefore, when transformation costs are filled with different meanings, it seems appropriate to consider some of the efficiency conditions in order to form own vision of the issue.

Socio-economic interaction as one of the forms of communication between individuals have no fundamental differences from the interaction between economic agents, therefore, the efficiency trends identified in public life can be successfully extrapolated to the relationships that develop in the economic mechanism. In an attempt to substantiate a new methodological paradigm of studying social interactions, Chernikov (2004) deduces one of the efficiency conditions: the lower the transformation and transaction costs, the more effectively the basic source of well-being is mastered, i.e., the higher the degree of non-equivalence of the exchange interaction between the collective human subject (society) and the source of well-being".

Chernikov's theoretical and methodological provisions contain a fundamental postulate that an individual is ontologically oriented towards an unequal exchange with their environment and, as a result, any human interaction is about certain sources of well-being, i.e., factors that can ensure the influx of resources. According to Chernikov's interpretation, the extent of mutual benefit and, accordingly, the strength of inter-subject interactions is determined by the concept of justice, which implies that (1) each participant in the exchange interaction should get more than they give, and (2) the rate of profit is equal for all. It is the gap between the two conditions of justice (to conclude a 'contract' on intersubjective interaction, it is enough that such interaction is beneficial to all its participants, but this by no means guarantees the equality of the rate of profit) that is viewed as the key to explaining all the contradictions and conflicts arising in the sphere of social relations.

Beyond the scope of social interaction, Buchanan and Tullock (1965) point to the favorability of "some significant investments in bargaining" which are partly related to transaction costs. The researchers believe that such a behavior is optimal for an individual participant since these investments will reduce the "negotiation set". In terms of external costs, Buchanan and Tullock (1965) suppose that "these costs can be reduced only by a change in decision-making rules" (p. 205).

Viewing efficiency in the context of the self-organization theory, Sammeck (2011) states that, given the certain benefits of secured self-regulation in relation to an economic agent, it can be argued that an increase in transformation costs leads to a decrease in the number of a company's incentives to contribute to self-organization. Elaborating this assumption, we can conclude that self-organization (as a process that signifies the constant striving for the optimal arrangement of the economic system) does not involve significant transformation costs, however, a close correlation between the size of transformation costs and the parameters of self-organization is unlikely to exist (self-organization can be observed both at significant and at low costs).

Following the discourse on the correlation between the efficiency of an economic agent and the direction of organizational change, we can refer to the works by Crase and Gandhi (2009), who interpreted optimality through "the minimization of the sum of all transaction costs (…) and transformation costs (static transformation costs, technological transition costs and intertemporal transformation costs)" (p. 36). This implies that the efficiency of economic agents (regardless of how transformation costs and transaction costs are interpreted) can be achieved by minimizing such costs to an acceptable and limited extent. Thus, the presence of a minimization limit, which is nothing but a 'norm', is identified. At that, it should be taken into account that efficiency as an economic category implies the result (effect) obtained being compared with the resources expended. Hence, cost efficiency of an economic agent should be accounted in a slightly different way than when evaluating any other efficiency-directed actions.

This is due to two factors. First, the object being assessed is an economic agent. Therefore, the definition of efficiency should not be isolated from the mutually determining relationship 'the state of the economic agent—activity—the result of activity—the state of the economic agent'. Second, the subject in relation to which the efficiency is evaluated is costs (productive and unproductive). On the one hand, the definition of efficiency is based on the extent to which costs will be tolerably minimized; on the other, cost reduction occurs due to the measures taken, for the implementation of which resources were spent, i.e., the same costs. In this case, the effect should be determined by identifying the difference between the potential reduction in production costs from their initial level and the amount of costs incurred in attaining this result. The difference obtained will be the net value of the effect, and it is this value that should be used in establishing cost efficiency of an economic agent.

Thus, the sum of transaction and transformation costs is of importance in the empirical comparison of organizations (Buchanan & Tullock, 1965). This once again confirms the idea that minimization of transaction costs seen as a direct source of the efficiency of institutions is partly untenable, due to the fact that cost minimization is an aspect of only one type of efficiency, i.e., the efficiency of economic agents. While functioning due to transaction costs, institutions cannot focus on their reduction, since the emergence of any institutional normative imperative, at the same time as a new institution, leads to an increase in the total transaction costs of economic agents.

5 Rethinking the Approach to Evaluating Transaction Costs

It is extremely important to take into account that economic agents united in different industries and operating within different territories differ in the background or natural levels of transaction intensity (i.e., the contribution of transaction costs to the total amount of costs incurred by economic agents). The use of the terms 'background' ('natural') level of transaction costs is not accidental: determining their value allows performing an adequate comparison of the results of economic entities' activities, making informed decisions in the field of cost management, assessing the risks of implementing economic activity, etc.

This regularity is noted in the work by Maher (1997). The researcher highlights that the size of transaction costs varies for different industries and for different firms operating within the same industry, while paying attention to the significance of the influence of the market structure's specificities on the logic of transaction costs in intercompany operations. This thesis is in many respects similar to Popov's idea about the close dependence of the transaction function on the parameters of the economic environment in which the transaction is carried out.

The background level of transaction costs plays a significant part in the mechanism for calculating the riskiness and the very risk of conducting economic transactions between business entities. The range of transaction costs' deviations from each other is the basis for detecting the allowable intervals of cost deviations, thereby identifying the zones of commitment to risk. The calculation of the share of transaction costs in its pure form (their normal value) can serve as a basis for determining the risk of effective implementation of production-economic activities by an economic entity.

It is worth noting that although a lot of scientific works are devoted to the issues of measuring transaction costs, the logic of the methodology for estimating such costs is still the subject of scientific discussion. One of the first ways to assess transaction costs was based on Kokorev's approach (Kokorev, 1996): it is founded on measuring the turnover (in terms of macroeconomics) or the overhead costs of firms (in terms of microeconomics). Giving his own interpretation of transaction costs, Radaev (1999) notes the particular type of costs that should be taken into account when making such calculations, these are "costs associated with entering the market and exiting it, access to resources, transfer, specification and protection of property rights, entering into and maintaining business relationships". Popov (2011) also draws attention to the need to consider various types of transaction costs, each of which is associated with the functioning of an individual economic institution (this approach allows one to consistently analyze all types of transaction costs applying its own methodological approach to evaluate each of them). Despite this approach is of undoubted interest, following it leads to ignoring those transaction costs that arise due to the interaction of an economic entity (enterprise or organization) and the state. Meanwhile, the significance of such transaction costs can be very considerable, e.g., some researchers believe taxes to be one of the forms of their manifestation (the volume of which has a significant weight in the share of firms' costs). For instance, Kuzminov and Yudkevich (2002) note that in exchange for paying taxes, we receive transaction benefits from the state. Auzan (2006) comes up with similar ideas and defines the role of taxes as transaction costs as payment for services related to the protection of property rights and specification. One of the varieties of transaction benefits is infrastructure that is created and updated, among other things, at the expense of the state as a guarantor of the normal life of the population and the functioning of enterprises and organizations.

It is worth mentioning that taxes perform a dual function, on the one hand, acting as a tool for creating infrastructure (by the state), on the other hand, reducing the level of side transaction costs (arising due to the imperfection of the communication and interaction environment). At the same time, paying taxes places an additional burden on enterprises and organizations, thereby contributing to an increase in the explicit transaction costs that they are forced to bear (explicit transaction costs are the costs that arise due to the implementation of production or manufacture of products). The ambiguous role of taxes in the transaction turnover is also mentioned in the study by Islamutdinov (n.d.).

The above example of taxes serves only as an illustration of the duality of the nature of transaction costs, which determines the complexity of their measurement and the importance of finding the optimal ratio of explicit and side transaction costs. In addition, an in-depth analysis of some transaction costs allows us to conclude that, along with transformation (production) costs, they can include costs that are transactional in relation to the seller organization.

The above allows concluding that, when establishing the size of costs, the hierarchical factor is necessary to be taken into account: both at the macro and micro levels, transaction costs should be calculated based on the identification of the same indicators. At that, the need to avoid double counting when assessing macroeconomic processes should be also considered: part of the transaction costs incurred related to the implementation of operations between economic agents is returned to business entities in the form of market revenue due to such a phenomenon as a "closed cycle of commodity circulation".

Hence, transaction costs that are incurred, or might be incurred, by an individual economic agent should be measured according to the presence (or absence) of a closed cycle of commodity circulation. For example, if there is no closed cycle of commodity exchange, the enterprise can be viewed as a conditionally closed economic system that does not enter into direct bilateral contacts with counterparties, but at the same time performs unidirectional operations with them without identifying a specific customer of goods and services. In this case, the calculation of transaction costs can be called autonomous. If there is a closed cycle of commodity exchange, the enterprise's transaction costs are transformed and returned to the actors in the form of proceeds from market operations, while passing through several iterations of exchange with other economic agents. In this case, the environment for the implementation of exchange operations can be regarded as conditionally open, and the algorithm for calculating the size of transaction costs should include an estimate of the value of the economic exchange multiplier, which, in turn, depends on the number of economic agents in the cycle, the share of transaction costs in the total volume of costs, the ratio of 'internal' and 'external' transaction costs, as well as the normalized level of intermediate consumption of transaction costs. This type of calculation can conditionally be called subordinate.

In this regard, the important aspects of the applied methodology for calculating transaction costs are the assumptions stated by the purpose of the study, as well as the specificity of the conditions prevailing in the economic system. In particular, when looking at economic agents as independent entities, the calculation should be carried out according to the autonomous type (if the subordinate calculation type is used, the value of transaction costs will be underestimated). The initial assessment base is also of great importance: in order to correctly calculate the transaction costs of enterprises and organizations, commercial and administrative expenses and the amount of income tax should be taken into account.

Similar, but incomplete ideas about the peculiarities of transaction costs calculation are given in the publications by Nikolaeva (2009) and Anikina (2011). In the former, the researcher does not consider tax payments, while in the latter the author does not substantiate the attribution of the analyzed expense items to transaction costs, in particular, the researcher proposes considering the costs of paying interest as transaction costs, which seems incorrect, since interest in this case acts as the price or cost of goods in the form of money. The approaches of some other scientists often cannot be used in the implementation of dynamic calculation or in practice (in real conditions), since in most cases they are associated with the need to refer to indicators for which it seems impossible to find their values in databases of different levels. Among such researchers are Iskokov (2011) who developed an open list of expenses, and Blokhin (2002), who proposed using indicators of the input–output balance of the system of national accounts.

In this regard, the development of a universal methodological approach to assessing transaction costs is of particular relevance, which makes it possible to evaluate and analyze transaction costs at the firm level and total transaction costs at the national level in the context of individual territories, while satisfying the conditions of compliance and accessibility of the total and regional statistical data.

6 Conclusion

Transaction costs are among the basic parameters of economic relations. They make it possible to characterize the efficiency of institutions and economic agents, give an idea of the complexity of doing business in the context of 'viscosity' and uncertainty of the environment. At the same time, there is some controversy in understanding the significance of transaction costs for these phenomena. We have made an attempt to substantiate a number of provisions that have allowed eliminating gaps in the methodological concept of transaction costs.

Minimization of transaction costs is believed to be the criterion for the efficiency of institutions in particular and the institutional environment as a whole. However, in the course of our study we have come to the opposite conclusion. The activity of the institutions of the economic mechanism is not subordinated to the goal of reducing transaction costs, but on the contrary it stimulates their growth. This is due to the fact that the functioning of such institutions is subject to the idea and conception of transaction costs: when, on the one hand, the emergence of institutions generates transaction costs, and, on the other hand, transaction costs are a necessary resource for them to exist. The functioning of institutions is conditioned by the role they play as a guarantor of the stability of organizational-economic systems, determining the operation order of economic mechanisms and the norms and rules of socio-economic processes, and thereby minimizing the uncertainty of the conditions in which business entities are forced to perform their activities. We believe that the efficiency of institutions cannot be assessed only through the transaction costs dynamics.

On the other hand, it is transaction costs (due to the change in the level of uncertainty) that establish for economic agents the special features of functioning in market conditions and competitive struggle. The desire of actors to increase their efficiency leads to the fact that the only means in this struggle is to reduce or minimize transaction costs, when the improvement of the meta-production function is already limited. The collision of economic agents with institutions (in the variety of their forms) is associated with some insurmountable minimum of transaction costs. Economic agents' attempts to reduce entropy encounter opposition from the very organizational-economic system and allow, at best, maintaining it at a certain level of acceptable stable self-organization.

Thus, the minimization of transaction costs is a manifestation of only one type of efficiency, that is the efficiency of economic agents. While functioning due to transaction costs, institutions cannot focus on reducing them, since the emergence of a new institutional normative imperative, at the same time as a new institution, only contributes to their increase. The dissonance between the criteria for the efficiency of institutions and economic agents determines the possibility of finding parity between such parameters of the economic mechanism as complexity and uncertainty.

References

Anikina, N. A. (2011). Tools for regulating transaction costs of agribusiness enterprises in the system of economic interaction in the region. *Fundamental Research, 12*(3), 618–622.

Arkhipov, A. I., & Bolshakova, A. K. (Eds.). (2009). *Economics*. Prospekt.

Arrow, K. (1969). The organization of economic activity: Issues pertinent to the choice of market versus non-market allocation. In *The analysis and evaluation of public expenditure: The PPB system*, 1.

Aubin, J.-P., Pujal, D., & Saint-Pierre, P. (2001). *Dynamic management of portfolios with transaction costs under tychastic uncertainty*. Université Paris-Dauphine, Scuola Normale Superiore, preprint.

Auzan, A. (Ed.). (2006). *Institutional economics: New institutional economics* (p. 2006). Moscow.

Blokhin, A. (2002). *Institutional conditions and factors of modernization of the Russian Economy*. MAKS Press.

Buchanan, J. M., & Tullock, G. (1965). *The calculus of consent: Logical foundations of constitutional democracy*. University of Michigan Press.

Chernikov, M. V. (2004). The logic of social interactions in the light of two conditions of justice. *Political Studies, 5*, 71–84.

Coase, R. H. (1937). The nature of the firm. *Economica, 4*(16), 386–405.

Commons, J. R. (1931). Institutional economics. *American Economic Review, 21*(4), 648–657.

Crase, L., & Gandhi, V. P. (2009). *Reforming institutions in water resource management: Policy and performance for sustainable development*. Earthscan.

Efimova, E. G., Bodrunova, S. A., Zaslavskaya, M. D., Potapova, I. S. (2008). *Economic theory. Part 1: Microeconomics*. MSIU.

Eggertsson, T. (2001). *Economic behavior and institutions*. Delo.

Fischer, T. (1999). Coordination of quality management in the light of the theory of transaction costs. *International Journal of Management Theory and Practice, 3*, 62–67.

Frolov, D. P. (2011). Institutions and transaction costs: Overcoming the quasi-Cowsian tradition. *Journal of Economic Regulation, 2*(4), 5–23.

Iskokov, M. O. (2011). Estimation of transaction costs in corporate structures. *Frontier Materials & Technologies, 2*(16), 246–251.

Islamutdinov, V. F. (n.d.). Institutional aspects of taxes. *Problems of accounting, analysis, audit and taxation*. http://econf.rae.ru

Kangoh, L. (1989). Transaction costs and equilibrium pricing of congested public goods with imperfect information. *BEBR Faculty working Paper № 89–1562*. College of Commerce and Business Administration, University of Illinois Urbana-Champaign.

Kokorev, V. (1996). Institutional transformations in modern Russia: Analysis of the dynamics of transaction costs. *Voprosy Ekonomiki, 12*, 61–72.

Kovalenko, B. B., Ponomarev, S., & Smeshko, O. G. (2010). *Building a corporate management structure for an entrepreneurial organization of a holding type*. Publishing house of St. Petersburg Academy of Management and Economics.

Kushlin, V. I. (2000). *Economic transformation: Goals, directions, dynamics*. RAPA.

Kuzminov, I. Y., Bendukidze, K. A., & Yudkevich, M. M. (2006). *Institutional economics: Institutions, networks, transaction costs, contracts*. HSE Publishing house.

Kuzminov, Ya. I., & Yudkevich, M. M. (2002). Institutional economics. PhysTech.

Kuzminov, Ya., Bendukidze, K., & Yudkevich, M. (2005). How market science becomes social science. *Voprosy Ekonomiki, 12*, 63–81

Litvintseva, G. P. (2003). *Institutional economics*. NSTU.

Maevsky, V. I. (2001). Evolutionary theory and institutions. *University Bulletin. Series: Institutional Economics, 1*(2), 73–107.

Maher, M. E. (1997). Transaction cost economics and contractual relations. *Cambridge Journal of Economics, 21*(2), 147–170.

Malahov, S. (1996). Some aspects of the theory of imperfect competitive equilibrium (two-factor model of transaction costs). *Voprosy Ekonomiki, 10*, 89–102.

Marschak, J. (1950). The rationale of the demand for money and of 'money illusion'. *Microeconomica, 2*(II).

Menger, C. (2007). *Principles of economics*. Ludwig von Mises Institute.

Milgrom, P., & Roberts, J. (1999). *Economics, organization and management* (Vol. 1). Ekonomicheskaya shkola.

Moiseev, N. N. (1998). *Parting with simplicity*. Agraf.

Niehans, J. (1987). *Transaction cost*. Macmillan Press.

Nikolaeva, E. V. (2009). The influence of transaction costs on the efficiency of a modern corporation. *Bulletin of Chelyabinsk State University, 2*(140), issue 18, 133–138.

North, D. (1990). *Institutions, institutional change and economic performance*. Cambridge University Press.

North, D. (1992). Institutions, ideology, and economic performance. *Cato Journal, 11*(3), 477–496.

North, D. (1997). *Institutions, institutional change and the functioning of the economy*.

Ostrom, E. (1990). *Governing the commons: The evolution of institutions for collective action*. Cambridge University Press.

Popov, E. V. (2011). *Transactions*. Ural Branch of the RAS.

Radaev, V. V. (1999). Russian business: Transaction cost structure. *Social Sciences and Modernity, 6*, 5–19.

Rudenkov, I. A. (2010). Economic efficiency of institutions: Assessments and factors. In *Institutionalistics: Theory, methodology, applied aspects—2009*. Proc. of Int. sci.-pract. conf. Brest.

Sammeck, J. (2011). *A new institutional economics perspective on industry self-regulation*. Springer.
Slater, G., & Spencer, D. A. (2000). The uncertain foundations of transaction costs economics. *Journal of Economic Issues, 34*(1), 61–87.
Solo, R. A. (2000). *Economic organizations and social systems*. University of Michigan Press.
Walker, G., & Weber, D. (1983). *Transaction cost approach to component make-or-buy decisions*. Working Paper № 1452–83. Massachusetts Institute of Technology in Cambridge.
Wallis, J. J., & North, D. (1986). Measuring the transaction sector in the American economy, 1870–1970. In S. L. Engerman & R. E. Gallman (Eds.). *Long-term factors in American economic growth*. University of Chicago Press.
Wang, N. (2003). *Measuring transaction costs: An incomplete survey*. Ronald Coase Institute Working Papers № 2.

Changing Growth Patterns of the Spanish Economy Attributable to the Consulting Sector in Context of Uncertainty

José Luis Ruiz Zapatero and Pedro Antonio Martín-Cervantes

Abstract Much has been discussed about the global financial crisis of 2007–2008, including its reasons and consequences on the productive fabric of international economies; however, the studies focused on highlighting the most resilient productive sectors are a significant minority. In this sense, this paper provides a novel analysis of the behavior of Spanish companies involved in the economic-legal consultancy sector throughout the course of the crisis. This manuscript emphasizes the relative strength of these kinds of firms, their eagerness for innovation and internationalization, as well as their ability to adapt to the needs of their clients at any given moment, especially during a period characterized by enormous uncertainty and insecurity, both on the part of the financial markets and of the political authorities who had to face the pernicious effects of the recession. Finally, a series of future lines of research that could be pursued on the basis of this manuscript are outlined. In summary, this paper shows how a service-based economy such as the Spanish one in the context of high uncertainty such as the 2007–2008 global economic crisis was able to obtain ample support through the consultancy services subsector and its internationalization to alleviate the effects of the crisis. It should be inferred that in those countries that, like Spain, boosted this sector (Italy, Greece or Turkey), this industry served to mitigate the effects of the crisis and define new market niches for all these economies.

Keywords Consultancy sector · Spain · Financial crisis

JEL Classification G01 · L84 · O11

J. L. Ruiz Zapatero · P. A. Martín-Cervantes (✉)
University of Valladolid, Campus "Duques de Soria", 42004 Soria, Spain
e-mail: pedroantonio.martin@uva.es

J. L. Ruiz Zapatero
e-mail: joseluis.ruiz.zapatero@uva.es

V. Kumar et al. (eds.), *Consequences of Social Transformation for Economic Theory*, Springer Proceedings in Business and Economics,
https://doi.org/10.1007/978-3-031-27785-6_10

1 Introduction

Nearly two thousand years have passed since the advent of the Antonine Plague (165–180 AD), and it is still remembered in the academic literature as the first great Pandemic that devastated the Western world (Harper, 2015), bringing a myriad of socio-economic repercussions that would eventually lead to the fall of the Roman Empire. "The Plague of Galen" also serves as an example that the causes of an economic crisis are quite complex and that the reasons given by researchers or by political powers do not always correspond exclusively to reality. In this sense, Roman historiography blamed the anger of the pagan gods, who were angry at the rise of the Christians (Horgan, 2019), a fact that is derisory nowadays, but which in truth was the official explanation for that tragedy for several centuries. This comparison has been drawn to justify why this research has been based on the global mortgage crisis and not on more recent crises such as the COVID-19 pandemic. It is true that nearly 20 years have passed, but this rationale should not detract from its significance. Indeed, the subprime crisis represented the worst sovereign debt crisis since the Great Depression and even though almost a century has passed following the Black Thursday, that debacle still attracts the interest of researchers, because of the reminiscences it left on the social collective of the countries of the 'capitalist sphere' (Holtzclaw, 2012). If we were to focus only on the economic-financial crises of the immediate present, essentially the COVID crisis, we would be giving rise to the argumentative fallacy "ad novitatem" (Duthel, 2015), that is, considering a certain event with special predilection, simply because it is new.

On the other hand, there have been economic crises due to pandemic phenomena before COVID (e.g. the Spanish Flu in the early twentieth century (Barro et al., 2020)), or the Black Death, which remain in the literature, among other things, for being much more pernicious to global economies than the SARS-CoV-2. Such is the case of the "1998 Russian financial crisis" (Chiodo & Owyang, 2002), in which Russia was able to emerge from the crisis with its own independent recipe (Gidadhubli, 2007), far away from the neoliberal dictates of the International Monetary Fund, which meant that the effects of the Financial Crisis of 2007–2008 did not affect Russia with the same severity as most developed countries (Åslund et al., 2010). Precisely, the independence of Russia's growth policies at the time suggests that, in the long run, the task of looking for similarities and analogies between countries in times of crisis often proves somewhat inefficient, given that not all nations chose to subrogate their sovereignty by bowing to the demands of supranational institutions such as the renowned European *Troika*. Moreover, the full extent of the 2007–2008 financial crisis will be difficult to understand because its origins are often confused. Just as Marcus Aurelius blamed the Christians for the Plague of Antonine, US policymakers blamed Europe for the outcome of the crisis (Hirsh, 2011) long after A. Greenspan underestimated the danger of the subprime mortgages.

The last major financial crisis before the devastating effects of the COVID-19 pandemic, the Financial crisis of 2007–2008, brought a large number of countries that had specifically opted for economic growth based on sectors such as construction or services to the brink of collapse. That not-too-distant era, characterized by mere speculation, was referred to by Shiller (2001) as "Irrational Exuberance". The uncertainty was particularly notable in the countries of southern Europe, especially Spain and Italy, as the financial bubble turned into a sovereign debt crisis (Barba et al., 2021; Quaglia & Royo, 2015) whose effects were comparable to the famous crash of 1929. The reconstruction of these economies was built on internationalization, as well as on the support of those sectors that were able to cope with global uncertainty. Such is the case of consulting firms, whether engineering consulting or economic-legal consulting, sectors in which Spain already had extensive experience. This paper analyzes in a novel way the resilience of the latter, highlighting their role in the post-crisis growth.

Certainly, the globalization process that had already begun before the crisis led to the proliferation of engineering consulting firms (da Silva, 2019). Regarding economic-legal consulting firms, although they have been able to adapt to the internationalization of their services, in the Spanish case, they continue to show a relatively "localist" character, based on their proximity to their clients, an aspect that is abundantly evident in the literature in other countries and contexts (Lopes da Costa et al., 2020a, 2020b; Nikolova et al., 2009).

In this sense, Cerruti et al. (2019) monographically determine the main characterizing features on which management consulting research has focused over the last fifty years, highlighting several explanatory elements or factors (Jang & Lee, 1998; Lopes da Costa et al., 2020c; Mas Machuca & Martínez Costa, 2012b). Among these factors could be mentioned the knowledge culture implemented in these organizations (Askegaard & Torp, 2020; Barthélemy, 2020; Mas Machuca & Martínez Costa, 2012a), the entry into the scene of digitalization (Betti et al., 2021; Bode, 2019; Bode et al., 2021) or the time factor by itself (Bedenk et al., 2022). From these starting points, other research has diversified, highlighting how knowledge is acquired by this type of organization (Aslam et al., 2022; Babío, 2009) or defining the role played by the leadership culture (Zerner et al., 2021). For their part, Gartzia (2021) and Blanchard (2022) analyze the relationship between gender equality and management consulting organizations. There is no single key factor that determines the performance of these organizations. While some studies ratify that the quality search is the basic approach of any activity belonging to the field of consulting (Gutiérrez et al., 2006), others opt for innovation processes (Cesário et al., 2015). A third way determines that, in reality, the economic compensation of the upper echelons of the organization chart is the raison d'être that shapes the behavior of these companies (Grosse et al., 2020), a perspective that contrasts clearly with Suárez-Albanchez et al. (2022), who focus their attention not on the earnings of the members of the consulting companies, but on how their operating organization chart is constituted.

In the case of Spanish companies, mainly those included in the economic-legal consulting sector, in the same way very similar parameters are presented with the companies of their closest geopolitical environment, such as the consulting companies of Turkey (Beldek et al., 2020; Erdost, 2005), it can be noted that they describe certain particularities that differentiate them from the rest of the nations. For example, for Spanish consulting firms, technology is essential, but so are other aspects such as dialogue with the clientele or between the different levels of the organization (Cayolla et al., 2021; Shoai et al., 2020). This is because they are organizations in which internal communication is paramount (Castro-Martínez & Díaz-Morilla, 2020), hence the high level of transparency defined by Zorio-Grima et al. (2018), this being another of the means by which Spanish consulting firms have traditionally tried to reduce the levels of risk management (Lozano-Torró et al., 2019), especially in times of financial turbulence such as those analyzed in this paper.

It is also interesting to note some studies that link consulting firms with the preponderant ideological component of each nation and/or power group. Some studies such as Binder et al. (2016) or Donnelly and Gamsu (2019) point out that already from student days, future members of consulting organizations belong to a certain social elite that protects them. Çalışkan and McGregor (2019) goes even further arguing that consulting firms are nothing but forms or instruments through which the Neoliberal superstructure of certain nations is perpetuated.

Given the multiple perspectives offered by the literature, this research has chosen to review how Spanish companies in the field of economic-legal consultancy were able to overcome with relative solvency the vicissitudes resulting from the Financial crisis of 2007–2008. To this end, this research has been structured as follows: in the subsequent section (materials and methods), the methodology implemented is defined, as well as the data used and their origin. Next, the results and discussion section lists the inputs obtained in this work and briefly discusses them in the light of the predominant literature. Finally, the conclusions section concludes this research, defining the main limitations inherent to it and proposing a series of future lines of research.

2 Materials and Methods

Regarding the data employed, this research has utilized data provided by the Spanish National Institute of Statistics (INE), gathering the most representative figures in the evolution of the Gross Domestic Product (2005–2016) and the economic-legal consultancy sector (2008–2016) (). For a greater degree of detail, additionally it has been used data obtained from the "Observatorio del Despacho Profesional" (ODP) throughout the final biennium of the Financial crisis of 2007–2008 (ODP, 2018). At the methodological level, this investigation has focused on visualizing the variables subject to analysis by means of their graphical representation, as well as on obtaining tables that have enabled to determine the specific weight of the Spanish consulting firms focused on the economic-legal area with regard to the economic growth of this nation during the aforementioned global crisis. As regards the characterisation of the data used in this report on the evolution of Spanish GDP, the table shows the main descriptive statistics of the time series, while Fig. 1 displays its histogram (Table 1).

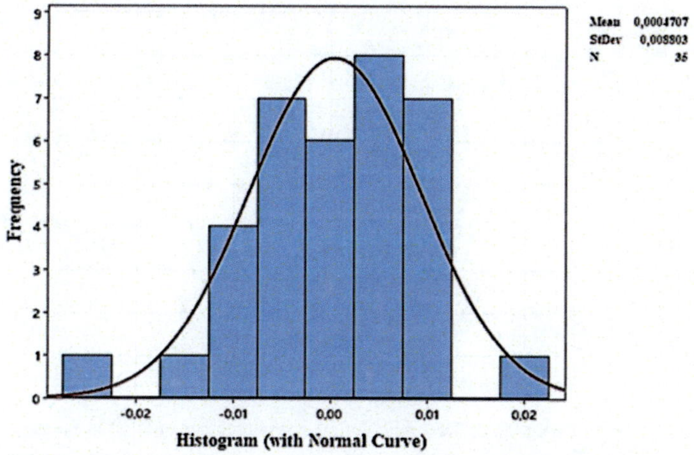

Fig. 1 Histogram of the time series of the quarterly percentage change in Spanish GDP (1Q-2008/4Q-2016). *Source* Authors' elaboration based on data obtained from INE (2022b)

Table 1 Main descriptive statistics of the time series for quarterly percentage changes in the Spanish GDP (1Q-2008/4Q-2016)

Mean	0.00047	Range	0.04274
SE mean	0.00149	Q1	−0.00535
TrMean	0.00076	Q3	0.00736
Median	−0.00077	IQR	0.01271
StDev	0.0088	MSSD	0.00004
Variance	0.00008	Sum	0.01647
CoefVar	1870.22	Sum of squares	0.00264
Maximum	0.02007	Kurtosis	0.42
Minimum	−0.02268	Skewness	−0.39

Source Authors' elaboration based on data obtained from INE (2022b)

3 Results and Discussion

Figure 2 is a masterly example of the crisis period under analysis. As it can be appreciated, we can roughly distinguish four main stages: (1) (2005–2006) final phase of Spanish economic growth based on the real estate sector, (2) (2007–2008) beginnings of the crisis coupled with the collapse of this nation's main macroeconomic indicators, (3) (2009–2011) phase of ephemeral growth supported by expansionary public spending policies that ultimately proved not to be particularly effective and (4) (2012–2016) phase of gradual recovery of the Spanish economy based on greater openness of the productive sectors, improvements in competitiveness and, fundamentally, a sustained process of internal devaluation.

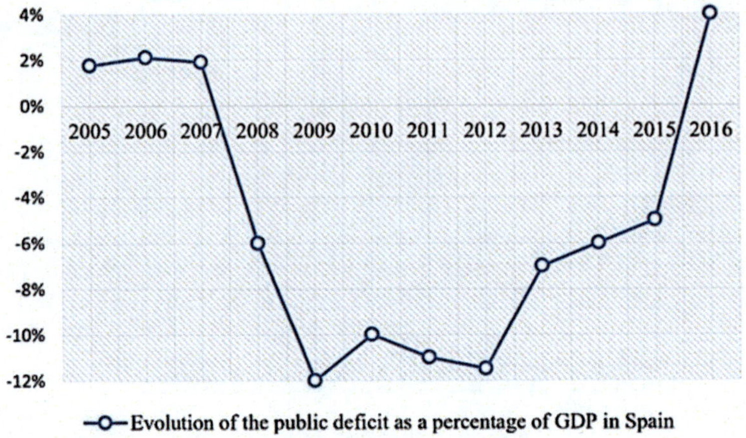

Fig. 2 Evolution of the public deficit as a percentage of GDP in Spain. *Source* Authors' elaboration based on data obtained from INE (2022b)

If we start with the number of companies engaged in accounting, auditing, and tax and legal consultancy in Spain, we can see in Fig. 3 all the companies, regardless of the number of employees or their legal status. As we can see in this chart, the period between 2008 and 2013 is characterized by a certain stability, in which, while in one year the figure increases, in the following year it decreases, and so on each year, but without suffering abrupt changes and with a figure close to 164,000 companies, both in 2008 and 2013. However, from 2014 onwards, there was a notorious decrease in the number of companies, since in that year the number of companies in this sector was reduced by 7.13% in just one year. However, both in 2015 and 2016 the trend is again towards an increase in the number of companies, although the figures are still far from those reached in 2013. With these data, we observe that, although the economic crisis did not initially affect the number of companies in Spain, in 2014 there was a significant destruction of these, which may be due to different reasons, such as the closure of the company or the merger with another because of the variety of activities they can develop. This merger of companies may be carried out in order to achieve a larger portfolio of services to be provided, since, as we will see below, one of the business strategies in this sector is to increase the variety of services provided to gain clients.

Another important issue is the size of the companies. The ideal way to analyze them would be to divide them into micro, small, medium and large companies. However, the data offered by the National Institute of Statistics does not allow this classification, since in one table it offers data from 101 to 200 workers and in the following table it shows from 201 to 499 workers. Thus, the medium-sized company is not completely included in a size range. As Fig. 4 exhibits, most tax, legal and accounting firms are microenterprises, i.e., they have no more than nine employees. The next largest group is that of small businesses and, lastly, small companies. As

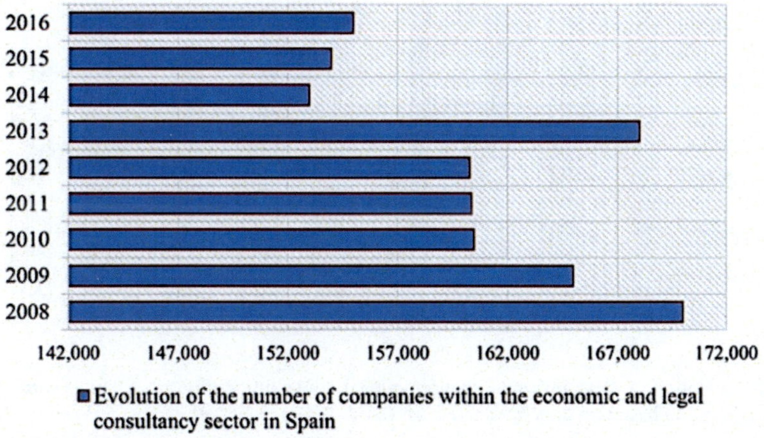

Fig. 3 Evolution of the number of companies within the economic and legal consultancy sector in Spain. *Source* Authors' own elaboration based on data obtained from INE (2022a)

can be seen in the evolution of the size of these companies, micro-companies have been the cause of the decrease in the number of companies in the sector, which is logical because they account for more than 98% of the companies in the sector.

To better analyze how this sector is composed, we can observe in Fig. 5 the evolution of the number of companies in this sector in Spain. As we can see, the subsector with the largest number of companies is the legal activities sector, but we can see that this number of companies has been decreasing over the years analyzed. Therefore, it is getting closer and closer to the number of economic activities, a subsector which, as Graph 2.4 shows, is growing in the number of companies, since in 2008 there was a total of 55,462 economic consultancies and in 2016 this number increased to 66,093. According with these data we can verify that the sector of

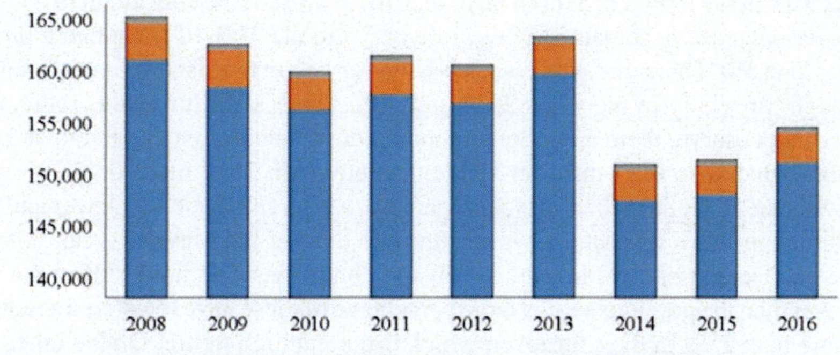

Fig. 4 Evolution of the size of companies within the economic and legal consultancy sector in Spain. *Source* Authors' own elaboration based on data obtained from INE (2022b)

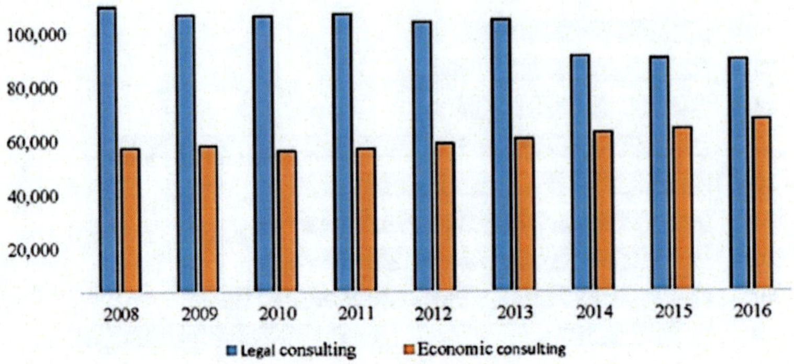

Fig. 5 Evolution of the number of economic-legal consulting entities in Spain. *Source* Authors' own elaboration based on data obtained from INE (2022b)

economic activities is booming while the opposite happens with the sector of legal activities, since, since 2014 it has significantly decreased its number of companies. The reason for this data may be due to several circumstances. A first reason can be related to the economic crisis, since as we have seen, the total number of companies in this sector has been reduced, and the reason may be due to the economic crisis that has caused many companies to have to cease their activity due to the decrease of their clients and therefore of their turnover. Another reason may be due to the fact that being a very fragmented sector, these consulting firms choose to associate, especially in small offices, in order to offer a better service and unite the client portfolio of both. As an example of this reason we can observe that these consultancies are in the situation of covering several activities, that is to say, to carry out fiscal activities, accounting activities, labor activities, etc. The problem with this is that small firms do not have a specialist in each activity, so they lose potential clients. Because of this, a possible solution is to associate with other firms to offer more specialized services by bringing companies together and thus, the business demographics of this sector are affected.

As we can see in Fig. 6, in both 2012 and 2013, most of the consultancies saw their turnover decrease or remain stable, while only around 10% of them had a turnover higher than 5%. This trend, however, has been varying in the last three years analyzed, although especially in the years 2014 and 2015, as in 2016 it remains more stable. As we can observe, there are more and more consultancies, reaching almost 50% of the total, that keep their turnover stable. Moreover, in 2016 more than 20% of the consultancies have seen their turnover increase, while, consequently, fewer and fewer consultancies have recorded a worse turnover than in the previous year. Although these data seem positive, in the case of the companies that have suffered a lower turnover than the previous year, a large percentage of these have registered a reduction of more than 25% in their turnover, which is quite a high figure. On the other hand, in the case of those that have achieved a higher turnover than the previous year, there has only been an increase of between 5 and 15% of turnover. Therefore, although the trend is positive, due to the fact that more and more companies are obtaining a

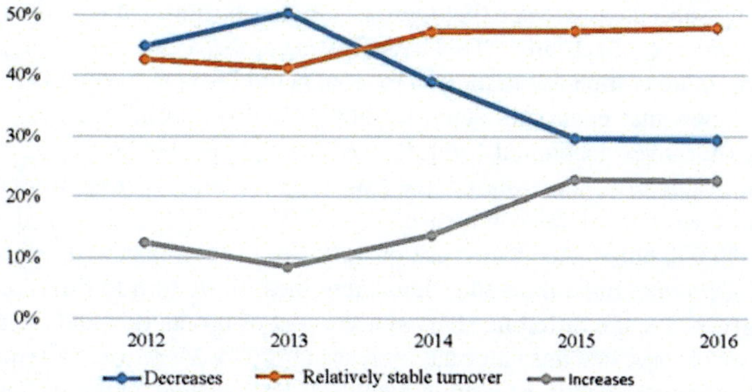

Fig. 6 Evolution of the turnover of economic-legal consultancy firms in Spain. *Source* Authors' own elaboration based on data obtained from ODP (2018)

higher turnover than in previous years, this trend is moderate. This trend should be taken with caution, since the current increase in turnover does not compensate for the previous years of decreasing turnover. Regarding a possible cause of this lower increase in turnover, we can find the price war that we often find in this sector, in which consulting firms lower their prices in order to attract more clients.

By its part, in Table 2 is verified that most of the companies engaged in legal activities in 2014 were individuals, while the economic activities sector is divided between individuals and limited liability companies. In addition, although it is not apparent in the table, a high percentage of the legal activities that have ceased their activity were natural persons, so it is possible that these persons have ceased their activity and have been integrated into firms engaged in economic activity and therefore moved from the legal activities subsector to the economic activities subsector. This reason can be justified in the above mentioned, where the firms try to offer a better portfolio of activities and integrate legal professionals in their offices.

Next, we can observe in Table 3 that the turnover of the sector in 20,141 was 19,316,457,000 euros, a figure higher than that obtained in 2013. If we analyze this

Table 2 Number of Spanish entities engaged in the field of economic-legal consultancy services in 2014 according to their statutory characterization

	Legal activities	Economic activities	Total
Individuals	72,555	29,115	101,670
Corporations	–	1,399	1,399
Limited liability companies	12,202	32,956	45,158
Other legal forms	4,220	2,623	6,843
Total	89,144	66,093	155,237

Source Authors' own elaboration based on data obtained from ODP (2018)

variable by subsectors, we see that there is a higher turnover of economic activities with respect to legal activities. This is interesting since, as we have seen previously, there were more companies dedicated to legal activities than to economic activities. All this shows that economic activities obtain higher income than legal firms. In 2014, this turnover accounted for 1.86% of the Spanish Gross Domestic Product. As for the value of production, i.e. the sum of goods and services produced by our sector, we see that this also increased from 2013 to 2014 reaching the figure of 17,162,906,000 euros. As in the case of turnover, economic activities had a higher volume of production compared to legal activities. If we turn to the value added at market prices, i.e. the difference between the cost of production and the sale of that service, we observe that this value has increased in 2014. Moreover, as expected, there is a higher value added in economic activities than in legal activities. On the other hand, investment in tangible assets, i.e., the investment of these companies in tangible assets such as furniture and real estate, has increased by around 12%, so that these companies are devoting part of their assets to renewing and acquiring assets to carry out their activity. Although we do not have data on what this investment is dedicated to, we can predict, if there is a responsible investment, that this investment is dedicated to the purchase or improvement of offices, to the improvement of technological elements and to the improvement of office elements. Finally, we have that the number of premises has been reduced in 2014 with respect to the previous year by almost 6%. This may be due to the reduction in the number of companies in the sector, specifically in the legal activities subsector, which as we have seen previously, in 2014 there was a considerable decrease in the number of companies in this subsector.

Another relevant aspect to analyze the turnover of consultancy firms is to find out whether it has increased, decreased or remained stable in recent years. For this purpose, we have divided the turnover according to whether they have suffered losses of more than 5% of turnover, whether turnover has remained at a threshold between 5 and −5% of turnover compared to the previous year or whether turnover has reached a level of more than 5%.

4 Conclusion

This contribution has analyzed the paper performed by the Spanish economic-legal consulting firms This contribution has analyzed the paper performed by the Spanish economic-legal consulting firms during the financial crisis of 2007–2008, confirming how these types of companies behaved in a relatively resilient way in response to the shocks of this downturn. On the other hand, the analysis certifies how the growth of the economic consulting firms evolved better than that of the legal consulting firms. In fact, as a whole, the growth of both types of companies was stronger than the growth of the Spanish gross domestic product during the study period in question. These effects are most likely the result of the high know-how of Spanish consulting firms in their different modalities (engineering, economic-financial, legal, etc.). Undoubtedly, these firms have an international reputation, which has also led them to provide their

Table 3 Revenue of Spanish companies engaged in the legal or economic-financial consultancy services per type of activity

Panel (A) Turnover of legal consulting firms per activity	2013	2014	Variation, %
Notary and registry services	2,048.01	2,193.42	7.10
Commercial law	1,817.59	1,735.92	−4.49
Civil law	1,505.40	1,371.33	−8.91
Labor law	760.07	689.73	−9.25
Tax law	550.55	559.48	1.62
Administrative law	499.71	473.32	−5.28
Criminal law	527.51	446.83	−15.29
Legal advice on patents	351.46	344.67	−1.93
Other branches of law	440.09	330.70	−24.86
Other legal activities	351.52	328.98	−6.41
Consulting services	146.84	138.67	−5.56
Mediation, arbitration and conciliation services	41.29	118.59	187.20
Business consulting services	51.57	41.68	−19.19
Other activities and services	35.65	32.52	−8.79
Legal services related to auctions	7.24	7.40	2.22
Total	9,134.50	8,813.23	−3.52
Average	608.97	587.55	
Panel (B) Turnover of economic-financial firms per activity	**2013**	**2014**	**Variation, %**
Accounting services	2,880.65	2,756.11	−4.32
Tax advisory services	2,444.97	2,492.97	1.96
Financial audit services	1,542.40	1,406.20	−8.83
Payroll management and labor administration	1,200.45	1,373.38	14.41
Business management services	640.62	532.43	−16.89
Insolvency and liquidation of companies	192.38	372.33	93.54
Other activities and services	1,138.25	1,306.73	14.80
Total	10,039.73	10,240.16	2.00
Average	1,434.25	1,462.88	

Source Authors' own elaboration based on data obtained from ODP (2018)

services abroad. Such expansion has taken place, especially for those companies with a larger relative size, and especially in Latin America, an area with obvious socio-cultural connotations and linkages with Spain in which direct communication with clients occupies a position almost as important as the implementation of the new technologies (Shoai, 2020; Shoai et al., 2020).

Certainly, since the beginning of the 1980s, the Spanish economy has gradually focused on the services sector at the sacrifice of its industrial structure. The risks of this decision were felt in the financial crisis of 2007–2008 when the financial and economic collapse of the European Union countries that had followed the same pattern as the Spanish economy in the past (mainly Italy, Greece, and, to a lesser extent, Ireland) took place. The solution was provided by the innovation and competitiveness of the Spanish services sector, a fact that was fostered by the readjustment of the banking sector to the dictates of the European Union and, as already indicated, to a broad knowledge of the companies within this sector (Álvaro-Moya et al., 2020).

Based on this contribution, new lines of research could be initiated. For example, repeating a similar analysis regarding the resilience of Spanish consulting firms by diversifying it towards other areas different from economic-financial or legal consulting such as engineering consulting, political consulting, etc. In the same way, analyses of similar nature could be implemented comparatively with countries of the Spanish socio-economic environment such as Portugal, Italy, or Greece. Consequently, similar studies could be carried out in which the economic and financial crisis of reference would be the COVID-19 shock, given the profound changes in the consumption patterns of the service sector clients (Toubes et al., 2021). The main limitations that this work has encountered have been operational, i.e., as this is eminently pioneering research of its kind, the available data are somewhat limited, hence a deep econometric analysis could not be undertaken and we had to opt for exploratory and descriptive analysis.

In the same way, and following the mainstream literature as a reference, the main guidelines of this paper could be replicated in different alternative lines of research. For example, the Economic History of Spain and its overseas possessions (Dobado & Marrero, 2011), the livestock sector (López et al., 2018), or the contributions of women to the recent Spanish economic growth (Duarte et al., 2019). Other lines of research may well be aimed at exploring the growth cycle of the Spanish economy over the last decades (García-Ferrer et al., 2001; Sánchez Chóliz et al., 2022), by defining its characterizing facts (Buendía & Molero-Simarro, 2018) or by determining the role played by the public sector (Flores De Frutos et al., 1998), while investigating the strong growth disparities between Spanish regions (Gutiérrez Posada et al., 2020), elements that hinder full economic convergence throughout the country (Díez-Minguela et al., 2016).

Funding This research received no external funding.

Conflict of Interest The author declares no conflict of interest.

References

Álvaro-Moya, A., Puig, N., & Torres, E. (2020). Managing foreign know-how and local human capital: Urquijo Group and the rise of Spanish engineering firms. *Business History, 62*(7), 1231–1253. https://doi.org/10.1080/00076791.2017.1413093

Askegaard, S., & Torp, S. M. (2020). Cultural corporate branding: An encounter of perspectives. In L. Peñaloza, N. Toulouse, & L. M. Visconti (Eds.), *Marketing management: A cultural perspective* (2nd ed., pp. 199–215). Routledge.

Aslam, M. S., Ali, I., Qammar, A., Kiwan, L., & Dhir, A. (2022). How knowledge acquisition creates a competitive edge? A qualitative inquiry from international consultancy alliance. *International Marketing Review*. https://doi.org/10.1108/IMR-03-2021-0111

Åslund, A., Guriev, S., & Kuchins, A. (2010). *Russia after the global economic crisis*. Columbia University Press.

Babío, N. C. (2009). Analysis of dynamic simulation as tool to support talent management in consulting firms [Análisis de la simulación dinámica como herramienta de apoyo directivo a la gestión del talento en organizaciones de consultoría]. *Revista Europea de Direccion y Economia de La Empresa, 18*(1), 135–154.

Barba, J. C., Laborda, J., & Laborda, R. (2021). The timely overestimation of Spanish GDP in the great recession. *Cambridge Journal of Economics, 45*(3), 427–456. https://doi.org/10.1093/cje/beab010

Barro, R. J., Ursua, J. F., & Weng, J. (2020). *The coronavirus and the great influenza epidemic—Lessons from the "Spanish flu"; for the coronavirus's potential effects on mortality and economic activity* (No. 8166; CESifo Working Paper Series).

Barthélemy, J. (2020). The impact of economic development and national culture on management consulting expenditures: Evidence from Europe and North America. *European Management Review, 17*(1), 185–196. https://doi.org/10.1111/emre.12352

Bedenk, S., Kunert, S., & Fietze, B. (2022). Time as a factor in systemic organisational consulting [Der Faktor Zeit: Impulse für Coaching, Teamentwicklung und Organisationsberatung]. *Gruppe. Interaktion. Organisation. Zeitschrift Fur Angewandte Organisationspsychologie, 53*(1), 39–48. https://doi.org/10.1007/s11612-022-00626-9

Beldek, T., Konyalıoğlu, A. K., & Camgöz-Akdağ, H. (2020). A fuzzy MCDM approach for project selection criteria prioritization in a big-four company: Evidences from Turkey consultancy sector. *Advances in Intelligent Systems and Computing, 1029*, 796–803. https://doi.org/10.1007/978-3-030-23756-1_95

Betti, N., Sarens, G., & Poncin, I. (2021). Effects of digitalisation of organisations on internal audit activities and practices. *Managerial Auditing Journal, 36*(6), 872–888. https://doi.org/10.1108/MAJ-08-2020-2792

Binder, A. J., Davis, D. B., & Bloom, N. (2016). Career funneling: How elite students learn to define and desire "prestigious" jobs. *Sociology of Education, 89*(1), 20–39. https://doi.org/10.1177/0038040715610883

Blanchard, S. (2022). Feminism through the market? A study of gender-equality consultants in France. *Gender, Work and Organization, 29*(2), 443–465. https://doi.org/10.1111/gwao.12770

Bode, M. (2019). Towards a formal description language for digital IT consulting products in decentralized IT consulting firms. In *Proceedings—IEEE International Enterprise Distributed Object Computing Workshop, EDOCW, 2019-October* (pp. 168–173). https://doi.org/10.1109/EDOCW.2019.00037

Bode, M., Deneva, M., & Van Sinderen, M. J. (2021). Requirements for digital IT consulting services and their provision through digital consulting platforms—Results from a focus group study. In *Proceedings—2021 IEEE 23rd Conference on Business Informatics, CBI 2021—Main Papers* (Vol. 1, pp. 111–120). https://doi.org/10.1109/CBI52690.2021.00022

Buendía, L., & Molero-Simarro, R. (2018). *The political economy of contemporary Spain: From miracle to mirage*. Taylor & Francis.

Çalışkan, G., & McGregor, A. J. (2019). 'You can change the world. We're just here to help': Activist consultancy firms as forms of neoliberal governmentality. *Globalizations, 16*(5), 625–643. https://doi.org/10.1080/14747731.2018.1562510

Castro-Martínez, A., & Díaz-Morilla, P. (2020). Internal communication and happiness and well-being management in Spanish companies [Comunicación interna y gestión de bienestar y felicidad en la empresa española]. *Profesional de La Informacion, 29*(3), 1–13. https://doi.org/10.3145/epi.2020.may.24

Cayolla, R. R., Martín, S. M., & Malone, C. (2021). It's the mindset, not the technology: The grass roots, Spain case study. In *Handbook of research on developing a post-pandemic paradigm for virtual technologies in higher education*. https://doi.org/10.4018/978-1-7998-6963-4.ch015

Cerruti, C., Tavoletti, E., & Grieco, C. (2019). Management consulting: A review of fifty years of scholarly research. *Management Research Review, 42*(8), 902–925. https://doi.org/10.1108/MRR-03-2018-0100

Cesário, M., Fernandes, S., Jesus, B., & Barata, J. M. (2015). Sources of innovation: The case of Portuguese consultancy sector. *Journal of Technology Management and Innovation, 10*(3), 44–52. https://doi.org/10.4067/S0718-27242015000300005

Chiodo, A. J., & Owyang, M. T. (2002). *A case study of a currency crisis: The Russian default of 1998* (No. 84; Federal Reserve Bank of St. Louis Working Papers).

da Silva, D. (2019). Launching a value program in a global engineering company. In *Proceedings of the SAVE 2019 Value Summit* (pp. 55–63).

Díez-Minguela, A., Martínez-Galarraga, J., & Tirado-Fabregat, D. A. (2016). Why did Spanish regions not converge before the civil war? Agglomeration economies and (regional) growth revisited. *Revista de Historia Económica/Journal of Iberian and Latin American Economic History, 34*(3), 417–448. https://doi.org/10.1017/S0212610915000300

Dobado, R., & Marrero, G. A. (2011). The role of the Spanish imperial state in the mining-led growth of Bourbon Mexico's economy. *The Economic History Review, 64*(3), 855–884. https://doi.org/10.1111/j.1468-0289.2010.00555.x

Donnelly, M., & Gamsu, S. (2019). The field of graduate recruitment: Leading financial and consultancy firms and elite class formation. *British Journal of Sociology, 70*(4), 1374–1401. https://doi.org/10.1111/1468-4446.12659

Duarte, R., Sarasa, C., & Serrano, M. (2019). Structural change and female participation in recent economic growth: A multisectoral analysis for the Spanish economy. *Economic Systems Research, 31*(4), 574–593. https://doi.org/10.1080/09535314.2019.1589425

Duthel, H. (2015). *Epistemoloía - Erkenntnistheorie: Wissenschaftslehre*. Books on Demand.

Erdost, H. E. (2005). Management consulting firms in Turkey. *Problems and Perspectives in Management, 3*(4), 173–180.

Flores De Frutos, R., Gracia-Díez, M., & Pérez, T. (1998). Public capital stock and economic growth: An analysis of the Spanish economy. *Applied Economics, 30*(8), 985–994. https://doi.org/10.1080/000368498325156

García-Ferrer, A., Queralt, R., & Blazquez, C. (2001). A growth cycle characterisation and forecasting of the Spanish economy: 1970–1998. *International Journal of Forecasting, 17*(3), 517–532. https://doi.org/10.1016/S0169-2070(01)00097-8

Gartzia, L. (2021). Gender equality in business action: A multi-agent change management approach. *Sustainability (Switzerland), 13*(11). https://doi.org/10.3390/su13116209

Gidadhubli, R. G. (2007). Putin's economic formula for Russia. *Economic and Political Weekly, 42*(49), 19–22. http://www.jstor.org/stable/40277017

Grosse, M., Ma, N., & Scott, T. (2020). Evidence on compensation consultant fees and CEO pay. *Australian Journal of Management, 45*(1), 15–44. https://doi.org/10.1177/0312896219837999

Gutiérrez, L. J. G., Martínez-López, F. J., & Molina Fernández, L. M. (2006). A dynamic evaluation of factors determining the quality of service perceived by clients: An empirical analysis focused on the consultancy sector. *International Journal of Services, Technology and Management, 7*(4), 369–382. https://doi.org/10.1504/IJSTM.2006.011003

Gutiérrez Posada, D., Rubiera Morollón, F., & Viñuela, A. (2020). Which places grow faster? In J.-C. Thill (Ed.), *Innovations in urban and regional systems: Contributions from GIS&T, spatial analysis and location modeling* (pp. 87–111). Springer International Publishing. https://doi.org/10.1007/978-3-030-43694-0_5

Harper, K. (2015). Pandemics and passages to late antiquity: rethinking the plague of c. 249–270 described by Cyprian. *Journal of Roman Archaeology, 28*, 223–260. https://doi.org/10.1017/S1047759415002470

Hirsh, M. (2011). *How much is Obama really to blame for the economy?* The Atlantic. Retrieved July 16, 2022, from www.theatlantic.com/politics/archive/2011/08/how-much-is-obama-really-to-blame-for-the-economy/243598/

Holtzclaw, K. (2012). *A childhood reminiscence of the great depression: A true story*. CreateSpace.

Horgan, J. (2019). *Antonine plague*. World History Encyclopedia. Retrieved July 16, 2022, from https://www.worldhistory.org/Antonine_Plague/

INE. (2022a). *Industria, energía y construcción*. Datos Por Temas - Instituto Nacional de Estadística. Retrieved June 7, 2022, from https://www.ine.es/dyngs/INEbase/es/categoria.htm?c=Estadistica_P&cid=1254735570688

INE. (2022b). *Producto Interior Bruto*. Datos Por Temas - Instituto Nacional de Estadística. Retrieved June 7, 2022, from https://www.ine.es/dyngs/INEbase/es/operacion.htm?c=Estadistica_C&cid=1254736164439&menu=ultiDatos&idp=1254735576581

Jang, Y., & Lee, J. (1998). Factors influencing the success of management consulting projects. *International Journal of Project Management, 16*(2), 67–72. https://doi.org/10.1016/S0263-7863(97)00005-7

Lopes da Costa, R., Ferreira Pereira, L., Lopes Dias, A., & Gonçalves, R. A. (2020a). Engage customers in co-creation: Is critical for projects success. *Journal of Modern Project Management, 8*(2), 66–75. https://doi.org/10.19255/JMPM02405

Lopes da Costa, R., Lopes Dias, A., Ferreira Pereira, L., Brás Dos Santos, J., & Miguel, I. (2020b). The basis for a constructive relationship between management consultants and clients (SMEs). *Business: Theory and Practice, 21*(2), 666–674. https://doi.org/10.3846/btp.2020.11872

Lopes da Costa, R., Santos Antonio, N., & Brás Dos Santos, J. (2020c). The Portuguese model of determinants that make up the management consultancy sector. *International Journal of Learning and Change, 12*(2), 209–229. https://doi.org/10.1504/IJLC.2020.106747

López, B., Lupi, T. M., León, J. M., López, F., Agudo, B., & Delgado, J. V. (2018). Characterization of the commercial growth curves of Spanish Merino, Fleischschaf, and crossbred lambs in an associative economy context. *Small Ruminant Research, 164*, 8–14. https://doi.org/10.1016/j.smallrumres.2018.04.009

Lozano-Torró, A., García-Segura, T., Montalbán-Domingo, L., & Pellicer, E. (2019). Risk management as a success factor in the international activity of Spanish engineering. *Administrative Sciences, 9*(1). https://doi.org/10.3390/admsci9010015

Mas Machuca, M., & Martínez Costa, C. (2012a). A study of knowledge culture in the consulting industry. *Industrial Management and Data Systems, 112*(1), 24–41. https://doi.org/10.1108/02635571211193626

Mas Machuca, M., & Martínez Costa, C. (2012b). Exploring critical success factors of knowledge management projects in the consulting sector. *Total Quality Management and Business Excellence, 23*(11–12), 1297–1313. https://doi.org/10.1080/14783363.2011.637778

Nikolova, N., Reihlen, M., & Schlapfner, J.-F. (2009). Client-consultant interaction: Capturing social practices of professional service production. *Scandinavian Journal of Management, 25*(3), 289–298. https://doi.org/10.1016/j.scaman.2009.05.004

ODP. (2018). *Revisando el modelo de negocio de nuestros Despachos* (10th ed.). Observatorio del Despacho Profesional.

Quaglia, L., & Royo, S. (2015). Banks and the political economy of the sovereign debt crisis in Italy and Spain. *Review of International Political Economy, 22*(3), 485–507. https://doi.org/10.1080/09692290.2013.877059

Sánchez Chóliz, J., Duarte, R., & Jiménez, S. (2022). Structural components of income growth: An application to the evolution of the Spanish economy, 1980–2014. *Economic Systems Research, 34*(2), 151–166. https://doi.org/10.1080/09535314.2021.1974353

Shiller, R. J. (2001). *Irrational exuberance*. Broadway Books.

Shoai, A. (2020). Dialogue between organizations and publics in the digital era: The "unfulfilled promise" of new media and the consultancy discourse in spain [Diálogo entre organizaciones y públicos en la era digital: La "promesa incumplida" de los nuevos medios y el disc. *Profesional De La Informacion, 29*(3), 1–14. https://doi.org/10.3145/epi.2020.may.21

Shoai, A., Ladevézeladevéze, L. N., & Acevedo, L. E. (2020). Combining dialogue and technology: Digital media and organization-public dialogue from the perspective of multinationals in Spain and Latin America [Conjugando diálogo y tecnología. Los medios digitales y el diálogo organizaciones-públicos desde la perspe. *Revista Latina de Comunicacion Social, 2020*(77), 309–327. https://doi.org/10.4185/RLCS-2020-1460

Suárez-Albanchez, J., Gutierrez-Broncano, S., Jimenez-Estevez, P., & Blazquez-Resino, J. J. (2022). Organizational support and turnover intention in the Spanish IT consultancy sector: Role of organizational commitment. *Cogent Social Sciences, 8*(1). https://doi.org/10.1080/23311886.2022.2051790

Toubes, D. R., Vila, N. A., & Fraiz Brea, J. A. (2021). Changes in consumption patterns and tourist promotion after the COVID-19 pandemic. *Journal of Theoretical and Applied Electronic Commerce Research, 16*(5), 1332–1352. https://doi.org/10.3390/jtaer16050075

Zerner, V., Marten, E., & Brandt, J. (2021). Commitment in the German banking and consulting industry: Influence of different leadership styles on employee commitment. *Central European Management Journal, 29*(4), 196–214. https://doi.org/10.7206/cemj.2658-0845.65

Zorio-Grima, A., García-Benau, M. A., Grau-Grau, A. J., & Paredes-Ojeda, F. (2018). The transparency report issued by audit firms: Evidence from the Spanish market 2010–2013 [El informe de transparencia de las firmas auditoras: Evidencia del mercado español 2010–2013]. *Revista Espanola de Financiacion y Contabilidad, 47*(2), 280–305.

Institutional Aspect of Assessing the Impact of Property Rights Protection on Economic Security

Irina Ferova, Ekaterina Tanenkova, and Svetlana Kozlova

Abstract Economic security, both at the national and regional levels, should be ensured by high-quality institutions that allow reducing the uncertainty of the environment and have mechanisms for the specification and protection of property rights. To assess the quality of institutions at the macrolevel, today there are many indices making it possible to compile a rough picture of the effectiveness of the institutional environment and institutional agreements in Russia. To date, there are no generally accepted methods that allow measuring individual institutions, including in the context of these mechanisms. However, many studies are reduced to assessing the quality of institutions through proxy indicators, which can only reflect approximate trends in the development of economic systems and economic security. At regional level, an institutional assessment of economic security can be made through the prism of mechanisms for the specification and protection of property rights, which are the main institutional tool for reducing risks and threats to economic security, both in the region and at the macrolevel. This paper proposes using indicators of the quality of the judicial system as one of the possible indicators of the provision of protection mechanisms and the specification of property rights.

Keywords Economic security · Institutions · Indicators · Property rights

JEL Classification D0 · D2 · D9

I. Ferova · E. Tanenkova · S. Kozlova (✉)
Siberian Federal University, 79 Svobodny Pr., 660041 Krasnoyarsk, Russian Federation
e-mail: svekozlova@sfu-kras.ru

I. Ferova
e-mail: iferova@sfu-kras.ru

E. Tanenkova
e-mail: etanenkova@sfu-kras.ru

V. Kumar et al. (eds.), *Consequences of Social Transformation for Economic Theory*, Springer Proceedings in Business and Economics,
https://doi.org/10.1007/978-3-031-27785-6_11

1 Introduction

The stable formation of the institutional environment today is a rather topical issue, since, on the one hand, the institutional environment creates opportunities for effective cooperation and coordination of individual actions, which are subsequently embodied in a common result; on the other hand, the institutional environment reduces uncertainty. The uncertainty of the environment increases the transaction costs of economic agents, preventing the free exchange of property rights in the economy, reducing the efficiency of individual economic relations and the economic system as a whole.

The importance of studying the issues of measuring the protection of property rights from the institutional point of view over the past twenty years is also confirmed by program documents in the field of socio-economic development of Russia: in the Program for the Socio-Economic Development of the Russian Federation for the Medium Term (2006–2008): "One of the most serious obstacles to economic growth in Russia at present is a weak institutional environment, including an insufficiently high level of protection of property rights and inefficient functioning of the judicial system…" (Kokorev, 2008); in the Concept of Long-Term Socio-Economic Development of the Russian Federation for the Period up to, 2020, it is noted that "The institutional environment necessary for an innovative socially oriented type of development will be formed in the long term within the following areas. First, political and legal institutions aimed at ensuring the civil and political rights of citizens, as well as the implementation of legislation. That is, the protection of basic rights, including the inviolability of the person and property, the independence of the judiciary, the effectiveness of the law enforcement system, and freedom of the media" (Concept, 2008).

Thus, the study of the institutional aspects of the protection of property rights is currently one of the key areas of state policy.

Institutional economics has been the leading direction of economic science for some time, since it has the necessary tools to study the nature of economic relations. Individuals need stable social institutions to reap the benefits of joint action. The organization of economic operation requires various institutional forms, as rules and procedures are established to regulate working conditions and distribution.

The institutionalization of political action is carried out through the creation of electoral and administrative rules. The structuring of social institutions in order to gain from cooperation, coordination, and exchange can be carried out in various ways. The structure of economic and political institutions is the fundamental basis of social life and can significantly affect the distribution of economic and political gains/losses in society.

Bondarenko (2018) notes that the neo-institutional economic theory, which studies the effectiveness of institutions, has a significant potential for analyzing economic security in terms of its quality. Institutions set a system of both positive and negative incentives for socio-economic activity, respectively reducing uncertainty and risks or making the institutional environment unpredictable and unsafe for vital interests, primarily economic.

The problem of the quality of economic security in this context is the threat of losing the "surplus" of productive activity, which can be appropriated without any compensation by any other individual, who has a higher potential for violence. The modern concept of "property rights" describes actions or a set of actions in relation to any type of resource that an individual or a group of individuals can carry out without being subject to the threat of sanctions from other parties, including the government (Bondarenko, 2018).

The uncertainty of the environment, unaccounted for by neoclassicists, is reduced due to institutions. However, this happens when institutions perform their functions and can be considered effective.

In modern conditions, sustainable socio-economic development is ensured mainly by preventing threats and identifying risks to economic security. This study considers the issues of identifying the degree of influence of economic institutions on economic security both at the macroeconomic and the regional level.

The authors assume that the institutional environment has a direct impact on economic interactions, thus the assessment and measurement of institutions can be considered a financial and economic component of security. The main purpose of this paper is to identify the role and place of various approaches to measuring institutions for the protection of property rights and the possibility of using theoretical methods for assessment to analyze the institutional impact on economic relations in particular and economic security in general.

One of the assumptions put forward in the paper is the idea that the measurement of institutions in the context of economic security can be carried out on the basis of parameters and indicators of the mechanisms for specifying and protecting property rights. This assumption is confirmed by modern research in the field of institutional economic theory and, as a first approximation, can be implemented through the analysis of parameters and indicators of the judicial system. For example, indicators of the judicial workload per judge in civil and criminal cases, as well as the cost per court day, can be used. Thus, one of the elements of measuring the institutional impact on economic security can be the ratio of the results of work (the number of cases considered) and the costs of their implementation.

In the course of the study, the following tasks were set and solved:

- to study and analyze the studies of Russian and foreign scholars devoted to the issues of assessing the measurement of institutions;
- to identify the most effective approaches and methods for measuring institutions in the context of assessing the economic security of economic entities;
- to offer the authors' approach to the assessment of economic security through the prism of the institutional approach;
- to assess the threats to economic security by measuring the effectiveness of the activities of the judiciary.

2 Literature Review

In order to identify which institutional factors have an impact on economic security, it is necessary to identify how this category is interpreted in the economic literature, including devoted to institutional research.

Afontsev (2001) points out that there are three main approaches to the definition of economic security in the literature. Thus, economic security is identified: through the protection of national interests, which is ensured by the state of the economy and government institutions; through the stability of the system, that is, reducing the impact of adverse factors on the functioning of the system; through independence, a set of factors and conditions that ensure the independence of the national economy.

From the authors' point of view, the main institutional prerequisites that affect the emergence of threats to economic security can be considered the following: the uncertainty of the environment, causing an increase in the transaction costs of economic agents in the implementation of transactions; insufficient specification and protection of property rights, which do not contribute to reducing the uncertainty of the environment.

The issues of efficiency and performance of economic relations have been analyzed by various academics throughout the history of the development of economic doctrine. However, it was the institutional theory that suggested analyzing economic relations from the standpoint of changes in the structure of property rights (Acemoglu et al., 2020; Cvetanović et al., 2019; Fedyunina & Oganesyan, 2022; Guerriero & Pignataro, 2021; Hodgson, 2019; Meramveliotakis, 2020; Murtazashvili & Murtazashvili, 2021; Slaev, 2019). In general, property rights can be defined as the ability to use a resource, possess, and alienate (dispose). The subject of economic relations today is property rights, their distribution among individuals, the conditions under which their alienation and appropriation are possible, and much more.

The specification of property rights in modern literature is understood as a procedure during which the composition and structure of possible obstacles to unauthorized access to a particular property right are identified.

Alchian (1965) and Eggertsson (2001) define property rights as "a set of methods for granting specific individuals 'authority' to choose any way to use particular goods from the class of non-prohibited ways to use these goods". Furubotn and Richter (2005) point out that when any property is exchanged, its value will depend on the bundle of property rights that are transferred during the transaction. North (1997) defines property rights as "the rights that individuals attribute to their labor and to the goods and services they own".

Kapelyushnikov (2008) notes that the theory of property rights is one of the most striking examples of economic imperialism, the purpose of which is to unify numerous sciences that study society through neoclassical analysis. This unification is expressed in the fact that various spheres of relations become the subject of study of economic science.

The problems caused by the erosion of property rights in the post-Soviet period in the Russian Federation are described by Stiglitz (2001). He, considering privatization in Russia as a factor in the development of market relations, believes that the inefficiency of building a market economy is caused by the lack of the necessary financial and legal structures.

Sonin (2003) in his study considers transition economies, in which the main emphasis was made towards liberalization, stability of the macroeconomic system, and privatization. He puts that "weak" institutions encourage economic agents to invest in protecting property rights, increase the corruption component of economic relations, and increase contracting costs.

Institutional change in general is a complex process. Aspects hindering effective institutional changes identified by North (2000) can be seen in the Russian reality. So, domestic small and medium-sized businesses today are experiencing very significant problems in adapting existing institutions that are not able to provide full specification and protection of property rights.

For example, Bednar and Page (2006) note that it is necessary to take into account the influence of culture on institutions and that of institutions on culture: "culture has both horizontal and vertical components". How agents interact depends on the current situation, for example, on how agents built interactions in the past, which norms and behaviors they adhered to. Under the vertical component, the authors understand the previous path of culture development in general and the institutional choice in particular. The set of existing institutions and the sequence in which they are created influence the culture. A rational choice between institutions can influence the set of existing institutions, as well as the sequence of their creation.

Rîșteiu et al. (2022) explores the opening a globally significant gold mine at Roşia Montană, in the Transylvanian region of Romania, which have led to decades of controversy and struggle. They note the different understandings of extraction amongst advocates for and opponents of the mine over the last two decades. The discussion of the paper is the shifting roles of capital, the state, civil society organizations, and the local community over time, the arguments for the need to distinguish between their different positions on mining. The authors showed that the understanding of extraction promoted by the owners of the mine, and by the local community, is fundamentally different in terms of cultural, social, and economic priorities. The local community argue for a traditional type of mining, embedded in local ownership and established labor identities, whereas the neoliberal vision of capital for the Roşia Montană site is that of a globally competitive, technologically advanced form of extraction. In uncovering and developing these hermeneutic differences, the paper reveals that pro-traditional development attitudes among economically marginalized groups are not necessarily attuned to the material global interconnections shaping neoliberal capitalism.

Nureev and Latov (2010) note that society at any given time faces the issue of choosing from a variety of institutional alternatives, among which there are short-term alternatives being ineffective in the long term and giving no positive effect in the future.

So, economic security both at the national level and at the level of regions and microstructures can be ensured by "good", stable, and efficient institutions. Suppose that, based on the analysis carried out above, one can conclude that formal institutions, which represent a rather weak institutional environment that does not adequately provide for the specification and protection of property rights, are replaced by institutional alternatives of an informal nature, the quality and effectiveness of which is significantly higher than those of formal institutions. Then the question arises as to why informal institutions cannot (or can, but not fully) ensure national economic security, as well as high-quality and sustainable economic growth.

First, as Nureyev and Latov have already shown, informal alternatives to existing formal institutions tend to be aimed at solving short-term problems in cooperation, reducing transaction costs, and also the uncertainty of the environment.

Second, if the choice occurs between two inefficient institutions, economic agents intuitively explore different equilibrium states. Thus, equilibrium in a formal institution is less effective for individuals, compared with the choice of equilibrium within an informal institution. That is, to a certain extent, equilibrium in informal institutions is a Pareto improvement. At the same time, one must understand that alternative institutions of a formal and informal nature in this case create "bad" equilibria.

Third, as Tambovtsev (2006) notes, in modern conditions, the state is the most massive guarantor of property rights, and therefore it may seem that formal property rights are usually better protected than informal ones. As he notes, this is not entirely true, since formal institutions are also created by economic agents, who at a certain point in time may believe that the "insecurity" or "blurring" of property rights reduces the state's monitoring and control costs. On this occasion, Tambovtsev (2006) writes: "However, the blurring of property rights, which is beneficial in the short term, creates difficulties in filling the treasury in the long term. After all, the weakening of the exclusivity of property rights reduces the degree of certainty of the future for economic agents, increases risks, thereby reducing incentives for investment activity".

In this regard, the specification and protection of property rights are closely related to the balance of the regional budget, the investment activity of economic entities, and their economic security.

But we should note that property rights as housing can be put in question when processes of desegregation appear in cities. Méreiné-Berki et al. (2021) note that policymakers are eager to create socially mixed neighbourhoods, even though evidence for the positive impact of social mixing is patchy. The authors examine the relationship between social mixing, social capital, and the lived experience of residents affected by the desegregation of an urban Roma area. The paper shows that desegregation has complex and contradictory impacts on lived experience, and that these relate to changes in social forms of capital. The presence of strong negative neighborhood effects, acknowledged by marginalized residents themselves, indicates that social mixing can contribute to the enhancement of wellbeing and social mobility for many segregated families. Desegregation alone is insufficient, and further policies are required to increase socio-spatial integration and deal with the social, economic, and cultural causes of extreme poverty.

Shastitko (2006) notes that the importance of the institutional environment in Russia, namely the role in improving welfare and economic growth, was underestimated, which "in practice turned into a protracted transformational recession and underutilization of significant development reserves in the relatively favorable last century".

An analysis of institutional changes, an assessment of their quality and effectiveness involves researching the states *before* institutional changes and *after* them. To date, there is no generally accepted approach that gives an unambiguous interpretation of the results obtained. A detailed analysis of existing approaches to the assessment of institutions was carried out by Tanenkova (2020).

Aron (2000) notes that it is necessary to distinguish between descriptions of institutions and measurement of institutions. The description of institutions is understood as a description of various characteristics of institutions (for example, the presence or absence of constitutional property rights). Under the measurement of formal and informal institutions, he understood the effectiveness of existing (and implemented) rules and norms. For example, measuring the quality of formal institutions may take the form of a subjective ranking of property rights in terms of their effectiveness, the presence of bureaucratic barriers, and other related characteristics. It is believed that such characteristics make it possible to measure institutions, but in their essence they are proxy variables and reflect the transaction costs of production, which affect the volume and efficiency of investments and, as a result, economic growth.

Alonso and Garcimartin (2009) point out that empirical assessments of institutional effectiveness are associated with the following difficulties: imperfection of indicators for measuring institutional quality; problems of studying endogenous variables; collinearity among explanatory variables, preventing them from being considered independent factors; variables not taken into account that bias the assessment results.

The assessment of economic security at the macrolevel does not have a generally accepted methodology, which causes numerous disputes and criticism from researchers. Various authors use different methods for assessing economic security, while using national macroeconomic indicators.

The issue of institutional assessment of economic security, both at the macrolevel and at other levels, remains open, among other things, for the following reasons:

First, there is a methodological problem of assessing not only economic security but also the problem of assessing institutions at all levels—from the micro to the macrolevel.

Second, the assessment of economic security through the specification of property rights also does not currently have universal methods.

Third, the assessment of institutions and the specification of property rights, for example, at the macroeconomic level, faces problems that have been formulated by Jütting (2003). He believes that such shortcomings include:

1. Evaluation of the "quality" of institutions is carried out on the basis of simple logic: effective institutions ensure the political and economic stability of the government.

2. Measurement of institutions is often based on “perceptions” and expert assessments of foreign agents. On the one hand, it can serve as a motivation for developed countries to further develop their institutions. On the other hand, for developing countries, “perception” characterizes only the quality of formal institutions.

The problems of evaluating institutions and their effectiveness are expressed not only in the definition and interpretation of appropriate criteria and indicators but also in how to identify different levels of the institutional environment. The basic theoretical problem is the need (or lack of it) to identify institutions of various levels. For example, the theoretical analysis, as a rule, is based on the division of institutions into macro- and micro-components, while empirical estimates of the regional context suggest the allocation of mesoinstitutions.

Shastitko (2019) notes that the use of the concept of “mesoinstitutions” is not new for economic analysis: “Note that the mesolevel has already been introduced into academic circulation in economic research when it comes to regions and individual industries—mesoeconomics, and not only in foreign but also in Russian literature”. In addition, he believes that the allocation of mesolevel institutions can become a “multiplication of entities”.

Nevertheless, there are many studies highlighting the institutions of the mesolevel. Representatives of the institutional direction of mesoeconomics research include Popov (2007), Keiner (2003), Kirdina-Chandler (2017).

However, despite the problems described above, most authors use various macroeconomic indicators and indices to assess the institutional impact on economic security at the macroeconomic level.

At the same time, macroeconomic indicators that could reflect the effectiveness of the institutional environment do not meet such expectations and distort the existing institutional and economic realities.

3 Materials and Methods

Economic security is a complex concept that includes an analysis of various components of the economic system. The definition of various specific areas of economic security is a very important aspect of its analysis. In this paper, the authors attempt to assess economic security through the prism of the institutional environment and its impact on the economic interaction of agents. Previously, the authors studied the applied aspects of assessing the financial security of the region (Ferova, 2021; Podtikhova & Ferova, 2021, 2021).

One of the popular assessment tools is macroeconomic indicators and indices for assessing the institutional impact on economic security at the macroeconomic level.

Let us analyze the Government Quality Indicators, which are formed by the World Bank (Kaufmann et al., 2009).

These indicators include: Control of corruption; Government effectiveness; Political stability and absence of violence, terrorism, peaceful power transfer via a constitutional way; Regulatory quality, understood as the absence of the burden of administrative regulation and the ability of the government to formulate and implement rational policies and legal acts that promote the development of the private sector; Rule of law, understood as fair and open rules on major social and economic issues, the independence of the judiciary and the police, the protection of property rights and the enforcement of contracts, etc.

To calculate the values of indicators, 441 variables are used, including statistical indicators, the results of sociological surveys and expert assessments.

Table 1 presents the dynamics of indicators from 1996 to 2020 (World Bank, 2022). The indices of this methodology take a value from −2.6 to 2.6, and the higher the index, the better the quality of public administration, that is, the more effective the work of institutions.

During this period, the performance indicators of institutions did not reach positive values, and in general, it can be noted that the growth in the quality of institutions over 23 years is not very significant.

The indicator of control of corruption in 2008 was estimated at the level of 1996, and in 2020—at the level of 2004 and 2016. It was (−0.9), while a similar indicator in China in 2020 was (−0.1).

The government effectiveness indicator changed in waves: in 2020 it was 0.0, while in the period from 1996 to 2000 being (−0.7), and then it tended to increase and in the period from 2004 to 2016 varied from (−0.4) to (−0.2). In China, the indicator for the specified period demonstrates a higher quality of institutions as it increases throughout the period under review: in 1996 being (−0.3) and in 2020, 0.6.

Table 1 Indicators of the quality of public administration in Russia and China from 1996 to 2020

Country	Worldwide governance indicators	1996	2000	2004	2008	2012	2016	2020
Russia	Control of corruption	−1.1	−1.0	−0.8	−1.1	−1.0	−0.8	−0.9
	Government effectiveness	−0.5	−0.7	−0.4	−0.4	−0.4	−0.2	0.0
	Political stability and absence of violence/terrorism	−1.2	−1.4	−1.5	−0.7	−0.8	−0.9	−0.7
	Regulatory quality	−0.4	−0.6	−0.1	−0.4	−0.3	−0.4	−0.4
	Rule of law	−0.8	−1.1	−0.9	−1.0	−0.8	−0.8	−0.8
China	Control of corruption	−0.3	−0.2	−0.6	−0.5	−0.4	−0.3	−0.1
	Government effectiveness	−0.3	−0.1	−0.1	0.2	0.0	0.4	0.6
	Political stability and absence of violence/terrorism	−0.1	−0.2	−0.4	−0.5	−0.5	−0.5	−0.3
	Regulatory quality	−0.3	−0.3	−0.3	−0.2	−0.2	−0.3	−0.1
	Rule of law	−0.5	−0.5	−0.5	−0.4	−0.5	−0.3	−0.1

Source Compiled by the authors based on: https://databank.worldbank.org/source/worldwide-governance-indicators

The indicator of political stability and the absence of violence/terrorism demonstrates a generally positive trend, and that of the effectiveness of institutions, regulating this area of economic, social, and other types of relationships almost doubled—from (−1.2) to (−0.7). For China, the indicator under consideration also decreased from (−0.1) in 1996 to (−0.3) in 2020.

The indicator of regulatory quality in 2020 coincides with the estimates of 1996 being (−0.4). The greatest efficiency was achieved in 2004. In China, the legislative quality indicator is also negative, in 1996 being (−0.3) and in 2020 being (−0.1).

The rule of law indicator in Russia had a minimum value in 2000 being (−1.1); in 2020, the indicator increased to (−0.8). In China, in 2020, the indicator was (−0.1), which indicates a positive trend compared to 1996 being (−0.5).

On the basis of data on the quality of public administration, conclusions can be drawn that Russia today has rather weak institutions especially when compared to developed countries. It should be noted that though a positive trend exists, the increase in the quality of institutions remains very insignificant. That is, in general, the quality of the institutional environment has changed in a very insignificant way without going beyond negative values. For example, Vaslavskaya (2012), examining the indicators of the quality of public administration, notes that "the economic growth which has been observed in the country since 1996 has not been accompanied by qualitative changes in institutions affecting guarantees of property rights and the quality of the regulatory environment. There has been no decrease in the level of corruption". The researcher calls the combination "economic growth—poor quality of the institutional environment" an institutional lag, which interferes with the conditions of multiplication of a positive effect in the process of socio-economic dynamics. Here one can state that weak institutions have a negative impact on the economic security of the country as a whole.

In China as a whole, according to all indicators, there is also a systemic lag in the quality of the institutional environment in comparison with many developed countries, which, however, does not hinder its economic growth. Cheung (1998), studying transaction costs and institutions supporting democratic societies, wrote the following about China: "In other words, in a Communist regime, transaction costs are very high compared to the benefits of specialization. Because of this, I'm sure, the Chinese are so poor …".

This way, it turns out that various macroeconomic indicators which could reflect the effectiveness of the institutional environment do not meet such expectations and distort the existing institutional and economic realities.

That is, the results of assessing macroeconomic indicators of institutional efficiency can be misleading and create false ideas about the level of not only national economic security but also economic development in general.

From the authors' point of view, the approach to assessing economic security from the standpoint of institutional analysis should include assessments and an analysis of the uncertainty of the environment and the possibility of reducing it through specification and protection of property rights.

So, the approach to the institutional assessment of economic security from the authors' position should be based on two components: modeling and evaluation of contractual relations between economic agents at the microlevel and then scaling to the level of the region; evaluation of effective conflict resolution, unforeseen by contracts.

As is known, the conclusion of institutional agreements (contracts as a type of agreements) creates prerequisites for reducing the uncertainty of the environment and transaction costs. In this regard, Pyzhev and Tanenkova (2022) proposed an original transaction-contract approach to measuring microeconomic institutions. Based on this approach, it becomes possible to identify the components of institutional norms and to model contractual relations, taking into account the transactional component.

Since the contracts concluded between counterparties are not fully fair, there is a risk of lack of mechanisms for resolving conflicts without resorting to the intervention of a third party. In this case, as noted by many studies, an important criterion for the effectiveness of the institutional environment as a whole becomes a mechanism for resolving conflicts.

On this case, Tambovtsev (2006) notes that in ensuring the protection of property rights for each level of economic relations, the judiciary and its independence play a significant role. Tambovtsev puts that the activities of the judiciary can be analyzed from the economic view in the context of the categories "performance" and "efficiency".

Performance here refers to "the degree of success in resolving conflicts".

Efficiency, according to the scholar, depends on two factors: (a) type of the legal system, namely, a system of common or codified law. Under the common law, the judiciary is given the function of making laws, within the framework of codified law—the function of creating laws belongs to the legislature. Courts implement these institutions despite the effect of their implementation; (b) independence of judges and the accountability of the court to the law and society at large.

Efficiency is understood as the ratio of costs for the implementation of results and obtaining performance results.

Some scientists are inclined to that idea that the efficiency of the work of courts is directly related to the indicators of the workload of judges. If the load is high, then there is a decrease in the quality of justice; low load indicates that budget funds are spent inefficiently. That is, there is an "overcrowding of the judiciary" (Mamotov, 2017).

The issues of the impact of the efficiency of the judicial system on the socio-economic development and economic security of the region were considered in the works by foreign scholars (Haisley, 2016; Jin & Amaral-Garcia, 2019; Manuel & Chen, 2021; Wolfgang, 2002).

Wolfgang (2002) investigates the empirical relationship between the quality of the Indian judicial system and the economic development of the Indian states and union territories. The quality of the judiciary is defined in terms of the speed of decision-making and the predictability of the trial outcome. Also, the relationship between the quality of the judicial system and production factors is investigated, such as agriculture, development of the private sector, capital accumulation, poverty level, public security and infrastructure, and per capita income level.

According to the results of the study, the author found that a weak judicial system has a negative impact on economic and social development, which leads to a decrease in per capita income; higher levels of poverty; decline in private economic activity: weak public infrastructure; higher crime rates.

Haisley (2016) notes that since the 1980s, academics and development banks have recognized the relationship between institutions and economic growth. He proposes to explore the role of judicial institutions in the efficiency of the economy and questions on whether the strengthening of judicial institutions can lead to an acceleration of the economic development of developing countries. The study showed that the strengthening of judicial institutions through judicial reform efforts both in the civil sector and in the criminal justice sector could potentially enhance economic development. To accelerate economic development, resources should be directed to strengthening judicial institutions so that they can effectively address both civil and criminal justice systems.

Therefore, studies confirm the role of the judiciary in economic growth and, consequently, economic security.

4 Results

In this study, the judicial system is considered as a mechanism for ensuring the economic security of the region since the accessibility of justice and the timing of decisions are the main factors affecting the ability of an economic entity to ensure the protection of property rights, while the effectiveness of the judicial system affects the willingness of economic entities to invest.

Data on the workload per judge in the Krasnoyarsk Territory in criminal and civil cases are presented in Tables 2 and 3.

It is noted that in general for a period of 9 months in 2020, the average monthly workload per judge of a district and city court decreased: in criminal cases from 3.4 to 3.2; in civil cases from 22.5 to 18.2. In 2018, the average monthly workload per judge was 2.6 criminal cases and 25.2 civil cases. So, one can see that in general there is a tendency to reduce the load on one judge of district and city courts in the Krasnoyarsk Territory. At the same time, absolute indicators, for example, received criminal cases during the year grew by almost 25% in 2020 compared to 2018. The data is presented in Fig. 1.

In general, it can be noted that the judicial workload is unevenly distributed. Obviously, it depends on the number of cases received in the period under review as well as the number of cases remaining in court operation.

Evaluation of efficiency, as shown above, is connected not only with the identification of the workload but also the cost of the administering justice. Some scholars point out that the cost of one hour of work of a judge is estimated at about 3 thousand rubles and one court day being at least 25 thousand rubles. Therefore, the cost of administering justice is higher than the value of the results.

Table 2 Minimum and maximum workload per judge of district and city courts of the Krasnoyarsk Territory in criminal cases for 9 months of 2020

District and city courts of the Krasnoyarsk Territory	Load of criminal cases per judge per month
Maximal load	
Sharypovsk district	6.2
Minusinsk district	5.3
Kansk district	5.3
Irbey district	5.1
Rybinsk district	4.9
Ilansk district	4.8
Zheleznogorsk district	4.5
Aban district	4.4
Dzerzhinsk district	4.4
Tyukhtet district	4.4
Minimal load	
Krasnoyarsk Central district	2.1
Nizhniy Ingash district	2.1
Dudinka district	1.8
Ust-Yeniseisk district	1.8
Igarka district	1.74
Turukhansk district	1.74
Baikit district	1.2
Dikson district	0.3
Tyukhtet district	4.4

Source Compiled by the authors based on materials: https://www.mirsud24.ru/start/sudebnaya-statistika/

So, regarding the institutional aspects of economic security, the following conclusions can be drawn. Economic security both at the national and the regional levels is ensured via good quality institutions allowing reducing the uncertainty of the environment and having some mechanisms for specification and protection of property rights. It should be noted that today there are no generally accepted methods that allow measuring individual institutions, including in the context of these mechanisms. To assess the quality of institutions at the macrolevel, today there are many indices that allow getting a rough picture of the effectiveness of the institutional environment and institutional agreements in Russia. So, looking at Governance Quality Indicators according to the World Bank estimates, most indicators of the quality of Russian institutions have a positive trend. However, these dynamics have a very low growth rate, which allows speaking about the difficulties and inefficiency of economic institutions, and, consequently, threats to economic security.

The specification and protection of property rights are the main institutional tool for reducing risks and threats to economic security both on the regional and the

Table 3 Minimum and maximum workload per judge of district and city courts of the Krasnoyarsk Territory in civil cases for 9 months of 2020

District and city courts of the Krasnoyarsk Territory	Load of civil cases per judge per month
Maximal load	
Krasnoyarsk Soviet district	27.9
Krasnoyarsk Oktyabrsky district	27.4
Bolsheuluysk district	27.2
Minusinsk district	24.3
Krasnoyarsk Central district	23.5
Yemelyanovo district	22.4
Sosnovoborsk district	22.3
Berezovsky district	21.9
Krasnoyarsk Sverdlovsk district	21.2
Zheleznogorsk district	21.2
Minimal load	
Yeniseisk district	10.7
Taseyevo district	9.7
Dudinka district	9.2
Turukhansk district	8.9
Baikit district	8.2
Nizhniy Ingash district	6.3
Ust-Yeniseisk district	4.3
Igarka district	3.8
Dikson district	1.9

Source Compiled by the authors based on materials: https://www.mirsud24.ru/start/sudebnaya-statistika/

macro level. The measurement should be made in the context of the categories: "performance" and "efficiency". So, for the Krasnoyarsk Territory, the minimum and maximum workloads for judges were considered and showed an uneven distribution within the region. In general, the methodology for assessing specifications and protecting property rights requires separate research and development. According to the data reviewed, it can be assumed that the efficiency of justice administration tends to increase, however, its performance may pose a threat to the economic security of the region.

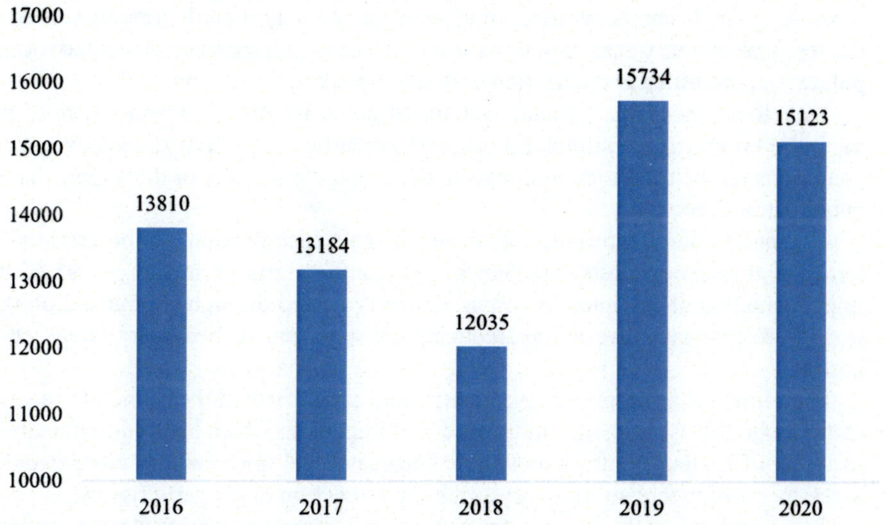

Fig. 1 Number of criminal cases received by the district and city courts in the Krasnoyarsk Territory in the period from 2016 to 2020

5 Discussion and Conclusion

This paper points to the importance of institutes in guarantees of property rights. Institutional environment has the main role in improving welfare and economic growth in transforming economy, ignoring can lead to protracted transformational recessions and underutilization of significant development reserves (Shastitko, 2006).

Our research based on suggestion that the state is the most massive guarantor of property rights (Tambovtsev, 2006). The blurring of property rights creates difficulties in filling the treasury in the long term, the weakening of the exclusivity of property rights reduces the degree of certainty of the future for economic agents, increases risks, reducing incentives for investment activity (Tambovtsev, 2006).

Our study confirms the findings of other research (e.g. Haisley, 2016; Jin and Amaral-Garcia, 2019; Mamotov, 2017; Manuel and Chen, 2021; Wolfgang, 2002), in that it suggests that there is a mutually influential relationship between economic development, economic security and efficiency of the work of courts, which directly related to the indicators of the workload of judges.

From the point of view of the institutional science, the situation with the specification and protection of property rights as one of the indicators of the absence of a threat to the economic security of micro, meso, and macrolevel looks like this: there is a lack of independence of the judiciary as a whole, which means a certain dependence on political decisions and lobbying by special interest groups;—the performance of courts can be assessed in terms of workload distribution. It can be noted here that in the Krasnoyarsk Territory, the distribution of the workload on judges is uneven, which can be explained by a number of factors, the analysis of which requires a separate study. It can be assumed that such factors may include: remoteness from the regional center; transaction costs of proceedings; competence characteristics of judges; opportunities in connection with the appealing a case, etc.

The efficiency of the judicial system, as noted by most researchers, does not meet the criteria for optimizing costs and performance, which obviously creates conditions for the formation of threats to the economic security of the region and the entire national economy.

In general, the effectiveness of property rights specification can be assessed in terms of transaction costs. So, part of the conflicts arising in the course of the implementation of economic relations can be protected through contractual obligations—effective incentive setting, reducing the opportunistic behavior of transaction parties.

Therefore, for a comprehensive institutional assessment of the economic security of the region, it is necessary to expand the boundaries of an institutional analysis in terms of scaling contract models to the mesolevel and conduct more detailed assessments of mechanisms for ensuring the protection of property rights.

Our research can be use for measuring indicators, evaluating performance in programs of development and digitalization of justice. The measurement can improve the efficiency, access to and quality of justice.

There is need for further research using quantitative approaches, collecting data from countries that have implemented programs of justice reform across justice systems. This may be important to public policy decision makers, economists, scholars and jurists.

For development of research it is necessary to consider the role of informal institutions in the protection of property rights in countries with different types of economy.

Acknowledgements The research was funded by RFBR, the Government of the Krasnoyarsk Territory and Krasnoyarsk Regional Fund of Science. Project number 20-410-242912.

References

Acemoglu, D., Egorov. G., & Sonin, K. (2020). *Institutional change and institutional persistence*. Elsevier.

Afontsev, S. A. (2001). Problems of Russia's economic security in the context of market transformation. *Socio-Economic Transformation in Russia: Scientific Reports of the Moscow Public Science Foundation, 131*, 15–42.

Alchian, A. (1965). Some economics of property rights. *Politico, 30*(4), 816–829. Retrieved August 3, 2022, from https://www.jstor.org/stable/43206327

Alonso, J. A., & Garcimartin, C. (2009). *The determinants of institutional quality. More on the debate*. CREDIT Research Paper. No. 09/04. The University of Nottingham, Centre for Research in Economic Development and International Trade (CREDIT).

Aron, J. (2000). Growth and institutions: A review of the evidence. *The World Bank Research Observer, 1*(15), 105–106. https://doi.org/10.1093/wbro/15.1.99

Bednar, J., & Page, S. E. (2006). *Culture, institutional performance, and path dependence*. University of Michigan. Retrieved August 3, 2022, from https://escholarship.org/content/qt1bq6d126/qt1bq6d126_noSplash_a133b46647b94e2a5f1caa54ac762380.pdf?t=krn8uw

Bondarenko, T. I. (2018). Specification of property rights as a necessary condition for ensuring the economic security of Russia. *Electronic Network Polythematic Journal "Scientific works of KubGTU", 6*, 60–68. https://elibrary.ru/item.asp?id=35382689

Cheung, S. N. S. (1998). The transaction costs paradigm. 1998 Presidential address. Western Economic Association. *Economic Inquiry, XXXVI*, 514–521.

Cvetanović, S., Mitrović, U., & Jurakić, M. (2019). Institutions as the driver of economic growth in classic, Neoclasic and Endogenous Theory. *Economic Themes. Sciendo, 57*(1), 111–125. https://doi.org/10.2478/ethemes-2019-0007

Eggertsson, T. (2001). *Economic behavior and institutions*. Delo.

Fedyunina, E., & Oganesyan, L. (2022). The concept of minimization of transaction costs of functioning of the dual market of agricultural lands. *St Petersburg University Journal of Economic Studies, 37*(4), 628–655. https://doi.org/10.21638/spbu05.2021.405

Ferova, I. S. (2021). Cluster model as a tool for economic security and strategic development of the region. *Innovative Development of the Economy, 2–3*(62–63), 388–398. https://doi.org/10.51832/2223-7984_2021_2-3_388

Furubotn, E., & Richter, R. (2005). *Institutions and economic theory*. St. Petersburg State University Publishing.

Guerriero, C., & Pignataro, G. (2021). Endogenous property rights and the nature of the firm. *SSRN*. https://doi.org/10.2139/ssrn.3547522

Haisley, S. A. (2016). *Enhancing judicial institutions: Enhancing economic development.* Duke University School of Law. Retrieved August 3, 2022, from https://scholarship.law.duke.edu/cgi/viewcontent.cgi?article=1009&context=mjs

Hodgson, G. (2019). Prospects for institutional research. *RAUSP Management Journal, 54*(1), 112–120. https://doi.org/10.1108/RAUSP-11-2018-0112

Jin, Y., & Amaral-Garcia, S. (2019). *Enhancing judicial efficiency to foster economic activity in Portugal*. OECD Economics Department Working Papers No. 1567. OECD Publishing. https://doi.org/10.1787/e8d8f103-en

Jütting, J. (2003). *Institutions and development: A critical review*. OECD Development Centre Working Papers, No. 210. OECD Publishing. https://doi.org/10.1787/341346131416

Kapeliushnikov, R. (2008). Ownership without Legitimacy? *Voprosy Ekonomiki, 3*, 85–105. https://doi.org/10.32609/0042-8736-2008-3-85-105

Kaufmann, D., Kraay, A., & Mastruzzi, M. (2009). Governance Matters VIII Aggregate and Individual Governance Indicators. 1996–2008. *World Bank Policy Research Working Paper 4978* (pp. 98–105). World Bank. https://documents1.worldbank.org/curated/en/598851468149673121/pdf/WPS4978.pdf

Keiner, G. (2003). Mesoeconomic problems of the Russian economy. *Economic Bulletin of the Rostov State University, 2*.

Kirdina-Chandler, S. (2017). Mesoeconomics and the economics of complexity: Actual going beyond orthodoxy. *Journal of Institutional Studies, 3*(10), 6–17.

Kokorev, R. A. (2008). *The role of institutions in the diversification of the Russian federation economy.* Retrieved August 3, 2022, from http://www.un.org/en/development/desa/policy/publications/general_assembly/eitconference/2apram_report_kokorev_eng.pdf

Manuel, R. M., & Chen, D. L. (2021). *The role of justice in development: The data revolution.* Policy Research Working Paper; No. 9720. World Bank. Retrieved August 3, 2022, from https://openknowledge.worldbank.org/handle/10986/35891

Meramveliotakis, G. (2020). Surveying the methodological and analytical foundations of the new institutional economics: A critical comparison with neoclassical and (old) institutional economics. *Economic and Business Review, 22*(3). https://doi.org/10.15458/ebr109

Méreiné-Berki, B., Málovics, G. & Creţan, R. (2021). "You become one with the place": Social mixing, social capital, and the lived experience of urban desegregation in the Roma community, *Cities, 117*. https://doi.org/10.1016/j.cities.2021.103302

Momotov, V. V. (2017). Economics of justice: About the good of the state and the benefit of a private person. *Journal of Foreign Legislation and Comparative Law, 3*(64). Retrieved July 14, 2021, from https://cyberleninka.ru/article/n/ekonomika-pravosudiya-o-blage-gosudarstva-i-polze-chastnogo-litsa

Murtazashvili, J. B., & Murtazashvili, I. (2021). *Land, the state, and war property institutions and political order in Afghanistan.* Cambridge University Press.

North, D. (1997). *Institutions, institutional change and economic performance.* Fond ekonomicheskoi knigi "Nachala".

North, D. (2000). Five theses about institutional changes. *Club's Quarterly Bulletin, 7.*

Nureev, R., & Latov, A. (2010). *Russia and Europe: The track effect (an experience of institutional analysis of the history of economic development).* Publishing House of the Kant Russian State University.

Podtikhova, N. N., & Ferova, I. S. (2021). Estimation of the financial security of a coal mining enterprise. *Business. Education. Law, 3*(56), 25–31. https://doi.org/10.25683/VOLBI.2021.56.328

Popov, E. (2007). *The evolution of mini-economy institutions.* Nauka.

Pyzhev, I. S., & Tanenkova, E. N. (2022). Evaluation of institutions of the microeconomic level: Transaction-contract approach and its implementation. *Journal of Institutional Studies, 14*(2), 36–46.

Rîşteiu, N. T., Creţan, R., & O'Brien, T. (2022). Contesting post-communist economic development: Gold extraction, local community, and rural decline in Romania. *Eurasian Geography and Economics, 63*(4), 491–513. https://doi.org/10.1080/15387216.2021.1913205

Shastitko, A. (2019). Meso-institutions: Multiplying entities or developing an economic research agenda? *Economic Issues, 5*, 5–26.

Shastitko, A. (2006). Problems of corporate governance and ways to solve them in corporate legislation. *Russian Journal of Management, 2*(4), 3–24. Retrieved August 3, 2022, from https://rjm.spbu.ru/article/view/660

Slaev, A. (2019). Complex private-common property rights in institutional and planning theories. *Planning Theory, 19*, 193–213. https://doi.org/10.1177/1473095219874832

Sonin, K. (2003). Why the rich may favor poor protection of property rights. *Journal of Comparative Economics, 31*(4), 715–731.

Stiglitz, J. (2001). Quis custodiet Ipsos custodes? Failures of corporate governance in the transition to the market. *Economic Science of Modern Russia, 4*, 108–146.

Tambovtsev, V. (2006). Improvement of property rights protection—Dormant reserve of Russia's economic growth? *Voprosy Ekonomiki, 1*, 22–38. https://doi.org/10.32609/0042-8736-2006-1-22-38

Tanenkova, E. N. (2020). The opportunities of measurement of institutions and institutional changes in modern economic science. *Herald of Omsk University. Series "Economics", 18*(1), 45–56. https://doi.org/10.24147/1812-3988.2020.18(1).45-56

The Concept of Long-Term Socio-Economic Development of the Russian Federation for the Period up to 2020. Decree of the Government of the Russian Federation of November 17, 2008 No. 1662-r. Retrieved August 3, 2022, from http://www.consultant.ru/document/cons_doc_LAW_82134/

Vaslavskaya, I. (2012). Indicators of the reliability of protection of property rights. *Bulletin of the Institute of Economics of the Russian Academy of Sciences, 6*, 108–120. Retrieved August 3, 2022, from https://cyberleninka.ru/article/n/idikatory-nadezhnosti-zaschity-prav-sobstvennosti

Wolfgang, K. (2002). *The economic consequences of a weak judiciary: Insights from India.* Law and Economics 0212001. University Library of Munich, Germany. Retrieved August 3, 2022, from https://EconPapers.repec.org/RePEc:wpa:wuwple:0212001

World Bank. (2022). *Worldwide Governance Indicators.* DataBank. Last Updated: July 27, 2021. Retrieved August 3, 2022, from https://databank.worldbank.org/source/worldwide-governance-indicators

Problems of a Comprehensive Assessment of the Socially Significant Investment Projects Amid a Pandemic

Tatyana S. Novikova, Olga I. Gulakova, and Tatyana V. Afanasyeva

Abstract The pandemic crisis has highlighted the need to rethink the priorities of economic decision-making and fundamentally change the emphasis towards the principles of sustainable development. To assess even commercially viable investment projects, it is necessary to take into account their impact on long-term economic growth and social development. Appropriate methods for evaluating socially significant investment projects, along with financial estimates, require an assessment of the economic efficiency of investment projects, which are in line with the priorities of sustainable development. The paper proposes an integrated approach to the evaluation of socially significant investment projects using the case of the tourism industry, combining the private interests of the business with the public interests of expanding investment in projects with significant social effects. To do this, when comparing cash flows of financial and economic efficiency, flows associated with specific public effects, primarily social and tax ones, are identified. The proposed methods were tested for a real water park project in Russia. As a result of the calculations, a significant gap was revealed between relatively low financial efficiency along with high economic efficiency. The project was evaluated under various scenarios, including those with and without a pandemic. All calculation variants, taking into account the pandemic, show negative financial net present values for the project. However, even under the most pessimistic scenarios simulating the pandemic crisis, the level of economic efficiency remained positive, indicating greater opportunities for investment agents to adapt to adverse negative changes and the importance of social priorities in the context of sustainable development.

T. S. Novikova · O. I. Gulakova (✉)
Institute of Economics and Industrial Engineering, Siberian Branch of the Russian Academy of Sciences, 17 Ac. Lavrentyeva Pr, 630090 Novosibirsk, Russian Federation
e-mail: olgulakova@yandex.ru

T. S. Novikova · O. I. Gulakova · T. V. Afanasyeva
National Research University "Novosibirsk State University", 1 Pirogova Str, 630090 Novosibirsk, Russian Federation

V. Kumar et al. (eds.), *Consequences of Social Transformation for Economic Theory*, Springer Proceedings in Business and Economics,
https://doi.org/10.1007/978-3-031-27785-6_12

Keywords Social effects · Economic effects · Tourism investment projects · Cost–benefit analysis · COVID-19 pandemic

JEL Classification C67 · D62 · H43

1 Introduction

The world faced a pandemic and was forced to respond to new challenges. How to look for and find ways out of this situation? How to prioritize decision-making? How to ensure sustainable development in the end? The answers to these questions are based on the appropriate methods for evaluating socially significant projects and the adequate coordination of investment activities of agents at the microeconomic level in the implementation of investment projects. The pandemic crisis has significantly updated the need to rethink the priorities of economic decision-making and fundamentally change the emphasis in favor of the principles of sustainable development and, above all, social justice. Modern methods for evaluating even commercially viable tourism projects require consideration of their impact on long-term economic growth and social development. Therefore, it is important to identify and measure in monetary terms social effects, which are the difference between private indicators of financial efficiency and the resulting indicators for society as a whole, and then evaluate the economic efficiency of projects along with financial one.

In this article, the search for answers to modern challenges is considered on the example of evaluating investment projects in the field of tourism and analyzing the possibility of adapting such projects to the conditions of the pandemic crisis. This is due to the distinctive features of tourism, on the one hand associated with its significant social significance, and on the other hand, with its relatively high profitability. However, when evaluating such projects, it is important to analyze whether there is a margin of safety for the tourism business in the new unfavorable conditions. To substantiate such estimates, it is necessary to apply cost–benefit analysis methods, which retain their leading role as a tool for monetary assessment of the impact of social factors. It is carried out whenever possible as an integral part of the assessment of social effects in economic analysis in combination with financial analysis (Asian Development Bank, 2017; European Commission, 2021; Novikova, 2022; Novikova & Tsyplakov, 2021).

The rapid development of tourism is one of the most important long-term global trends and is ensured through the implementation of relevant investment projects that require the development of special methods of project analysis. The tourism industry affects the change in living standards in some regions. To increase the tourist flow, these regions receive an influx of funds that are used to develop infrastructure and increase jobs. All this has a positive effect on the socio-economic situation enhancing the quality of life in the region. However, the steady progress of tourism was suddenly and decisively interrupted by the onset of the pandemic crisis. Consider in more detail the impact of COVID-19 on the tourism market. In 2020, the whole world is faced with infections caused by the coronavirus infection (Bruhn et al., 2021; Dasgupta &

Wheeler, 2020). The example of tourism activity shows especially clearly how the first outbreak was recorded in December 2019 in the Chinese city of Wuhan. As early as January 30, 2020, the World Health Organization declared that this outbreak is a public health emergency of international concern. On March 11, 2020, the World Organization declared the COVID-19 pandemic. The COVID-19 pandemic has had a severe negative impact on the economy and especially on employment around the world (Economics, 2021).

To combat the coronavirus infection, the policies implemented have resulted in the closure of international borders and jeopardized an overly national approach to crisis management that hinders global cooperation (Fang et al., 2022). The rise of isolationist politics and rapid reflex reactions have hampered cooperation and coordination both in initial efforts to repatriate citizens of other countries and in the wider opening of borders to support international mobility (World Travel & Tourism Council, 2021).

Undoubtedly, the closure of borders has practically paralyzed international tourism. As the situation improved, the governments of various countries were looking for a way to return the normal functioning of the tourism business, but without aggravating the epidemiological situation (World Bank Group, 2020). For example, in the European Union in 2020, countries sought to reopen for the summer tourism period to take advantage of the historically lucrative season. To avoid the spread of the disease, various entry requirements have been introduced in these countries. For example, testing was carried out and quarantine was introduced for arrivals. However, testing and quarantine requirements differed from country to country, and these measures were often applied arbitrarily and without much notice. Many tourists were not ready to overcome these difficulties. Some tourists have chosen to refrain from tourist travel during the pandemic, so the decline has occurred across the board. According to a study by Sheresheva, international tourism among citizens of the Russian Federation decreased by 2.7 times, while trips within Russia decreased by only 1.4 times (Sheresheva, 2020). An analysis of the tourist flows of international and domestic tourism allows us to conclude that among Russian tourists, domestic tourism has suffered to a lesser extent than international tourism. This can be explained by the fact that the closure of the borders led to the reorientation of Russian tourists to the domestic market, thereby reducing losses from the reduction in the tourist flow in general.

The purpose of the proposed work is an attempt to apply an integrated approach to the evaluation of socially significant projects, combining the private interests of the business with the public interests of expanding investment in projects with significant social effects.

2 Literature Review

The theoretical foundations of the methods of economic analysis of socially significant investment projects were originally developed at the beginning of the twentieth century as part of the Cost Benefit Analysis (CBA) for evaluating public sector projects in developed countries (Boardman et al., 2018). Since the middle of the twentieth century, similar approaches have been used by international financial organizations (the World Bank, the Asian Development Bank, the European Investment Bank) to evaluate projects not only in the public sector, but also in the private sector. The term economic analysis began to be used to designate them. The justification for promoting the economic growth of developing countries, and then countries with economies in transition, required a significant improvement in traditional methods. Economic analysis as a separate area of investment project evaluation, supplementing financial analysis, has been formed in the context of solving development problems (OECD, 2018; World Bank, 2017). It reached its peak in the early 1980s. Project evaluation methods were modified again in the 1990s to adapt to market transition conditions in Russia and other former socialist countries. At the same time, the combination of two types of analysis began to be denoted by the concepts of commercial and public efficiency (Novikova, 2022).

In the twenty-first century, at a new stage of scientific and technological development, corresponding to the realities of the fourth industrial revolution, attention to the economic evaluation of projects has increased again and has led to the development of new methods (Bonner, 2022; Sunstein, 2018). At the turn of the millennium, the priorities of sustainable development have changed significantly, which predetermined the transformation of methodological approaches to justifying investments in socially significant projects, which include tourism development projects. There was a transition from the assessment of development results in purely economic indicators (primarily GDP) to a multidimensional system of indicators (Stiglitz et al., 2015) consistent with the goals of sustainable development and the goals of the new millennium (WECOOP, 2021).

In the new system for evaluating investment projects, social and environmental indicators have come to the fore. In particular, the names of the main documents and the adopted project evaluation standards began to include the indicated pair of terms (World Bank, 2017). The priorities and methods of evaluating projects have changed accordingly. One of the latest project analysis techniques, the Investor's Guide to Help Professionals Prepare Environment, Climate Change and Water Investment Projects in Central Asia [The project investors are the nine largest international financial institutions united within the framework of the European Union—Central Asia: Cooperation in the field of water resources, environment and climate change (WECOOP)], emphasizes that funding is only allocated to projects that contribute to sustainable development. To determine such a beneficial impact, all projects require a social impact assessment (impact assessment) as part of an appropriate social analysis, supplemented by the measurement of social effects in monetary terms as part of the economic aspect of the analysis. Even under the Paris Agreement, which initially (following the Kyoto Agreement) focused on emissions of harmful substances, the focus is now shifting to adaptation to climate change and funding projects that ensure such adaptation (Porfiriev, 2019).

The new priorities do not mean abandoning the development of projects on the main aspects and, above all, economic (or cost–benefit analysis) and financial (or capital budgeting). In the Investor Guide 2021 (WECOOP, 2021) mentioned above, when answering the question of what makes a successful project proposal and a promising project, one of the six main arguments is "description of *financial* and *economic* factors" (highlighted by the authors) (WECOOP, 2021, p. 52). In another part of the document, which is devoted to the presentation of the approach of the World Bank, it is noted "an independent analysis of the project … on technical, institutional, *economic and financial* issues" (highlighted by the authors) (WECOOP, 2021, p. 24).

The methods for conducting financial and especially economic analysis are noticeably more complicated, and not only due to the addition of impact assessment of social and other public effects. As noted in the updated 2021 EU Guidelines on cost–benefit analysis, "Economic analysis in the initial stages (corresponding to the 2008–2014 editions of the EU Guidelines) can be considered as simplified, based on rough indicative estimates of benefits and costs" (European Commission, 2021, p. 20). The depth and complexity of economic analysis is significantly increased compared to the corresponding traditional methods.

Tourism has traditionally been singled out in all international methodologies as one of the sectors for which methods of economic analysis should be applied (World Bank, 2017; European Commission, 2021). However, in practice, financial analysis methods were mainly used (with the exception of regional tourism projects with a significant environmental impact). This was due to the high financial return of the respective investments. All over the world, private investment in the tourism business usually provides a fairly high return (Strapko, 2021). Nevertheless, this industry belongs to the areas of activity supported by international financial organizations on a preferential basis (WECOOP, 2021, p. 24). States in all countries of the world provide tourism with state support and consider the development of tourism activities as the most important strategic direction. For example, the Tourism Development Strategy sets out the task of increasing investment in tourism by 3 times by 2035. This is due to the most important modern trends towards reorientation in the direction of social development and stimulating the outstripping growth of industries associated with the formation and expansion of investment in human capital.

Social effects include the consequences of an increase in people's well-being as a result of participation in tourism programs, an increase in human capital, primarily an improvement in people's health, broadening their horizons and creative abilities, as a result of an increase in labor productivity (Avdeeva et al., 2021). This important result of the implementation of projects in the field of tourism is the increase in human capital by improving people's health, which is confirmed by the results of recent empirical studies (Lysikova & Kerimi, 2021; Masters et al., 2017; Marshall et al., 2018).

Corresponding features of investment projects in the field of tourism predetermine the need for the use of special methods of economic analysis in general and calculation of social effects in particular (Pleshakova et al., 2020; Yang et al., 2019). One of the most famous operational methods for such calculations was the technique set out in the European manual (European Commission, 2021). It uses the multiplication of private benefits by conversion factors. This approach is also applied to social effects. In the twentieth century, methods for calculating social benefits in monetary terms were improved and widely used in practice (JSC "CORPORATION TOURISM.RF", 2021; UNWTO, 2020).

3 Proposed Methods for Evaluating Investment Projects for Tourism Development

The identified trends in the transformation of methods and techniques for evaluating tourism projects indicate the need to develop economic and mathematical tools that allow in monetary terms measuring the consequences of their implementation at various levels in accordance with ethical imperatives.

The proposed methods for assessing social effects are based on the financial and economic model of the microeconomic level with the definition of cash flows and related project performance indicators within the framework of financial and economic analysis and with a detailed presentation of social effects (Novikova, 2022; Suslov et al., 2021)

The central place in the financial and economic model of the project model is occupied by two groups of project cash flows used to calculate its efficiency in the financial and economic blocks. The first group is determined to assess the financial efficiency of the project based on benefits and costs, easily observable in the process of budgetary and market interaction of participants. They are calculated by traditional methods and during the investment period include capital costs and investments in the growth of working capital, during the operational period proceeds from the proceeds minus operating expenses and taxes, and during the liquidation period (the period of conditional closing of the project) the value of the terminal (liquidation) value. The second group of cash flows is used in the economic block of the model to assess economic efficiency and is determined by adding to the cash flows of the first group of specific cash flows associated with social benefits and costs, which are difficult to observe as a result of the project and even more so to measure in monetary terms. For tourism projects, such specific cash flows arise in the case of positive social effects. They also include tax effects (occurring in all projects) and other specific public effects: environmental, price, indirect and other specific social effects (significant to varying degrees for different projects). The final total cash flows, on the basis of which the project performance indicators are calculated in the economic block of the model, are presented in the ratio (1). To obtain discounted indicators on their basis, a special social discount rate is applied.

The leading role in the considered model complex is played by the calculation of the cash flows of the project and the corresponding net present value (NPV^E) as the difference between discounted benefits and costs in the relevant time periods, determined in the framework of financial and economic analysis and serving as the basis for determining the social and other pubic effects of the project.

$$NPV^E = \sum_{t=0}^{T} \frac{(B_t - C_t) + \sum_{f=1}^{F}\left(\Delta B_t^f - \Delta C_t^f\right)}{(1 + r - \Delta r)^t}$$
$$= \sum_{t=0}^{T} \frac{(B_t - C_t) + \left(\Delta B_t^{soc} - \Delta C_t^{soc}\right) + \left(\Delta B_t^{oth} - \Delta C_t^{oth}\right)}{(1 + r - \Delta r)^t}, \quad (1)$$

where $(B_t - C_t)$ is benefits and costs in period t in the framework of financial analysis; $\left(\Delta B_t^f - \Delta C_t^f\right)$ is public effects as a result of adjustment within the economic analysis for each factor (f), including social (soc) and other (oth) factors and related effects (tax, environmental, price and indirect); $(r - \Delta r)$ is the social discount rate taking into account its difference from the financial discount rate (r).

In this paper, a combination of the conversion rate method and the fiscal multiplier method is used to assess social effects. At the same time, the value of operating expenses, excluding depreciation and VAT, is multiplied by a given multiplier at each point in time.

To assess the impact of medical expenses on economic growth, the method of budgetary social multipliers is used quite widely, especially recently (Stuckler et al., 2017; Vlasov & Deryugina, 2018; Mitsek & Mitsek, 2020). It calculates the change in the resulting economic indicators (for example, regional value added) per 1 RUR of the increase in expenditures of various sectors and for the economy as a whole, while the resulting values differ markedly. Estimates of fiscal multipliers in the United States range from 0 to 2, including taking into account differences between states, the most well-known level is 1.5 (Auerbach et al., 2020; Kudrin & Sokolov, 2017). According to the calculations of the International Monetary Fund, the overall fiscal multiplier in Europe was 1.7, and in the sectors of health, education and social protection it was estimated at a significantly higher level to 3.0. Available estimates for Asian countries range from 0.73 to 0.88 (Reeves et al., 2013). For Russia, the spread of results is even more significant (Zyablitsky, 2020). According to the Center for Strategic Studies, the Russian budget multiplier for health care is 1.25, which corresponds to a total value for total government spending of 0.91 (Kudrin & Sokolov, 2017). To assess social effects, the impact of human capital growth on labor productivity is used, at a 31% level according to a study by the Higher School of Economics (Avdeeva et al, 2021). Among the important consequences of socially oriented projects, incl. tourism, refers to the positive impact of improving the mood of people on the return of human capital. Sean Achor, in his study, noted the impact of reducing stress symptoms on a 23% increase in output (Achor, 2013).

4 Results of Testing the Proposed Methods Using the Case of the "RusTropic" Investment Project

The investment project "RusTropic" is a project of a park-hotel with a water park in the style of the Asian tropics. The initial data for the experimental calculations were based on the project application in the database of investment projects and the presentation of a preliminary feasibility study, author's data on the values of the financial coefficients of the model (Suslov et al., 2021); Novikova, 2022) and open information on the development of the pandemic crisis (Economics, 2021; Norheim et al., 2021). The facility includes a hotel building, a water park with areas of entertainment, water attractions, health and relaxation, as well as a man-made tropical natural area. This project is focused on providing tourist and entertainment services throughout the year. It is planned to implement this project in the Moscow region or in cities with a population of more than 1 million people on a site of at least 10 hectares. As the analysis of the tourism market showed, this region remained in demand even during the pandemic.

The implementation of the project under consideration corresponds to the general trends in the development of tourism in Russia and the world as a whole. A study by the World Travel and Tourism Council showed that in 2017 the tourism market was the fastest growing industry worldwide. It has overtaken industrial production, agriculture and forestry, fishing, retail and wholesale trade, and financial services. There is a steady positive trend in the world towards the expansion of the influence of tourism on economic growth. The authors estimate that the total contribution of travel and tourism to global GDP could grow by 1% by 2030 compared to 2019. If this forecast comes true, the number of jobs will increase by 95 million worldwide (World Travel & Tourism Council, 2020).

Tourism can be attributed to one of the main components of the income of some open economies. So in some states, tourism accounts for from a fifth to a half of the gross national product (Alyakina & Shpilina, 2019).

The contribution of tourism to the GDP of the Russian Federation is 5%. The country's economy is not heavily dependent on tourism, but nevertheless there is a contribution. Tourism also provides 5.6% of total employment in the Russian Federation (Zajcev & Tixonov, 2020). The main resort areas of the country are the Krasnodar Territory, Altai Territory, the Republic of Crimea. Thus, tourism in the Russian Federation is poorly developed, however, long-term trends and prospects for its development are quite favorable.

To assess the project under consideration, a separate area for assessing socially significant projects during the pandemic crisis was used. Tourism projects have become one of the most vulnerable during this period. The decrease in the tourist flow and the introduction of epidemiological restrictions had a negative effect on the activities of tour operators. Tour operators specializing in international outbound tourism have suffered the most. So, for example, their number in the Unified Federal Register of the Russian Federation decreased by about 1.3 times in 2020 compared to 2019. In total, 315 tour operators ceased their activities on the Russian market during pandemic period (Ovcharov & Malkina, 2021).

The structure of tour operators focusing on domestic tourism is dominated by small and medium-sized businesses that have suffered less losses thanks to state support programs. As noted above, the government introduced various support measures for the tourism business. From July 1, 2021, various benefits and subsidies were introduced to support tour operators specializing in domestic and inbound tourism. These support measures helped reduce the negative impact of the pandemic on the tourism industry. The cost of the service package will include: accommodation, meals, relaxation and health services, sports and entertainment events and other variants that are similar and imitate the rest of a tropical resort. The capacity of the complex is 200 people at a time.

To take into account unfavorable changes in experimental calculations, a scenario approach was used. In this investment project, three stages of its implementation can be distinguished. The first stage consists in the selection of a land plot, the development of an architectural and artistic concept with the preparation of the main structural units and types of buildings and structures, the preparation of algorithms for the synchronous activity of all implementers of the project for the construction and operation of the facility. This stage takes 6 months. During the second stage, a land plot is acquired, engineering surveys are carried out, a building permit is obtained and directly access to the site. 12 months are allotted for the implementation of the second stage. The longest stage in time is the third. Its implementation takes from 24 to 36 months. During this period, the construction of buildings, structures, the installation of internal and external networks and communications, the implementation of various works on the improvement of the territory, as well as the implementation of all measures for the fire and anti-terrorist safety of the facility, the registration of the facility with all supervisory authorities and the direct commissioning of the facility.

The evaluation of the efficiency of the "RusTropic" investment project was carried out on the basis of multivariate calculations according to the financial and economic model of the project under various scenarios. The projected cash flows were built for the project implementation in the period of 2017–2036, including with the allocation of a separate period of conditional liquidation of the project (for which the value of the terminal value was calculated). All indicators are calculated at constant 2017 prices. The main results of financial (commercial) efficiency are presented in Table 1. The discount rate was set at 17%, corresponding to the cost of capital of similar travel companies and used by the project developers.

The initial first variant corresponds to the prediction of creating a water park in favorable conditions without a coronavirus pandemic (see the first line of Table 1). The resulting return on investment is set at an acceptable but rather low level. When calculated without discounting, the project would seem to bring a significant net present value (NPV) in the amount of 2117.3 million RUR. However, when discounted, it drops to almost zero, amounting to only 82.1 million RUR. The corresponding level of internal rate of return (IRR) is also at a level close to the discount rate and is 18.3%.

Table 1 Key indicators of the financial efficiency of the "RusTropic" project

Variant	NPV ($r = 0\%$, million RUB)	NPV ($r = 17\%$, million RUB)	IRR, (%)
First variant (initial)	2,252.0	20.2	17.5
Second variant (basic with pandemic)	1,001.2	−572.8	6.3
Third variant (with 30% of the basic with pandemic)	293.9	−858.1	1.7
Fourth variant (pessimistic with pandemic)	176.8	−758.9	1.2
Fifth variant (capital grant under the conditions of the Second variant)	2,576.2	229.0	23.4
Sixth variant (capital grant under the conditions of the Third variant)	1,868.9	−56.2	36.2
Seventh variant (capital grant under the conditions of the Fourth variant)	1,751.8	43.0	18.5%

Source authors' calculations. Investment project Park-hotel with water park "RusTropic". https://rusinvestproject.ru/projects/ishhu-soinvestora-kredit-dlya-realizacii-proekta-park-otel-s-akvaparkom-rustropik/

If we turn to the analysis of economic (public) efficiency, we get completely different results of evaluating the implementation of the project in the considered first scenario. And this mainly depends on the significant social health effects of tourism activities. In the base case for calculating social effects, a conversion factor at the test case level for services in the European Community methodology was used, equal to 1.2. This coefficient was multiplied by indicators of benefits in the cash flow of the project to calculate the financial efficiency, in our case, revenues without VAT. As a result, the efficiency of the project increases dramatically (see the first line of Table 2).

Table 2 The main indicators of the economic efficiency of the "RusTropic" project in the basic version of the calculation of social effects

Variant	NPV ($r = 0\%$, million RUR)	NPV ($r = 17\%$, million RUR)	IRR, (%)
First variant	6,329.9	1,431.8	53.5
Second and fifth variant	4,271.6	466.3	25.3
Third and sixth variant	3,584.4	182.1	20.1
Fourth and seventh variant	3,058.3	218.6	22.0

Source authors' calculations

When calculated without discounting, the implementation of the project provides a net present value (NPV) in the amount of 6,329.9 million RUR in the conditions without a pandemic, which is noticeably higher compared to financial efficiency. It is noteworthy that when discounted, the economic NPV reaches a significant positive level of 1,431.8 million RUR. The corresponding IRR of 53.5% also indicates a significant margin of safety for the project in relation to adverse changes and significantly exceeds the discount rate.

When calculated using simple methods (without discounting), the share of social effects in the total economic NPV amounted to 25.8%, and tax effects—38.6%. As you can see, tax effects make a significant positive contribution to the increase in economic efficiency compared to financial efficiency, since they are added with a plus to the initial cash flow determined as part of the financial efficiency analysis. However, this is done to level redistribution processes, and as a result, the contribution of taxes as part of econoimic efficiency indicators becomes zero, since at the same time they are taken into account with a minus as part of costs when calculating cash flows to assess financial efficiency.

Now let's look at how the efficiency of the "RusTropic" project has changed during the pandemic. To this end, several scenarios for the development of events have been developed. In the second version of the model, revenue in 2020 becomes zero, and later gradually increases to the level without a pandemic over two years. This variant indicates serious losses for business during a pandemic. The discounted financial NPV of the project for the entire period of its implementation becomes negative and brings a net loss of 572.8 million RUR (despite the recovery in sales two years after the start of the crisis). However, although the economic NPV of the project is decreasing, it remains positive in the amount of 4,271.6 million RUR. without discounting and 466.3 million RUR with discounting (see the second line of Table 2). The third variant was considered as an intermediate one, in which revenue during the pandemic decreased by 30% compared to its volumes in the Second variant (see the third rows of Tables 1 and 2).

Fortunately for the project under consideration, the most difficult period of loss of revenue falls on the first years of the project, when the enterprise has not yet reached its design capacity. In the Fourth variant, the most pessimistic scenario was assessed, in which the project is being implemented in a different time schedule, and zero revenue falls on the first year of the expected design capacity with subsequent recovery in a year.

As a result, the financial NPV of the project indicates a significant increase in net losses to the level of −758.9 million RUR with discount. When calculated without discounting, it remains positive in the amount of 176.8 million RUR, but this level is insufficient for doing business. In particular, the IRR of 1.2% is well below the normal rate of return on investment with a corresponding level of 17% (discount rates). The economic NPV of the project remains positive at 3,058.3 million RUR without discounting and 218.6 million RUR with discount. From the point of view of society, the project remains effective even in the context of the pandemic crisis, despite the negative results of its evaluation in terms of financial efficiency.

In the Fifth, Sixth and Seventh variants, the consequences of providing state support to the project in a pandemic (based on variants 2–4) were assessed by providing a capital grant from the regional budget in the amount of 50% of the investment in fixed assets. As a result, significantly more favorable conditions are created for private investment in the project (see the financial NPV values in the corresponding rows of Table 1). The main thing is that there are significant social effects and opportunities are realized for improving the health of residents, improving their well-being and mood, as a result, conditions for increasing labor productivity are created. Since state support is redistributive in nature, the total indicators of economic efficiency and the corresponding NPV values completely coincide with those given in the corresponding lines 2–3 of Table 2.

Social effects were calculated using the transition coefficients of different levels, which led to a corresponding change in the indicators of the economic efficiency of the project. At the same time, the indicators of financial efficiency remained at the same level. Three levels of cash flow adjustment due to social effects were estimated in the main calculations: along with the baseline 20% level of the European Community methodology, the 23% level of the impact of reducing stress symptoms (close to the estimates of the Center for Strategic Studies) and the 31% level impact on labor productivity growth according to HSE research.

To assess the level of economic efficiency of the project in a pandemic, nine variants were calculated. The indicators of the discounted economic NPV, coinciding for the Second and Sixth variants (considered as the base ones), with a 23% level of social effects, amounted to 532.0 million RUR and increased by 13.9% compared to the corresponding indicators of the original variant, and by 13.9% for the Third and Seventh variants. For the Second and Sixth variants, with a 31% level of social effects, the economic NPV amounted to 703.5 million RUR and increased by 50.9% compared to the corresponding indicators of the original version. In all variants, taking into account the impact of the pandemic crisis, the level of economic efficiency remains at a high level and indicates the creation of stabilizing conditions for the development of the economy and the creation of the foundations for further successful social and economic development.

5 Conclusion

In the face of adverse changes during the period of COVID-19, tourism has become one of the most vulnerable industries, despite a long-term trend towards a stable growth.

Tourism development projects are characterized by a significant gap between the levels of financial and economic efficiency, mainly associated with a remarkable positive contribution of social effects. Theoretical and managerial implications of this paper are connected with an urgent need to conduct a comprehensive assessment of two types of efficiency at the same time, in order to take into account the interests of both the private tourism business and society as a whole.

The application of the proposed methods for the economic evaluation of investment projects with an appropriate system of indicators of economic (public) efficiency, complementing the methods for assessing the financial (commercial) efficiency, is in line with the priorities of sustainable development and has become more relevant in the context of the pandemic crisis.

The calculation results showed that in a pandemic, the financial efficiency of tourism projects is characterized by a negative net present value, and economic efficiency shows positive results in all the considered options, indicating the importance of social priorities in the context of sustainable development. The limitations of the considered experimental calculations are largely related to the initial stage of the project life cycle. In the future, it is planned to trace the actual implementation of the project and assess the extent to which the contribution of social factors ensured the degree of its success for business and society as a whole.

The proposed methods for assessing social effects are based on the allocation of these social effects as part of economic (public) efficiency; analysis and monitoring of the distribution of these effects among the participants, taking into account the creation of mechanisms that provide favorable institutional conditions for investing in investment projects characterized by positive environmental and high social effects.

Acknowledgements The article was prepared with the support of the Russian Foundation for Basic Research (project No. 20–010–00377).

References

Achor, Sh. (2013). *Before happiness: The 5 hidden keys to achieving success, spreading happiness, and sustaining positive change hardcover*. Random House.

Alyakina, E. A., & Shpilina, T. M. (2019). International tourism as a form of foreign economic activity. *Open Science, 1*(2), 90–96.

Asian Development Bank (2017). *Guidelines for the economic analysis of projects* (Vol. 170). Asian Development Bank. https://www.adb.org/sites/default/files/institutional-document/32256/economic-analysis-projects.pdf

Auerbach, A. J., Gorodnichenko, Y., & Murphy, D. (2020). Local fiscal multipliers and fiscal spillovers in the United States. *IMF Economic Review, 68*, 195–229. https://doi.org/10.1057/s41308-019-00102-3

Avdeeva, D. A., Akindinova, N. V., Voskoboynikov, I. B., Gimpelson, V. E., Denisenko, M. B., Simachev, Yu. V., Travkin, P. V., & Fedyunina, A. A. (2021). Labor productivity and human capital: paradoxes of interconnection? Report by April 22 *International scientific Conference on Problems of Development of Economy and Society*, Moscow, 13–30 April. 2021. National research University Higher School of Economics. HSE.

Boardman, A. E., Greenberg, D. H., & Vining, A. R. (2018). *Cost-benefit analysis*. Cambridge University Press.

Bonner, S. (2022). *Social cost benefit analysis and economic evaluation*. The University of Queensland. https://doi.org/10.14264/2c7588c

Bruhn, M., Demirguc-Kunt, A., & Singer, D. (2021) *Competition and firm recovery post-COVID-19*. Policy Research Working Paper 9851, World Bank. https://openknowledge.worldbank.org/handle/10986/36604

Economics and economic policy in a pandemic. (2021). In Kudrin A. & L. Moscow (Ed.) Gaidar Institute Publishing House, 344. https://www.iep.ru/files/text/Gaidar_IEP_monographs/Ec_virus-text.pdf

European Commission. (2021). *Economic appraisal: Vademecum 2021–2027. General principles and sector applications.* EC, 98. https://ec.europa.eu/regional_policy/sources/docgener/guides/vademecum_2127/vademecum_2127_en.pdf

Dasgupta, S, & Wheeler, D. (2020). *Modeling and predicting the spread of Covid-19: Comparative results for the United States, the Philippines, and South Africa.* Policy Research Working Paper 9419, World Bank. https://openknowledge.worldbank.org/handle/10986/34590

Fang, S., Goh, C., Li, S., & Xu, L. C. (2022). *Private sector development firm resources, strategies, and survival and growth during COVID-19: Evidence from two-wave global surveys.* Policy Research Working Paper 9997. World Bank. https://openknowledge.worldbank.org/handle/10986/37294

Suslov, V.I., Novikova, T.S., Gulakova, O.I. (2021). Price effects in the evaluation of investment projects. *Economy of regions, 17*(1), 16–30. https://doi.org/10.17059/ekon.reg.2021-1-2

JSC "Corporation Tourism.RF". (2021). *Requirements for the design, composition and content of the business plan of the investment project.* https://kislovodsk-kurort.org/uploads/images/docum/ekonomika/3_2021/----.docx-1.pdf

Kudrin, A., & Sokolov, I. (2017). Budget maneuver and structural restructuring of the Russian economy. *Questions of Economics, 9*, 5–27.

Lysikova, O. V., & Kerimi, K. M. (2021). Regional tourism: From human potential to human capital and quality of life. *Bulletin of the Association of Universities of Tourism and Service, 15*(1), 23–32.

Marshall, L., Finch, D., Cairncross, L., & Bibby, J. (2018). The nation's health as an asset. The Health Foundation. https://www.health.org.uk/publications/the-nations-health-as-an-asset

Masters, R., Anwar, E., Collins, B., Cookson, R., & Capewell, S. (2017). Return on investment of public health interventions: A systematic review. *Journal of Epidemiology and Community Health, 71*(8), 827–834.

Mitsek, E. B., & Mitsek, S. A. (2020). Analysis of the factors of the dynamics of the main macroeconomic variables of the Russian Federation. *Management Issues, 1*(62), 47–62. https://doi.org/10.22394/2304-3369-2020-1-47-62

Norheim, O. F., Abi-Rached, J. M., & Bright, L. K. (2021). Difficult trade-offs in response to COVID-19: The case for open and inclusive decision making. *Nature Medicine, 27*(1), 10–13.

Novikova, T. S. (2022). Investments in research infrastructure on the project level: Problems, methods and mechanisms. *Evaluation and Program Planning, 91*, 102018.

Novikova, T. S., & Tsyplakov, A. A. (2021). Development of social policy based on agent-based and cross-sectoral approaches. *Journal of the New Economic Association, 4*(52), 12–36. https://doi.org/10.31737/2221-2264-2021-52-4-1

OECD. (2018). *Cost-benefit analysis and the environment: Further developments and policy use.* OECD Publishing. https://doi.org/10.1787/9789264085169-en

Ovcharov, A., & Malkina, M. (2021). The impact of economic instability on the development of the European tourism market. *Contemporary Europe, 2*(102), 75–88 https://doi.org/10.15211/soveurope220217588

Pleshakova, M. A., Khudik, A. A., & Khoreeva, N. K. (2020). Using econometric models for solving problems in the tourism industry. *Tourism Industry: Opportunities, Priorities, Problems and Prospects, 17*(2), 130–137.

Porfiriev, B. N. (2019). Economic dimension of the climate challenge to Russia's sustainable development. *Herald of the Russian Academy of Sciences, 89*(4), 400–407. https://doi.org/10.31857/S0869-5873894400-407

Reeves, A., Basu, S., McKee, M., Meissner, C., & Stuckler, D. (2013). Does investment in the health sector promote or inhibit economic growth? *Globalization and Health, 9*(43). https://globalizationandhealth.biomedcentral.com/articles/https://doi.org/10.1186/1744-8603-9-43

Sheresheva, M. (2020). Coronavirus and tourism. *Population and Economics, 4*(2), 72–76. https://doi.org/10.3897/popecon.4.e53574

Stiglitz, J. E., Fitoussi, J., & Durand, M. (2015). *Measuring what counts: The global movement for well-being*. The New Press.

Strapko, D. A. (2021). *Impact of the tourism industry on the economic country and the socio-cultural sphere. Per Aspera Ad Astra—through thorns to the stars. Collection of scientific articles of international scientific student hearings «Law. Economy. Control»*. Stavropol, pp. 258–261.

Stuckler, D., Reeves, A., & Mckee, M. (2017). Social and economic multipliers: What they are and why they are important for health policy in Europe. *Scandinavian Journal of Public Health, 45*(18), 17–21. https://doi.org/10.1177/1403494817707124

Sunstein, C. R. (2018). *The cost-benefit revolution*. MIT Press.

The World Bank. (2017). *Environmental and social framework*. International Bank for Reconstruction and Development. The World Bank. https://documents1.worldbank.org/curated/en/383011492423734099/pdf/The-World-Bank-Environmental-and-Social-Framework.pdf

UNWTO. (2020). *Recommendations on tourism and rural development. A guide to making tourism as an effective tool for rural development*. UNWTO. https://doi.org/10.18111/9789284422173

Vlasov, S. A., & Deryugina, E. B. (2018). Fiscal multipliers in Russia. *Journal of the New Economic Association, 2*(38), 104–119. https://doi.org/10.31737/2221-2264-2018-38-2-5

WECOOP. (2021). *Investor guide for preparation of investment projects in environment, climate change and water in Central Asia*. https://wecoop.eu/wp-content/uploads/2020/04/Investor-guide-EN_2021.pdf

World Bank Group. (2020). *Protecting people and economies: Integrated policy responses to COVID-19*. International Bank for Reconstruction and Development. The World Bank Washington. https://documents1.worldbank.org/curated/en/879461587402282989/pdf/Protecting-People-and-Economies-Integrated-Policy-Responses-to-COVID-19.pdf

World Travel & Tourism Council. (2020). *The importance of Travel & Tourism in 2019*. https://wttc.org/Portals/0/Documents/Reports/2020/EIR%202020%20Importance%20of%20Travel%20and%20Tourism%20Infographic.pdf?ver=2021-02-25-183030-667

World Travel & Tourism Council. (2021). *Lessons learnt during COVID-19*. https://wttc.org/Portals/0/Documents/Reports/2021/Lessons-Learnt-%20COVID-19.pdf?ver=2021-08-19-095731-037

Yang, Ch., Lukash, S., & Guo, Q. (2019). Econometric analysis on the relationship between agritourism development and economic growth—the case of central plains economic zone of China. *Agribusiness Economics and Management, 2*(151), 33–42. https://doi.org/10.33245/2310-9262-2019-151-2-33-42

Zajcev, A. A., & Tixonov, A. A. (2020). Review of the impact of the coronavirus pandemic on the tourism industry. *HSE Analytical Bulletin on the Economic and Social Consequences of the Coronavirus in Russia and in the World, 6*, 57–66.

Zyablitsky, I. E. (2020). Evaluation of fiscal multipliers in the Russian economy. *Higher School of Economics Economic Journal, 24*(2), 268–294. https://doi.org/10.17323/1813-8691-2020-24-2-268-294

Consumer Equilibrium Conditions in the Cardinal Versus Ordinal Approaches: Any Difference?

Khandakar Elahi and Jack Reardon

Abstract 'Utility' is the foundational concept in modern consumer theory. Currently, two consumer theories have entered into textbooks—cardinal and ordinal approaches—which describe the derivation of the law of market demand. The cardinal approach assumes that consumers can measure utility quantitatively in the theoretical sense. This assumption is conceptually incorrect because 'utility' is a psychological phenomenon. To rectify this theoretical weakness, Hicks developed the ordinal utility approach, which he claims does not require quantifying utility. This paper disputes Hicks' claim. The cardinal approach indicates consumer equilibrium by the equality among all marginal utilities to price ratios, while the same condition is suggested by the tangency between the budget line and the indifference curve in the ordinal approach. These two conditions are not, and cannot be, different because the slope of the indifference curve is the ratio of two marginal utilities, which are cardinal concepts.

Keywords Microeconomics · Consumer equilibrium · Cardinal approach · Ordinal approach

JEL Classification A1 · B1 · B2 · D1

This paper's debate is two and a half centuries old, entailing a large literature. A review of the literature might be productive, but we cannot do so at this time. Barnett (2003), Hands (2010), Moscati (2013), Read (2004) have analyzed this issue from different angles. This paper examined the issue from a new perspective, with any similarities in the few pieces of the literature surveyed and credited.

K. Elahi (✉)
Bangladesh Agricultural University, Mymensingh 2202, Bangladesh
e-mail: kelahi53@gmail.com

J. Reardon
University of Wisconsin-Eau Claire, 127 Roosevelt Avenue, Eau Claire, WI 54701, USA

V. Kumar et al. (eds.), *Consequences of Social Transformation for Economic Theory*, Springer Proceedings in Business and Economics,
https://doi.org/10.1007/978-3-031-27785-6_13

1 Introduction

Modern microeconomics theoretically explains how goods and services are produced, distributed, exchanged, and consumed in an economy founded mainly on the institution of private property. Prices of goods and services are assumed to be determined by the free interplay of the forces of demand and supply. The following graph, simple indeed, describes the gist of this model (Fig. 1).

In this model, the market demand curve, D, is downward sloping, meaning consumers ordinarily buy more quantities of a commodity when its price falls. Just the opposite happens in the case of supply; the profit-maximizing firms supply more when prices increase. We are here interested only in the demand side of the market.

The demand for a commodity, it's an ordinary experience of life, falls when its price increases and vice versa. As a social scientist, Marshall describes this common experience theoretically with help of the *utility* conception that Bentham (1781) used to reform the legal system of sentencing different kinds of criminals, and Jevons (1871) adapted it to fit into the discourse of political economy. Both Bentham and Jevons attached subjective value to the conception of utility. Marshall retained the term in his consumer theory but made it scientific by redefining it. The creation of value, this is how he defined utility, is free from subjective implications. Nevertheless, he retained the Benthamite and Jevonsian conception of cardinal utility.

In criminal laws, Bentham observed, the severity of publishment varies with the nature of the crime. The utility is the property of an object that gives pleasure to an individual or lessens her pain, meaning the concept is directly related to the prison period. A criminal found guilty gets maximum pleasure and no pain if he/she is freed from the charge. However, his/her pleasure declines and the pain increases when the prison period increases.

Jevons applied this idea to political economy, referring specifically to necessary commodities. For example, as a hungry person begins eating, she receives the highest level of pleasure or satisfaction from the initial doses which then decreases. Thus,

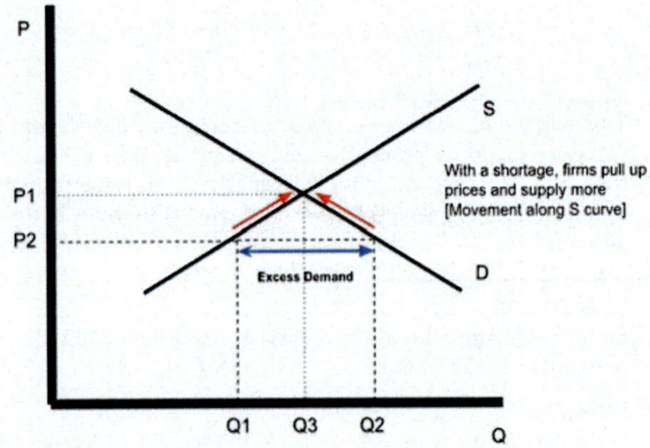

Fig. 1 Equilibrium in the X commodity market

he developed the concepts of total utility (TU) and marginal utility (MU) to articulate the law of diminishing marginal utility (LDMU). TU increases with additional procurement of the same commodity but at a decreasing rate, signifying that MU decreases continuously. The downward-sloping law of the individual demand (LoID) is the outcome of this LDMU.

The utility is a psychological phenomenon that cannot be measured scientifically—this is the general objection to this approach. Thus, an alternative technique that does not require measuring MU directly is preferable. Edgeworth (1881) and Pareto (1906) significantly developed this alternative approach. Edgeworth developed the indifference curve technique to resolve resource allocation problems in a two-dimensional closed economy model, i.e., the *Edgeworth box*. Pareto borrowed this technique to formulate an efficiency criterion that modern economists have accepted as a principle. Finally, Hicks (1939) brought Pareto's indifference curve analysis to the present level of popularity by developing the ordinal utility concept that, in his opinion, does not require quantification.

In both cases, a consumer reaches an equilibrium position in choosing a commodity bundle, which gives a maximum level of utility. However, the equilibrium conditions are different in the two approaches. For the cardinal approach, the equimarginal principle states that the ratio of marginal utility of a commodity and its price must be equal for all commodities included in the consumption basket. For the ordinal approach, the consumer equilibrium is given by the tangency between an indifference curve and the budget line that does not require measuring utility quantitatively.

It is generally believed that the consumer equilibrium conditions offered by the two approaches are different. This paper intends to prove that this common belief needs critical review. More specifically, they are identical both algebraically and economically.

The article is organized as follows: Sect. 2 summarizes the cardinal utility approach to describe the equimarginal principle. Section 3 does likewise for the ordinal utility approach to describe the consumer equilibrium articulated in terms of the tangency between the budget line and an indifference curve. The two conditions are then contrasted in Sect. 4, and Sect. 5 concludes the paper.

2 Marshall: Total Utility, Marginal Utility, and the Equimarginal Utility Principle

The cardinal approach, which Jevons developed and Marshall popularised, has now been archived. Modern textbooks concentrate on the ordinal approach to derive the needed market demand curve with some passages on the former (Case et al., 2012; Mankiw et al., 2019; Nicholson & Snyder, 2008; Perloff, 2018; Varian, 2010). Therefore, some details of this approach might help understand the difference between the two approaches.

Marshall organizes his treatise into six books, of which Book 3 is devoted to the theory of demand. However, we need to visit the Preface to the first edition and Chap. 1 to understand the meanings and messages of his text. First, he begins the Preface with the observation that each generation of economists examines economic issues in the light of their own political and social environment, which, at first sight, seems to contradict the old studies. However, these similarities between old and new theories and opinions become clearer after the due debate. Thus, he claims that the fundamental feature of his book is the *Principle of Continuity*, i.e., he explains and refines the old ideas in the light of the new social situation and scientific development.

The second point concerns his conception of the nature and scope of economic analysis. He defined *Political Economy* or *Economics* as a study of mankind in the ordinary business of life, which examines that part of individual and social action which is most closely connected with the attainment and with the use of the material requisites of wellbeing. Thus, it is on the one side a study of wealth; and on the other, economics, and more important side, a part of the study of man (Marshall, 1920).

These two points are critical to assessing Marshall's viewpoints about consumer behavior. Moreover, his reasonings might help us understand the meaning of Hicks' ordinal approach to be described in the following section.

Book 3, titled 'On Wants and Their Satisfaction,' is divided into six chapters. The topic of our interest is developed in Chap. 3, briefly summarized below. This chapter begins with the idea of a commodity market borrowed from the French economist Cournot (Robinson, 2017). A market consists of a region in which buyers and sellers 'are in such free intercourse with one another that the prices of the same goods tend to equality easily and quickly'. This tendency bears a positive relationship with the degree of market perfection. The other concept borrowed from Jevons is diminishing marginal utility. However, he freed *utility* from all moral implications by redefining it as changing form, time, or place to make the product more beneficial to the consumer.

With these premises, he assumes that the want of a single commodity is satiable, but not all want simultaneously. Given that the marginal utility of a commodity diminishes with increased consumption, the total utility must increase but at a diminishing rate. Thus, the relationship between TU and MU can be described with the following diagram.

In Fig. 2, the '0x' axis represents the total quantity of food consumed, while the '0y' axis represents utility derived from incremental amounts of food. TU increases at a decreasing rate, which means that MU decreases in the language of differential calculus. At a certain level of food intake, the MU curve touches 0x, meaning TU is maximum. Any additional increase in food intake will cause disutility as MU will be negative, meaning TU declines. Alternatively, we can say that the negative MU has contributed to the fall in TU.

This relationship between TU and MU makes the individual demand curve downward-sloping. Since the market demand curve is a horizontal aggregation of the individual demand curves, it must slope downward too. This demand theory is called cardinal because the consumer is assumed to know the amount of utility she obtains from the increased consumption in terms of utils, an imaginary unit.

Fig. 2 Relations between TU and MU

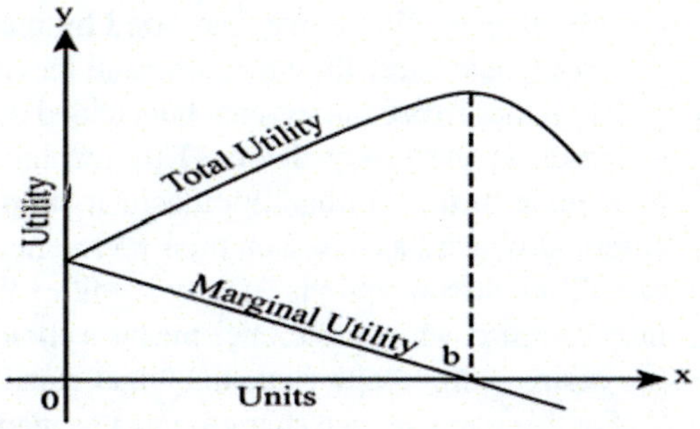

However, this theory does not describe the equilibrium of a consumption bundle consisting of all the commodities she wants for a specific time. This is because MU deals with one commodity. The rule that the consumer can use to attain equilibrium is called the equimarginal principle.

The fundamental condition of maximum satisfaction or utility is the equimarginal principle. It states that a consumer achieves maximum satisfaction or utility when the marginal utility-price ratio of each commodity is equal to the marginal utility of the last dollar spent on it.

The common marginal utility per dollar of all commodities in consumer equilibrium is called the marginal utility of income. It measures the additional utility that would be gained if the consumer could enjoy an extra dollar's worth of consumption (Samuelson & Nordhaus, 2010, p. 87).

Algebraically, this equilibrium condition may be written as:

$$\frac{MU_1}{P_1} = \frac{MU_2}{P_2} \cdots \frac{MU_n}{P_n} = MUI \tag{1}$$

where MU = marginal utility; P = price; and the numbers indicate commodities.

3 Hicks: Consumer Equilibrium in the Ordinal Approach

The cardinal approach suffers from two difficulties. First, utility is a psychological phenomenon, which means that no practical measurement unit, like a liter and kilogram, is available to determine its value. Second, the real objection against Marshall's theory is the last argument in the equimarginal formulae—marginal utility of income (MUI). When prices of critically essential commodities increase substantially, like food and healthcare, this assumption becomes untenable. It may mean nothing to a billionaire whether the food prices double or quadruple. However, this price change might cause dramatic readjustments in the family life of a low-income household. Pareto's efficiency criterion, which measures substitution effects due to a price change, will be overshadowed by income effects. His efficiency and equity theories would carry little meaning and message.

Both these difficulties can be tackled by introducing the indifference curve approach in the utility theory. This technique does not require counting utilities as is done in the cardinal approach; it simply requires the consumer to rank two commodity bundles based on their preference. Here utility and preference represent two different conceptions. Utility signifies the property of a commodity to satisfy human desire, while preference means a choice that the consumer must make among her desired commodities due to budget constraints.

For this purpose, two changes must be made in the cardinal utility approach. First, include a second commodity, which allows the consumer to rank different commodity bundles according to her preference instead of comparing the utilities provided by the two. Second, introduce the budget to obtain consumer equilibrium through tangency between the indifference curve and the budget line.

These changes introduce a mathematical feature in the consumer theory that was not present before. Marshall's model was not axiomatic because he did not impose any condition on consumer behavior other than assuming that MU must decline. However, Hicks' model is thoroughly axiomatic because it derives all its inferences by imposing three "consistency" assumptions on consumers' preference-making process: completeness, reflectivity, and transitivity.

Modern economists have accepted this transition as a legitimate way to derive the market demand curve of a commodity. However, we would deceive ourselves if we failed to note two features of the ordinal approach that distinguish it from the cardinal approach. First, in social sciences, we explain the consumer's behavior, e.g., why and how the consumer buys a certain quantity of a specific commodity. The consistency condition imposed by the indifference curve does not create any difficulty in the two-commodity case, but it does when the number of commodities increases (Appendix 1). Second, we study consumer behavior to find regularities in their buying activity so that we can use this general pattern for future analysis. However, when the consistency conditions are imposed, our study loses its social science characteristics and becomes a topic in formal sciences. We see long chains of mathematical reasoning in many books, including Arrow (1951), Arrow and Debreu (1954), and Samuelson (1947). These reasonings are possible because the variables under investigation are not actual; mathematical symbols have been used to represent them.

The reason for doing this is that we cannot do mathematical manipulations by using the name of an actual variable. For example, consider an indifference curve $U_0 = f(X, Y)$ where f' is positive. We can manipulate this function any way we can.

However, this may not be possible if we use actual commodity names instead of X and Y because the commodity characteristics will interrupt our faculty of understanding (Elahi, 2017) (Appendix 2).

Tangency between the budget line and the indifference curve

Hicks explains his ordinal approach to consumer equilibrium in Chap. 1, Sect. 3: Suppose that we have a consumer with a given money income, who is spending the

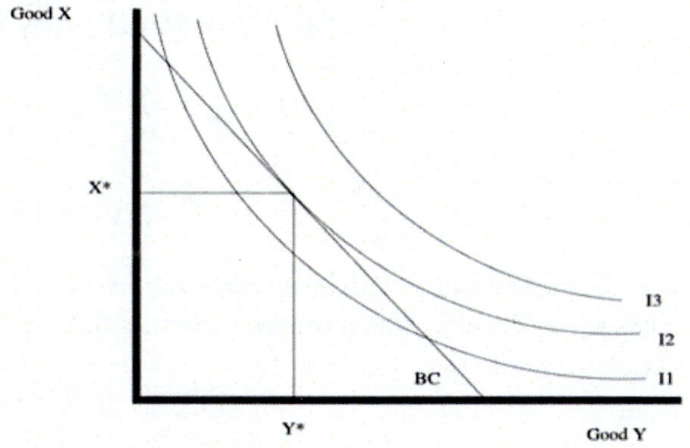

Fig. 3 Tangency between the budget line and the indifference curve. *Source* Wikipedia (n.d.)

whole of that income upon the two commodities X and Y, with no others entering into the picture. Suppose that the prices of those commodities are given on the market. Then we can read off the amounts that he will buy directly from his indifference map, without any information about the amounts of utility he derives from the goods (Hicks, 1939).

Modern texts use this statement in more standard forms to explain Hicks' theory geometrically and algebraically. Figure 3 shows that the indifference curve I2 is tangent to the budget line BC. Any indifference curve below I2 represents low utility, while any above is not affordable. Therefore, this tangency point must be the preferable commodity bundle for our consumer.

At this point, the condition of equilibrium is given by Eq. (2):

$$\frac{MU_1}{MU_2} = \frac{P_1}{P_2} \tag{2}$$

This same condition can be obtained through the Lagrangian multiplier approach (Nicholson & Snyder, 2008; Perloff, 2018). The decision problem is stated as follows:

$$\text{Maximize U} = \text{f (X, Y) subject to } P_X X + P_Y Y = M^0 \tag{3}$$

where X and Y are two commodities, P_X and P_Y are their prices, M^0 is the total budget available for a certain period, and U is the total utility derived from the consumption of a given bundle. There are two variables, X and Y, and two parameters in this function. When this function is set as a Lagrangian, we will have another variable λ, the marginal utility of income (MUI):

$$L = \text{Max U} = f(Y, X) + \lambda\left(M^0 - P_Y Y - P_X X\right). \tag{4}$$

Since this Lagrangian function contains three unknowns: Y, X and λ, we need to differentiate it with respect to each unknown to determine optimal value.

$$\delta L/\delta Y = \delta U/\delta Y - \lambda P_Y = 0 \tag{5}$$

$$\delta L/\delta X = \delta U/\delta X - \lambda P_X = 0 \tag{6}$$

$$\delta L/\delta \lambda = M^0 - P_Y Y - P_X X = 0 \tag{7}$$

These first-order derivatives give us the necessary conditions of the optimum values X, Y and λ, which can be written as follows:

$$\lambda = \frac{MU_Y}{P_Y} = \frac{MU_X}{P_X} \tag{8}$$

Equation (8) repeats the consumer equilibrium condition obtained in Eqs. (1) and (2), suggesting that the consumer equilibrium condition is the same in both approaches. In the cardinal approach, we set all marginal utilities divided by their prices equal to a common term, which Marshall called marginal utility of income (MUI). Samuelson rephrased it as the marginal utility of the last dollar spent on all commodities. We have λ in the ordinal approach. What is λ? Is it different from the marginal utility of income?

Few texts elaborate on the meaning λ, perhaps because it is difficult to give a different explanation from that of the cardinal approach. Let us examine the explanations offered by Nicholson and Snyder (2008), and Perloff (2018). First, consider Nicholson and Snyder (2008) for the n-commodity case, where we can rewrite (8) as

$$\lambda = \frac{U_1}{P_1} = \frac{U_2}{P_2} \dots \frac{U_n}{P_n} \tag{9}$$

Equation (9) says that each good purchased should yield the same marginal utility per dollar spent on that good at the utility-maximizing point, meaning the commodity should have an identical (marginal) benefit-to-(marginal)-cost ratio. This equation can also be expressed as

$$\frac{U_i}{U_j} = \frac{P_i}{P_j} \tag{10}$$

Here, the left-hand side is the absolute value of the marginal rate of substitution (MRS), while the right side is the absolute value of the marginal rate of transformation (MRT). In other words, the geometric and the calculus techniques give us the same condition of the consumer equilibrium: The indifference curve must be tangent to the budget constraint, signifying equality between the MRS and the MRT. Because of this relationship between the budget line and the utility function, the ordinalists argue that the MRT of the budget line may be used to represent MRS at that point, meaning we need not measure the MRS.

Finally, this equation can also be rewritten as:

$$P_i = U_i/\lambda, \quad \text{for } i = 1 \ldots n \tag{11}$$

Nicholson and Snyder interpret Eq. (11) by assuming that the consumer's marginal utility of income (λ) is constant over some range. In other words, $\Delta\lambda = 0$, meaning the price variation is directly proportional to the extra utility derived from that good.

At the margin, therefore, the price of a good reflects an individual's willingness to pay for one more unit. This is a result of considerable importance in applied welfare economics because the willingness to pay can be inferred from market reactions to prices (Nicholson & Snyder, 2008, p. 122).

Perloff (2018) manipulates the first-order derivatives differently as he does not pretend to interpret λ in the light of Hicks. Equation is copied below from his book:

$$\lambda = U_1/P_1 = U_2/P_2 \tag{12}$$

He explains the optimal value of λ as the consumer's extra pleasure from the last dollar of expenditure on each good. This value must be the same for all commodities, and this is precisely the same condition given by Eq. (1).

4 Consumer Equilibrium: Cardinal Versus Ordinal Approach

Let us now compare and contrast the nature of consumer equilibriums suggested by the two utility approaches. Is there any difference between the two equilibrium conditions?

Based on the preceding analysis, the answer is 'no.' First, in the two-commodity case, the consumer equilibrium contains four arguments: MU_X, MU_Y, P_Y, and P_X. The first two are choice variables, while the last two are parameters. We can rearrange them in different ways, which does not change the fact that they are cardinal concepts. The difficulty, therefore, remains with the justification of interpreting a cardinal concept in ordinal terms.

Second, Hicks' (1939) theory is that we are not required to measure MRS because each point on the budget line specifies the exact amounts of the two commodities contained in the bundle. In other words, we can use the MRT to represent the MRS. This argument is contestable because the MRS and the MRT represent two very different ideas concerning consumer choice. The commodity prices are fixed, suggesting that the consumer has no control over them. In other words, MRT is predetermined; it has no relation to the consumer's choice, which is assumed to be *voluntary*. Our consumer may be bound by the budget constraint to choose the commodity combination suggested by an MRT on the budget line.

For example, assume that our consumer is a heart patient who needs immediate bypass surgery, which she has to forgo if her budget does not permit it. On the other hand, MRS is a behavioral variable whose value is determined by the utility of the commodity in question. It will be ridiculous to think that our patient consumer will voluntarily give up a choice to save her life. In consumer choice, the budget is the binding constraint, which removes all the freedom from the consumer. On the contrary, the consumer can choose any commodity combination she likes based on her preferences. In other words, MRS represents a conjectural concept, meaning it may not be represented by a market variable (MRT).

Third, we also need to examine the meaning of Eq. (10). We might interpret it via the slopes of the two curves, but we cannot give them any economic sense. We can rearrange (10) as:

$$U_iP_j = U_jPi \tag{13}$$

Equation (11) has no economic meaning. Remember that marginal utilities come directly from the cardinal approach, which deals with one commodity, and derives the demand curve directly from the MU curve. Here, the demand curve is price-dependent. Marshall did not face the difficulty that Hicks encountered because the equimarginal utility principle does not involve the market variable MRT. This problem crops up in the indifference curve approach because Hicks draws his demand curve as price-dependent. To maintain this functional relationship in the context of the indifference curve approach, we need to reverse the right-hand side of Eq. (10), which gives us:

$$U_i/U_j = P_j/P_i \tag{14}$$

Equation (14) can now be rearranged as:

$$U_i \times P_i = U_j \times P_j \tag{15}$$

In Eq. (15), the left-hand side represents the value of the marginal utility of the commodity X_i, while the same value, indicated by the right-hand side, signifies X_j. Thus, the values of marginal utilities of the two commodities must be equal at the point of tangency. We will get the same equilibrium condition if the equation of the equimarginal principle is manipulated.

Thus, Eq. (15) makes perfect economic sense. However, the difficulty with this interpretation is that it invariably involves the interpersonal comparison of utility. The traditional conceptual value used in the n-commodity case is the marginal utility of income, a cardinal concept. We cannot be satisfied that the ordinalists have succeeded in vanishing interpersonal comparison of utility from the consumer theory.

5 Conclusion

It is a common belief in our profession that the conditions of consumer equilibrium suggested by the cardinal and ordinal approaches are different. This paper examined this the foundation of this belief and concluded that they are not, and cannot be different. This is because both conditions involve the ratio of marginal utilities of two goods, MU_1/MU_2. The two terms, MU_1 and MU_2 are conjectural variables, which cannot be represented by the slope of the budget line, MRT.

And, this is the principal theoretical finding of this paper, which has two far-reaching implications. First, our textbooks do not discuss this similarity, meaning their treatment of the cardinal and the ordinal approaches is incomplete. Second, In his book, Hicks justifies why he does not think it necessary to measure MRS, which is the ratio two cardinal quantities MU_1/MU_2. The literature in this paper does not discuss Hicks' explanations, which is an explicit weakness of the utility literature.

Appendix 1

Consistency Conditions Under n-Commodity Case

In the late eighteenth century, Marquis de Condorcet (1743–1794), a French philosopher and mathematician, introduced the voting paradox when the number of candidates exceeded two (Herings & Houba, 2016). Arrow (1950) applied this paradox in economics to explain the problems of social choice in a democratic society. In the case of consumer theory, we have only one consumer, meaning the issues Arrow dealt with do not apply to this inquiry. However, this does not suggest that the methodology of the indifference curve can be extended to the n-commodity case without any consistency issue.

It is conventional to extend the indifference curve analysis to an n-commodity model keeping all the axioms of the former intact. Mathematically, this practice may not raise any issue because mathematics deals with variables whose definitions are unique. However, economics is a social science, which studies human behavior related to the production, distribution, exchange, and consumption of wealth. Here, our consumers enjoy all the volitions to make their preferences under the condition of income constraints.

This situation does not seem much different from hundreds of other choices that we make in daily affairs. For example, as law-abiding citizens, we choose all courses of action based on the laws of the land. In the same way, our income constraints regulate our choices; this choice-making is a part of life that we inherit from our ancestors. The manifestations of the scarcity condition have changed during our rough journey to civilized life, but not its essence.

Thus, it is not the budget constraint that transforms economics into a formal science; rather, the axioms of the model. The axioms of the indifference curve are often generally accepted because most make sense. However, we may not retain the same confidence when extending our model to the n-commodity case. The following is an exploratory attempt to highlight this problem.

Let us consider the preference problem of our consumer who has to choose a combination of commodities belonging to three commodity groups: food and shelter, comfort goods, and healthcare. We can analyze this economic problem in two different ways: symbolically or using the actual names of the commodity groups.

First, let us do it symbolically, as is traditionally done in our textbooks. We can write the utility function of our consumer as:

$$U = f(X,\ Y,\ Z),\ \text{where } X = \text{food};\ Y = \text{comfort goods};\ \text{and } Z = \text{healthcare}$$

Because the bundle consists of three commodities, the indifference curve technique is no longer applicable. This problem should be solved by the Lagrangian method, and the solution will give us the equilibrium values of X, Y, Z, and λ.

So far, there have been no complications because all our attention is focused on following the rules of calculus. However, this is a problem in economics, not mathematics, meaning we need to explain the results we obtain in plain English. The difficulty starts when we try to do that.

Let us look at our model's completeness and transitivity conditions to see this difficulty. There are six mathematically possible ways to rearrange the objects of this function, i.e., we are supposed to get six preference orderings. However, because of the transitivity restriction, we will only have one preference ordering, which, let us suppose, is given by:

$$X\,\boldsymbol{P}\,Y\,\boldsymbol{P}\,Z$$

We do not ask why our consumers made this preference scale, and as long we keep these symbols, we need not ask this question. This is not a subjective statement because it is standard practice in modern microeconomics. However, if we want to translate these mathematical results into English, we need to use the actual names:

U = f(food and shelter, comfort goods and healthcare), and the preference scale is:

Food and shelter ***P*** comfort goods ***P*** healthcare

We can now explain this preference scale in English. Food and shelter are necessary for survival. Therefore, the consumer must satisfy this need before spending her budget on comfort commodities. Finally, the consumer is not sick, meaning she does not need any healthcare. Accordingly, any rational consumer would make this preference scale.

Appendix 2

Symbolic Logic in Social Sciences

Marshall, a mathematician, thought that mathematics could not be a language for deriving theories of economics, although it should be used as a short-hand method for clarity and conciseness. Accordingly, he discouraged its extensive use as a chain of illustration. However, Edgeworth, Menger, Walras, and Pareto, disagreed and developed economic models in terms of symbols and equations. Hicks and Allen solidified their works, and Samuelson, Arrow, and others converted economics into applied mathematics.

This is the trend we follow nowadays. However, the fundamental features of mathematics, a formal science, put certain limitations on its use and applicability in social sciences. Elahi (2017) explains them in the context of Arrow's impossibility theorem. The following paragraphs elaborate on the idea in the context of consumer theory.

Logic plays the role of grammar in literary compositions. It is a branch of philosophy that studies the methods of correct reasoning without judging whether the inference is favorable or unfavorable. On the other hand, symbolic logic is a branch of mathematics. It uses symbols to express logical ideas, allowing researchers to manipulate ideas mathematically in much the same way that numbers are manipulated (Symbolic Logic, 2022). Methods of logic are classified as inductive and deductive, distinguishing between logic and symbolic logic. Deductive logic is the primary method of drawing inferences in formal sciences, while inductive is used in the social sciences. In deductive logic, the truth value of the conclusion is conditional upon the realism of its primary premise, i.e., the conclusion is either true or false. On the other hand, all conclusions in inductive logic are probable; the intensity of this probability is determined by experience deductively inferred.

Accordingly, we deviate from the methods of social sciences when we use axioms to rationalize consumer behavior. For example, we cannot change the preference pattern used in Footnote 1 unless we change the health status of our consumer, i.e., making him a sick person.

References

Arrow, K. (1950). A difficulty in the concept of social welfare. *The Journal of Political Economy, 58*(4), 328–346.

Arrow, K. (1951). *Social choice and individual values.* Wiley.

Arrow, K., & Debreu, G. (1954). Existence of an equilibrium for a competitive economy. *Econometrica, 22*(3), 265–290.

Bentham, J. (1781). *An introduction to the principles of morals and legislation.* Retrieved January 21, 2021, from https://www.utilitarianism.com/jeremy-bentham/#one

Barnett, W. (2003). The modern theory of consumer behavior: Ordinal or cardinal? *The Quarterly Journal of Austrian Economics, 6*(41). https://doi.org/10.1007/s12113-003-1012-4

Case, K., Fair, R., & Oste, S. (2012). *Principles of economics* (10th ed.). Prentice-Hall.

Edgeworth, F. (1881). *Mathematical psychics: An essay on the application of mathematics to the moral sciences.* Retrieved May 5, 2022, from https://ia800206.us.archive.org/25/items/mathematicalpsy01goog/mathematicalpsy01goog.pdf

Elahi, K. (2017). A difficulty in Arrow's impossibility theorem. *International Journal of Social Economics, 44*(12), 1609–1621.

Hands, D. W. (2010). Economics, psychology and the history of consumer choice theory. *Cambridge Journal of Economics, 34*(4), 633–648. https://doi.org/10.1093/cje/bep045

Herings, P. J. J., & Houba, H. (2016). The condorcet paradox revisited. *Social Choice and Welfare, 47*, 141–186. https://doi.org/10.1007/s00355-016-0950-7

Hicks, J. R. (1939). *Value and capital: An inquiry into some fundamental principles of economic theory.* Retrieved May 10, 2022, from https://archive.org/stream/in.ernet.dli.2015.223876/2015.223876.Value-And_djvu.txt

Jevons, W. (1871). *The theory of political economy.* Retrieved April 08, 2022, from https://archive.org/stream/theoryofpolitica00jevouoft/theoryofpolitica00jevouoft_djvu.txt

Mankiw, N. G., Kneebone, R., & McKenzie, K. (2019). *Principles of microeconomics* (8th ed.). Cengage.

Marshall, A. (2013). [1920] *Principles of economics* (8th ed.). Palgrave classics in economics. Macmillan Publishers Limited. Retrieved Feb 21, 2022, from http://www.library.fa.ru/files/marshall-principles.pdf

Moscati, I. (2013). How cardinal utility entered economic analysis: 1909–1944. *The European Journal of the History of Economic Thought, 20*(6), 906–939. https://doi.org/10.1080/09672567.2013.825001

Nicholson, W., & Snyder, C. (2008). *Microeconomic theory: Basic principles and extensions* (10th ed.). Thomson South-Western.

Pareto, V. (1971). [1906] *Manual of political economy.* Augustus M. Kelley Publishing.

Perloff, J. (2018). *Microeconomics* (8th ed.). Pearson.

Read, D. (2004). *Utility theory from Jeremy Bentham to Daniel Kahneman.* Working Paper No: LSEOR 04-64. http://eprints.lse.ac.uk/22750/1/04064.pdf

Robinson, J. (2017). 'Market' *Encyclopedia Britannica.* Retrieved May 15, 2022, from https://www.britannica.com/topic/market

Samuelson, P. (1947). *Foundations of economic analysis.* Harvard University Press.

Samuelson, P., & Nordhaus, W. D. (2010). *Economics* (9th ed.). McGraw-Hill/Irwin. Retrieved Feb 27, 2021, from http://pombo.free.fr/samunord19.pdf

Symbolic Logic. (2022). *UXL Encyclopedia of science.* Encyclopedia.com. Retrieved May 22, 2022, from https://www.encyclopedia.com

Varian, H. (2010). *Intermediate microeconomics a modern approach* (8th ed.). W. W. Norton & Company.

The Role of Social Networks in Shaping up the Consumer Behavior of Young People

Ulviyya Rzayeva, Veronica M. Grebennikova, Oksana A. Us, and Alexander A. Malkov

Abstract This paper examines the role that social networks play in the creation and sustaining of the consumer behavior of young people. Nowadays, social networks such as Facebook, Twitter, or Instagram became an important part of the social and economic life and providing information and data for the decisions many people make in the market. The primary objective of the present research is to investigate the reasons why the young people purchase products recommended on social media platforms by social influencers and how social networks can shape up their decisions or alter them completely. Social factors have always played a role in consumers purchasing habits, but the widespread availability of smartphones and social media has taken word-of-mouth advertising to the completely new levels. Business companies are now realizing that sharing brands messages and consumers experiences is a new path to brand marketing because of widespread smartphone usage and internet, and because a majority of people now depend on brands via social media. Consumers do not need to rely on traditional media outlets for information on products prior to making their purchases anymore, as social media outlets are effective and easy for accessing that information. In addition, social networks are now widely used by the governments for spreading the information to the wider audience as a part of the political marketing campaigns or for communicating political decisions to the masses. We argue that social networks represent an enormous potential in manipulating the consumer behavior and that their relevance is especially important in the case of young people.

U. Rzayeva (✉)
Faculty of Digital Economy, Azerbaijan State University of Economics, 6 Istiglaliyyat Str., AZ1001 Baku, Azerbaijan
e-mail: ulviyya.rzayeva@unec.edu.az

V. M. Grebennikova · O. A. Us · A. A. Malkov
Kuban State University, 149 Stavropolskaya Str., 350040 Krasnodar, Russian Federation
e-mail: oxi79@yandex.ru

A. A. Malkov
e-mail: goal444@malkov-aleksandr.ru

V. Kumar et al. (eds.), *Consequences of Social Transformation for Economic Theory*, Springer Proceedings in Business and Economics,
https://doi.org/10.1007/978-3-031-27785-6_14

Keywords Social networks · Consumer behavior · Economic theory · Youth

JEL Classification C8 · D11 · M20 · M31

1 Introduction

Social networking sites (SNSs) represent online networks or communities where users can meet and interact with each other by creating and sharing their profiles, as well as uploading of photos and statuses (Horng & Wu, 2020; Starr et al., 2020). Researchers define SNSs as services based on the Internet that help users to build their profiles which are either locked or open to the public inside the predefined system, chose with users they can interact with or share their information as well as set how the information about them should be visible online and accessible for other users (Aichner et al., 2021). Social networking bases core interactions on a user's profile, a personal homepage providing the ability to personalize one's page with self-directed information, images, quotes, and widgets that contribute to the construction of one's online identity. Those people who are in advance of social network sites tend to say that online information sharing is fast and efficient and that it helps people to quickly interact ideas and views with each other, as well as to enhance family and friends networks and sharing of information that can help to enhance human interaction and communication (Kumar et al., 2019; VanMeter et al., 2018).

Social networks are considered to be the most important channel for communicating brands messages because of its interactive characteristics, which allow for knowledge exchange, collaboration, and participative activities, which are accessible to larger communities compared with media formats like radio, television, and print) (Strielkowski et al., 2022). Social media allows consumers to interact with businesses and interact in many ways, from liking posts and following their accounts, sharing content related to the brand, yelling brand love, or asking product questions (Ali et al., 2022; Huerta-Álvarez et al., 2020). Nowadays, social is often the preferred option for consumers to share reviews or contact with customer service issues or questions (Abrhám & Wang, 2017). With the social distance and increased telecommuting, consumers are largely reliant on social channels to talk, interact, and conduct transactions (Toleikienė et al., 2020). Marketers are making social spaces more transparent, sharing reviews, comments, likes, tweets, and pins from their satisfied customers in order to build trust in their brands and improve conversion rates. As customers, people are sharing product reviews, service insights, nutrition or health tips, product alerts, tips for using specific products, and much more which is often used by the modern consumers, even though the widespread use of SNNs is particularly liked and appreciated by the Millennials (people born in the 1980s and 1990s).

If a business company is not having its brands presence in the social media, then it is surely missing an important opportunity to influence its consumers purchasing behaviors. Brands need to make sure their target audiences are seeing company's products, liking and sharing them on social media, all of which helps to influence consumers behaviors (Al-Zyoud, 2018). Social marketers looking to sell their products need to have strong social proof, in the form of case studies, images, videos, podcast interviews, and influencers, as part of their sales strategy. Influence can be so strong that a large share of consumers is more likely to buy the same day they use social media. Social media marketing communication is now being used by all sorts of corporations and firm with some of them lacking the understanding about the true impact that these digital ICT channels exert on the young consumers attitude responses, or if and which use and demographic variables are having favorable effects on their attitudes (Creevey et al., 2022; Koudelková & Svobodová, 2014; Yessenbekova, 2020). Companies and their brands need to evaluate their usage and/or adapt strategies in light of social media marketing communications diminishing impact on young consumers hierarchy-attitude stages and varying impact on usage and demographic variables in targeting profitable consumers (Kashintseva et al., 2018; Litau, 2018). A plethora of papers in the fields of economics, sociology, or computer sciences confirmed that social networks are beneficial for helping to form the positive attitudes among young consumers, but at a declining scale, consistent with a purchasing funnel model (Schaefers et al., 2021). They also examine the impact of several complementary factors, such as access and usage as well as the demographic variables influencing the social media marketing communications for the consumers (Joshi et al., 2019).

As a comparison of the various forms of the social media and its impacts on the social interactions and ties, businesses publicize products via social media platforms like Instagram, Twitter, YouTube, or Facebook, with brands acting to manage and enhance their reputation on the internet through the creation of partnerships with social personalities. Most companies tend to benefit from the online marketing strategies, in order to create brand recognition with consumers (Argyris et al., 2020). Integrated marketing activities can be done at lower costs and efforts due to the important role of the social media in facilitating interactions, collaborations, and the exchange of important information (Tafesse & Wien, 2018). Social commerce makes it infinitely easier for brands to provide a seamless shopping experience that buyers desire, all in one place. Networks are now experiencing and formalizing the power of commerce, both bringing convenience to consumers and providing brands with a new source of revenue (Weber & Chatzopoulos, 2019). Operators are in a position to learn about consumer behaviors while maintaining social interactions with customers. Social proof has emerged from people's tendency to emulate behavior from those around them, or from those with influence over them. As concrete objectives, this is intended to examine the concepts, evolution, and operations of social media advertising; to observe and analyze management patterns and strategies chosen by the cellular telephone companies on social media (Sima et al., 2020). Furthermore, it is set to compare different behaviors of each of the analyzed companies in the various social media; to attempt to detect similarities or differences in communications among analyzed brands; to gain insights that can inform decisions made about the social media strategies of other companies; and to analyze the effect of social media on the mobile telephone companies. Social media can even be used in armed conflicts and in political campaigns, as well as for political purposes (Besenyő & Sinkó, 2021).

Thence, main focus of this paper is to assess the role of the social media marketing and its impacts on the consumer behavior. Moreover, this paper would attempt to study and to scrutinize the relationships between different social media marketing activities, client activities, as well as consumer behaviors.

2 Social Networks and Customer Behavior

Social media allows a lot of information to be shared about a business or a product. Before making a purchase, a consumer may go to a social media site and find out what others are saying about your product, as well as how well customer service is handled (Dabija et al., 2018). Analyzing consumer behaviors is the main task of selling products and services, as the majority of consumers are using online tools and online social networks. It is difficult to tell precisely how much customers are affected by social media, not only by the things they purchase, but also by their general consumption habits (Agnihotri et al., 2022). Logically, a lot of consumers purchasing decisions are also made on the internet, where people spend the majority of their online time: social media. Social media is an enormous influence for consumers as they try to raise awareness for a specific product. Therefore, many marketing specialists tend to forget that social networks constitute a powerful weapon in the marketing agenda through influencing consumers purchasing decisions (Cooley & Parks-Yancy, 2019). Brands need to make sure the target audience is seeing your products, liking and sharing it on social media, all of which helps influence the consumers behavior. Retailers need to learn how to boost their knowledge of the social media in order to increase the interest, enhance brand recognition, and generate traffic to their sites. Social marketers looking to sell their products need to have strong social proof, in the form of case studies, images, videos, podcast interviews, and influencers, as part of their sales strategy (Guan et al., 2022). Marketers are making social media more transparent, sharing reviews, comments, likes, tweets, and pins from their satisfied customers in order to build trust with their brands and improve conversion rates. Nowadays, social is consumers preferred choice for sharing reviews or reaching out to address an issue or query in customer service. Consumers are just as likely to share a positive customer feedback on social media as a negative one. Research shows consumers are still looking at social media for product reviews and recommendations rather than buying direct from a website (Yi et al., 2019). The impact may be so great that almost half of the consumers are more likely to purchase the same day they used social media (Shanahan et al., 2019).

Social media marketing is the current innovative approach in doing business, especially in the services market, because marketers are moving from one strategy (such as fan building) to another (6-s videos), or yet to another (social-local-mobile), which relates to progressively omni-directional forms of driving, ranging from expanding the neighborhood sections, to the results from the web scrapers, to the other (messaging bots), looking for the right innovative strategies for improving the brand health (Nuseir & Refae, 2022). However, it needs to be remembered that social media is not the only means how to keep in touch with one's loved ones. They also have become powerful digital marketing tools for building brand recognition and interacting with customers. Social media also allows for two-way communication, creating an interactivity between businesses and customers, which has had some direct effects on consumer behavior (Kovač & Žabkar, 2020). Social allows consumers to interact with businesses and engage in many ways, from liking posts and following their accounts, sharing content related to the brand, yelling about the brands love, or asking questions about products. Social media, including content, images, promotions, discounts, and influencers, has the power to impact consumers purchasing behavior.

Social media influencers significantly impact the behavior of consumers of various social media is a large part of everyone's life today, and it is an important avenue for brands to reach new customers (Appel et al., 2020). The so-called Millennials are the largest consumer group that is eager to spend and to invest and their focus has shifted from the traditional means of spreading news and information to the new platforms of social media (Munsch, 2021). People can forget about going into stores to find out about new products, consumers nowadays can simply browse through their social feeds to find inspiration. Today's consumers can type the exact kind of product they are looking for in an online search engine, and make their decisions really fast, depending on the products price-sensitivity, quality, price-to-value ratio, user reviews, and so on. For instance, if customers see the product on Instagram, they can instantly search for the hashtag in order to see more reviews, and make up their mind if they should purchase or not. Consumers who have product questions or ordering issues are far more likely to contact you through a brands Facebook page, Twitter mention, or Instagram. Consumers turn to channels such as Twitter and review sites such as Yelp to praise, and critique various products and businesses. Modern consumers, particularly Millennials, are increasingly using online tools, such as blogs, Facebook, and YouTube, to voice opinions on products and services that they consume (Wielki, 2020). Social media has allowed marketers to gain continuous and immediate access to and monitoring of consumers opinions through the ability to listen and engage with the conversations taking place on the Internet. Digital consumers on social media are looking to shop and the demand is rising (Zhang et al., 2021) suggesting that steps taken by social platforms to make products more buyable in line with the digital behaviors of the pandemic-era are working.

3 Business Organizations and Their Use of Social Networks

Social media represent a crucial marketing tool for today's businesses, but it also has the potential to improve the customer experience of businesses (Keiningham et al., 2020). Social platforms can help people to communicate with customers, raise brand awareness, and boost leads and sales. Social networks have become the epicenter of businesses building credibility, thanks to their built-in ability to virtually remove barriers to engagement (Fry et al., 2021). Now more than ever, businesses around the world are using digital platforms such as Facebook and Twitter as a tool to conduct business, raise brand awareness, sell products, and interact with customers—both existing and prospective. Social media tools such as Facebook and Twitter are replacing traditional marketing techniques, and helping more businesses utilize social media in their customer experience in order to create a cohesive brand on multiple platforms (Killian & McManus, 2015).

There are plenty of other ways that any business company could be using social media for building a client relationship, but the social networks marketing might give it a few ideas to explore. While there are plenty of channels that a company can use to help build its client relationships—forums, own website, email marketing, blog, and many others—many more things can be achieved via the social media platforms. The company has to nurture its customers relationships through social media, so that they come back over—they will begin to be advocates for the business they like and assist with its marketing (Li et al., 2021). When customers reach out to companies, they have to show that they can be a useful resource for their customers. Brands are often at a loss in terms of customer support in social media because they are not listening to and actively engaging with customers. Because a company cannot see customers the way it does in traditional corporate settings, it needs to take full advantage of tools that get it close to users of social media. Using tracking tools such as Facebooks Pixel, a company can display those prospects with social media ads about the exact products that they browsed its site for, or put into their cart (Diba et al., 2019). Social ads also provide powerful targeting options, so the company can reach the right audience and get the most out of its budget. Any business, no matter its size or budget, has an opportunity to increase its audience and achieve its goals with ads on social platforms such as Facebook and Instagram. While some might not think social media is the most personal platform for building relationships with customers, a company can build meaningful connections with its audience online when done the right way (Hofacker & Belanche, 2016). Providing its audience with an excellent social media experience can improve customer satisfaction and brand loyalty. When a company provides value for its customers through social media, it is likely to create a lasting relationship—and that, in turn, drives brand recognition and growth.

Social media engagement with customers has the potential for high success, particularly if the company outsources social media management to a third-party company, or if it dedicates an employee to creating content and moderating accounts (Dabbous & Barakat, 2020). One good way to start relationship-building on social media is by creating a dedicated customer support channel. Introducing the followers to the people that make up the business, and show existing customers using and benefiting from the existing products. By showing what a company offers and values, it builds trust with its prospects (Wongkitrungrueng et al., 2020). Offering a free value helps demonstrate how useful its products should be, attract new customers, and establish rapport that helps these customers stay. Making sure customers know that they are appreciated helps keep them happy, and it gives a company a leg up on competitors. Whether it is posting about the latest sales, or responding to customers questions, a business can engage easily with its current, past, and future customers. No doubt, the competitors are trying to establish strong customer relationships too, responding to users and engaging in 1-on-1 conversations (Čikošev, 2019).

Any company needs to realize that a lot of CEOs and other high-ranking executives at large brands are taking to Facebook and Twitter to interact directly with customers that may buy their products. Customers are not only sharing updates about their lives, but also searching businesses, products, and services, as well as connecting with brands via their own social channels. Social media gives a company a way to engage with its customers and fans directly, and it gives them the same way, to engage directly with its brand. Along with the two-way communication social media provides, it also offers the unique ability to up the company's customer service game and deliver instant gratification to its target audience and engaged users (Mulyana et al., 2020). To take advantage of this strategy, the company needs to get it right—failing to carefully manage its social media presence could hurt its existing brand and turn potential paying customers away. The majority of the profiles at the social media sites is public which means search engines can track and locate them. This can ensure that when there is a question or a problem, the company or organization shows up as an answer. Social accounts are a crucial part of the sales pipeline. This also represents a process by which a new contact becomes a customer. Thence, social media's role accounts activity level on their probability and time at which they would be repurchased is quite significant.

4 Interactive Nature of Social Networks

Social media and other online media are excellent tools for engagement and two-way communication, but given the nature of these real-time, two-way communications, the potential exists for substantial risks associated with their improper use (Ewing et al., 2019). Internet-based social media occurs via various web-based platforms, which enable users of similar interests to share content and interact on the Internet. Often defining themselves as websites that facilitate establishing contact networks for sharing different types of content on the Internet, social networking sites provide spaces for interactions that extend beyond face-to-face interactions. The online discussion fora and communities that existed in the old days used to be arranged by topics, while today's but social networks are individual-based with individual users being fed the topics and contents they like which can be achieved using complicated artificial intelligence-riven algorithms (Chen et al., 2018; Waniek et al., 2018). Social media is the collective term for websites and applications focusing on communications, input from communities, interactions, content-sharing, and collaboration. Social media is fundamentally a digital space created by users for the other users with the purpose of facilitating interactions at various levels (e.g., personal, professional, commercial, marketing, political, and societal) (Matušková & Strielkowski, 2014).

Moreover, social platforms allow businesses to rapidly promote their products and services to large audiences. As communication platforms, social media fosters customer reviews and makes it easier for customers to share their experiences with the business (Ye et al., 2021). Companies use social applications to promote and advertise their products, as well as monitor customer concerns. People use social networks for expressing themselves as well as for reaching out to other users, while also keeping in touch with their friends, families, and relatives. Social media initially existed to help users digitally interact with all kinds of kindred spirits that they may have never met in person. Early social media networks drew millions of users and allowed for the recording of e-mail addresses and basic networking (Maffie, 2020). Some 20 or 30 years ago, at the tech news website Digital Trends, growth in the Internet allowed for online communications services like CompuServe, America Online, and Prodigy (Kozinets, 2019). While earlier generations wrote notes in one another's printed yearbooks at the end of their school years, modern technology and the Internet have brought about new, vibrant ways for individuals to interact socially. While the roots of digital communications go back far, most modern accounts of the modern origins of the Internet and today's social media cite the emergence of the Advanced Research Projects Agency network (ARPANET) in 1969. At the same time as technology is expanding the boundaries of our social circles, different media are changing how we experience and engage with one another (Paloque-Bergès & Schafer, 2019).

In general terms, social media is changing economic relationships in a very meaningful way, from improving customer service, for example allowing users to send money to others through online platforms. We are seeing a lot of examples of social media, and digital communications in general, helping respond to catastrophes. Social networks are also becoming more common for school libraries, which are used to connect with potential library patrons, and also to expand on services provided by individual school libraries (Lovari & Bowen, 2020). Providing facilitates promoting e-commerce websites or using e-commerce tools that expand online social networks capabilities into e-commerce. Social networks also become a very important part of the cryptocurrencies and crypto economy that is the new and rapidly expanding field (Lu & Strielkowski, 2022). Social networks are also used for communicating research findings by academics and, as public communications tools, as well as to link individuals with similar professional interests, the benefits may differ by discipline. According to Schlagwein and Hu (2016), social media comprise Internet-based channels for communication and collaboration that have been in wide use since 2005, and in terms of information systems, the tools of social media and the surrounding organizational and management structures form a social information system. In their research, they argue that social media tend to have some features in common, such as: user profiles, users access to digital content, users' relationship link lists, as well as the users' ability to see and navigate relationship links (Wakefield & Wakefield, 2016). A social media service (also social media sites or social networks) is an online platform that individuals use to form social networks or social relationships with others with whom they share personal or professional profiles. Online dating sites are similar to social networks in the sense that users build profiles in order to meet and interact with others, but their activities on such sites are for the sole purpose of finding someone to date. These sites use graphics and text to enable users to share photos and information about themselves, communicate, and play games. Interactive media allows individuals to communicate with others whether people or organizations which is making them an active part of the media they consume.

5 Conclusion

Overall, social media can be confirmed as an important promotional strategy, however, improvements are needed regarding their utility aspects as an advertising tool. The social media's advantage encompasses different aspects, such as social interactions, maintaining connections to friends, sharing helpful information with others via social media sites, and having access to sites that enable students to find support online that might otherwise be absent from traditional relationships.

At the moment, engaging with digital media and social media is not only advantageous, it facilitates personal social interactions and communications, as well, by allowing users to build brands and generate career opportunities. Content generated by social media users, such as comments, posts, digital photos, video shares, and all data from online interactions, is crucial and represents the lifeblood of social media sites and social media. Since the introduction of SNS technologies, teens usage of these technologies has expanded, and is now a predominant mode for communicating with and getting information about others within their social networks. Although computers were originally developed for adults, adolescents have fully embraced these technologies for their social purposes, and are often family experts in the use of electronic media and social networking sites. Constant online communications are maintained mainly through the Internet (social media sites like Facebook, status update sites like Twitter, and media-sharing sites like Instagram) and through current mobile phones (in the form of instant messaging and image sharing). It becomes clear that messages via social media resulted in in-person interactions when plans were made through the sites, and that social media users sent messages to close friends more than seeing them in person.

Our research demonstrates the effects of increased information access and social media use on respondents, including questions about social media structures and use, reasons respondents used social media, and how respondents perceived the positive and negative aspects of social media sites. Overall, adolescents and young adults stated that their motives for using (social media sites) were rather similar to those of more traditional forms of communication: keeping in touch with friends, making plans, getting to know people better, and representing on social media identified similar ideas about the cultural and experiential states of engagement among young people, While specific systems can come and go, the way in which young people are engaging through social network sites today provides long-lasting insights about identity formation, status negotiations, and peer-to-peer sociality.

Evidence suggests that social networks are differentially associated with adolescent social connectedness and identity development, with sociability, self-esteem, and the nature of feedback from social networks serving as important potential moderators. After introducing theoretical perspectives that offer a basis for the uses of and implications of social networks in adolescents, we then examine extant literatures about social networks and adolescents' social relationships, and identity development. Next, taking the societal changes occurring during adolescence as the background, we consider how social networks overlap with core tasks in the psychosocial development of adolescents, particularly peer identification and quality of friendship, and identity development. We examined various social networks and social media from every possible angle and can summarize that their positive outcomes probably outweigh those negative ones.

Social networks can also help users to socialize, much like unmediated public spaces. Contradictory data has been found regarding younger individuals; adolescents who are socially anxious are just as likely as their peers who are not to have a Facebook account, and their social anxiety does not affect the way that they use social networks, nor the amount of time that they spend using them. Many researchers have found that socially anxious people use the Internet to manage their social and anxious counterparts who use Facebook or Instagram to interact with others online for extending their examination of other people's behavior and comparing themselves to the others, at least in the online environment.

Our results also demonstrated that social networks and social media have profound effects on whether users saw the social network contribution, and if they forwarded it. Social media opponents claim social media sites discourage face-to-face interaction; occupy time with frivolous activities, change the brains and behaviors of children, making them more susceptible to various psychological diseases, expose users to predators such as pedophiles and thieves, and disseminate false and potentially harmful information. In summary, policymakers and lawmakers should remember about that when regulating the contents of the social networks and mediating their influence on young consumers.

Acknowledgements The research is carried out with the financial support of the Kuban Scientific Foundation within the framework of the scientific project No. PPN-21.1/51 "Mechanisms and technologies to counteract the influence of the content of Internet resources and social networks on the national consciousness of young people".

References

Abrhám, J., & Wang, J. (2017). Novel trends on using ICTS in the modern tourism industry. *Czech Journal of Social Sciences, Business and Economics*, *6*(1), 37–43. https://doi.org/10.24984/cjssbe.2017.6.1.5

Agnihotri, R., Kalra, A., Chen, H., & Daugherty, P. J. (2022). Utilizing social media in a supply chain B2B setting: A knowledge perspective. *Journal of Business Logistics, 43*(2), 189–208. https://doi.org/10.1111/jbl.12289

Aichner, T., Grünfelder, M., Maurer, O., & Jegeni, D. (2021). Twenty-five years of social media: A review of social media applications and definitions from 1994 to 2019. *Cyberpsychology, Behavior, and Social Networking, 24*(4), 215–222. https://doi.org/10.1089/cyber.2020.0134

Ali, R., Komarova, V., Aslam, T., & Peleckis, K. (2022). The impact of social media marketing on youth buying behaviour in an emerging country. *Entrepreneurship and Sustainability Issues, 9*(4), 125–138. https://doi.org/10.9770/jesi.2022.9.4(6)

Al-Zyoud, M. F. (2018). Social media marketing, functional branding strategy and intentional branding. *Problems and Perspectives in Management, 16*(3), 102–116. https://doi.org/10.21511/ppm.16(3).2018.09

Appel, G., Grewal, L., Hadi, R., & Stephen, A. T. (2020). The future of social media in marketing. *Journal of the Academy of Marketing Science, 48*(1), 79–95. https://doi.org/10.1007/s11747-019-00695-1

Argyris, Y. A., Wang, Z., Kim, Y., & Yin, Z. (2020). The effects of visual congruence on increasing consumers' brand engagement: An empirical investigation of influencer marketing on Instagram using deep-learning algorithms for automatic image classification. *Computers in Human Behavior, 112*, 106443. https://doi.org/10.1016/j.chb.2020.106443

Besenyő, J., & Sinkó, G. (2021). The social media use of African terrorist organizations: A comparative study of Al-Qaeda in the Islamic Maghreb, Al-Shabaab and Boko Haram. *Insights into Regional Development, 3*(3), 66–78. https://doi.org/10.9770/IRD.2021.3.3(4)

Chen, T., Drennan, J., Andrews, L., & Hollebeek, L. D. (2018). User experience sharing: Understanding customer initiation of value co-creation in online communities. *European Journal of Marketing, 52*(5/6), 1154–1184. https://doi.org/10.1108/EJM-05-2016-0298

Čikošev, T. C. (2019). Development and implementation of the integrated marketing communications concept. *Economic Analysis, 52*(1), 36–47. https://doi.org/10.28934/ea.19.52.12.pp36-47

Cooley, D., & Parks-Yancy, R. (2019). The effect of social media on perceived information credibility and decision making. *Journal of Internet Commerce, 18*(3), 249–269. https://doi.org/10.1080/15332861.2019.1595362

Creevey, D., Coughlan, J., & O'Connor, C. (2022). Social media and luxury: A systematic literature review. *International Journal of Management Reviews, 24*(1), 99–129. https://doi.org/10.1111/ijmr.12271

Dabbous, A., & Barakat, K. A. (2020). Bridging the online offline gap: Assessing the impact of brands' social network content quality on brand awareness and purchase intention. *Journal of Retailing and Consumer Services, 53*, 101966. https://doi.org/10.1016/j.jretconser.2019.101966

Dabija, D. C., Bejan, B. M., & Tipi, N. (2018). Generation X versus millennials communication behaviour on social media when purchasing food versus tourist services. *E+M Ekonomie a Management, 21*(1), 191–205. https://doi.org/10.15240/tul/001/2018-1-013

Diba, H., Vella, J. M., & Abratt, R. (2019). Social media influence on the B2B buying process. *Journal of Business & Industrial Marketing, 34*(7), 1482–1496. https://doi.org/10.1108/JBIM-12-2018-0403

Ewing, M., Men, L. R., & O'Neil, J. (2019). Using social media to engage employees: Insights from internal communication managers. *International Journal of Strategic Communication, 13*(2), 110–132. https://doi.org/10.1080/1553118x.2019.1575830

Fry, S. W., Brown, D., & Sass, M. S. M. (2021). Parent first, essential worker second, student third: Lessons learned from an underrepresented student's journey in a service-learning course during COVID-19. *Journal of Higher Education Outreach and Engagement, 25*(3), 107–124.

Guan, J., Lau, Y.-Y., Yang, H., & Ren, L. (2022). To buy or not to buy: How young consumers approach new smart products in the social media context. *Young Consumers, 23*(1), 90–111. https://doi.org/10.1108/YC-12-2020-1272

Hofacker, C. F., & Belanche, D. (2016). Eight social media challenges for marketing managers. *Spanish Journal of Marketing-ESIC, 20*(2), 73–80. https://doi.org/10.1016/j.sjme.2016.07.003

Horng, S. M., & Wu, C. L. (2020). How behaviors on social network sites and online social capital influence social commerce intentions. *Information & Management, 57*(2), 103176. https://doi.org/10.1016/j.im.2019.103176

Huerta-Álvarez, R., Cambra-Fierro, J. J., & Fuentes-Blasco, M. (2020). The interplay between social media communication, brand equity and brand engagement in tourist destinations: An analysis in an emerging economy. *Journal of Destination Marketing & Management, 16*, 100413. https://doi.org/10.1016/j.jdmm.2020.100413

Joshi, Y., Sangroya, D., Srivastava, A. P., & Yadav, M. (2019). Modelling the predictors of young consumers' sustainable consumption intention. *International Journal of Nonprofit and Voluntary Sector Marketing, 24*(4), e1663. https://doi.org/10.1002/nvsm.1663

Kashintseva, V., Strielkowski, W., Streimikis, J., & Veynbender, T. (2018). Consumer attitudes towards industrial CO2 capture and storage products and technologies. *Energies, 11*(10), 2787. https://doi.org/10.3390/en11102787

Keiningham, T., Aksoy, L., Bruce, H. L., Cadet, F., Clennell, N., Hodgkinson, I. R., & Kearney, T. (2020). Customer experience driven business model innovation. *Journal of Business Research, 116*, 431–440. https://doi.org/10.1016/j.jbusres.2019.08.003

Killian, G., & McManus, K. (2015). A marketing communications approach for the digital era: Managerial guidelines for social media integration. *Business Horizons, 58*(5), 539–549. https://doi.org/10.1016/j.bushor.2015.05.006

Koudelková, P., & Svobodová, P. (2014). Knowledge creation & sharing as essential determinants of SMEs innovation. *International Economics Letters, 3*(1), 12–20. https://doi.org/10.24984/iel.2014.3.1.3

Kovač, M., & Žabkar, V. (2020). Do social media and e-mail engagement impact reputation and trust-driven behavior? *Market-Tržište, 32*(1), 9–25. https://doi.org/10.22598/mt/2020.32.1.9

Kozinets, R. V. (2019). *Netnography: The essential guide to qualitative social media research*. Sage.

Kumar, B., Jensen, M. M., Strielkowski, W., Johnston, J. T., Sharma, V., Dandara, C., Shehata, M., Micarelli Struetta, M., Nikolaou, A., Szymanski, D., Abdul-Ghani, R., Cao, B., Varzinczak, L., Kerman, B., Arthur, P., Oda. F., Bohon, W., Ellwanger, J., Tyner, Jordan. E., & Murphy. C. (2019). NextGen voices: Science-inspired sustainable behavior. *Science, 364*(6443), 822–824. https://doi.org/10.1126/science.aax8945

Li, F., Larimo, J., & Leonidou, L. C. (2021). Social media marketing strategy: Definition, conceptualization, taxonomy, validation, and future agenda. *Journal of the Academy of Marketing Science, 49*(1), 51–70. https://doi.org/10.1007/s11747-020-00733-3

Litau, E. (2018). Information flows management as a way to overcome "Puberty challenges" of a small enterprise. *ACM International Conference Proceeding Series*, 34–38. https://doi.org/10.1145/3278252.3278259

Lovari, A., & Bowen, S. A. (2020). Social media in disaster communication: A case study of strategies, barriers, and ethical implications. *Journal of Public Affairs, 20*(1), e1967. https://doi.org/10.1002/pa.1967

Lu, J., & Strielkowski, W. (2022). Russia: Could cryptocurrency mining exploit unsold fuel? *Nature, 605*(7909), 225–225. https://doi.org/10.1038/d41586-022-01267-0

Maffie, M. D. (2020). The role of digital communities in organizing gig workers. *Industrial Relations: A Journal of Economy and Society, 59*(1), 123–149. https://doi.org/10.1111/irel.12251

Matušková, A., & Strielkowski, W. (2014). Technology applications in Czech presidential elections of 2013: A story of social networks. *Mediterranean Journal of Social Sciences, 5*(21), 419–424. https://doi.org/10.5901/mjss.2014.v5n21p419

Mulyana, A., Briandana, R., & Rekarti, E. (2020). ICT and social media as a marketing communication platform in facilitating social engagement in the digital era. *International Journal of Innovation, Creativity and Change, 13*(5), 1–16.

Munsch, A. (2021). Millennial and generation Z digital marketing communication and advertising effectiveness: A qualitative exploration. *Journal of Global Scholars of Marketing Science, 31*(1), 10–29. https://doi.org/10.1080/21639159.2020.1808812

Nuseir, M., & Refae, G. (2022). The effect of digital marketing capabilities on business performance enhancement: Mediating the role of customer relationship management (CRM). *International Journal of Data and Network Science, 6*(2), 295–304. https://doi.org/10.5267/j.ijdns.2022.1.008

Paloque-Bergès, C., & Schafer, V. (2019). Arpanet (1969–2019). *Internet Histor-DRFTGY7UH87ies, 3*(1), 1–14. https://doi.org/10.1080/24701475.2018.1560921

Schaefers, T., Falk, T., Kumar, A., & Schamari, J. (2021). More of the same? Effects of volume and variety of social media brand engagement behavior. *Journal of Business Research, 135*, 282–294. https://doi.org/10.1016/j.jbusres.2021.06.033

Schlagwein, D., & Hu, M. (2016). How and why organisations use social media: Five use types and their relation to absorptive capacity. *Journal of Information Technology, 32*(2), 194–209. https://doi.org/10.1057/jit.2016.7

Shanahan, T., Tran, T. P., & Taylor, E. C. (2019). Getting to know you: Social media personalization as a means of enhancing brand loyalty and perceived quality. *Journal of Retailing and Consumer Services, 47*, 57–65. https://doi.org/10.1016/j.jretconser.2018.10.007

Sima, V., Gheorghe, I. G., Subić, J., & Nancu, D. (2020). Influences of the industry 4.0 revolution on the human capital development and consumer behavior: A systematic review. *Sustainability, 12*(10), 4035. https://doi.org/10.3390/su12104035

Starr, R. G., Jr., Zhu, A. Q., Frethey-Bentham, C., & Brodie, R. J. (2020). Peer-to-peer interactions in the sharing economy: Exploring the role of reciprocity within a Chinese social network. *Australasian Marketing Journal (AMJ), 28*(3), 67–80. https://doi.org/10.1016/j.ausmj.2020.06.002

Strielkowski, W., Zenchenko, S., Tarasova, A., & Radyukova, Y. (2022). Management of smart and sustainable cities in the post-covid-19 era: Lessons and implications. *Sustainability, 14*(12), 7267. https://doi.org/10.3390/su14127267

Tafesse, W., & Wien, A. (2018). Implementing social media marketing strategically: An empirical assessment. *Journal of Marketing Management, 34*(9–10), 732–749. https://doi.org/10.1080/0267257x.2018.1482365

Toleikienė, R., Rybnikova, I., & Juknevičienė, V. (2020). Whether and how does the crisis-induced situation change e-leadership in the public sector? Evidence from Lithuanian public administration. *Transylvanian Review of Administrative Sciences, 16*(SI), 149–166. https://doi.org/10.24193/tras.si2020.9

VanMeter, R., Syrdal, H. A., Powell-Mantel, S., Grisaffe, D. B., & Nesson, E. T. (2018). Don't just "Like" me, promote me: How attachment and attitude influence brand related behaviors on social media. *Journal of Interactive Marketing, 43*(1), 83–97. https://doi.org/10.1016/j.intmar.2018.03.003

Wakefield, R., & Wakefield, K. (2016). Social media network behavior: A study of user passion and affect. *The Journal of Strategic Information Systems, 25*(2), 140–156. https://doi.org/10.1016/j.jsis.2016.04.001

Waniek, M., Michalak, T. P., Wooldridge, M. J., & Rahwan, T. (2018). Hiding individuals and communities in a social network. *Nature Human Behaviour, 2*(2), 139–147. https://doi.org/10.1038/s41562-017-0290-3

Weber, M., & Chatzopoulos, C. G. (2019). Digital customer experience: The risk of ignoring the non-digital experience. *International Journal of Industrial Engineering and Management, 10*(3), 201–210. https://doi.org/10.24867/ijiem-2019-3-240

Wielki, J. (2020). Analysis of the role of digital influencers and their impact on the functioning of the contemporary on-line promotional system and its sustainable development. *Sustainability, 12*(17), 7138. https://doi.org/10.3390/su12177138

Wongkitrungrueng, A., Dehouche, N., & Assarut, N. (2020). Live streaming commerce from the sellers' perspective: Implications for online relationship marketing. *Journal of Marketing Management, 36*(5–6), 488–518. https://doi.org/10.1080/0267257x.2020.1748895

Ye, G., Hudders, L., De Jans, S., & De Veirman, M. (2021). The value of influencer marketing for business: A bibliometric analysis and managerial implications. *Journal of Advertising, 50*(2), 160–178. https://doi.org/10.1080/00913367.2020.1857888

Yessenbekova, U. M. (2020). Social media and slacktivism in young people's life. *Media Watch, 11*(3), 515–524. https://doi.org/10.15655/mw/2020/v11i3/202950

Yi, C., Jiang, Z., Li, X., & Lu, X. (2019). Leveraging user-generated content for product promotion: The effects of firm-highlighted reviews. *Information Systems Research, 30*(3), 711–725. https://doi.org/10.1287/isre.2018.0807

Zhang, X., Liu, H., & Yao, P. (2021). Research jungle on online consumer behaviour in the context of web 2.0: Traceability, frontiers and perspectives in the post-pandemic era. *Journal of Theoretical and Applied Electronic Commerce Research, 16*(5), 1740–1767. https://doi.org/10.3390/jtaer16050098

The Impact of Internet Content Regulation Policies on the Promotion of Targeted Consumer Behavior

Jing Wang, Veronica M. Grebennikova, Snezhana A. Khazova, and Alexander A. Malkov

Abstract This paper focuses on the impact of various Internet content regulation policies on the promotion of targeted consumer behavior. Humanity's ability to connect and transmit across global boundaries, and the data economy that has grown up around that environment, has been so influential that governments worldwide are now struggling with whether to set limits for the extent of social media and social networks that has become so ubiquitous that few people would be capable of imagining their lives without them. At the same time, social media users are learning more about their roles in the data economy. Social and digital marketing provide organizations with considerable opportunities to drive lower costs, increase brand recognition, and boost sales. Recognizing the influence that Internet content has on consumers attitudes and decisions, brands have begun approaching social media influencers (i.e., powerful users of social media who have managed to generate large audiences of followers) and offering incentives for social media influencers (i.e., creating and sharing content related to the relevant, authentically-appearing brand, a practice known as influencer marketing). We determine long-run platform effects for both direct and spillover communication, by dividing the estimates for direct and spillover communications by the decline in intermedia engagement. We determine consumer engagement with brand activity on the Internet-based resources. Due to log–log specifications, estimates also reflect elasticities between the brand-generated content and the consumers engagement. Once the brand's goal is decided, the team must talk with employees, partners, and customers to understand the employee's interests in the social causes. Our results show that strengthening stakeholders' relationships with the company by conducting a reciprocal corporate social responsibility initiative can be beneficial. Social impact by consumers engagement with network-based and small-group-based virtual communities can also be useful.

J. Wang (✉)
School of Management, Shandong University, 27 Shandu Nanlu Jinan, 250 100 Shandong, People's Republic of China
e-mail: jingwang@sdu.edu.cn

V. M. Grebennikova · S. A. Khazova · A. A. Malkov
Kuban State University, 149 Stavropolskaya Str., 350040 Krasnodar, Russian Federation
e-mail: goal444@malkov-aleksandr.ru

V. Kumar et al. (eds.), *Consequences of Social Transformation for Economic Theory*, Springer Proceedings in Business and Economics,
https://doi.org/10.1007/978-3-031-27785-6_15

Keywords Internet regulation · Consumer behavior · Economic theory

JEL Classification C88 · D10 · O33

1 Introduction

The Internet has evolved as a means for conducting business, making consumers data privacy an increasingly important issue. However, the advent of Internet commerce and Big Data in the early twenty-first century has put the consumer data privacy problem in a new light (Aho & Duffield, 2020; Sollins, 2019). As consumers increasingly embrace digital technologies, the data they produce presents both opportunities for businesses to enhance consumer engagement, as well as liabilities for keeping consumers data secure (Čábelková et al., 2021).

Consumer data is obviously changing businesses, and companies are accountable for managing the data that they capture. The shift to the wide-scale sharing and collection of personal data on the Internet has given marketers unprecedented insights into individual consumers, allowing them to deliver solutions that are precisely tailored to the needs of every person (Lobschat et al., 2021). For instance, the U.S. in 2017 rescinded federal efforts to expand data privacy protections, by requiring Internet Service Providers (ISPs) to get consent from customers before using their personal data for advertising and marketing (Minow, 2021).

In the recent years, people have begun to learn what causes consumers to oppose targeting, and how marketers can leverage personalization while still respecting individuals' privacy (Thomaz et al., 2020). Research has shown that digital targeting significantly increases responses to ads, and ad effectiveness decreases when marketers have less access to consumers data (Hosťovecký & Poláčik, 2016). As targeted ads get more sophisticated and more targeted and consumers become increasingly aware of how their privacy can be compromised giving people meaningful control over their information is likely to increase advertising effectiveness (Liu-Thompkins, 2019). Digital marketers must be aware of when using consumers data to tailor ads will meet with adoption or irritation, so that they can respect consumers expectations for how their information should be used (Brinson & Britt, 2021).

There is a lot that we still do not know about how people react to data collection and advertising targeting online, and privacy norms are likely to shift over time as younger digital natives grow into consumers and as technology becomes more pervasive in our lives (Kumar et al., 2019; Yessenbekova, 2020). This includes potential uses for online advertising within off-label promotional activities (based on research findings showing industry sponsored links in search engines are inadequate for providing drug-indication information), how the dynamic nature of these technologies can affect consumers differently from traditional forms of advertising, and how marketers can alter the tactics to harness the power of these platforms to reach consumers directly and establish relationships in new and different ways (Wong et al., 2022).

These practices have grown in importance to businesses and consumers alike, as the consequences of breaches have grown, and as greater regulations govern how long to disclose a data breach. In the United States, the reduction of use of the Federal Trade Commission's rulemaking authority over the past few years has similarly contributed to growing weaknesses in online consumer protections. Consumer Privacy Issues Personal information, when improperly used or inadequately protected, leads to identity theft, financial fraud, and other problems, which together cost individuals, businesses, and governments millions of dollars each year (Schein et al., 2022). Consumer privacy, also known as customer confidentiality, involves managing and protecting the sensitive personal information customers provide during routine transactions (not speaking about the weird world of cryptocurrencies (Lu & Strielkowski, 2022)). Consumers are exercising greater control over their personal information through the myriad privacy tools that are now available, including web browsers with built-in cookie blockers, ad-blocking software (used by over 600 million devices worldwide), and incognito browsers (used by more than 40% of Internet users worldwide) (Dodel & Mesch, 2018). Understanding helps develop new products and services, and customizes advertising and marketing (the total value of digital advertising worldwide is now estimated to be $300 billion (Redjeki & Affandi, 2021)). The results are partly due to more data leading to better tracking, profiling behavior and targeted data-driven marketing on the Internet. The U.S. Food and Drug Administration perceives electronic direct-to-consumer advertising (eDTCA) as highly interactive, with a high degree of multimedia content and user-generated content, and as engaging consumers in social ways, with eDTCA campaigns typically being coordinated strategically through shared online resources and linked together (Aikin et al., 2019). This may be accomplished by adapting marketing campaigns and scheduling content schedules, evaluating language and images used in advertising and marketing materials, and being aware of consumers increased anxieties during these times.

2 Consumer Responses to Marketing Communications

Customer engagement marketing represents a marketing strategy for communicating timely, relevant, and personal messages to consumers. Customer engagement is the way customers engage with an experience and a brand, including their decisions, as well as the way they talk about and respond to a company's products and services (Hollebeek & Macky, 2019). Customer engagement is no longer limited to sales, support, or services; rather, it as the continuous practice by which brands anticipate customer's needs and stay connected to them in order to cultivate lasting relationships, loyalty, and thus, growth of the business. Customer engagement gives customers a sense of power and purpose in the process, making them active decision-makers rather than just recipients of experiences. Customer engagement captures the quality of customer relationships at different points in time, as opposed to customer satisfaction, which indicates how the customer feels after engaging with the brand (Liu et al., 2019).

Consumer engagement refers to the efforts a business or brand makes to develop relationships with individuals by customizing interactions on multiple channels, with the aim of winning and keeping customers (Čábelková et al., 2015). Integrated marketing communications is the process of communicating one consistent message through multiple channels in order to foster higher levels of customer engagement for the company's products and solutions. Moreover, integrated marketing communications has exponential benefits to businesses, provided that they place sufficient importance on capturing customer engagement with coherent, crisp messaging (Kwangyong et al., 2021). While marketers may be using an integrated marketing communications plan to sell products and gain new customers, increasing retention and loyalty must be the main goal. Instead, well-planned integrated marketing communications strategies can lead to sustained engagement, building a relationship with customers on the basis of a consistent brand experience. To reach engagement goals, a company wants to make sure that its content marketing strategy is highly consumer-centric, so it publishes only valuable content customers can take advantage of. Businesses should think strategically about what needs to go into marketing content, appropriate channels of distribution, and how that might impact customer engagement (Lopes et al., 2022). They have to get creative in engaging customers, particularly in social media, and do not restrict outreach and marketing campaigns only to Twitter and Facebook. Social media is a great way to reach customers who might not have discovered or connected with any given brand. Social media platforms offer customers many features designed to support engagement within the brands community (Weismueller et al., 2020). Companies can interact with customers through social media, emails, websites, community forums, or any other spaces they interact with or consume content. Customers want and expect to engage with brands and companies wherever they are comfortable. Every marketer knows that they need to be on social media, but the question is how best to reach customers once they are there. To increase consumer engagement, brands should be proactive about connecting with customers and engaging them, whenever possible (Zlyvko et al., 2014). They need to use insights and data about customers to build positive brand perceptions and increase engagement on all channels (Haenlein et al., 2020).

In general, every brand has the opportunity to implement engagement strategies that will benefit their current and prospective customer bases. A marketing engagement strategy must strongly consider existing and potential customers needs during their purchasing journey. From data gathering (via sales engagement platform or sales automation tools) to customer reviews and forums, creating an engagement strategy involves just as much social listening and research as brand advocacy (Ancillai et al., 2019). Listening is a critical component to engaging customers, and improving any company's services or products on the basis of customer feedback can do much to build confidence in its brand. An effective customer engagement strategy can be crucial to helping brands connect with customers better, in ways that will keep them wanting to continue being customers. By measuring customer engagement over time, brands can understand user reactions, as well as adjust and optimize their activities for the best results.

A customer engagement platform can also test marketing, sales, and customer service campaigns to provide optimal customer engagement (Zhong & Schweidel, 2020). The integrated marketing communications process maximizes individual and aggregate efforts across all channels, including print media, advertising, digital media, social media, events, public relations, and mobile for engaging customers. The process involves the use of all communications channels for building relationships, improving satisfaction, and actively nurturing the customer base. Making means optimizing the team structure, operations, and technology in order to build a positive feedback loop with customers. In order to do that, a business company must be aware of its customer's evolving needs, preserve and strengthen brand integrity, and use data ethically to assist customers in appropriate ways. From tailored communications to curating online and virtual events, build individualized customer experiences that make consumers feel like the business is responsive to their needs and interests (Manita et al., 2020). The customer experience is the way consumers experience a company's brand, or the way this brand is seen and received, from their point of view. Customer experience forces companies to wear their consumers hats, and to approach sales and marketing from their buyers' point of view. Whether it is a chatbot greeting a potential customer on a company's landing page or a hand-written note thanking her or him for a purchase, marketers can use customer engagement to optimize the customer experience and improve customer loyalty and customer retention. This is fantastic news for customer engagement, as marketers now have a lot more ways, they can leverage native ads to grab customers attention and keep users engaged with their content and brands (Leung et al., 2022). Targeting relevant videos at customers segments through social media or video YouTube ads means that any company is more likely to be successful at getting them interested and engaged. Including these tactics in the marketing strategy will make sure that the customers willingly spend more time on the company's website/app, and that engagement levels skyrocket.

Whether we want it or not, it is the Social Media Age, and, for better or worse, social media engagement accounts for a significant proportion of the overall engagement efforts a business makes, and for the overall interactions a customer has with the brand (Fakunle & Ajani, 2021). A thoughtful, multichannel engagement strategy that keeps customer needs front of mind and lays a clear road map for ongoing, relevant engagement can set a unique tone of engagement that allows customers to differentiate your brand and define themselves through it.

3 Consumers' Social Media Engagement Behavior

The effect of perceived marketing elements on social media consumers brand participation and brand knowledge. In the present study, the engagement behavior was a reaction; online social media are generally observed to induce emotions in consumers, and influence their behavior (Shahbaznezhad et al., 2021). Rational social media calls had superior effects on the facilitation of both active and passive participation in social media users, while emotional calls promoted passive, not high-active, participation behavior, in spite of the social and interactive nature of digital media landscape (Dolan et al., 2019).

One of the ways in which customers engage more in social media is to make content more approachable and easier to consume. Sentiment analytics allows businesses to understand the type of content that their customers are interested in, so that they can build more campaigns that they will like and find engaging. This information can help them to build tailored campaigns that generate engagement, get positive reviews, and build better relationships with their customers. That is why it is essential to know where a firm's brand is mentioned, and where its various target personas are spending their time, so that it can reach its audience in the right places, at the right times, with the right content (Gruss et al., 2020). Even the biggest brands, those with millions of followers, are usually investing in the resources and investing in the necessary technologies to filter all the messages and mentions coming in across social media, to ensure that they get back 100% of the time on the big inquiries (customer service questions for technology brands, complaints about the food for chain restaurants, etc.) (Montag et al., 2019). A quick response time does not only apply to questions directed at your brand on social, it can be generic comments, or even compliments. Based on personal experiences, almost half of consumers think that social media has introduced them to new people, and an equal part thinks that social media has helped them learn about another person's perspective. More than half of consumers wish brands would use social to help them connect with like-minded individuals, and more than one-third are looking for communities to which they can belong. Eighty-one percent of consumers think brands could serve as good connectors, as they offer products and services that attract a wide variety of customers (Bharucha, 2018).

In other words, while the direct impact of the focal social media platform might be smaller in magnitude, posts in this media outlet can have a significant impact on brand messaging engagement in other social networks because of a stronger spillover effect from the focal media outlet.

4 Consumer Engagement Varies Across Social Media

Whether a business company is publishing content or engaging in social media, it is going to want to know how well its social media marketing is performing. Social media marketing involves publishing awesome content to a company's social media profiles, listening and engaging with its followers, analyzing its results, and running ads on social media (Zuhdi et al., 2019). A focus on users leads to users of social media posting related, quality content, and engaging consumers. Publishing content that encourages users to participate and engage increases rankings and fosters brand loyalty. With effective social marketing strategies in place, companies can increase their chances of engaging customers via personalized interactions on social media.

An effective customer engagement strategy can prove critical to helping brands connect with customers more effectively, in ways that will keep them wanting to remain customers (Wang, 2021). A clearly defined engagement strategy also helps you, as a company, to recognize and understand the customers main pain points when using your products/services, so that a company can address those efficiently and keep customers around. When it comes to the marketing channels, like emails, push notifications, social media, and chatbots, a company needs to make sure that it is tracking and rigorously analyzing interactions and engagements across all its campaigns, so that it has a definitive place to start and a clear understanding of areas to improve (Li et al., 2021; Litau, 2018). All of the above ultimately affects everything from its marketing messaging to the way it will approach customer support or selling on social. As the company grows, so does its social media following, conversations around its brand will also grow. Social media can also help any company to build engagement around its brand, build community, and act as a customer service channel to its customers. Social media also allows companies to reach out to a wide range of customers at once, run surveys, and make patients feel like part of the community (Matušková & Strielkowski, 2014). Another way marketers are using social media is by monitoring cultural trends, and when appropriate, including brand-specific concepts that capitalize on these trends in order to attract customers to participate in a company's content (Reagan et al., 2020).

On one side, firms create content through their efforts in social media (referred to as company-generated content or tag-generated content) in order to engage consumers in an active manner. This has significant implications for brands, especially for brands who create content collaboratively with consumers. While influencers give companies a layer of built-in trust from consumers, social media platforms such as Facebook and LinkedIn offer deep analytics that enable digital marketers to target particular demographic groups with ads. Whether through traditional channels such as email and social media, or emerging ones including voice assistants and videos, it has become nearly standard practice for brands to establish and thoroughly maintain an online presence in order to attract an audience and attain first-in-mind awareness (Argyris et al., 2020). Digital marketing, also called online marketing, is branding that targets prospective customers using the Internet and other forms of digital communications. As a marketer, it is essential to leverage the digital world through online advertising, building the brand, providing an excellent customer experience, which will attract even more potential customers, and so on, through digital strategies.

Social media ads boost brand awareness and engagement across their respective social media platforms. While social media ads need to be paid for, the act of creating and sharing informative or interesting content on Facebook, Instagram, Twitter, and other platforms is the brands effort to organically grow their audience in other words, without paying directly (Raji et al., 2019). Moreover, social media enable individuals and communities to aggregate and connect and, in some cases, to work collaboratively with other users in real-time (Prandi et al., 2020). Other public health organizations have used key worded content from Wikipedia and other social media, combined with location-tracking technologies, to rapidly respond to disasters and to track the health and well-being of populations.

5 Conclusion

In the light of our findings from the economic, social, and organizational sciences reviewed in the previous sections, we have previously analyzed an agent-based model applying the evolutionary framework introduced previously to simulate collective decision-making processes in a fine-grained, well-connected social network framework. The evolutionary framework and subsequent computational models allow advances in understanding collective decisions made in dynamic, complex social systems. Some computational agent-based models focused on evolutionary considerations of collective decisions made in groups and social networks are developed and tested, with the variety of decision making, behavioral patterns, and social network structures being manipulated as experimental variables. In other words, agent-based modelling (ABM) helps understand how humans actually make decisions in dynamic, real-world environments (naturalistic decision making) through its requirement that computational agents behave explicitly. During experiments, decisions and interventions that are developed based on their mental models are tested against real-world dynamics. As discussed before, to develop an autonomous virtual person, a decision-making action choice mechanism must be implemented in order to simulate dynamic decision-making. An alternative is to perform computational pre-tests on what is often called micro-worlds, which respond to possible actions in a similar way as real-world ones, in order to explore various dynamic decision-making strategies within this model-free, modeling-and-simulation framework. The simulation approach is expected to yield insights into the actual cognitive processes that underlie dynamic decision-making by humans.

The goal of the present work is to analyze approaches to incorporating general processes that are relevant to all types of dynamic decision-making and through this to see how the impact of Internet content regulation policies influences on the promotion of targeted consumer behavior.

Simulation models addressing the dynamics of populations with disease features are valuable to identify preferred policies, enhance the understanding of the consequences of policy decisions, and bridge gaps in emergency response plans and public health policies. Differential equation-based compartmental models are also differentiated from other compartmental models in that they do not simulate an intervention with the population dynamics in one compartmental model, but instead generate multiple baseline models running in parallel for the various subpopulations generated during the implementation of a policy.

To overcome limitations of the earlier models, researchers develop compartmental models which yield insights on mitigation policy implementation within the local communities, and these models are also easier to apply to live exercises to inform consumer decisions. The major feature of compartmental models based on differential equations is robustness in moving individuals from one subpopulation to another in response to implemented decisions. In contrast, a model built around an underlying rule is capable of modeling segregated neighborhoods emerging from urban areas of varying populations, as the result of dynamic, collective decision-making processes.

Because these single-rule models need computational resources for running multiple scenarios, they might be less efficient for a real-time decision-making exercise in planning a pandemic. The models are unsurprising, as problems occur in collective decision models in the common assumption that each individual agent has, or makes, their own decisions. These models are used for specific analysis at a sub-level on how the homogeneity or heterogeneity in goals and decision utility functions between participants influence dynamics and final outcomes of their collective decision-making, and predictions made from this model were also confirmed in experiments on human subjects. The goals included learning about the process of developing the simulation model and how it could be used to inform decision-making. Because of the substantial time commitment involved in developing dynamic, participatory modeling models, opportunity costs and the likely outcomes from a modeling project were important factors in decision making by policymakers about participating in this process. Model outputs were described as engaging and helpful, with some of a bit of science as well as wizardry (or computer wizardry).

However, concerns are expressed about model outputs being interpreted as fact by those outside of the participatory process, instead of being used as a decision-support tool for comparisons between alternative strategies. For instance, if regulating interventions are being considered, stakeholders with oversight over the regulation of an issue must be included in developing participative dynamic modeling models in order to build confidence and mitigate risk that such stakeholders will resist using models to support policymaking. The development of communications tools, such as interactive tools and presentations which can easily adapt to various audiences, was considered crucial for the facilitation of using the model during policy and program discussions for the purpose of forming decisions. Models distinguishing between decision making and navigation and locomotion, served to enlarge the microworlds in computerized environments, which allowed for the conducting of risk-free experiments using agent-based models to explore how individuals make decisions repeatedly within complex environments that evolve over time. It is a fascinating approach that uses concepts of system dynamics to simulate decision-making by virtual humans living out their lives within microworlds. A range of predictions can be made based on the specific implementations of the model we presented, including on how we should expect individual characteristics (e.g., exploration tendencies, precision, and selectivity) to influence the decision-making quality, as well as on what circumstances we should expect maladaptive phenomena such as precipitous decision-making and contemplative exploring to arise, and when they are in fact useful for the decision-making quality.

All in all, we can conclude that Internet content regulation policies really might have a series impact as well as profound implications on the promotion of targeted consumer behavior. This can be done using a plethora of Internet-based technologies that are not limited to information and communications technologies (ICTs) but can also include artificial intelligence (AI) and other innovative elements. Policymakers and government need to be cautious about the manipulation of consumers' knowledge and free will, thence some regulations and restrictions are needed. However, the field is so new that possible economic regulations and implications need to be properly studied before they can be applied.

Acknowledgements The research is carried out with the financial support of the Kuban Scientific Foundation within the framework of the scientific project No. PPN-21.1/51 "Mechanisms and technologies to counteract the influence of the content of Internet resources and social networks on the national consciousness of young people".

References

Aho, B., & Duffield, R. (2020). Beyond surveillance capitalism: Privacy, regulation and big data in Europe and China. *Economy and Society, 49*(2), 187–212. https://doi.org/10.1080/03085147.2019.1690275

Aikin, K. J., Boudewyns, V., Betts, K. R., Southwell, B. G., & Williams, P. (2019). Individual- and ad-level predictors of perceptions of serious and actionable risks in direct-to-consumer prescription drug TV advertising. *Journal of Health Communication, 24*(5), 536–546. https://doi.org/10.1080/10810730.2019.1632396

Ancillai, C., Terho, H., Cardinali, S., & Pascucci, F. (2019). Advancing social media driven sales research: Establishing conceptual foundations for B-to-B social selling. *Industrial Marketing Management, 82*, 293–308. https://doi.org/10.1016/j.indmarman.2019.01.002

Argyris, Y. A., Wang, Z., Kim, Y., & Yin, Z. (2020). The effects of visual congruence on increasing consumers' brand engagement: An empirical investigation of influencer marketing on Instagram using deep-learning algorithms for automatic image classification. *Computers in Human Behavior, 112*, 106443. https://doi.org/10.1016/j.chb.2020.106443

Bharucha, J. (2018). Social media and young consumers behavior. *International Journal of Supply Chain Management, 7*(6), 72–81.

Brinson, N. H., & Britt, B. C. (2021). Reactance and turbulence: Examining the cognitive and affective antecedents of ad blocking. *Journal of Research in Interactive Marketing, 15*(4), 549–570. https://doi.org/10.1108/JRIM-04-2020-0083

Čábelková, I., Pogorilyak, B., Strielkowski, W., Stříteský, V., & Tahal, R. (2015). Customer store loyalty determinants: A case of the czech republic. *DLSU Business & Economics Review, 25*(1), 28–44.

Čábelková, I., Strielkowski, W., Streimikiene, D., Cavallaro, F., & Streimikis, J. (2021). The social acceptance of nuclear fusion for decision making towards carbon free circular economy: Evidence from Czech Republic. *Technological Forecasting and Social Change, 163*, 120477. https://doi.org/10.1016/j.techfore.2020.120477

Dodel, M., & Mesch, G. (2018). Inequality in digital skills and the adoption of online safety behaviors. *Information, Communication & Society, 21*(5), 712–728. https://doi.org/10.1080/1369118x.2018.1428652

Dolan, R., Conduit, J., Frethey-Bentham, C., Fahy, J., & Goodman, S. (2019). Social media engagement behavior: A framework for engaging customers through social media content. *European Journal of Marketing, 53*(10), 2213–2243. https://doi.org/10.1108/EJM-03-2017-0182

Fakunle, S., & Ajani, B. (2021). Peculiarities of ICT adoption in Nigeria. *Insights into Regional Development, 3*(4), 51–61. https://doi.org/10.9770/IRD.2021.3.4(4)

Gruss, R., Kim, E., & Abrahams, A. (2020). Engaging restaurant customers on Facebook: The power of belongingness appeals on social media. *Journal of Hospitality & Tourism Research, 44*(2), 201–228. https://doi.org/10.1177/1096348019892071

Haenlein, M., Anadol, E., Farnsworth, T., Hugo, H., Hunichen, J., & Welte, D. (2020). Navigating the new era of influencer marketing: How to be successful on Instagram, TikTok, & Co. *California Management Review, 63*(1), 5–25. https://doi.org/10.1177/0008125620958166

Hollebeek, L. D., & Macky, K. (2019). Digital content marketing's role in fostering consumer engagement, trust, and value: Framework, fundamental propositions, and implications. *Journal of Interactive Marketing, 45*, 27–41. https://doi.org/10.1016/j.intmar.2018.07.003

Hosťovecký, M., & Poláčik, M. (2016). Communication skills as the competitive advantage of sellers. *Czech Journal of Social Sciences, Business and Economics, 5*(1), 18–26. https://doi.org/10.24984/cjssbe.2016.5.1.2

Kumar, B., Jensen, M. M., Strielkowski, W., Johnston, J. T., Sharma, V., Dandara, C., Shehata, M., Micarelli Struetta, M., Nikolaou, A., Szymanski, D., Abdul-Ghani, R., Cao, B., Varzinczak, L., Kerman, B., Arthur, P., Oda. F., Bohon, W., Ellwanger, J., Tyner, Jordan, E., & Murphy, C. (2019). NextGen Voices: Science-inspired sustainable behavior. *Science, 364*(6443), 822–824. https://doi.org/10.1126/science.aax8945

Kwangyong, S., Shen, Z., Shin, H., Zhang, S., Chen, K., & Li, L. (2021). The mechanism of how integrated marketing communications influence on the Chinese online customer's repurchase intention. *Science Journal of Business and Management, 9*(1), 26–38. https://doi.org/10.11648/j.sjbm.20210901.13

Leung, F. F., Gu, F. F., & Palmatier, R. W. (2022). Online influencer marketing. *Journal of the Academy of Marketing Science, 50*(2), 226–251. https://doi.org/10.1007/s11747-021-00829-4

Li, F., Larimo, J., & Leonidou, L. C. (2021). Social media marketing strategy: Definition, conceptualization, taxonomy, validation, and future agenda. *Journal of the Academy of Marketing Science, 49*(1), 51–70. https://doi.org/10.1007/s11747-020-00733-3

Litau, E. (2018). Information flows management as a way to overcome "Puberty challenges" of a small enterprise.*ACM International Conference Proceeding Series*, 34–38. https://doi.org/10.1145/3278252.3278259

Liu, W., Moultrie, J., & Ye, S. (2019). The customer-dominated innovation process: Involving customers as designers and decision-makers in developing new product. *The Design Journal, 22*(3), 299–324. https://doi.org/10.1080/14606925.2019.1592324

Liu-Thompkins, Y. (2019). A decade of online advertising research: What we learned and what we need to know. *Journal of Advertising, 48*(1), 1–13. https://doi.org/10.1080/00913367.2018.1556138

Lobschat, L., Mueller, B., Eggers, F., Brandimarte, L., Diefenbach, S., Kroschke, M., & Wirtz, J. (2021). Corporate digital responsibility. *Journal of Business Research, 122*, 875–888. https://doi.org/10.1016/j.jbusres.2019.10.006

Lopes, A. R., Porto, I. P. A. M., & Casais, B. (2022). Digital content marketing: Conceptual review and recommendations for practitioners. *Academy of Strategic Management Journal, 21*(2), 1–17.

Lu, J., & Strielkowski, W. (2022). Russia: Could cryptocurrency mining exploit unsold fuel? *Nature, 605*(7909), 225. https://doi.org/10.1038/d41586-022-01267-0

Manita, R., Elommal, N., Baudier, P., & Hikkerova, L. (2020). The digital transformation of external audit and its impact on corporate governance. *Technological Forecasting and Social Change, 150*, 119751. https://doi.org/10.1016/j.techfore.2019.119751

Matušková, A., & Strielkowski, W. (2014). Technology applications in Czech presidential elections of 2013: A story of social networks. *Mediterranean Journal of Social Sciences, 5*(21), 419–424. https://doi.org/10.5901/mjss.2014.v5n21p419

Minow, M. (2021). *Saving the news: Why the constitution calls for government action to preserve freedom of speech.* Oxford University Press.

Montag, C., Lachmann, B., Herrlich, M., & Zweig, K. (2019). Addictive features of social media/messenger platforms and freemium games against the background of psychological and economic theories. *International Journal of Environmental Research and Public Health, 16*(14), 2612. https://doi.org/10.3390/ijerph16142612

Prandi, C., Monti, L., Ceccarini, C., & Salomoni, P. (2020). Smart campus: Fostering the community awareness through an intelligent environment. *Mobile Networks and Applications, 25*(3), 945–952. https://doi.org/10.1007/s11036-019-01238-2

Raji, R. A., Rashid, S., & Ishak, S. (2019). The mediating effect of brand image on the relationships between social media advertising content, sales promotion content and behavioral intention. *Journal of Research in Interactive Marketing, 13*(3), 302–330. https://doi.org/10.1108/JRIM-01-2018-0004

Reagan, R., Filice, S., Santarossa, S., & Woodruff, S. J. (2020). #ad on Instagram: Investigating the promotion of food and beverage products. *The Journal of Social Media in Society, 9*(2), 1–28.

Redjeki, F., & Affandi, A. (2021). Utilization of digital marketing for MSME players as value creation for customers during the COVID-19 pandemic. *International Journal of Science and Society, 3*(1), 40–55. https://doi.org/10.54783/ijsoc.v3i1.264

Schein, M., Avery, R. J., & Eisenberg, M. D. (2022). Missing the mark: The long-term impacts of the Federal Trade Commission's Red Flag Initiative to reduce deceptive weight loss product advertising. *Journal of Public Policy & Marketing, 41*(1), 89–105. https://doi.org/10.1177/0743915620984116

Shahbaznezhad, H., Dolan, R., & Rashidirad, M. (2021). The role of social media content format and platform in users' engagement behavior. *Journal of Interactive Marketing, 53*, 47–65. https://doi.org/10.1016/j.intmar.2020.05.001

Sollins, K. R. (2019). IoT big data security and privacy versus innovation. *IEEE Internet of Things Journal, 6*(2), 1628–1635. https://doi.org/10.1109/jiot.2019.2898113

Thomaz, F., Salge, C., Karahanna, E., & Hulland, J. (2020). Learning from the dark web: Leveraging conversational agents in the era of hyper-privacy to enhance marketing. *Journal of the Academy of Marketing Science, 48*(1), 43–63. https://doi.org/10.1007/s11747-019-00704-3

Wang, C. L. (2021). New frontiers and future directions in interactive marketing: Inaugural Editorial. *Journal of Research in Interactive Marketing, 15*(1), 1–9. https://doi.org/10.1108/jrim-03-2021-270

Weismueller, J., Harrigan, P., Wang, S., & Soutar, G. N. (2020). Influencer endorsements: How advertising disclosure and source credibility affect consumer purchase intention on social media. *Australasian Marketing Journal, 28*(4), 160–170. https://doi.org/10.1016/j.ausmj.2020.03.002

Wong, L. W., Tan, G. W. H., Hew, J. J., Ooi, K. B., & Leong, L. Y. (2022). Mobile social media marketing: A new marketing channel among digital natives in higher education? *Journal of Marketing for Higher Education, 32*(1), 113–137. https://doi.org/10.1080/08841241.2020.1834486

Yessenbekova, U. M. (2020). Social media and slacktivism in young people's life. *Media Watch, 11*(3), 515–524. https://doi.org/10.15655/mw/2020/v11i3/202950

Zhong, N., & Schweidel, D. A. (2020). Capturing changes in social media content: A multiple latent changepoint topic model. *Marketing Science, 39*(4), 827–846. https://doi.org/10.1287/mksc.2019.1212

Zlyvko, O., Lisin, E., Rogalev, N., & Kurdiukova, G. (2014). Analysis of the concept of industrial technology platform development in Russia and in the EU. *International Economics Letters, 3*(4), 124–138. https://doi.org/10.24984/iel.2014.3.4.2

Zuhdi, S., Daud, A., Hanif, R., Nguyen, P. T., & Shankar, K. (2019). Role of social media marketing in the successful implementation of business management. *International Journal of Recent Technology and Engineering, 8*(2), 3841–3844. https://doi.org/10.35940/ijrte.b1507.0982s1119

The Influence of the Consumer Society on the Education System

Elena Korneeva, Oleg V. Grebennikov, Vladlen K. Ignatovich, and Liliya Yu. Averina

Abstract This paper focuses on the aspects of influence of the consumer society on the education system and the financial literacy which represents an important aspect for the personal development of young individuals. It also analyses the importance and usefulness of the financial education that can help to prepare young people for existing in the modern world distinguished by the globalization, social networks, as well as various fintech and crypto products. Financial education, or the act of providing consumers with financial literacy, is a growing, novel, but at the same time very important issue for various banking and financial institutions, and financial education programs are becoming an important component of marketing, financial communication, as well as customer service for financial services. Our results confirm the considerable growing influence of the consumer society on the education systems across countries and regions. Moreover, the findings show that with a growing complexity more efforts and support should be provided by the governments and stakeholders in order to embed such issues as financial literacy into the modern educational systems. We argue that all the measures might contribute to the creation of the better consumer society that would adhere to the principles of balanced economic growth compatible with the Sustainable Development Goals (SDGs).

Keywords Education system · Consumer society · Economic theory

JEL Classification D11 · I2 · H40

E. Korneeva (✉)
Prague Business School, Werichova 1145/29, 152 00 Prague, Czech Republic
e-mail: korneeva@pbs-education.cz

O. V. Grebennikov · V. K. Ignatovich · L. Yu. Averina
Kuban State University, 149 Stavropolskaya Str, 350040 Krasnodar, Russian Federation
e-mail: olegvlad@inbox.ru

V. Kumar et al. (eds.), *Consequences of Social Transformation for Economic Theory*, Springer Proceedings in Business and Economics,
https://doi.org/10.1007/978-3-031-27785-6_16

1 Introduction

Consumer education is a branch of philosophy, the study of how people might educate themselves about the real character, the constitutive features of good living and observing the principles of sustainable economic behavior (Khoshnava et al., 2019; Shutaleva et al., 2020). To achieve that, students are capable of participating and shaping the community, consumer education should be incorporated into the cultural development of institutions and education curricula, right from the start, and in every level of the educational system. Consumer education cannot be assigned to one particular discipline, but it is an assignment that can be contributed by each subject (Tasdemir & Gazo, 2020).

Educational processes related to a citizens' role of consumers occur both informally and in formal education (Nureev et al., 2020). Education systems can support students to develop consumer skills necessary to handle daily life as well as transform consumption systems and environments (Cieslik et al., 2016; Malik, 2018). According to the principles of economic theory, people must go through the consumer education process, defined as the art of better understanding the connection between what they spend and what they feel. The concept of consumer education has been confusing, to date, with the notion of auditing (Rahman et al., 2020). Not all individuals or societies are on board with the goal and role of higher education in today's world. In general terms, higher education constitutes a complex institution that features lecturers, students, administrators, decision makers, workers, entrepreneurs, marketers, and, in general, individuals with a variety of societal roles, diverse demographic characteristics, and even diverse socioeconomic backgrounds (Kumar et al., 2019). For example, U.S. schools, and especially schools established by and located within the cities, are typically perceived as the examples of institutions in which social discrimination is promoted, and in which their higher education systems are now functioning as mechanisms for reproducing social inequalities (McCallen & Johnson, 2020). In fact, that U.S. educational systems, in addition to preparing students for labor markets, also serve social roles. Much of this education system is designed to provide individuals with skills for obtaining a good job with stable income (Bol et al., 2019).

In general terms, when education, especially higher education, is considered as a social right that is a public right to which all people must be entitled, then human capital, if it is only informed by the approach to it as a form of investments, cannot be regarded as the best tool for explaining the benefits to individuals and societies from education (Gruzina et al., 2021; Williamson et al., 2020). Some authors emphasized the necessity of higher education institutions serving public purposes beyond narrow self-interested concerns, and also for forcing societal changes in order to reflect the character of a society desired by its members (Brown & Hobbs, 2022). People must become better at sending signals into the marketplace that will aid in the evolution of capitalism (Moskalenko & Yevsieieva, 2015). There is surely no problem with this, except that it ensures they keep enough in the purse (by which they mean, always more). The instinct to go with what other people are doing is a sure-fire way of survival for nearly all of us outside modern societies (Ford et al., 2021). Originals are individuals who are safe and secure enough to not care very much about what others think of them, and who allow their own pleasures to guide their lifestyle. Yet beneath this appearance of individuality, the patterns of consumption were strikingly standardized. People are often not as strong as it is required since they are not enamored with fighting the dominant trends of our time.

2 Financial Education and Its Impacts on Students' Consumer Choices

Financial education is good in teaching students to make the right choices. Generally, financial education programs help consumers learn about their finances and the choices that go into having a good and balanced portfolio and cash flow (Madeira & Margaretic, 2022). Teaching consumers how to be financially literate can help them to learn about investing and saving programs, giving them tools to build a better, financially secure future (Kalyugina et al., 2015). Because high-school-age students are also worried about their own skills related to how to invest money and assets for their future, or even college, providing financial literacy starting from the early stages of life will help consumers develop confidence, along with skills (Litau, 2018; Totenhagen et al., 2015).

As discussed above, financial literacy is lower for high-school students, although these youngsters will need to make major decisions such as whether or not to attend college and how to fund an education shortly. In many countries, high school students are responsible for making some of the most critical financial decisions of their lives, namely, whether or not to attend college, and, if so, what to study (Lambrechts, 2020). New international evidence for secondary students that is based on the findings discussed thus far have mostly concerned adult populations, but data that was recently collected by the OECD as part of its PISA survey includes an international assessment among secondary students. The PISA Financial Literacy Assessment provides a rich comparative dataset for policymakers and other stakeholders to use in making evidence-based decisions regarding financial education. The purpose was to assess the young (age 15) students' knowledge about finance, as well as their ability to apply this knowledge in making financial decisions and planning for their future (Moreno-Herrero et al., 2018). Here, the effects of parent involvement on the student learning of financial education courses are apparent. Results from many studies indicate that financial mathematics positively affected students' knowledge of financial products and offers at the banking and financial market in the short run, increasing their knowledge about the concepts (related to mathematics) in financial literacy, as well as applying the methods of financial mathematics in the financial world (Cordero et al., 2022).

Some economists synthesized multiple studies linking financial and education measures to behaviors, with financial literacy may account for little variance in financial behaviors, particularly among low-income individuals (Kaiser et al., 2021). For instance, increasing financial literacy is not likely to result in higher savings when consumers do not earn enough to save. With an array of investments and savings products in an array of complexity, many consumers simply lack the financial literacy education needed to make good choices. Taken together, financial literacy has material implications for families in trying to balance a budget, purchase a home, finance a child's education, and secure a stream of income for retirement (Dew et al., 2020). While debt is typically associated with the high costs of housing and higher education, providing consumers the financial literacy needed to make better choices with their money can lower overdrafts, increase consumers investment capacity, and lead to a generally higher quality of life. The high proportion of teachers who do not meet a threshold that indicates sufficient capacity for providing financial education is concerning, since the quality of teachers is a major contributing factor for financial educations effectiveness (Herawati et al., 2018). The above findings suggest that, as an alternative to efforts taken to promote financial literacy, policymakers could efficiently influence investors risk assessments by providing a risk metric that simplifies decision-making frameworks for all investors, regardless of their financial literacy levels.

3 Financial Literacy, Household Decision and Consumption

Nowadays, in a climate of rapid change and ongoing developments within the financial industry and broader economy, it is important to know if individuals are equipped to navigate efficiently through the maze of financial decisions that confront them daily. Decisions on financial issues are often influenced by the context or the circumstances under which they are presented. The choices made from among complicated financial instruments, which have an extensive array of options, may affect the consumers ability to purchase a house, fund education, or save for retirement, adding stress to decision-making (Hendershott et al., 2021). And this is not to mention the bizarre world of crypto currencies (Lu & Strielkowski, 2022). To summarize, a knowledge about financial products and the way banking and financial institutions work can help the consumers to plan their budgets throughout their lives and to build their retirements plans with a purpose to have enough funds to cover their spendings and prevent themselves from going into debts. Unfortunately, many individuals do not possess these skills and are not keen on acquiring them which makes them vulnerable to the new challenges posed by the financial markets and advertised by banks, saving societies, and other similar institutions.

In Switzerland, only 45% of people aged 35 years and younger were able to answer the standard battery of questions correctly, and while individuals can potentially learn by making financial decisions, this learning seems to be limited (Kendzia & Borrero, 2022). In the United States, fewer than 30% of respondents are able to answer a standard set of questions correctly by the age of 40, although many consequential financial decisions are made long before this age. The standard set of questions has been administered in a number of surveys in the U.S., including the National Financial Capability Survey (NFCS) and, more recently, the Survey of Consumer Finances (SCF), as well as many domestic surveys worldwide (Lusardi, 2019).

Financial literacy is a convergence of knowledge about finance, credit, and debt management necessary for making financially responsible decisions—in short, the choices integral to our daily lives. To be financially literate, a person needs to know key components regarding investments (Dewi et al., 2020). Taking steps toward becoming financially literate is a vital component in living a life that can provide financial stability, decrease anxiety, and spur achievement of financial goals. Becoming financially literate allows the individual to better prepare themselves against particular financial obstacles, which, in turn, decreases the likelihood of experiencing economic hardship on an individual level (Kurowski, 2021). Learning about the critical components of investing allows individuals to make wiser financial decisions, potentially leading to increased revenue streams. Some components to be learned in order to make profitable investments are interest rates, price levels, diversification, risk reduction, and indices (Shaheen et al., 2020).

Recognizing that knowledge about the financial products and services might be important for young people, as well as accounting for the unique potential for improving knowledge and skills for generations to come, more countries are beginning to develop financial education programs for children and youth. It is notable that the financial literacy (or being able to navigate among various financial products and services) is quite similar in case of quite different countries distinguished by the varying levels of economic development—indicating that, from a financial knowledge perspective, the world is truly flat—suggests that levels of income or omnipresence of sophisticated financial products alone are not equivalent to more financially competent populations (Lopus et al., 2019). The knowledge and awareness of financial products and services can differ with education levels and income levels, but the evidence shows that consumers that are better educated and tend to have higher incomes may be just as clueless on financial matters as consumers that are not that well education and have lower incomes (although, overall, the least educated generally do tend to be less financially literate). Being financially literate is a skill that brings an array of benefits that may enhance one's standard of living (Fu, 2020). The standard of living is a term used to describe levels of income, necessities, luxury items, and other goods and services generally enjoyed by individuals, as the result of increased financial stability. It also provides the first detailed guidelines to national authorities about the extent and the criteria how to assess person's knowledge of financial products and services, contributing to both national and international frameworks.

4 Consumption Decisions and Utility Maximization

In order to figure out how households make their choices, economists often look at what consumers can afford, shown by a line of budget constraints, as well as the total utility, or the sense of well-being, that comes with these choices (Collins & Urban, 2020). To understand this, one needs to recall the incremental process for finding choices that have higher total utility, by comparing the marginal utilities gained and lost by the various choices along a budget constraint that is a part of the classical economic theory (Cheung, 2020).

The combination of goods or services that maximizes utility is determined by comparing the marginal utilities of the two choices and finding the alternative with highest total utility within the budget limit (Bechler et al., 2021). Economists sometimes refer to this as an equivalent bang-for-the-buck condition, since the equation indicates that in an optimal choice, a consumer should receive exactly the same marginal utility per dollar for consuming goods A and B. At the final item purchased, the marginal utility per dollar spent for the two goods is equal, there is no other combination of pizza and milkshakes that would provide us with more utility given $11 spent. The budget lines provide combinations of two goods a consumer could buy given a given budget. To maximize utility, a consumer selects a combination of the two goods where the inequality curve is tangent to the budget line (Erfle, 2019). The direction the indifference curves bend yields the two goods could be traded without making the consumer worse off and decreasing her or his utility. Here comes the point when the consumer's utility is maximized which is the rate at which a consumer is willing to trade in one good for another is therefore equal to the rate at which two goods are interchangeable at the existing market. When the utility is at its maximum, the consumers marginal rate of exchange (represented by the position of the slope of the curve in question) is the same as the ratio of existing prices between the two goods. It needs to be remembered too, that the slope of the equilibrium curve is the economy's rate of substitution (ERS) which represents the rate at which the consumer is willing to exchange one good for another, given the current prices (Syverson, 2019).

We can infer a demand curve from an indifference diagram by looking at the quantities consumed for goods at various prices. The maximum that consumers will pay for any product or service is the sum of the highest bid that they are willing to pay for the first unit and the lowest bid they are willing to pay for the second unit (McLure & Montesano, 2019). The prices of those bids are typically downturn and are based on the individual demand curves that are characterized by the traits of the consumers under the constraints on their budget. Given the consumers objective to maximize utility given their budget constraints, they look for the combination of goods which allows them to achieve the highest inequality curve given their budget constraints. As one can deduct from all that discussion, consumers consider their income, as well as the relative prices of all possible goods that they might purchase, and thus select from among all the possible combinations of goods their budget will support. Just as we can discuss making consumption choices within a budget constraint using utilities and marginal utilities, we can also use these ideas to think about how consumers choices shift as their budget constraints change as incomes or prices change. Application in government and business is such that the framework of the budget constraint provides a reminder that individuals may respond to changes in prices or incomes in many different ways. To solve a consumers choice problem, one has to combine the understanding of budget constraints with preferences represented by utility functions (Bejaković, 2020). The revolving nature of the budget constraint means that as individuals pursue their highest utility, the amount demanded for the good will vary.

We can therefore make certain conclusions about the choices a utility-maximizing consumer might be expected to make. Solving the optimal set of consumptions of the ideal complement starts by controlling for, meaning that we are asking how much utility the consumer gets by spending all his or her income on a single good (Guerrieri et al., 2022). Since we have a better-is-better assumption, the consumer is always going to spend all of his or her budget on good goods A and B. If the price of one bundle produces a lower cost per unit, then the consumer will buy that good alone, and thus consumption will occur in either of two intercepts. The more general pattern for total utility, as shown here, is that the consumption of more goods leads to higher total utility, but at a declining rate (Kryscynski et al., 2021).

If a particular goods utility decreases as it is consumed in every additional unit, the consumer will stop once the marginal utility has reached zero or becomes negative. In brief, general rules give us a utility-maximizing choice, called a consumer's equilibrium. Generally, the consumers behavior is to maximize the total utility, acquiring units that allow consumers to obtain maximum utility from the amount of money spent. Therefore, consumers analyze optimal ways of using their purchasing power in order to maximize utility and minimize opportunity costs.

5 Consumers and Consumerism Knowledge

Consumer education is preparing individuals so that they are capable of making conscious decisions in purchasing products within the consumer culture. To teach consumers properly, activities should relate to them and to the items that they consume (Fernandes & Oliveira, 2021). The purpose of teaching consumerism education is to help individuals see how we, as humans, have traditionally made mistakes when it comes to making decisions, so we can become more self-aware, and attempt to use this information to make more crucial, helpful decisions. Traditionally, the subjects taught in consumer education would have been found under the rubric of household economics (Wong & Faikhamta, 2021). Creating opportunities for students to practice applying the content, as through games or incentives, may close the gap between learning concepts presented in class and using this information to address the problems encountered in their actual situations. With careful, creative planning, consumerism in the classroom can become an enriching experience for students, today and in the future. Fostering intrinsic motivation for becoming a wise consumer requires some balanced and well-designed strategies (Bin Saeed et al., 2019).

What is for sure, however, is that the theories of consumer studies cannot continue to be focused exclusively on the behavior of consumers in formal markets, while neglecting consumers making purchases in informal economies. It could be argued, likewise, that those consumers making purchases in the informal economy are making a rational decision in moving into the informal economy because the supply in or absence of supply available in the formal market is so poor, giving consumers little other option but to enter into transactions in the informal economy (Narula, 2019). Another explanation of consumers purchasing from the informal economy is that such transactions are occurring because of imperfections in the formal economy. It could be asserted that not all transactions in the informal economy are made intentionally by consumers, as assumed in the previous view. The results show that consumers frequently engage in unreported transactions in order to help somebody from their immediate network (i.e., for social reasons), because they cannot find the goods or services that they want on the official market, or just because they are unaware of making purchases in the informal market. For consumers of goods and services from the informal market, education and outreach campaigns can focus on improving their tax morale, which has been shown to be strongly related to these informal transactions, and focusing on benefits of purchasing goods and services from the formal sector versus costs of purchasing them from the informal economy (e.g., absence of insurance, absence of guarantees of meeting required health and safety standards). Using a multilevel mixed-effects logistic regression analysis on Eurobarometer interviews conducted in 27 EU Member States and the United Kingdom conducted in 2019, it is clear how prevalence of these motivations varies considerably between populations and regions (Williams & Horodnic, 2018). When students are faced with high-stakes purchases (full degrees) and an information overload, they will typically narrow down to known institutions, or those ranked in the top pages of search results. Given the potentially delicate topics involved, it is necessary to discuss data trustworthiness prior to getting started with results. This would be the situation when the grant-giving authority does not have any control over the research, the selection of study subjects, the processing of data, as well as the data analysis and the interpretation of the results stemming from this data.

The framework postulates that consumption ideology arises out of conflicts between consumerism and consumers desires. In accordance with some authors, a consumerist system appropriates and sets rules and regulations of consumption, both unofficially and formally. Consumerism constrains an individual who acts as a consumer, providing both formal and informal rules and regulations about consumption (Thompson & Kumar, 2021).

Consumerism also structures the knowledge in consumers' minds (e.g., of desired bodies) such that it supports products, brands, and whole industries (e.g., diet and weight, plastic surgery, fitness and health, and self-help). When consumers desires as consumers are unmet, there can be conscious dissatisfaction with the system of consumerism, potentially leading to deliberate motivations to change (Lin et al.,

2018). Neoliberal reforms of developed markets have frequently led to shared, socio-ideological sensitivities, which inform consumers reconciliation with markets.

6 Conclusion

To summarize our findings, we can state that evidence from numerous sources shows financial literacy-enhancing programs help teenagers and young adults to better learn how to navigate themselves in the complex world of banking and finance. Therefore, we can advise advanced pathways for further research related to the financial literacy, financial education, as well as other related fields. It appears that it might be desirable to invest into the state-supported initiatives aimed at enhancing the awareness of financial products and services that would help to create more responsible and focused citizens that would be better aware about their personal finance as well as their pensions and savings. All of that would help the states and governments to achieve a more balanced public finances and to have healthier public finances in the future. As stated in the national financial literacy strategies of many countries, youth who build on foundations of financial competence are more likely to be financially stable adults. With regard to that, a survey of fifteen-year-olds in the U.S. can be recalled that found that one-fifth of respondents had not learned basic financial skills, which are frequently applied to everyday situations, such as creating a simple budget, making comparisons between purchases, and understanding bills. Another report of the results of a financial literacy test found that seniors scored on average around 50 percent right, suggesting that there is a great need for broader financial education among youths at high school.

Unfortunately, many young people do not get any guidance, either formal or informal, about finances. Fortunately, it is not necessary for the school and universities to be financial gurus to use their after-school programs to help students and their families understand financial concepts. In fact, many of the existing activities can be modified to help even younger students develop financial literacy in an age-appropriate manner.

Research and policy recommendations underscore the value of targeting parents simultaneously with youth, making twenty-first century financial literacy programs perfect settings to promote this financial literacy. These programs can offer age-appropriate, practice-based activities and dialogues that help parents and caregivers encourage their children to build positive financial knowledge, skills, habits, and attitudes. Using an intelligent mix of entertainment and education, episodes can be prepared to shows children and young adults how to create and manage money while introducing concepts of financial literacy and entrepreneurship. All of that can equip youth and adults with financial tools and education to ensure a better future—coaching them through their personal ambitions and life challenges, while also making the path to financial independence easier. Diverse stakeholders dealing with financial literacy are working together to train and equip the nations young people for financial success throughout life.

It goes on to say that public controllers should review methods and tools aimed at teaching consumers to manage their personal finances, and provide recommendations to develop programs that will efficiently enhance the positive results stemming from financial literacy.

All in all, it appears that making good financial decisions also requires twenty-first century skills like researching, analyzing, and problem-solving. Setting goals, making a budget, saving, spending, borrowing, using credit—setting goals is only one of the types of knowledge, skills, and behaviors that individuals must have in order to effectively manage their resources.

Acknowledgements The research is carried out with the financial support of the Kuban Scientific Foundation within the framework of the scientific project No. PPN-21.1/46 "Designing and psychological and pedagogical support of joint creative activity of high school students and students in informal educational environments as an innovative form of continuity of school and university in the development of creative talent of children and youth of Kuban".

References

Bechler, G., Steinhardt, C., Mackert, J., & Klein, R. (2021). Product line optimization in the presence of preferences for compromise alternatives. *European Journal of Operational Research, 288*(3), 902–917. https://doi.org/10.1016/j.ejor.2020.06.029

Bejaković, P. (2020). How to achieve efficiency and equity in the tax system? *Revija Za Socijalnu Politiku, 27*(2), 137–150. https://doi.org/10.3935/rsp.v27i1.1690

Bin Saeed, B., Afsar, B., Shahjeha, A., & Imad Shah, S. (2019). Does transformational leadership foster innovative work behavior? The roles of psychological empowerment, intrinsic motivation, and creative process engagement. *Economic Research-Ekonomska Istraživanja, 32*(1), 254–281. https://doi.org/10.1080/1331677x.2018.1556108

Bol, T., Ciocca Eller, C., Van De Werfhorst, H. G., & DiPrete, T. A. (2019). School-to-work linkages, educational mismatches, and labor market outcomes. *American Sociological Review, 84*(2), 275–307. https://doi.org/10.1177/0003122419836081

Cheung, S. L. (2020). Eliciting utility curvature in time preference. *Experimental Economics, 23*(2), 493–525. https://doi.org/10.1007/s10683-019-09621-2

Cieslik, A., Michalek, J., & Mycielski, J. (2016). Globalization, international trade, and human development: A case of Central and Eastern Europe. *Czech Journal of Social Sciences, Business and Economics, 5*(2), 6–15. https://doi.org/10.24984/cjssbe.2016.5.2.1

Collins, J., & Urban, C. (2020). Measuring financial well-being over the lifecourse. *The European Journal of Finance, 26*(4–5), 341–359. https://doi.org/10.1080/1351847x.2019.1682631

Cordero, J. M., Gil-Izquierdo, M., & Pedraja-Chaparro, F. (2022). Financial education and student financial literacy: A cross-country analysis using PISA 2012 data. *The Social Science Journal, 59*(1), 15–33. https://doi.org/10.1016/j.soscij.2019.07.011

Dew, J., Dean, L., Duncan, S. F., & Britt-Lutter, S. (2020). A review of effectiveness evidence in the financial-helping fields. *Family Relations, 69*(3), 614–627. https://doi.org/10.1111/fare.12445

Dewi, V. I., Febrian, E., Effendi, N., Anwar, M., & Nidar, S. R. (2020). Financial literacy and its variables: The evidence from Indonesia. *Economics & Sociology, 13*(3), 133–154. https://doi.org/10.14254/2071-789x.2020/13-3/9

Erfle, S. (2019). Discussing substitutes and complements in an economics principles classroom with discrete choice consumer utility tables. *Journal of Economics Teaching, 4*(2), 93–114.

Fernandes, T., & Oliveira, E. (2021). Understanding consumers' acceptance of automated technologies in service encounters: Drivers of digital voice assistants adoption. *Journal of Business Research, 122*, 180–191. https://doi.org/10.1016/j.jbusres.2020.08.058

Ford, A., De Togni, G., & Miller, L. (2021). Hormonal health: period tracking apps, wellness, and self-management in the era of surveillance capitalism. *Engaging Science, Technology, and Society, 7*(1), 48–66. https://doi.org/10.17351/ests2021.655

Fu, J. (2020). Ability or opportunity to act: What shapes financial well-being? *World Development, 128*, 104843. https://doi.org/10.1016/j.worlddev.2019.104843

Gruzina, Y., Firsova, I., & Strielkowski, W. (2021). Dynamics of human capital development in economic development cycles. *Economies, 9*(2), 67. https://doi.org/10.3390/economies9020067

Guerrieri, V., Lorenzoni, G., Straub, L., & Werning, I. (2022). Macroeconomic implications of COVID-19: Can negative supply shocks cause demand shortages? *American Economic Review, 112*(5), 1437–1474. https://doi.org/10.1257/aer.20201063

Hendershott, T., Zhang, X., Zhao, J. L., & Zheng, Z. (2021). FinTech as a game changer: Overview of research frontiers. *Information Systems Research, 32*(1), 1–17. https://doi.org/10.1287/isre.2021.0997

Herawati, N. T., Candiasa, I. M., Yadnyana, I. K., & Suharsono, N. (2018). Factors that influence financial behavior among accounting students in Bali. *International Journal of Business Administration, 9*(3), 30. https://doi.org/10.5430/ijba.v9n3p30

Kaiser, T., Lusardi, A., Menkhoff, L., & Urban, C. (2021). Financial education affects financial knowledge and downstream behaviors. *Journal of Financial Economics, 145*(2), 255–272. https://doi.org/10.1016/j.jfineco.2021.09.022

Kalyugina, S., Ushvitsky, L., Astachova, E., & Strielkowski, W. (2015). Sustainable and secure development: Facet of personal financial issues. *Journal of Security and Sustainability Issues, 5*(2), 297–304. https://doi.org/10.9770/jssi.2015.5.2(14)

Kendzia, M. J., & Borrero, Y. S. (2022). Financial Literacy among the Youth in Switzerland. *Journal of Financial Risk Management, 11*(2), 323–341. https://doi.org/10.4236/jfrm.2022.112017

Khoshnava, S. M., Rostami, R., Zin, R. M., Štreimikienė, D., Yousefpour, A., Strielkowski, W., & Mardani, A. (2019). Aligning the criteria of green economy (GE) and sustainable development goals (SDGs) to implement sustainable development. *Sustainability, 11*(17), 4615. https://doi.org/10.3390/su11174615

Kryscynski, D., Coff, R., & Campbell, B. (2021). Charting a path between firm-specific incentives and human capital-based competitive advantage. *Strategic Management Journal, 42*(2), 386–412. https://doi.org/10.1002/smj.3226

Kumar, B., Jensen, M. M., Strielkowski, W., Johnston, J. T., Sharma, V., Dandara, C., Shehata, M., Micarelli Struetta, M., Nikolaou, A., Szymanski, D., Abdul-Ghani, R., Cao, B., Varzinczak, L., Kerman, B., Arthur, P., Oda, F., Bohon, W., Ellwanger, J., Tyner, J., & E., & Murphy. C. (2019). NextGen Voices: Science-inspired sustainable behavior. *Science, 364*(6443), 822–824. https://doi.org/10.1126/science.aax8945

Kurowski, Ł. (2021). Household's overindebtedness during the COVID-19 crisis: The role of debt and financial literacy. *Risks, 9*(4), 62. https://doi.org/10.3390/risks9040062

Lambrechts, A. A. (2020). The super-disadvantaged in higher education: Barriers to access for refugee background students in England. *Higher Education, 80*(5), 803–822. https://doi.org/10.1007/s10734-020-00515-4

Lin, S. T., & Niu, H. J. (2018). Green consumption: E nvironmental knowledge, environmental consciousness, social norms, and purchasing behavior. *Business Strategy and the Environment, 27*(8), 1679–1688. https://doi.org/10.1002/bse.2233

Litau, E. Y. (2018). Cognitive science as a pivot of teaching financial disciplines. In *Proceedings of the 31st International Business Information Management Association Conference, IBIMA 2018: Innovation Management and Education Excellence through Vision 2020*, 72–80.

Lopus, J. S., Amidjono, D. S., & Grimes, P. W. (2019). Improving financial literacy of the poor and vulnerable in Indonesia: An empirical analysis. *International Review of Economics Education, 32*, 100168. https://doi.org/10.1016/j.iree.2019.100168

Lu, J., & Strielkowski, W. (2022). Russia: Could cryptocurrency mining exploit unsold fuel? *Nature, 605*(7909), 225–225. https://doi.org/10.1038/d41586-022-01267-0

Lusardi, A. (2019). Financial literacy and the need for financial education: Evidence and implications. *Swiss Journal of Economics and Statistics, 155*(1), 1–8. https://doi.org/10.1186/s41937-019-0027-5

Madeira, C., & Margaretic, P. (2022). The impact of financial literacy on the quality of self-reported financial information. *Journal of Behavioral and Experimental Finance, 34*, 100660. https://doi.org/10.1016/j.jbef.2022.100660

Malik, R. S. (2018). Educational challenges in 21st century and sustainable development. *Journal of Sustainable Development Education and Research, 2*(1), 9–20. https://doi.org/10.17509/jsder.v2i1.12266

McCallen, L. S., & Johnson, H. L. (2020). The role of institutional agents in promoting higher education success among first-generation college students at a public urban university. *Journal of Diversity in Higher Education, 13*(4), 320–332. https://doi.org/10.1037/dhe0000143

McLure, M., & Montesano, A. (2019). Thinking outside the box: Edgeworth, pareto and the early history of the box diagram. *Economic Record, 95*(310), 301–311. https://doi.org/10.1111/1475-4932.12489

Moreno-Herrero, D., Salas-Velasco, M., & Sánchez-Campillo, J. (2018). Factors that influence the level of financial literacy among young people: The role of parental engagement and students' experiences with money matters. *Children and Youth Services Review, 95*, 334–351. https://doi.org/10.1016/j.childyouth.2018.10.042

Moskalenko, V., & Yevsieieva, I. (2015). Effective leadership conflict management in food technology enterprises. *International Economics Letters, 4*(2), 91–102. https://doi.org/10.24984/iel.2015.4.2.4

Narula, R. (2019). Enforcing higher labor standards within developing country value chains: Consequences for MNEs and informal actors in a dual economy. *Journal of International Business Studies, 50*(9), 1622–1635. https://doi.org/10.1057/s41267-019-00265-1

Nureev, R., Volchik, V., & Strielkowski, W. (2020). Neoliberal reforms in higher education and the import of institutions. *Social Sciences, 9*(5), 79. https://doi.org/10.3390/socsci9050079

Rahman, M., Aziz, S., & Hughes, M. (2020). The product-market performance benefits of environmental policy: Why customer awareness and firm innovativeness matter. *Business Strategy and the Environment, 29*(5), 2001–2018. https://doi.org/10.1002/bse.2484

Shaheen, R., Ağa, M., Rjoub, H., & Abualrub, A. (2020). Investigation of the pillars of sustainability risk management as an extension of enterprise risk management on Palestinian insurance firms' profitability. *Sustainability, 12*(11), 4709. https://doi.org/10.3390/su12114709

Shutaleva, A., Nikonova, Z., Savchenko, I., & Martyushev, N. (2020). Environmental education for sustainable development in Russia. *Sustainability, 12*(18), 7742. https://doi.org/10.3390/su12187742

Syverson, C. (2019). Macroeconomics and market power: Context, implications, and open questions. *Journal of Economic Perspectives, 33*(3), 23–43. https://doi.org/10.1257/jep.33.3.23

Tasdemir, C., & Gazo, R. (2020). Integrating sustainability into higher education curriculum through a transdisciplinary perspective. *Journal of Cleaner Production, 265*, 121759. https://doi.org/10.1016/j.jclepro.2020.121759

Thompson, C. J., & Kumar, A. (2021). Beyond consumer responsibilization: Slow Food's actually existing neoliberalism. *Journal of Consumer Culture, 21*(2), 317–336. https://doi.org/10.1177/1469540518818632

Totenhagen, C. J., Casper, D. M., Faber, K. M., Bosch, L. A., Wiggs, C. B., & Borden, L. M. (2015). Youth financial literacy: A review of key considerations and promising delivery methods. *Journal of Family and Economic Issues, 36*(2), 167–191. https://doi.org/10.1007/s10834-014-9397-0

Williams, C. C., & Horodnic, A. V. (2018). Explaining informal payments for health services in central and Eastern Europe: An institutional asymmetry perspective. *Post-Communist Economies, 30*(4), 440–458. https://doi.org/10.1080/14631377.2018.1442051

Williamson, B., Eynon, R., & Potter, J. (2020). Pandemic politics, pedagogies and practices: Digital technologies and distance education during the coronavirus emergency. *Learning, Media and Technology, 45*(2), 107–114. https://doi.org/10.1080/17439884.2020.1761641

Wong, Y. Y., & Faikhamta, C. (2021). Reconnecting self, others and nature. *Cultural Studies of Science Education, 16*(3), 867–880. https://doi.org/10.1007/s11422-021-10033-z

The Role of Education-Based Migration in the Country's Economic Development

Wadim Strielkowski, Oleg V. Grebennikov, Elena A. Baydetskaya, and Juliet A. Kuraeva

Abstract Education-based migration plays a decisive role in any country's economic development from the traditional agricultural society to the modern globalized and industrialized economy, which is confirmed by the numerous provisions of economic theory. In this paper, we focus on the multigenerational overlapping pattern framework for educational-based migration occurring before labor market involvement, and examine its roles and pathways in economic development, urbanization, and workforce composition. Given the rapid changes in both the numbers of foreign-born people and in their composition across European countries and other Western developed economies over the past few decades, it is important to explore not only the extent to which mechanisms shaping associations between education and anti-migration attitudes vary between countries, but also how these differences develop over time, and whether these differences are systematically related to economic factors, such as levels of income inequality or economic development, or the stocks of immigrant communities. Our results demonstrate that education-based migration might increase the intellectual potential and innovations in the incumbent countries, as visible from the examples of Erasmus student exchange program in the European Union. Moreover, this migration can be induced using the targeted economic policies such as maintained by Canada or Australia. These findings can be used as guidelines for stakeholders and researchers focusing on deriving the strategies of economic growth.

Keywords Education-based migration · Economic development · Economic theory · Labor market participation

JEL Classification B50 · I25 · J08 · O10

W. Strielkowski (✉)
University of California Berkeley, 303 Giannini Hall, Berkeley, CA 94720, USA
e-mail: strielkowski@berkeley.edu; strielkowski@pef.czu.cz

Czech University of Life Sciences, Kamýcká 129, 16500 Prague, Czech Republic

O. V. Grebennikov · E. A. Baydetskaya · J. A. Kuraeva
Kuban State University, 149 Stavropolskaya Str., 350040 Krasnodar, Russian Federation
e-mail: olegvlad@inbox.ru

V. Kumar et al. (eds.), *Consequences of Social Transformation for Economic Theory*, Springer Proceedings in Business and Economics,
https://doi.org/10.1007/978-3-031-27785-6_17

1 Introduction

According to the paradigms of the economic theory, natural increase of the human population and rural–urban (as well as, most recently, international) migration become the major components of urban growth (Jedwab et al., 2017; Jiang et al., 2022; Strielkowski & Weyskrabova, 2014). A growing population in any city means that this city needs more housing units as well as other related facilities required by the dwellers, which causes a rapid urban land expansion and the demand for construction and developer projects (Gao et al., 2022; Metcalf, 2018). Once a rural place or a site becomes urbanized, it can start thriving because of a few advantageous characteristics—the majority of which are the things that draw people more into it (such as new jobs, good schools and educational systems in general, or the way of life distinguished by the opportunities for leisure activities modern urban centers tend to provide for their citizens) (Angelo, 2021). When urban areas develop into vibrant cities and towns, they also come through the process of morphing into cultures societies, which may and often really foster economic and educational growth (Brennan & Cochrane, 2019; Li, 2020). As industrialization generates economic growth, the demand increases for improved educational facilities and government employment agencies, which are characteristic for many urban areas (Cieślik et al., 2016). Industrialization has aways historically led to the urbanization and thence to creating economic growth and employment opportunities that attract people to cities (Boateng, 2021; Jandová, 2012). The economic growth experienced over the last decade has been mostly from the city-based sectors (industry and services), and that is particularly the case for better-performing economies such as the developed Western countries (Carson & Carson, 2021).

This is where the migration comes in into the picture. In order to attract new labor force that would be educated and qualifies, those economies in question have to either engage into the brain-drain snapping the skilled individuals from the other countries, or to attract students that would obtain higher education on site and integrate into their societies (Demintseva, 2021).

Group threat theory provides a useful framework for identifying factors shaping attitudes towards migration as well as the ways in which these attitudes might vary depending on individuals' education levels, and external conditions, such as the size of the migration community and economic conditions of the country (García-Muñoz & Milgram-Baleix, 2021). Education also cultivates individuals ability to information-process, and consequently, individuals with higher levels of education are likely to be in better positions to interpret and assess the phenomena of migration, by being able to take into account the potentially long-term positive economic effects migration may have on the receiving countries, through taxes and social contributions, that are generally comparable or even exceed the number of benefits to individuals they derive (Čábelková & Strielkowski, 2013; Conrad & Openo, 2018; Litau, 2018; Vuong & Napier, 2015). The departure of more highly educated individuals from a giving country can also result in a brain drain effect, providing access for the local and incumbent population of the receiving country to the knowledge built up abroad

(Vazzana & Rudi-Polloshka, 2019). The adverse developmental consequences of this type of recruitment to a poorer country could potentially be mitigated through supporting education and training in source countries, especially in fields in which needed skills are scarce. There are arguments for developing countries to compensate developing countries for emigrating their best-educated professionals (Norton, 2020; Waller et al., 2020). The most commonly quoted support for the positive side of this argument is the observation that the returns on the remittances from international migrants have played a phenomenally large part of many developing countries economic accounts, much more so than formal development aid (Emara & Zhang, 2021).

This remittances' role is particularly significant in those countries in which credit markets are not well developed. Remittances, which are the more concrete consequences of international migration for developing countries, have reached significant dimensions globally. If remittances are migrations main benefits in terms of the destination countries, then human resources losses–particularly of highly qualified individuals are its most significant costs (Jushi et al., 2021). This human capital flight can be a substantial economic burden on developing countries, since migrants bring the cost of their education, often subsidized by governments with limited resources. Migration can have high costs for developing countries, leaving a country with insufficient human capital needed for sustained economic growth (Bajra, 2021). In addition, development does not always result in lower migration, brain drain may not be harmful for migrant-sending countries human capital levels, and remittances may not always benefit receiving economies. The development effects of brain drain are more serious in source countries, which have a weaker human resources base, and in which education systems are unable to substitute those emigrating (Yoshino et al., 2020). Often, it is those from developing countries who emigrate are the best-educated. Ironically, migrants from countries where very few people have received higher education are not only more highly educated than their countrymen, they also generally have far higher levels of skills than people from the target countries. Concerning developing countries, it is often discussed how the remittances may result in private investments in education, but little is known about the impact of remittance flows on government spending on education (Eggoh et al., 2019).

Our findings are consistent with findings from earlier works, which, on the basis of country-specific data, showed positive relationships between remittances and private investments in education (Ali Bare et al., 2022; Su et al., 2021; Zhunio et al., 2012). Based on many empirical studies, the empirical support for a reverse-U relationship between the level of remittances and per capita expenditures on education can be found and confirmed. This is due to the fact that education subsidies and remittances can jointly be determined (as shown in the theoretical section), the changes in the real exchange rate can be viewed as an exogenous source of change in the purchasing power of a host countries migrant currency vis-a-vis its purchasing power in its origin country.

2 Economic Theory and Migration

According to the provisions on economic theory, Rogers and Williamson (1982) as well as Todaro (1969) have asserted that rural–urban migration is the main cause of urban growth in developed countries. Regression analyses results from the works of many researchers suggest that over half the differences in GDP levels, and roughly half of the difference in GDP growth rates, between the most and least urbanized regions, are explained by metropolitan regions having residents who are, on average, better educated (Dadashpoor et al., 2019; Marshall & Dumbaugh, 2020). In other words, economies of agglomeration and human capital attracted, stored, and generated are all roughly equally important factors explaining why metro areas tend to be wealthier. Technology-based industrial centers attract workers from other areas just as factories once did, contributing to urbanization (Sabatini-Marques et al., 2020).

There appears to be no straightforward linear link between urbanization and economic growth, nor is there any link between urban area and productivity. Insufficient attention is paid to urbanization dynamics and to the nature of growth, including different ways cities may sustain growth, and different forms or components of this growth (Diao et al., 2019). A good example of this is China which is a country of rapid urbanization, strong economic growth rates, and a natural low rate of population increase (Guan et al., 2018). While urbanization offers a number of economic, social, and ecological opportunities, the urban growth in lower-middle-income countries is also one of the key global challenges of the twenty-first century. The growing concentration of the global population in large cities and towns of low- and middle-income countries means that the link between urbanization and development has become a critical policy issue (Cattaneo et al., 2021). Some regions such as Sub-Saharan Africa experienced a large increase in the population in cities in the last half-century, drastically changing the region's economic and spatial profiles. No country has thrived without urbanization, and all developing countries are overwhelmingly urban (Henderson & Kriticos, 2018). The migration of rural populations into urban areas is due in large part to urban predispositions regarding economic development and opportunities. There are economic, political, and social issues that combine with the circumstances of modernization to cause individuals to wish to move from rural areas to urban areas (Zukin, 2020). Structural changes in or lower incomes in rural areas drive migrants away from agriculturally-intensive places toward urban areas. With so many moving out of rural areas, many urbanized cities are starting to experience an overcrowding problem (Bennett et al., 2018). Another negative is the rise of poor neighborhoods in urban fringes, occupied mainly by lower-income residents, which are slowly becoming a part of these cities. Custom, kinship networks, and voluntary associations are generally enough to meet collective social welfare needs in settlements of low densities and in rural areas, but government growth seems an inevitable consequence of an urban, industrialized society (Mođai-Snir & Van Ham, 2018). In developed economies, it has been observed that urban residents enjoy higher standards of living, levels of food, and the provision of services compared with those of rural inhabitants (Gebre & Gebremedhin, 2019). Economic, social, and ecological outcomes all seem influenced by the form, or quality, of urbanization, and by its level (the share of the population that lives in urban areas) or its rate (the rate at which urbanization levels are increasing each year) (Yu, 2021). Here, the term urbanization means an increasing share of the population in the country living in cities. Additionally, area annexation means extending the boundaries of cities, thereby increasing urban populations, which becomes a major driver in individual cities growth (Newman et al., 2019).

According to economic theory, metropolitan areas are larger than city proper, and may be as large as urban agglomerations, but they are different. Urban centers may also be shaped like stars, either if they are in the form of a circular street grid, or if the zoning has been done, with villages being swallowed up within city limits. Such movements are called urbanization–essentially, increasing population in rural areas (an area of 2500 inhabitants or less) to convert it to an urban area (a central city, with surrounding areas, of over 50,000 inhabitants) (Bonnell et al., 2018).

It will be important for urbanized cities to promote job growth and job creation, working with emerging technologies, creating new, innovative companies in their cities, and considering new global markets (Čábelková et al., 2015). Removing barriers to rural–urban mobility can drive economic growth, but the benefits would be far greater if supported with policies, markets, and infrastructure investments. If cities are going to embrace urbanization and its rapidly growing populations, they are going to have to figure out what works, what does not, and how to deal quickly with negative consequences of urbanization in order to survive (Corsini et al., 2021).

In general terms, some limitations of data about immigration and data linking immigration to urbanization make it difficult for researchers and policymakers to fully understand the effects of immigration on cities, as well as the ways that moving to cities impacts migrants. Rural jobs, such as agriculture and mining, are likely to be labor-intensive (that is, unless taken over by machines or automated devices), whereas opportunities for employment in cities–such as health care, commerce, and education–will require significant numbers of individuals with different skillsets to fill the myriad jobs. It can be expected that the children and grandchildren of mid-nineteenth-century urban residents in countries such as the United States would be far more likely to enter industrial jobs than would descendants of farmers. It can be also expected third-generation immigrants to be far more likely than older-born American-born birth cohorts of the late nineteenth and early twentieth centuries to have been exposed to emerging opportunities in urban industrial economies (Bolzani, 2020). In the 1880s, on the eve of the Industrialization era, when nearly half the wage-earning labor force in the United States was in the farm sector, immigrants and their children made up roughly a third of all workers (Husband & O'Loughlin, 2019). The workforce that made industrialization possible consisted of millions of recently arrived immigrants, and still larger numbers from rural areas. This shows the positive impact of migration on the economic prosperity and growth.

3 Student Migration and Country's Intellectual Potential

The conditions of changing human capital can be best explained using the example of migration potential of students. It appears interesting to examine the potential for students to migrate in regions of differing conditions on economic, cultural, scientific, and educational fields. The factors determining domestic and international migration as well as student migration potential can help researchers to understand these processes (França et al., 2018). The research of the factors that develop human capital in relation to migration processes trends is highly important nowadays. One factor that influences migration behaviors of students is regional differentiation of human and intellectual capital stocks. This metric is important to investigate students' migration potential. The results from some studies also suggest that non-observed factors have played non-negligible roles in the assortative of young people between families who migrate and those who do not (Tosi et al., 2019). Although it is impossible to determine the precise nature of the selection mechanism based on these data, it is evident that the unobserved factors are selected in non-random ways, which dampens negative associations that might otherwise emerge between family migration and labor force participation among young people (Jones et al., 2020).

Insofar as the outcome variables in question are not likely to directly affect whether or not a family member migrated, the results are at the very least suggestive of causal effects—in the classical counterfactual sense of the term—from the immigration of a family member on non-migrants' educational outcomes and economic activities (Triventi et al., 2021). Here, too, the parameter estimates on control variables for migrants and non-migrants tend to track each other fairly closely, suggesting that the net effects of familial, demographic, geographic, and socioeconomic characteristics on young adults' labor force participation are broadly uniform in relation to family migration. Socioeconomic factors that play an important role in examining student migration, concepts like inequality are important because students' decision to migrate are dependent on resources, school achievement, motivation, and values formed within their families (Tu & Nehring, 2020). Since the mid-twentieth century, a large variation of the economic development in the developing countries has made migration studies for students and educated, skilled people feasible.

4 International Student Mobility: A Case of Erasmus

One of the best examples of the international student mobility in the world is the Erasmus Student Mobility Program that supports the exchange of students among European universities, in particular through student grants that facilitate intra-European international mobility. The long history and widespread recognition of success of the Erasmus Program provides a solid basis for European higher education policymaking in other areas, especially in the field of interregional mobility (Cairns, 2017).

Unlike the Erasmus Student Mobility Program and Erasmus Mundus, the European Higher Education Area is not a European Commission (EC) initiative, though the EC has been involved directly in it since its creation, and has provided support for it (Brooks, 2018). Since the establishment of the Erasmus Student Mobility Program in 1987, over three million students and 350,000 higher education employees have participated in mobility funded under this program. The Erasmus student mobility flows since 1987 have reached the respective levels of two million, which has been increased in recent years due to an expansion of the program into Eastern countries (Jacob et al., 2019). While international student mobility is not an accrual phenomenon, it is no longer merely an exotic choice. Today, we are inclined to think international student mobility has increased significantly over recent years. This is the reason why the European Union has promoted the mobility of students on temporary basis under the framework of the Erasmus program since the late 1980s, based on the idea that mutual exchange is very desirable (Arnaldo Valdés & Gómez Comendador, 2022).

For instance, both the successful history of the Erasmus program, which has in particular supported temporary student mobility across Europe, as well as the focus placed on student mobility as the one and only important goal in the Bologna reform process, highlight the critical role of student mobility in the policies and activities on internationalization in Europe. Indeed, using network analysis allows not only for evidence on structural features of international flows for disabled Erasmus students, but also, in this case, for insights into the connections between universities. These results suggest that there is a cluster of inclusive universities, which are hosting students with disabilities at high rates (De Benedictis & Leoni, 2021). The growing strength of this network with time indicates that Erasmus has been becoming more inclusive as student participation with disabilities has increased.

The student network is characterized by modest assortative between 2008 and 2013, while the women's network corresponds with a trend towards increasing assortative over time, shown by the entire network of Erasmus students. Twenty-six percent of the male participants studied in STEM disciplines in 2008, while 14% of female participants did; this imbalance persisted in 2013, when 17% of males and 11% of females studied in STEM disciplines, also showing a general reduction of Erasmus students with disabilities within STEM disciplines (De Benedictis & Leoni, 2020). The growth of international students across regions within the European Higher Education Area and to Erasmus Program countries is continuing. One can therefore see that the key goal of both the Erasmus Student Mobility Program and of the European Higher Education Area is the increased attractiveness of European higher education, which is often operationalized by its selection as an international student destination. Even in the United Kingdom which has always been a smaller participant in the Erasmus Program because of an imbalance between the continent-based students who are interested in studying in the UK, the limited mobility ambitions of British students (twice as many Erasmus students studying in the UK as going to the continent for studies) and the prioritization of recruiting students as a source of revenue–interest for the program is growing. There are concerns about low levels of external mobility among British students, suggesting universities and the EU

Commission should facilitate opportunities for mobility and make placements under Erasmus more flexible (Ballatore & Ferede, 2013).

There are some novel mobility projects such as the adoption of the European Student Card initiative, which would promote the online administration of mobility cycles, and other more eco-friendly, inclusive approaches, consistent with the Erasmus Charter for Higher Education (ECHE) and ECHE guidelines. This higher education mobility action supports intensive blending programs, which allows groups of higher education institutions to co-develop blending mobility curricula and activities for students and for academics and administration staff.

In addition, HEIs from third countries not associated with the program can send participants under Erasmus spin-off programs (such as Erasmus+), provided that the receiving institution has, simultaneously, an ongoing mobility program funded with external policy funds funding the inbound students and staff of those countries. Mobility over a full academic program is distinguished by the fact that many students are mobile abroad over the full academic program, for example, over a period of three to four years, in order to undertake an entire Bachelor's degree course in a different country. Temporarily mobile students wish to experience another education system for a time, but generally to devote most of the time of study in their country of origin; studying abroad provides contrasts or supplements to studying at home of roughly equivalent quality, and most hope that their home institutions recognize their studies undertaken during their overseas time as equivalent to their own, and therefore not compel them to study any longer than a non-mobile student in order to obtain their degrees.

5 Skill-Based Migrants and Canadian Immigration Policy

One of the best examples of the skill-based migration is the making is the Canadian immigration policy. Canada has explored the merits of a skills-based points system for handling a large share of regular migration (Ellermann, 2020). Canada's system created for attracting highly qualified migrants for boosting its labor market and increasing the potential of its economic development is so good that it is used as an example for the same policies in the neighboring United States. There are in fact proposals that would move the United States away from a system where the majority of immigrants are granted entry on the basis of family reunification, and only marginally via green card and refugee status lottery, toward more of a skills-based system like that of Canada (Walsh, 2014). However, it took Canada some time to build an effective and smooth-functioning system and this work started over fifty years ago, back in 1967 (Krysa et al., 2019). Stating its intent to cut the backlog in all classes of immigration applicants, as well as to better address Canada's desired skills needs, the Canadian Federal government passed legislation in 2008 giving the Minister of Immigration new powers to change the immigration intake. Many expected these powers would be used to favor workers in skilled trades, rather than immigrants selected based on education via a points-based system.

According to Ferrer et al. (2014), Canada's implementation of a points-based system—which made skills selection stricter—accounted for a short-run shift in immigrant composition away from the lower-skilled to the higher-skilled. Most of the evidence indicates that immigrant selection on the basis of skills requirements—for example, the points-based systems in Canada and Australia—may have been effective at producing more highly skilled immigration flows than the United States. Overall, the evidence from Australia and Canada highlights the higher human capital endowment for immigrants selected by skills-based policies compared to migrants selected under other policies. There is evidence, at least in the U.S., that lower-skilled citizens are more skeptical about economic immigration generally, and the more skilled someone is, the less skeptical he or she is. In short, a lot of working-class people are skeptical about immigrants, since there is often an argument that immigrants are depressing wages and placing them under stress. The seeming inconsistency of skill levels and educational attainment among working-class migrants with labor market outcomes in Canada is an issue that highlights both the challenges of integration in the post-industrial economy, as well as a stark divide between immigration policy intentions and outcomes.

Some other countries also follow the example of Canada and the points-based system. For example, Tani (2020) confirmed that the policy changes in 1990s Australia improved the quality of affected migrants but had no meaningful effect on measures measuring immigrants' skills, suggesting that this alone might have failed to address labor market-related issues. Furthermore, recent work by Bertoli and Stillman (2019) found that points-based systems, heavily reliant on education, might fail to significantly improve immigrant skills. The complex nature, variety, and relative novelty of skills-based selection criteria might also weaken the effect of information, in contrast with the explicit, transparent information from the immigration racism criteria.

In summary, while skills-based selection would seem to have intuitive effects on social bases for respect, there are other underlying concerns that reduce the effects of such policies. We might be concerned that skills generally serve as proxies for the most problematic bases for selection. As noted, many draw distinctions between legal immigration restrictions on the basis of skills, and illegal discrimination based on factors such as race. For while advocates will claim that skill-based regulations are fair, objective, and transparent, in practice, these types of immigration rules often tend to favor certain groups over others in overly large numbers.

Most of the studies focus more on the evaluation of the efficacy of skills-based immigration policies rather than on the empirical consideration of their role in the selectiveness of immigrants between countries. Despite Canadian immigration policies favoring skilled professionals and those with high levels of education, our skilled immigrants frequently end up in disadvantageous positions when they seek jobs corresponding to their skills and career experiences. Even when performing jobs at similar levels of skills, immigrants are paid far less than their native-born counterparts. The high numbers of Asian immigrants, particularly those from the Peoples Republic of China, Hong Kong, and India, are due largely to the Canadian government's emphasis on skills, education, and language skills in their independent-candidate selection formula, and the consequent sponsorship of dependents in their families. The rate of immigration per capita to Canada has been relatively steady since the 1950s, with the first and second decades of the twenty-first century seeing steady increases in education and skills levels among immigrants in Canada, as the emphasis is placed on applicants with higher mean productive capacity, and therefore immigrants in Canada are on average more highly educated than Canadians. In the 1990s, Canada had pursued a more aggressive immigration plan, with approximately 200,000 individuals—primarily skilled economic migrants admitted through a points-based system—arriving each year (Hiebert, 2006). The first detailed analysis of Canadian immigration policy came from the Council of Canadian Economics; it called for an increase in immigration, eventually to raise the Canadian population to 100 million. Originally, a skills-based system was focused partly on trying to target immigration to fill cyclical labor shortages, but this approach was cumbersome and was abandoned for a more general skills-based agreement. Canada Citizenship and Immigration Canada (CIC) has significant statutory discretion in setting the levels of targeting and making changes to the skills base system. Recent policy initiatives focus on refining the immigration system so that it best meets the needs of Canadians economy (Sidney, 2014). In recent times, Canadian immigration policy has focused on designated profession immigration, aimed at attracting high-skilled workers with post-secondary education credentials and career experience, in order to best meet Canadas economic needs (Kaushik & Drolet, 2018). To put it differently, Canadian immigration policy has been emphasizing the points-based system, designed to attract skilled immigrants who demonstrate a commitment to being able to participate and contribute in Canadas economy and society. There might be a disconnect between skilled immigrants needs in Canada and the existing supports offered to them, and indicates that skilled immigrants require effective needs-based settlement services when first choosing to migrate to Canada, and language- and culturally-appropriate health-care services as they move through the settlement and integration processes into their new surroundings.

In this context, it is important to note that the distinction between skilled and unskilled immigrants entered British immigration law with the 1962 introduction of the Commonwealth Immigrants Act, which differentiated skilled workers, those skilled or unskilled workers who had secured employment, and those who were unskilled. All these political decisions appeared to help in increasing the qualified migration to the country and fostering its economic growth and welfare.

6 Conclusion

Overall, based on our results and discussion as well as the provisions of classic economic theory outlined above, we can conclude that the country's economic development is likely to be correlated with the education-based migration. Economic theory favors the international migration of the skilled specialists and views it as a beneficial tool for boosting economic growth. All of this might be particularly important in today's globalized world and Industry 4.0 when intellectual capital and acquired skills become the key elements in creating the innovative and competitive economy.

Our results also show, backed up by the examples of the Erasmus student mobility program and the Canadian immigration policy, that education-based migration might be a good option for increasing the human capital potential and creating economic competitive advantage.

However, policymakers and stakeholders should also remember that in order to attract bright young people, proper and transparent immigration rules should be established. It is quite a paradox that the immigration system of the United States is often called "Byzantine" for its complexity and absurdism—sometimes it is hard to obtain a visa for students and highly-qualified professionals, while in the same time it is possible to win the lottery and receive a Green Card on a random basis (the drawing is random and is done by computer).

To sum this all up, education-based migration needs to be shaped up based on each country's needs and perspectives, it needs to reflect its political goals and desires and it needs to be backed up by both public and business support. Nevertheless, if implemented properly, it can foster economic growth and development, help the economy to survive the shocks, and increase the intellectual capital that is often depleted through the brain-drain. Countries that face such threats as the decrease in population, economic downturns, and other similar issues (the examples include most of the developed Western economies and Russia) need to seriously think over their immigration policies and to attempt to attract perspective students from abroad. In order to do so, they also need to offer a good quality education that would provide necessary knowledge and skills to the newcomers and lure them to enroll into the study programs, either free or paid ones. Good education system means good workforce on the labor market that would mean higher salaries and more taxes collected from the wealthy taxpayers. Those should be the priorities of today's governments all around the world.

Acknowledgements The research is carried out with the financial support of the Kuban Scientific Foundation within the framework of the scientific project No. PPN-21.1/46 "Designing and psychological and pedagogical support of joint creative activity of high school students and students in informal educational environments as an innovative form of continuity of school and university in the development of creative talent of children and youth of Kuban".

References

Ali Bare, U. A., Bani, Y., Ismail, N. W., & Rosland, A. (2022). Does financial development mediate the impact of remittances on sustainable human capital investment? New insights from SSA countries. *Cogent Economics & Finance, 10*(1), 2078460. https://doi.org/10.1080/23322039.2022.2078460

Angelo, H. (2021). *How green became good: Urbanized nature and the making of cities and citizens*. University of Chicago Press.

Arnaldo Valdés, R. M., & Gómez Comendador, V. F. (2022). European universities initiative: How universities may contribute to a more sustainable society. *Sustainability, 14*(1), 471. https://doi.org/10.3390/su14010471

Bajra, U. Q. (2021). The interactive effects of remittances on economic growth and inequality in Western Balkan countries. *Journal of Business Economics and Management, 22*(3), 757–775. https://doi.org/10.3846/jbem.2021.14587

Ballatore, M., & Ferede, M. K. (2013). The Erasmus programme in France, Italy and the United Kingdom: Student mobility as a signal of distinction and privilege. *European Educational Research Journal, 12*(4), 525–533. https://doi.org/10.2304/eerj.2013.12.4.525

Bennett, A., Ravikumar, A., & Cronkleton, P. (2018). The effects of rural development policy on land rights distribution and land use scenarios: The case of oil palm in the Peruvian Amazon. *Land Use Policy, 70*, 84–93. https://doi.org/10.1016/j.landusepol.2017.10.011

Bertoli, S., & Stillman, S. (2019). All that glitters is not gold: Wages and education for US immigrants. *Labour Economics, 61*, 101749. https://doi.org/10.1016/j.labeco.2019.101749

Boateng, F. G. (2021). A critique of overpopulation as a cause of pathologies in African cities: Evidence from building collapse in Ghana. *World Development, 137*, 105161. https://doi.org/10.1016/j.worlddev.2020.105161

Bolzani, D. (2020). Thirty years of studies on migrant entrepreneurship: New opportunities for management scholars. *Migrant Entrepreneurship, 1*, 11–54. https://doi.org/10.1108/978-1-83867-491-520211003

Bonnell, K. J., Hargiss, C. L., & Norland, J. E. (2018). Understanding how large metropolitan/inner city, urban cluster, and rural students perceive food systems. *Urban Agriculture & Regional Food Systems, 3*(1), 1–10. https://doi.org/10.2134/urbanag2017.06.0001

Brennan, J., & Cochrane, A. (2019). Universities: In, of, and beyond their cities. *Oxford Review of Education, 45*(2), 188–203. https://doi.org/10.1080/03054985.2018.1551198

Brooks, R. (2018). Higher education mobilities: A cross-national European comparison. *Geoforum, 93*, 87–96. https://doi.org/10.1016/j.geoforum.2018.05.009

Čábelková, I., & Strielkowski, W. (2013). Is the level of taxation a product of culture? A cultural economics approach. *Society and Economy, 35*(4), 513–529. https://doi.org/10.1556/SocEc.2013.0007

Čábelková, I., Abrhám, J., & Strielkowski, W. (2015). Factors influencing job satisfaction in post-transition economies: The case of the Czech Republic. *International Journal of Occupational Safety and Ergonomics, 21*(4), 448–456. https://doi.org/10.1080/10803548.2015.1073007

Cairns, D. (2017). The Erasmus undergraduate exchange programme: A highly qualified success story? *Children's Geographies, 15*(6), 728–740. https://doi.org/10.1080/14733285.2017.1328485

Carson, D. B., & Carson, D. A. (2021). Demographic instability as a barrier to remote economic development in the north: Are cities the answer? *Sustainability, 13*(15), 8566. https://doi.org/10.3390/su13158566

Cattaneo, A., Nelson, A., & McMenomy, T. (2021). Global mapping of urban-rural catchment areas reveals unequal access to services. *Proceedings of the National Academy of Sciences, 118*(2), e2011990118. https://doi.org/10.1073/pnas.2011990118

Cieślik, A., Michałek, J., & Mycielski, J. (2016). Globalization, international trade, and human development: A case of Central and Eastern Europe. *Czech Journal of Social Sciences, Business and Economics, 5*(2), 6–15. https://doi.org/10.24984/cjssbe.2016.5.2.1

Conrad, D., & Openo, J. (2018). *Assessment strategies for online learning: Engagement and authenticity*. Athabasca University Press.

Corsini, M., Schöll, E. M., Di Lecce, I., Chatelain, M., Dubiec, A., & Szulkin, M. (2021). Growing in the city: Urban evolutionary ecology of avian growth rates. *Evolutionary Applications, 14*(1), 69–84. https://doi.org/10.1111/eva.13081

Dadashpoor, H., Azizi, P., & Moghadasi, M. (2019). Analyzing spatial patterns, driving forces and predicting future growth scenarios for supporting sustainable urban growth: Evidence from Tabriz metropolitan area, Iran. *Sustainable Cities and Society, 47*, 101502. https://doi.org/10.1016/j.scs.2019.101502

De Benedictis, L. D., & Leoni, S. (2020). Gender bias in the Erasmus network of universities. *Applied Network Science, 5*(1), 1–25. https://doi.org/10.1007/s41109-020-00297-9

De Benedictis, L., & Leoni, S. (2021). Inclusive universities: Evidence from the Erasmus program. *Applied Network Science, 6*(1), 1–21. https://doi.org/10.1007/s41109-021-00419-x

Demintseva, E. (2021). Understanding Russia's Brain Drain in the 2010s. *Problems of Post-Communism, 68*(6), 521–530.https://doi.org/10.1080/10758216.2021.1905533

Diao, S., Yuan, J., & Wu, Y. (2019). Performance evaluation of urban comprehensive carrying capacity of Harbin, Heilongjiang Province in China. *Chinese Geographical Science, 29*(4), 579–590. https://doi.org/10.1007/s11769-019-1056-9

Eggoh, J., Bangake, C., & Semedo, G. (2019). Do remittances spur economic growth? Evidence from developing countries. *The Journal of International Trade & Economic Development, 28*(4), 391–418. https://doi.org/10.1080/09638199.2019.1568522

Ellermann, A. (2020). Discrimination in migration and citizenship. *Journal of Ethnic and Migration Studies, 46*(12), 2463–2479. https://doi.org/10.1080/1369183X.2018.1561053

Emara, N., & Zhang, Y. (2021). The non-linear impact of digitization on remittances inflow: Evidence from the BRICS. *Telecommunications Policy, 45*(4), 102112. https://doi.org/10.1016/j.telpol.2021.102112

Ferrer, A. M., Picot, G., & Riddell, W. C. (2014). New directions in immigration policy: Canada's evolving approach to the selection of economic immigrants. *International Migration Review, 48*(3), 846–867. https://doi.org/10.1111/imre.12121

França, T., Alves, E., & Padilla, B. (2018). Portuguese policies fostering international student mobility: A colonial legacy or a new strategy? *Globalisation, Societies and Education, 16*(3), 325–338. https://doi.org/10.1080/14767724.2018.1457431

Gao, S., Li, C., Rong, Y., Yan, Q., Liu, W., & Ma, Z. (2022). The places-people exercise: Understanding spatial patterns and the formation mechanism for urban commercial fitness space in Changchun City, China. *Sustainability, 14*(3), 1358. https://doi.org/10.3390/su14031358

García-Muñoz, T. M., & Milgram-Baleix, J. (2021). Explaining attitudes towards immigration: The role of economic factors. *Politics and Governance, 9*(4), 159–173. https://doi.org/10.17645/pag.v9i4.4487

Gebre, T., & Gebremedhin, B. (2019). The mutual benefits of promoting rural-urban interdependence through linked ecosystem services. *Global Ecology and Conservation, 20*, e00707. https://doi.org/10.1016/j.gecco.2019.e00707

Guan, X., Wei, H., Lu, S., Dai, Q., & Su, H. (2018). Assessment on the urbanization strategy in China: Achievements, challenges and reflections. *Habitat International, 71*, 97–109. https://doi.org/10.1016/j.habitatint.2017.11.009

Henderson, J. V., & Kriticos, S. (2018). The development of the African system of cities. *Annual Review of Economics, 10*, 287–314. https://doi.org/10.1146/annurev-economics-080217-053207

Hiebert, D. (2006). Winning, losing, and still playing the game: The political economy of immigration in Canada. *Tijdschrift Voor Economische En Sociale Geografie, 97*(1), 38–48. https://doi.org/10.1111/j.1467-9663.2006.00494.x

Husband, J., & O'Loughlin, J. (2019). *Daily life in the industrial United States, 1870–1900*. ABC-CLIO Publishing.

Jacob, M., Kühhirt, M., & Rodrigues, M. (2019). Labour market returns to graduates' international experience: Exploring cross-country variation in Europe. *European Sociological Review, 35*(4), 491–505. https://doi.org/10.1093/esr/jcz022

Jandová, P. (2012). Migration and economic conditions in the EU: A case study of immigrants in Germany. *International Economics Letters, 1*(1), 41–48. https://doi.org/10.24984/iel.2012.1.1.4

Jedwab, R., Christiaensen, L., & Gindelsky, M. (2017). Demography, urbanization and development: Rural push, urban pull and... urban push? *Journal of Urban Economics, 98*, 6–16. https://doi.org/10.1016/j.jue.2015.09.002

Jiang, L., Jones, B., Balk, D., & O'Neill, B. C. (2022). The importance of reclassification to understanding urban growth: A demographic decomposition of the United States, 1990–2010. *Population, Space and Place*, e2562. https://doi.org/10.1002/psp.2562

Jones, A. M., Rice, N., & Zantomio, F. (2020). Acute health shocks and labour market outcomes: Evidence from the post crash era. *Economics & Human Biology, 36*, 100811. https://doi.org/10.1016/j.ehb.2019.100811

Jushi, E., Hysa, E., Cela, A., Panait, M., & Voica, M. C. (2021). Financing growth through remittances and foreign direct investment: Evidences from Balkan Countries. *Journal of Risk and Financial Management, 14*(3), 117. https://doi.org/10.3390/jrfm14030117

Kaushik, V., & Drolet, J. (2018). Settlement and integration needs of skilled immigrants in Canada. *Social Sciences, 7*(5), 76. https://doi.org/10.3390/socsci7050076

Krysa, I., Paludi, M., & Mills, A. J. (2019). The racialization of immigrants in Canada—A historical investigation how race still matters. *Journal of Management History, 25*(1), 97–113. https://doi.org/10.1108/JMH-09-2018-0048

Li, J. (2020). Culture and tourism-led peri-urban transformation in China—The case of Shanghai. *Cities, 99*, 102628. https://doi.org/10.1016/j.cities.2020.102628

Litau, E. Y. (2018). Cognitive science as a pivot of teaching financial disciplines. In *Proceedings of the 31st International Business Information Management Association Conference, IBIMA 2018: Innovation Management and Education Excellence through Vision 2020* (pp. 72–80).

Marshall, W. E., & Dumbaugh, E. (2020). Revisiting the relationship between traffic congestion and the economy: A longitudinal examination of US metropolitan areas. *Transportation, 47*(1), 275–314. https://doi.org/10.1007/s11116-018-9884-5

Metcalf, G. (2018). Sand castles before the tide? Affordable housing in expensive cities. *Journal of Economic Perspectives, 32*(1), 59–80. https://doi.org/10.1257/jep.32.1.59

Modai-Snir, T., & van Ham, M. (2018). Neighbourhood change and spatial polarization: The roles of increasing inequality and divergent urban development. *Cities, 82*, 108–118. https://doi.org/10.1016/j.cities.2018.05.009

Newman, G., Lee, R. J., Gu, D., Park, Y., Saginor, J., Van Zandt, S., & Li, W. (2019). Evaluating drivers of housing vacancy: A longitudinal analysis of large US cities from 1960 to 2010. *Journal of Housing and the Built Environment, 34*(3), 807–827. https://doi.org/10.1007/s10901-019-09684-w

Norton, G. W. (2020). Lessons from a career in agricultural development and research evaluation. *Applied Economic Perspectives and Policy, 42*(2), 151–167. https://doi.org/10.1002/aepp.13052

Rogers, A., & Williamson, J. G. (1982). Migration, urbanization, and third world development: An overview. *Economic Development and Cultural Change, 30*(3), 463–482. https://doi.org/10.1086/452572

Sabatini-Marques, J., Yigitcanlar, T., Schreiner, T., Wittmann, T., Sotto, D., & Inkinen, T. (2020). Strategizing Smart, Sustainable, and Knowledge-Based Development of Cities: Insights from Florianópolis, Brazil. *Sustainability, 12*(21), 8859. https://doi.org/10.3390/su12218859

Sidney, M. (2014). Settling in: A comparison of local immigrant organizations in the United States and Canada. *International Journal of Canadian Studies, 49*, 105–134. https://doi.org/10.3138/ijcs.49.105

Strielkowski, W., & Weyskrabova, B. (2014). Ukrainian Labour Migration and Remittances in the Czech Republic. *Tijdschrift Voor Economische En Sociale Geografie, 105*(1), 30–45. https://doi.org/10.1111/tesg.12052

Su, C. W., Sun, T., Ahmad, S., & Mirza, N. (2021). Does institutional quality and remittances inflow crowd-in private investment to avoid Dutch Disease? A case for emerging seven (E7) economies. *Resources Policy, 72*, 102111. https://doi.org/10.1016/j.resourpol.2021.102111

Tani, M. (2020). Migration policy and immigrants' labor market performance. *International Migration Review, 54*(1), 35–57. https://doi.org/10.1177/0197918318815608

Todaro, M. P. (1969). A model of labor migration and urban unemployment in less developed countries. *The American Economic Review, 59*(1), 138–148.

Tosi, F., Impicciatore, R., & Rettaroli, R. (2019). Individual skills and student mobility in Italy: A regional perspective. *Regional Studies, 53*(8), 1099–1111. https://doi.org/10.1080/00343404.2018.1528008

Triventi, M., Barone, C., & Facchini, M. (2021). Upper secondary tracks and student competencies: A selection or a causal effect? Evidence from the Italian case. *Research in Social Stratification and Mobility, 76*, 100626. https://doi.org/10.1016/j.rssm.2021.100626

Tu, M., & Nehring, D. (2020). Remain, return, or re-migrate? The (Im)mobility trajectory of Mainland Chinese students after completing their education in the UK. *International Migration, 58*(3), 43–57. https://doi.org/10.1111/imig.12589

Vazzana, C. M., & Rudi-Polloshka, J. (2019). Appalachia has got talent, but why does it flow away? A study on the determinants of brain drain from rural USA. *Economic Development Quarterly, 33*(3), 220–233. https://doi.org/10.1177/0891242419844320

Vuong, Q. H., & Napier, N. K. (2015). Acculturation and global mindsponge: An emerging market perspective. *International Journal of Intercultural Relations, 49*, 354–367. https://doi.org/10.1016/j.ijintrel.2015.06.003

Walsh, J. (2014). From nations of immigrants to states of transience: Temporary migration in Canada and Australia. *International Sociology, 29*(6), 584–606. https://doi.org/10.1177/0268580914538682

Waller, R., Hodge, S., Holford, J., Milana, M., & Webb, S. (2020). Lifelong education, social inequality and the COVID-19 health pandemic. *International Journal of Lifelong Education, 39*(3), 243–246. https://doi.org/10.1080/02601370.2020.1790267

Yoshino, N., Taghizadeh-Hesary, F., & Otsuka, M. (2020). Determinants of international remittance inflow in Asia-Pacific middle-income countries. *Economic Analysis and Policy, 68*, 29–43. https://doi.org/10.1016/j.eap.2020.08.003

Yu, B. (2021). Ecological effects of new-type urbanization in China. *Renewable and Sustainable Energy Reviews, 135*, 110239. https://doi.org/10.1016/j.rser.2020.110239

Zhunio, M. C., Vishwasrao, S., & Chiang, E. P. (2012). The influence of remittances on education and health outcomes: A cross country study. *Applied Economics, 44*(35), 4605–4616. https://doi.org/10.1080/00036846.2011.593499

Zukin, S. (2020). Seeing like a city: How tech became urban. *Theory and Society, 49*(5), 941–964. https://doi.org/10.1007/s11186-020-09410-4

Effects of Longevity on Changes in Returns to Education, Human Capital, and Economic Growth

Aysel Guliyeva, Natalya I. Nikitina, Zhanna R. Gardanova, and Vyacheslav I. Ilgov

Abstract This paper focuses on the effects of longevity on the changes in returns to education, as well as human capital and economic growth. Health issues and the quality of life may reduce human capital which can be defined loosely and thus decrease income over the lifetime. The income effects of health are likely to vary depending on how health changes (for example morbidity vs. mortality) and at what time of life (for instance, infancy, working age or older). In this paper, we show that higher rates of longevity improvements would also boost economic growth, even if we eliminate the human capital formation mechanism and only look at the growth effects from higher rates of longevity improvements due to investments in physical capital. We show that some researchers find large labor market returns on height in adulthood, which is to a certain extent a proxy for early-life health. In addition, we deduct the trend that while lower mortality moves populations to a new path of growth, where that path ultimately lands depend on how fertility adjusts to changes in health. By these extrapolations, improved health would inevitably lead to larger gains for unhealthy regions, even though the gaps between rich and poor countries are orders of magnitude larger than gains estimated in the micro-literature. Furthermore, we discuss in detail the aggregate implications of the micro-estimates and point out the complications when extrapolating to the aggregate equilibrium, particularly due to the effects of health status on the population size.

Keywords Longevity · Human capital · Education · Economic growth

A. Guliyeva (✉)
International Economy Department, Azerbaijan State University of Economics, 6 Istiglaliyyat Str., AZ 1001 Baku, Azerbaijan
e-mail: aguliyeva@unec.edu.az

N. I. Nikitina
Moscow University Named After A. S. Griboyedov, 21 Entuziastov Highway, 111024 Moscow, Russian Federation

Z. R. Gardanova · V. I. Ilgov
Pirogov Russian National Research Medical University, 1 Ostrovityanova Str, 117997 Moscow, Russian Federation
e-mail: zanna7777@inbox.ru

V. Kumar et al. (eds.), *Consequences of Social Transformation for Economic Theory*, Springer Proceedings in Business and Economics,
https://doi.org/10.1007/978-3-031-27785-6_18

JEL Classification J01 · J24 · O38

1 Introduction

The issue of longevity, the health status and the quality of life have troubled the economists for decades. Most importantly, the link between longevity and the changes in returns to education, human capital, and economic growth are in the focus of economic theory (Ahmad & Khan, 2019; He & Li, 2020). In general, in all countries—low, middle, or high-income—there are always large and quite substantial differences in health outcomes across all social groups. On one hand, low-income and middle-income countries also have to solve the issues of nutrition as a part of healthy diet and thence a healthy way of living (Bennett et al., 2018). On the other hand, some middle-income and most of the high-income countries have to face the issue of obesity which represents a serious health risk, shortens the life span, and becomes a serious financial burden for the healthcare system and thence for the whole economy, as taxpayers have to cover the costs of healthcare for obese people suffering from such common civilization diseases as diabetes, high blood pressure, various form of cancer, or cardiovascular diseases (Ameye & Swinnen, 2019).

Some studies examine long-term associations between nutrition during the intrauterine period or in early infancy and non-health-related outcomes later in life in low-income and middle-income countries (Washio et al., 2021). Economists study the effect of early-life nutrition on adult health, education, marriage, and economic outcomes. Despite the potential for significant health, education, and economic benefits, the efficacy nationally has been often challenged (Lu et al., 2020). Other components can also reinforce potential nutritional effects, improving children's general health and nutrition. The use of other community-based health programs may have increased after nutrition was introduced to intervention villages, leading to a possible confounding effect on adult outcomes. The lower rates of marriage across the settlements might have been associated with significant effects on women's health and demography, as well as children's health. This is in line with studies showing different effects of men's and women's labor market conditions on other children's outcomes (Moskvina, 2022; Reichelt et al., 2021). Overall, the results stemming from many related studies suggest that increased child weights with an improvement in female labor markets may result from decreased household time to prepare meals. In particular, an increase in the amount of time spent paying for childcare and medical care suggests that improvements in the male labor market had beneficial effects on the children's weight (a reduction in body mass) by increasing the health investments in children (Bertrand et al., 2021). In terms of predicted growth rates of men's employment, economists find substantial effects of time spent buying prepared foods and time spent paying for child care and medical care. When looking at effects of female labor markets, we find a one-percentage-point increase in predicted female employment growth rates is significantly and positively associated with BMI, the probability of being overweight or obese, and the probability of being obese. Besides the fixed effects at individual, county, and time, the models for the linear county-specific trend over time are built in order to capture existing parallel trends of women's labor market participation and increased overweight and obesity. In both extended and within-sibling models, there appears to be no effects of the poor child health of one spouse on labor supply for the other (Fang & Zhu, 2022).

The standard expectation is that, because of the usual non-observed household effects that are related both to child health and to adult outcomes, estimates of within-family effects of child health will be smaller. The standard expectation is that due to common unobserved family effects, correlated both with childhood health and adult outcomes, that within family estimates of impacts of childhood health would be smaller. Although this is frequently claimed as an advantage for using schools as a proxy, these findings suggest this argument is likely to be exaggerated, because health at an earlier age (which is related to later health) can modify educational attainment at a later age (Levasseur, 2020). One challenge with attributing effects to childhood health is the high likelihood that other, yet-to-be-measured, dimensions of the family environment may still exist, and these dimensions could relate both to education at an earlier age to health at an earlier age (Mishra & Singhania, 2014).

To fully understand how education influences economic growth, we must be able to understand more comprehensively its effects on a country's economy. However, economic models have left out indirect relationships between the cognitive effects from education (Litau, 2018) to labor supply via health. Economists suggest that an education-enhanced-health model of human capital provides a stronger political case for education, by capturing both educations direct effects on labor supply as well as indirect effects on labor supply via its effects on health. Education appears to affect the supply overlabor directly as well as indirectly via improvements in adult health (Setzler & Tintelnot, 2021).

In order to fully measure the indirect effects of education via adult health on labor force supply, education level and health status in adulthood are often included. Since labor force supply and adult health are the main variables, inclusion of both father's and mother's education is essential to the model construction. Father's education has a large effect on labor force supply, while, in the same time, mother's education has significant effects on health during childhood and early adulthood (Mörk et al., 2020).

Some researchers in the fields of economics or sociology explore the effects of child health on the observed economic and social outcomes in adulthood—education levels and trajectories, household income, family wealth, personal earnings, as well as labor supply. They present evidence that even nutrient intake during infancy influences health outcomes well after the individuals own adulthood (Cheng & Song, 2019). Although these studies generally control for an array of observed socioeconomic and demographic factors, the ordinary least squares (OLS) regression models typically used for them cannot resolve the possibility for reverse causation, or a third factor driving both obesity and labor market outcomes. When significant on-observable factors are temporally variable, or if reverse causality is suspected, studies may employ instrumental variables to examine both obesity and labor market outcomes. Finding that is strongly predictive of an individual's obesity, but is not related to labor market outcomes other than by its impact on obesity, is quite challenging. Although its validity would be compromised if the multitude of genes that are associated with obesity were also associated with other factors affecting labor market outcomes, such as the desire to postpone gratification (time-discounting), most studies failed to find any effects of common family environments on bodyweight. This approach will produce distorted estimates of the effects of obesity on earnings insofar as those factors are not captured by observable factors, such as education, or parents respond differentially to children's early signs of academic potential in ways related to future earnings.

2 Health Status and Income

There is some evidence stemming from the economic theory that income is correlated with the health status. People with various degrees of income tend to have varying degrees of health issues and problems (Strielkowski et al., 2022). This is explained by differences in the overall educational attainment, the distribution of resources and wealth, as well as in the strengths of health systems (Chvátalová, 2016). Given this, the utility of these measures when reviewing and assessing gender equality across higher-income countries is limited, and can obscure significant gender inequalities within these countries. This is also related to the differences in job satisfaction and thence mental health and happiness (Čábelková et al., 2016). Our literature review conducted in this section of our paper using a vast body of the economic literature identified only a few studies applying multidimensional measures of gender equality in relation to health outcomes in high-income countries. Given the motivations highlighted in the above points, the aim of the present paper is to first, systematically review multidimensional measures of gender equality across countries that have been used as the outcome of exposures in studies on health outcomes in high-income countries, and second, assess to what extent they are related to health outcomes.

In general terms, the assessment and monitoring of gender inequalities in high-income countries remains a priority. Here, we can compare inequalities between income levels in health and perceptions of health in high-income countries and in middle-income countries around the world. Many related studies focus on differences between individuals in their countries highest share of household income versus their countries lowest share, comparing respondents' experiences and views in the two-thirds with respect to their own health and healthcare (Kansiime et al., 2021).

To examine how the extent of the tolerance of income-based disparities in health care might differ across nations and regions, it is possible to compare the proportion of people in each country morally concerned about unequal access to health care among income groups given that country's level of perceived unmet health care needs. In all other high-income countries with similar low to moderate levels of concern about income-based health care inequality compared with the U.S. (such as Australia, Finland, Great Britain, and Taiwan) most respondents typically feel that their basic health needs are being met (Hero et al., 2017).

Variation among countries in the disparities in health care and medical assistance did not seem to be driven by differences in the level of wealth across various states. Moreover, it appeared that the ways people self-reported their health status differed considerably in the countries with high income and middle income. A review of papers examining income inequality and health among populations yield some interesting results that health was generally worse in societies with lower levels of inequality, particularly when the inequality was measured on larger geographical scales. In addition to that, it appears that the determinants of population health can differ from those for individual health (Abulibdeh, 2020; Alfani, 2022).

Although we know that individuals who are unemployed and low-income experience higher mortality, that does not necessarily imply that populations experiencing higher levels of unemployment or lower average income experience higher mortality. Therefore, it is important to understand population health on the social dimension, taking into account the total context that populations are living in. Even though the existence of health inequalities is an almost universal issue, it has been shown that the degree to which societal factors are relevant for health differs across countries. Health disparities negatively impact groups of individuals who systematically have experienced greater barriers to health on the basis of their race or ethnicity, religion, socioeconomic status, gender, age, mental health, as we as many other characteristics (Vela et al., 2022).

Researchers suggest that in United States racism which has produced segregated neighborhoods with few hospitals, higher rates of chronic illnesses, and uneven access to care is a major culprit. For the majority of African-Americans, American government's promises for improving access to healthcare still cannot be fully materialized (Manuel & Herron, 2020). In addition, African Americans are more likely to suffer adverse income shocks, and are less likely to have the ability to rely on savings or access to financial help from friends or relatives when emergencies arise, like when an illness strikes. For instance, 30 percent of older African American married couples and 50 percent of older black singles were dependent on social security schemes for the lion's shares of their incomes. The initiatives by the American law-makers aimed at raising the retirement age above 67 years of age will disproportionately hurt African American citizens and all Americans regardless with lower well-being or worsening health outcomes, serving as benefit cuts (Park et al., 2019).

This is a reflection of the 10/90 divide, wherein less than 10 percent of the funding allocated for healthcare research in developed countries is directed at problems that impact 90 percent of the global population, with even smaller proportions going to funding researchers and healthcare issues that are native to developing countries. Given the quality of evidence found, we can state that countries with social democratic institutional arrangements, higher government expenditure, lower income inequality, and policies to provide safer workplaces and access to education and housing tend to have better-health populations.

3 Improving Longevity and Reducing Mortality

Across the world, economist observe some differences in the mortality structures of populations. A drop in the death rate, unless it is accompanied by, or preceded by, a corresponding drop in fertility, will precipitate rise in the population, possibly leading to lower output per capita (Cazalis et al., 2018). Higher longevity can result in a larger population, which can reduce income per capita if there are Malthusian (congestion) effects. The tool takes advantage of what is called the epidemiological transition following the Second World War, which led to an exogenous decrease in deaths due to several major infectious diseases. The results obtained in a number of studies document that higher life expectancy has little impact on growth of total income, but has large effects on the increase of population, thus leading to substantial decreases in income per capita (Sharma, 2018).

Moreover, other results suggest that introducing a government-run healthcare system leads to substantial reductions in infant mortality and crude death rates, which, in turn, has significant positive effects on growth. Mackenbach et al., (2015), for example, linked rising national well-being with decreased deaths from infectious diseases across European countries from 1990–2008, when they examined the upward shift in the Preston Curve (the relationship between real income and life expectancy) across set of European countries. The association of health and GDP for Organization for Economic Co-operation and Development (OECD) countries during the past two centuries shows that GDP per capita and gross domestic product had significant impacts on life expectancy in most countries (Stefko et al., 2020), which was then followed by lower death rates. Early studies typically found strong positive associations between health and economic outcomes, defined as the level of either GDP growth per capita or per capita. Superior longevity and health were associated with increased productivity, which is the essential stimulus to sustained economic expansion. While among working-age populations primarily captures the impact of health on economic growth, which is mediated by labor supply and productivity, mortality across populations also accounts for macroeconomic effects from the survival rates in older populations, via savings, investment decisions, and welfare spending, among others (Kudins, 2022; Strielkowski & Weyskrabova, 2014). In terms of income inequality, Yapp and Pickett (2019) found that those states that yielded larger disparities in income also tended to exhibit worse results in terms of such health indicators as years of age, obesity, premature death, increased rates of homicide, and higher rates of mental illness.

4 General Equilibrium Model of Health Capital

The impact of health-related issues on the economic growth and well-being is often calculated using the General Equilibrium Models. Using these economic models allows the researchers to grasp the relevance of a feedback effect on the health-related benefits from an environmental policy (Kang et al., 2019; Kumar et al., 2019). The results stemming from these calculations that is reported in numerous studies suggest that explicitly modeling the health-related effects of air pollution on consumers and producers allows for more accurate estimates of the effects of an environmental policy on private consumption and employment (Brodeur et al., 2021; Shan et al., 2021). One of the types of models that is used widely by the economists for estimating the full-scale effects of changes in trade policies, for example, as the outcome of the round of multilateral trade negotiations, is the applied general equilibrium model (often called the "computed general equilibrium" (CGE) model). Computable General Equilibrium models constitute an important part of the development of economic science in the last two centuries or so (Nugroho et al., 2021; Soummane & Ghersi, 2022).

Another common type isa partial equilibrium model, which estimates the effect of a trade policy measure on specific sectors rather than on the overall economy (Chodorow-Reich, 2020; Ferraro & Cristiano, 2021). Partial equilibrium models do not capture the connection to other sectors, and are therefore useful where spillover effects are expected to be small. The dynamic general equilibrium models for the four European Union economies presented in some studies are based on the intertemporal optimization decisions of households and firms. In the present framework, the models break down household sectors in these four economies according to their income deciles. In this type of models, food for direct human consumption is projected in per capita terms using base-year data on income per capita. For instance, the growth in food consumption following growth in per capita income only, independent of changes in the distribution of income, is almost 50% during a 40-year period (Baarsch et al., 2020). Given the estimated spending elasticity of global food consumption as well as the increase in food consumption obtained by the more optimistic forecast of a five-per-cent decline in the Gini coefficient over 40 years could have been achieved by just slightly more than 2 years of growth of per capita income to its present level. Under the assumptions made, a rise of 8 per cent in the Gini coefficient over 40 years would produce a decrease of around 5 per cent in food demand per capita, whereas a 5 per cent drop in the Gini coefficient would produce an increase of around 2–3 per cent in per capita food consumption in 40 years, relative to an income distribution-neutral growth scenario (Lakner et al., 2022). Paradoxically, over the short-term to medium-term, a poor-friendly growth scenario, which decreases inequality through faster increases in per capita incomes in developing countries, results in higher growth of demand, as incomes increase most for those households that have higher elasticity of demand. Other factors may change demand; for instance, rising incomes shift the demand curve of an ordinary good outward from its origin.

Demand functions are programs that indicate what households will want to purchase at given prices using their income. Demand theories describe the rational choice by individual consumers to purchase a most preferable amount of each good given their income, prices, tastes, and so on. Public-sector fiscal and transfer policies influence households' incomes by their effects on those relative prices (Shulman & Geng, 2019). Governments that deliver public goods and transfer revenue to households raise revenues through direct and indirect taxes, although the former is more significant than the latter for the four European Union economies. Households accept commodity prices as given, and they discount future earnings using the reference rate in order to arrive at a present value of lifetime earnings. Neoclassical economics perceives its main tools, supply and demand, as the main price and quantity settlers in the market that is set in its equilibrium state, which influences both output distribution and income distribution. Modern mainstream economics builds upon neoclassical economics, but with a number of refinements either complementing or advancing in the novel realms of economic science such as the econometrics, game theory, as well as economic growth models (e.g., Solow model) to analyze the long-run variables that influence national income.

Macroeconomic analysis also looks at factors that influence long-run levels and growth in national income. Growth economics studies factors explaining economic growth—the growth in a nation's per capita income over an extended time frame. They are also used when attempting to assess the differences in per capita output in different countries, growth rates inside and across countries and groups of countries. In addition, they are employed to measure the convergence rates of different economies. Here is where the overall output of goods and services such as the country's GDP is used to measure the economic welfare, or the amount of wealth a given country produces on average per person. As Joseph Stiglitz has pointed out (Stiglitz, 2019), measuring GDP fails to capture some factors that matter to people's lives and contribute to their well-being, such as safety, leisure, distribution of income as well as sustainable development and growth per se needs in order to be sustained.

5 Conclusion

All in all, we show that longevity has some profound effects on the changes in returns to education, human capital, and economic growth regardless of the countries and regions in question. The duration and the quality of life of any country's citizens shape up the economic priorities, the tax collection system, as well as the spending on such important but vulnerable areas as education and healthcare that depend on the state budgets. It is also important to remember that returns to education are also higher in case people live longer and healthier. This helps to foster the creation of the high-quality human capital as well as to preserve it for a longer span of time. All of this might be quite important in the times of the decline in the population due to the falling birth rates in many developed economies. People in those economies tend to live longer but they also tend to settle down in older age in order to start a family. Yet many have few or no children which negatively impacts the population prognoses.

Furthermore, it is a well-known fact that the majority of health-related expenses for any individual falls into the last years of her or his life and might include hospital bills, various expensive treatments, or medicine. The aim of any government is to promote the healthy style of life among the population in order to minimize these costs and to save these money for other purposes.

While low-income and middle-income countries often struggle with malnutrition issues, some middle-income and the majority of high-income countries face the issues of obesity and the health risks it creates. Therefore, the approaches and policies aimed at prolonging the length of healthy and productive lives of the citizens might differ with goals set specifically for each concrete situation.

The impact of education on longevity is also considerable and notable. More investments into human capital means better educated population which can perform better in economic sense and spend more funds on promoting its healthcare and wellbeing.

Therefore, academics, business stakeholders, as well as governmental officials need to support factors leading to the support of the increasing longevity and its beneficial accompanying factors as far as they help to increase the economic growth of the society and increase the prosperity of the whole society.

References

Abulibdeh, A. (2020). Can COVID-19 mitigation measures promote telework practices? *Journal of Labor and Society, 23*(4), 551–576. https://doi.org/10.1111/wusa.12498

Ahmad, M., & Khan, R. E. A. (2019). Does demographic transition with human capital dynamics matter for economic growth? A dynamic panel data approach to GMM. *Social Indicators Research, 142*(2), 753–772. https://doi.org/10.1007/s11205-018-1928-x

Alfani, G. (2022). Epidemics, Inequality, and Poverty in Preindustrial and Early Industrial Times. *Journal of Economic Literature, 60*(1), 3–40. https://doi.org/10.1257/jel.20201640

Ameye, H., & Swinnen, J. (2019). Obesity, income and gender: The changing global relationship. *Global Food Security, 23*, 267–281. https://doi.org/10.1016/j.gfs.2019.09.003

Baarsch, F., Granadillos, J. R., Hare, W., Knaus, M., Krapp, M., Schaeffer, M., & Lotze-Campen, H. (2020). The impact of climate change on incomes and convergence in Africa. *World Development, 126*, 104699. https://doi.org/10.1016/j.worlddev.2019.104699

Bennett, S., Glandon, D., & Rasanathan, K. (2018). Governing multisectoral action for health in low-income and middle-income countries: Unpacking the problem and rising to the challenge. *BMJ Global Health, 3*(Suppl 4), e000880. https://doi.org/10.1136/bmjgh-2018-000880

Bertrand, M., Cortes, P., Olivetti, C., & Pan, J. (2021). Social norms, labour market opportunities, and the marriage gap between skilled and unskilled women. *The Review of Economic Studies, 88*(4), 1936–1978. https://doi.org/10.1093/restud/rdaa066

Brodeur, A., Gray, D., Islam, A., & Bhuiyan, S. (2021). A literature review of the economics of COVID-19. *Journal of Economic Surveys, 35*(4), 1007–1044. https://doi.org/10.1111/joes.12423

Čábelková, I., Abrhám, J., & Strielkowski, W. (2015). Factors influencing job satisfaction in post-transition economies: The case of the Czech Republic. *International Journal of Occupational Safety and Ergonomics, 21*(4), 448–456. https://doi.org/10.1080/10803548.2015.1073007

Cazalis, V., Loreau, M., & Henderson, K. (2018). Do we have to choose between feeding the human population and conserving nature? Modelling the global dependence of people on ecosystem services. *Science of the Total Environment, 634*, 1463–1474. https://doi.org/10.1016/j.scitotenv.2018.03.360

Cheng, S., & Song, X. (2019). Linked lives, linked trajectories: Intergenerational association of intragenerational income mobility. *American Sociological Review, 84*(6), 1037–1068. https://doi.org/10.1177/0003122419884497

Chodorow-Reich, G. (2020). Regional data in macroeconomics: Some advice for practitioners. *Journal of Economic Dynamics and Control, 115*, 103875. https://doi.org/10.1016/j.jedc.2020.103875

Chvátalová, I. (2016). Social policy in the European Union. *Czech Journal of Social Sciences, Business and Economics, 5*(1), 37–41. https://doi.org/10.24984/cjssbe.2016.5.1.4

Fang, G., & Zhu, Y. (2022). Long-term impacts of school nutrition: Evidence from China's school meal reform. *World Development, 153*, 105854. https://doi.org/10.1016/j.worlddev.2022.105854

Ferraro, O., & Cristiano, E. (2021). Family business in the digital age: The state of the art and the impact of change in the estimate of economic value. *Journal of Risk and Financial Management, 14*(7), 301. https://doi.org/10.3390/jrfm14070301

He, L., & Li, N. (2020). The linkages between life expectancy and economic growth: Some new evidence. *Empirical Economics, 58*(5), 2381–2402. https://doi.org/10.1007/s00181-018-1612-7

Hero, J. O., Zaslavsky, A. M., & Blendon, R. J. (2017). The United States leads other nations in differences by income in perceptions of health and health care. *Health Affairs, 36*(6), 1032–1040. https://doi.org/10.1377/hlthaff.2017.0006

Kang, M. Y., Myong, J. P., & Kim, H. R. (2019). Job characteristics as risk factors for early retirement due to ill health: The Korean longitudinal study of aging (2006–2014). *Journal of Occupational Health, 61*(1), 63–72. https://doi.org/10.1002/1348-9585.12014

Kansiime, M. K., Tambo, J. A., Mugambi, I., Bundi, M., Kara, A., & Owuor, C. (2021). COVID-19 implications on household income and food security in Kenya and Uganda: Findings from a rapid assessment. *World Development, 137*, 105199. https://doi.org/10.1016/j.worlddev.2020.105199

Kudins, J. (2022). Economic usefulness of older workers in terms of productivity in the modern world. *Insights into Regional Development, 4*(1), 40–56. https://doi.org/10.9770/IRD.2022.4.1(3)

Kumar, B., Jensen, M. M., Strielkowski, W., Johnston, J. T., Sharma, V., Dandara, C., Shehata, M., Micarelli Struetta, M., Nikolaou, A., Szymanski, D., Abdul-Ghani, R., Cao, B., Varzinczak, L., Kerman, B., Arthur, P., Oda, F., Bohon, W., Ellwanger, J., Tyner, J., & E., & Murphy. C. (2019). NextGen voices: Science-inspired sustainable behavior. *Science, 364*(6443), 822–824. https://doi.org/10.1126/science.aax8945

Lakner, C., Mahler, D. G., Negre, M., & Prydz, E. B. (2022). How much does reducing inequality matter for global poverty? *Journal of Economic Inequality*. https://doi.org/10.1007/s10888-021-09510-w

Levasseur, P. (2020). Fat black sheep: Educational penalties of childhood obesity in an emerging country. *Public Health Nutrition, 23*(18), 3394–3408. https://doi.org/10.1017/S1368980020002906

Litau, E. Y. (2018). Cognitive science as a pivot of teaching financial disciplines. In *Proceedings of the 31st International Business Information Management Association Conference, IBIMA 2018: Innovation Management and Education Excellence through Vision 2020*, 72–80.

Lu, J., Zhang, C., Ren, L., Liang, M., Strielkowski, W., & Streimikis, J. (2020). Evolution of external health costs of electricity generation in the baltic states. *International Journal of Environmental Research and Public Health, 17*(15), 5265. https://doi.org/10.3390/ijerph17155265

Mackenbach, J. P., Kulhánová, I., Bopp, M., Borrell, C., Deboosere, P., Kovács, K., & De Gelder, R. (2015). Inequalities in alcohol-related mortality in 17 European countries: A retrospective analysis of mortality registers. *PLoS Medicine, 12*(12), e1001909. https://doi.org/10.1371/journal.pmed.1001909

Manuel, T., & Herron, T. L. (2020). An ethical perspective of business CSR and the COVID-19 pandemic. *Society and Business Review, 15*(3), 235–253. https://doi.org/10.1108/SBR-06-2020-0086

Mishra, U., & Singhania, D. (2014). contrasting the levels of poverty against the burden of poverty: an Indian case. *International Economics Letters, 3*(2), 26–35. https://doi.org/10.24984/iel.2014.3.2.1.

Mörk, E., Sjögren, A., & Svaleryd, H. (2020). Consequences of parental job loss on the family environment and on human capital formation-Evidence from workplace closures. *Labour Economics, 67*, 101911. https://doi.org/10.1016/j.labeco.2020.101911

Moskvina, J. (2022). Work after retirement: The evidence of sustainable employment from Lithuanian enterprise. *Insights into Regional Development, 4*(2), 52–62. https://doi.org/10.9770/IRD.2022.4.2(4)

Nugroho, A., Amir, H., Maududy, I., & Marlina, I. (2021). Poverty eradication programs in Indonesia: Progress, challenges and reforms. *Journal of Policy Modeling, 43*(6), 1204–1224. https://doi.org/10.1016/j.jpolmod.2021.05.002

Park, S. S., Wiemers, E. E., & Seltzer, J. A. (2019). The family safety net of black and white multigenerational families. *Population and Development Review, 45*(2), 351. https://doi.org/10.1111/padr.12233

Reichelt, M., Makovi, K., & Sargsyan, A. (2021). The impact of COVID-19 on gender inequality in the labor market and gender-role attitudes. *European Societies, 23*(sup1), S228–S245. https://doi.org/10.1080/14616696.2020.1823010

Setzler, B., & Tintelnot, F. (2021). The effects of foreign multinationals on workers and firms in the United States. *The Quarterly Journal of Economics, 136*(3), 1943–1991. https://doi.org/10.1093/qje/qjab015

Shan, Y., Ou, J., Wang, D., Zeng, Z., Zhang, S., Guan, D., & Hubacek, K. (2021). Impacts of COVID-19 and fiscal stimuli on global emissions and the Paris Agreement. *Nature Climate Change, 11*(3), 200–206. https://doi.org/10.1038/s41558-020-00977-5

Sharma, R. (2018). Health and economic growth: Evidence from dynamic panel data of 143 years. *PLoS ONE, 13*(10), e0204940. https://doi.org/10.1371/journal.pone.0204940

Shulman, J. D., & Geng, X. (2019). Does it pay to shroud in-app purchase prices? *Information Systems Research, 30*(3), 856–871. https://doi.org/10.1287/isre.2019.0835

Soummane, S., & Ghersi, F. (2022). Projecting Saudi sectoral electricity demand in 2030 using a computable general equilibrium model. *Energy Strategy Reviews, 39*, 100787. https://doi.org/10.1016/j.esr.2021.100787

Stefko, R., Gavurova, B., Ivankova, V., & Rigelsky, M. (2020). Gender inequalities in health and their effect on the economic prosperity represented by the GDP of selected developed countries – Empirical study. *International Journal of Environmental Research and Public Health, 17*(10), 3555. https://doi.org/10.3390/ijerph17103555

Stiglitz, J. E. (2019). *Measuring what counts: The global movement for well-being*. The New Press.

Strielkowski, W., & Weyskrabova, B. (2014). Ukrainian labour migration and remittances in the Czech Republic. *Tijdschrift Voor Economische En Sociale Geografie, 105*(1), 30–45. https://doi.org/10.1111/tesg.12052

Strielkowski, W., Zenchenko, S., Tarasova, A., & Radyukova, Y. (2022). Management of smart and sustainable cities in the Post-COVID-19 Era: Lessons and implications. *Sustainability, 14*(12), 7267. https://doi.org/10.3390/su14127267

Vela, M. B., Erondu, A. I., Smith, N. A., Peek, M. E., Woodruff, J. N., & Chin, M. H. (2022). Eliminating explicit and implicit biases in health care: Evidence and research needs. *Annual Review of Public Health, 43*, 477. https://doi.org/10.1146/annurev-publhealth-052620-103528

Washio, Y., Atreyapurapu, S., Hayashi, Y., Taylor, S., Chang, K., Ma, T., & Isaacs, K. (2021). Systematic review on use of health incentives in US to change maternal health behavior. *Preventive Medicine, 145*, 106442. https://doi.org/10.1016/j.ypmed.2021.106442

Yapp, E., & Pickett, K. E. (2019). Greater income inequality is associated with higher rates of intimate partner violence in Latin America. *Public Health, 175*, 87–89. https://doi.org/10.1016/j.puhe.2019.07.004

The Role of Open Innovation in Governmental Sustainability

Grigorios L. Kyriakopoulos

Abstract Open innovation is an emerging practice in the public sector, requiring time and energy from public officials and managers. Therefore, it is an imperative need to highlight the problem of how to legitimate open innovation cases in the public sector and the implications for their institutionalization. In this context, public managers need to keep the momentum inside and outside their organizations. Open innovation processes do need suitable managerial tools to develop their full potential, enabling public managers to lead innovation initiatives within their organizations. This study covered instances where open innovation and governance are co-functional and provided evidence of future avenues of public management, based on open innovation. Such future endeavors involve the collaboration of citizens with public authorities, pinpointing the social implications and challenges of open-innovation structured governance. The managerial legitimacy and the procedural accountability were assessed by defining two decades of analysis: the pre-COVID-19 pandemic period and the COVID-19 pandemic crisis. In this emergency the long period of confinement posed challenges and opportunities to develop initiatives, channeling the civic energy to co-produce solutions among a wide range of actors. The key features of collaborative governance that guided open innovation initiatives in public sector were also denoted.

Keywords Governmental sustainability · Open innovation · Public management · Organizational collaboration · COVID-19 pandemic

JEL Classification L1 · O3 · N4

G. L. Kyriakopoulos (✉)
School of Electrical and Computer Engineering, National Technical University of Athens, 15780 Zografou, Greece
e-mail: gregkyr@chemeng.ntua.gr

V. Kumar et al. (eds.), *Consequences of Social Transformation for Economic Theory*, Springer Proceedings in Business and Economics,
https://doi.org/10.1007/978-3-031-27785-6_19

1 Introduction

Nowadays it has been encouraging to see people from different backgrounds joining forces to serve the common good. A paradigm of this has been illustrated by two initiatives whereby public sector bodies are collaborating with various other actors to find solutions to problems occurring as a result of the expanding pandemic. The measures of lockdowns and severe restrictions to mobility are obviously challenging, thus, motivating them to create these open innovation systems (Criado & Guevara-Gómez, 2021a). Such innovation programs aim at fostering productive partnerships and addressing public health issues. These past examples can explain why such initiatives were able to be developed and launched so swiftly especially among developed economies, as in the case of Spain (Criado & Guevara-Gómez, 2021a).

Historical Context of Open Innovation into the Information Age

The Information Age refers to gathering and control of information, thus, defining characteristic of the current era in human civilization. The start period of Information Age began was around the 1970s and is still going on to date. The Information Age is also termed as Computer Age, Digital Age, or New Media Age, and it covers a historical period that began in the mid-twentieth century, which has been characterized by a rapid epochal shift from traditional industry established by the Industrial Revolution to a primarily informatics-structured and technological-driven economy. The Information Age has coupled with the advent of personal computers, while other researchers and computer historians trace its beginnings dating back to the studies of American mathematician Claude E. Shannon, who proposed that information can be quantitatively encoded as a series of binary digits of ones and zeroes. Shannon, the "father of Information Theory", investigated how all information media, from telephone signals to radio waves to television, are transmitted without error through a single framework (Tucci, 2014).

The advent of Internet since the 1970s by the US Department of Defense and the subsequent adoption of personal computers a decade later- enabled the ongoing development of Information or Digital Revolution up to date. Striking technological changes, such as the development of fiber optic cables and faster microprocessors, accelerated the transmission and processing of information. The World Wide Web was initially utilized by companies as an electronic billboard for their products and services, being morphed into an interactive consumer exchange for goods and information. Then, electronic mail (email) supported near-instant exchange of information and it was widely adopted as the primary platform for labour and office needs of communication. In this context of contemporary digitization of information, there exists a tremendous impact on traditional media businesses, at almost the whole spectrum of entrepreneurial activities, including book publishing, music industry, as well as the leap frog technologies' evolution, from cable- to wi-fi telecommunication. As information is increasingly described in digital form businesses across many industries have sharpened their focus on how to capitalize on the Information Age (Tucci, 2014).

However, despite the fact that companies whose businesses are built on digitized information they have become valuable and powerful in a relatively short period of time, there are researchers who argued that just as land owners held the wealth and wielded power in the Agrarian Age and manufacturers such as Henry Ford and Cyrus McCormick accumulated fortunes in the Industrial Age, the current Information Age has spawned its own breed of wealthy influential brokers, especially from well-known and widely utilized communication modes and commercialized applications through the today social media platforms (Tucci, 2014).

Thematic Context of Open Innovation Development as Part of the Information Age

Focusing on technological leadership in this Information Age it is important to signify the role of the chief technology officer (CTO) who entails in today's ever-changing landscape. The CTO position is the highest of the technological leadership roles in the organization, overseeing all technology that drive value for customers. Especially at the widespread of the COVID-19 pandemic users' demands are sharply evolved, but the CTO roles is a trend that shows no sign of ceasing any time soon. A major duty undertaken by the CTO is to plan out and implement a technological strategy for the organization, thus, driving maximum value from the capabilities at the company's assets. The success of such a strategy is associated with clear allocation of responsibilities and joint collaboration/communication among board, leadership team, and labor workforce, so no one can be left behind (Hurst, 2022).

In response to the today entrepreneurial reality to a rapidly changing environments it is a further imperative need to constantly link information based on open systems with open innovations. Therefore, to successfully stay in tune with consumer requirements, constant and open innovation plays a pronounced role, especially considering the cases where the rapid evolution of the CTO role can (or should) ensure that an organization maintains a competitive edge (Hurst, 2022).

Such an achievement is related to fluctuated behavior of demand that transforms the current market and technology innovation, necessitating that companies are firmly attached to the forefront of innovation and development. In such a goal the future strategies are implying the shift of companies' mission to provide cutting-edge solutions, to drive to disruptive technology, and to deliver changes and innovation from both peoples' and processes' perspectives (Hurst, 2022). New technologies can take data from multiple sources in order to provide a realistic appreciation of the risks someone faces, enabling companies to develop their developmental models and plans at a proactive and predictive way, rather than a reactive one (Hurst, 2022). CTO must consider all the surrounding process and infrastructure needed to mitigate the security risks of an initiative (Hurst, 2022).

Definition and Functional Characteristics of Innovation in Governmental and Business Environments

In the last century—due to rapid, unexpected, and unpredictable changes in local societies—public and private organizations, as well as management systems, they are transformed by either choice or pressure or adaptation for survival (Farazmand, 2004). Governmental transformation is accompanied by citizens' roles who express transforming attitudes from that of traditional, passive, or receptive, towards highly demanding, challenging, and participatory attitudes. Subsequently new technologies and organizational networks enable citizens to play a more decisive role in the governmental and the administrative processes that further affect their everyday lives (Farazmand, 2004).

It is crucial to note that national prosperity is certainly characterized by persistent inequality that in fact widens rapidly between the rich and the poor, and between the rich nations of the industrialized world and those of the developing and less developed countries. Therefore, governments are constantly facing challenges in administration and management, while developing nations are far more seriously side-affected and vulnerable than those in industrialized nations (Farazmand, 2004). Subsequently, challenges present opportunities as well as severe constraints to the governments in developing nations that are making efforts to develop their economies, to utilize or manage their resources, to promote the social welfare of their citizens, to advance in science and technology, as well as to improve their capacity in both governability and service delivery to their citizens. To meet these challenges, all developed and developing economies are forced to rethink the philosophy of governments, to reconsider the modes of governance, and to redesign new systems and organizations of public administration and management (Farazmand, 2004). In this context strategic planning and management has proven to play a decisive role for economies to accomplish developmental goals, but strategic human resources development and management are key-aspects to the design and to the implementation of developmental plans focusing on national prosperity and economic growth, especially in those fields where these strategic plans can be accomplished through innovation (Farazmand, 2004).

Innovation refers to novelty in ideas, approaches, methods, processes, structures, behaviors, attitudes, and cultures, as well as in technologies and skills. It also refers to the knowledge background that is used to produce new products and deliver services (even at niche markets), to govern and administer societies, and to manage organizations of all types. This broad definition is not conclusive but it covers the main terminology and characteristics attributed to the innovation concept. Generally, the versatile conceptualization of innovation is able to serve several functions as follows:

- It is a useful way of expressing creativity through modeling and establishing frames of reference that serve as guideposts to observation and experiential as well as metaphorical phenomena.
- It serves as a guide to explanations, but it also serves as a transition to reality, to practice, and future actions.
- It is a problem-solving approach, when the old notion that "need and necessity lead to creativity and invention" holds true in case of innovations.
- Conceptualizing innovations in human resources development and management is both helpful and necessary for national development process especially in large-scale contexts/sectors, as that of construction and public services. In this respect household and international environmental considerations are causing uncertainties and demand for innovations, creativity, and self-reliance, which itself serves as a key impetus for further innovations to promote capacity enhancement in all areas of science, governance, management, and administration.

Innovation is an answer to constantly challenging problems and changing needs and expectations, individual obligations, and sharing responsibilities that citizens and governments face all the time, especially in the today rapidly globalized era. The imperative need to innovate means to invent as well as to create the means of progress and advancement. In business terms innovation makes highly caliber and niche markets, such as medical breakthroughs, new types of computer software, new advancements discovered at the space industry, enabling these markets to stay on top and be dynamic (Farazmand, 2004).

In real world condition there is actually no limit to the areas of innovation in human resources development and management. However, these areas may be grouped into the following three categories: (a) human resources or personnel area, including general management and leadership, (2) technological and financial resources necessary to sustain and promote strategic human resources, (3) organizational settings covering the areas of structure, process, and value system or culture. Organizational settings provide structure through which processes of innovation take shape, while the norms and values help shaping a system of organizational culture that can promote or hinder strategic innovations. Once institutionalized, the new culture of innovation can shape and reshape the process and the structure of an organization. Institutionalization is key to the legitimacy and support systems that innovative ideas can enjoy as a strategic instrument toward capacity building and enhancement in human resources development and management (Farazmand, 2004).

The suitability of selecting an open- versus closed-innovation it is shaped by the interplay between firms' analytical orientation and the institutional conditions within the operation entrepreneurial environments. Whereas there is a well-developed research production in the field of innovation performance, there is sparsely investigation of the factors that affect and influence innovation governance (Liedong, 2020). In this context, regulatory, normative, and cognitive institutional voids are variably impacting on the choice of open versus closed innovation. The analytical orientation of firms, their political connections, and the collaborating partnership developed among home country institutions, they can moderate the effect of institutional voids on innovation governance (Liedong, 2020).

Open innovation has always been centered on the organization especially where innovation is involved. Inflow and outflow of knowledge into organizations have addressed the concept around business (or government) organizations and their research and development (R&D) activities. The open innovation framework can be especially suitable for a better operation of focal organization, which is usually a business organization that offers a platform for other organizations to collaborate, by supporting the focal organization to commercialize its knowledge and to gain economic benefits or vice versa. In this respect Omar et al. (2017) argued the versatile role of an open innovation platform that functions as 'supplier-driven', that is, 'supplier' indicating the focal organization where innovation occurs. Another approach for open innovation it is its 'customer-driven' framework, where the customer organization or demand-creating organization can provide a platform for open innovation. This framework of a 'customer-driven' open innovation platform was explored in the case of Malaysia's Multimedia Super Corridor (MSC Malaysia) where the customer, in this case the Malaysian government provides the demand pull for creating an open-innovation platform. Based on this case valuable lessons were drawn for other emerging economies to understand how their governments can play a more active role, as policymakers and demand-generating entities to create a platform for open innovation (Omar et al., 2017).

Governance of open innovation networks should play a crucial role for their innovation performance in the feature, thereby providing some explanations for the differentiated performance reported between certain networks. Moreover, the effects of governance mechanisms depend on the scope of the network. By understanding that the effect of governance mechanisms varies under different contextual conditions this knowledge should creatively contribute to the ongoing debate on combined effects of governance mechanisms (Clauss & Spieth, 2017).

2 Materials and Methods

Various types of open innovation can be envisaged taking into common action public governments and administrations, private firms, universities, non-profit organizations and activists among other parties who are collaborated in these initiatives. The public sector bodies can advocate collaboration through public_private-people_partnership (4P). Such open innovation programs emerged during the initial stages of the pandemic, in early 2020. These endeavors' funding can be provided by the main public bodies involved, while resources in the shape of mentoring and digital tools are also made available. The latter aspect it is especially important especially with minimal in-person contact during the lockdown periods. Consequently, these programs are relied heavily upon information and communication technologies (ICTs) to organize and execute the different activities involved (Criado & Guevara-Gómez, 2021a). The ICTs-open innovation relationship has been also proven by

Čirjevskis (2021), who developed a research proposition that justified the role of dynamic capabilities as antecedents of the success of open innovation-typed merger and acquisition (M&A) deals in the ICT industry, constituting a real options' application to measure M&A synergies. It was also argued that important empirical evidence can bear on the literature on open innovation theory, dynamic capabilities framework, and real options theory (Čirjevskis, 2021).

In a wider organizational framework open innovation cannot be envisaged only as a developmental tool of contemporary businesses within central governments, but also as a precautionary tool in response to better understanding the dynamics of crises and emergency management. Crises are viewed as economic, environmental (ecology), organizational and leadership, labor, culture, traditions, governance, administration, politics/political, all being potential to cause severe decline and human deaths, being also vulnerable to moral bankruptcy and unethical conduct in public service transactions. Most crises sustain trigger points so critical as to leave historical marks on nations, groups, and individual lives. In the relevant literature a critique of our predatory globalization age has been developed, having many expected and unexpected detrimental effects on the world's environment, social systems, and governance and public administration systems, which have deteriorated human conditions, widened the gap between the rich and the poor and increased the chances of disasters and of violent conflicts (Farazmand, 2014).

In such a way understanding of crises can also develop a better understanding those crises' evolution and the management suited. It is further required serious crisis analysis, which, in turn, needs to go beyond a focus on human error as the origin of the crisis. Organizational, leadership, and systemic deficiencies ought to be diagnosed as effective approaches to crisis management, pointing out that numerous organizations develop over time a culture devoid of ability to detect environmental threats challenging their survival, and many crises develop as a result of managerial and leadership incompetence (Farazmand, 2014). It can be also recognized that public organizations are not immune from this mal-adaptation or bureaucratic culture inflicted by many bureau organizational deficiencies and vulnerabilities. Subsequently, crises are destructive but they reveal also opportunities to be developed for a new order, while changes may produce positive results. Therefore, a crisis can create its own antithesis, which may dialectically reinforce and complement positive forces of nature (Farazmand, 2014).

In the relevant literature crisis and emergency management have generally been neglected as a field of study in public administration, since only recently have they been recognized and pursued as an important area of public administration. Nevertheless, the dual fields of crisis and emergency management are least recognized as areas of scholarly activity among the public administration and public policy communities. In the steady evolving and rapidly changing uncertain conditions that characterize the current world, crisis and emergency management become central to all activities of public and private organizations. Massive corporate and government downsizing should be proven as a short-term solution to the long-term problems of economy and society, creating a creeping crisis that might be triggered by even small events in the future (Farazmand, 2014).

Not all emergency situations are caused by crises. Contrarily, all crises cause emergency situations, which must be dealt with very carefully. As a central activity of public administration, emergency management is considered a significant process of developing and implementing policies and actions that involve (a) mitigation, a course of action to detect the risk to society or the health of people and to reduce the risk; (b) preparedness, a response plan of action to reduce loss of life and to increase the chance of successful response to the disaster or catastrophe, (c) response, provision of emergency aid and assistance, and (d) recovery, provision of immediate support to return life back to normalcy (Farazmand, 2014). In this organizational framework crisis and emergency management require strategic, long-term vision, as well as creative thinking for the common good, appreciating and motivating all the members of the community to cooperate (Farazmand, 2014).

At this point of the analysis it is interesting to explore the main trends followed by the public administration over time. The development of public administration has attracted the scientific interest up to recent years (Yu, 2022). In this analysis it was adopted a bibliometric methodology to estimate the development of the field of public administration. However, it is noteworthy that only a small scope of journals has been currently covered in these research studies, while only few of those have investigated the evolution of the entire field. The majority of active institutions are from the US and the UK, which indicates their dominant position over others. In a methodological point of view the applied bibliometrics, as statistical methods to research and measure bibliographic information, they can objectively address the subjective bias from the typical and traditional evaluation in the field of public administration. Both the activity and the quality indicators were applied to various articles at a long-run period, to better reflect influence through a large-scale empirical analysis conducted. It was shown that an emerging "resident" journal concept was proposed to explore differences between traditional and emerging research forces. Resident journals maintain a large advantage over other journals in terms of higher quality journal indicators and citation impact indicators, providing more comprehensive comparisons through large-scale data and acknowledged methods to explore the research development of public administration (Yu, 2022).

In addressing societal issues, the collaboration between diverse actors plays a fundamental role to the smooth running of open innovation projects. This necessity is partly driven by the realization of public administration for which effective response would demand capabilities in addition to their own. Regarding the roles and the implications of governance for scheduled initiatives, even though open innovation projects can initiate by state organizations, some diversification it is apparent in terms of governance and liaisons between different actors (Criado & Guevara-Gómez, 2021a). Another useful tool of approaching governance operations through open innovation it is the modelling of self-determination theory, which can analyze the motivations offered to citizens, enabling them to participate in an open government platform while focusing on how these motivations can influence participation quantity (Schmidthuber et al., 2019). Schmidthuber et al. (2019) surveyed several platform users and argued that motivation of citizens' participation in public administration it is greatly varied across various forms of participation. Indicatively, at the relevant literature it was stressed out that public administration agencies can organize thematic meetings to express their needs and to select targeted managerial solutions such as the co-innovation lab and third-parties that best suited their needs (Cavallo et al., 2021). It is further important to note that intrinsic motivation can be positively associated with producing and consuming platform content, while external regulation can be positively associated with evaluation behavior. Contrarily, external and introjected regulation could be negatively related to individuals' active contribution (Schmidthuber et al., 2019).

The implementation of open innovation projects entails members of the public who took part in the initiatives to use social media channels, digital platforms and instant messaging services to contribute and collaborate. In this context meeting in virtual settings soon became the norm. Similarly, objectives of the respective programs are largely comparable but they appear to be devised with different audiences in mind, nonetheless. Moreover, citizens can be invited to post information about key issues and program leaders then engaged in a process of elimination to ascertain those deemed high priority. At a methodological overview digital maps can be used to align needs with offers of assistance. It is noteworthy that a huge number of projects emerged from the suggestions offered by citizens. All participants can also develop a range of other projects, linked to such as science, technology and innovation. Interestingly, such solutions are in fact secondary to the goal of creating a network within which a diverse range of actors could collaborate (Criado & Guevara-Gómez, 2021a).

In the relevant literature research exploration has been also engaged on how intellectual property rights and central government support are impacting on green innovation through open innovation at firms level. In this context a structural model that compared open innovation's direct and mediating roles it was applied by using data from the manufacturing sector in South Korea for the period 2014–2016. A partial least square structural equation method (PLS-SEM) was deployed, revealing that a firm's intellectual property rights and government support significantly affect open innovation, green process innovation, and green product innovation while open innovation played a mediating role between each. From a methodological side it is also proven challenging to provide a supplementary analysis following a sample-split test and comparing what should be the sensitivity of selecting partnership associates and deploying multigroup tests in alignment with firm size (Roha et al., 2021).

Indeed, enterprises growth is also implying that some subgroups have been formed to manage the logistics for different activities. Similarly, a smart move to empower participants to make decisions has been reported with support from institutions if needed. It is commonly occurred that participants do not share a common budget, thus, each organization is accountable for its role in the collaborations. Subsequently, it is apparently needed the creation of new strategies for accountability that are specifically designed for open innovation, while control and monitoring must be integral to new systems that utilize public resources for open innovation projects of implementation (Criado & Guevara-Gómez, 2021a).

Two important indicators of enabling appropriate responses as the pandemic unfolds and new challenges arise, they are that of agility and quick decision-making.

However, the decision-making process it is often and negatively affected due to constraints of time, resources, planning and energy. The divulged discussion about sustainability of public sector-driven open innovation processes suggest that procedural legitimacy has been attained for public-driven open innovation projects. Moreover, while foundations are clearly in place, doubts do persist though as the uniqueness of the pandemic generates the necessary time, commitment and intensity that might not transpire in future situations (Criado & Guevara-Gómez, 2021a).

Interestingly, a significant methodological application of open innovation to governance, it is the role of open government data (OGD) policy towards innovation diffusion. Indeed, open government data (OGD) policy differs substantially from policies referring to freedom of information disclosure (Chatfield & Reddick, 2018). Consequently, OGD can be considered as a policy innovation, which can be approached by innovation diffusion theory (Chatfield & Reddick, 2018). OGD initiatives are also vulnerable to lack of participation by public agencies in such efforts. It is also challenging researches to be motivated by this challenge and develop theoretically grounded models to explain what aspects are motivating public agencies to share their data on OGD platforms (Zhenbin et al., 2020). In approaching such a challenge:

- Zhenbin et al. (2020) deployed a model testing with survey and objective data from almost one hundred of public agencies, founding that agencies' resource dependence on external innovators significantly impacted on their data sharing behavior. Furthermore, the main influential factors of agencies' data sharing behavior were that of the conformity need and the sensitivity of their function (Zhenbin et al., 2020).
- Chatfield and Reddick (2018) examined Australia's OGD policy diffusion patterns at federal and state government levels based on the policy adoption timing and CKAN portal "Organization" and "Category" statistics. It was argues that those state governments that had adopted OGD policies earlier they had active policy entrepreneurs (or lead departments/agencies) responsible for the policy innovation diffusion across the different government departments. Moreover, efficacy ranking was shorted as relatively high in terms of OGD portal openness when openness is measured by the higher volumes of datasets that are proactively and systematically published through their OGD portals (Chatfield & Reddick, 2018).

3 Results

The today situation of using open innovation towards governance in national and international contexts revealed that public services will be shaped increasingly by the evolution of global, Internet-enabled, digital platforms, while supporting two distinctive technical and commercial features (Fishenden & Thompson, 2013):

(a) the use of open standards and architectures will separate standard business logic from supporting applications, enabling government to become technology-

and vendor-agnostic, freeing it from its bounding on proprietary systems and suppliers

(b) over time the open standards and the increased market choices available they will drive both innovation and progressive convergence on cheaper, standard "utility" public services (Fishenden & Thompson, 2013).

These two facts can firstly cause an disintegration of traditional "black box" technologies and services, traditionally organized around "systems integrators" and departmental structures and, secondly, cause re-aggregation around a customer-centrism scheme in the form of services. Such re-aggregation entails sharp distinctions between niche/innovative and commodity/standard offerings, supplied by a pluralistic, innovative, and cost-effective marketplace, altering ways of buying and deploying technology by the state (Fishenden & Thompson, 2013). A literature panorama in the field of open innovation in governance has been collectively represented in two distinct periods: the 2000s' decade (Table 1), and the 2010s' decade (Table 2). At both Tables 1 and 2 the relevant entries have been placed in reverse chronological order, from the newest to the earliest, as well as in first-author alphabetical shorting out per same year of publication.

Based on Tables 1 and 2 it can be denoted (a) the thriving literature production on open innovation-governance relationship within the last decade of publication, which counts for almost 3 times higher than that of the previous decade 2000s', and, (b) the relevant literature of open innovation projects in governance they supported endeavors of diversifying capabilities and effectiveness, from region to region and from decade to decade. However, for all cases, it can be inferred that not consensus has been reached in their efficacy and feasibility by all these studies conducted.

Evolutionary Characteristics from Traditional Governance Towards Open Innovation Governance

In recent years it is an imperative need to advance our understanding of the evolution of open innovation governance beyond the linear mechanism of technology transfer based on a supplier–buyer type of relationship in which both the business and the industry partner learn how to collaborate as peers. In this research setting it is notably investigating how does the governance of an open innovation collaboration between companies evolve over time? (Cavallo et al., 2021). Prior to focus on the evolutionary characteristics from traditional governance to open innovation governance it is noteworthy defining what is "open innovation in governance". In the relevant literature:

- Open innovation is commonly considered as a distributed innovation process based on the purposive use of knowledge flows across organizational boundaries (Cavallo et al., 2021). To result in positive outcomes, such collaborations transcending organizational boundaries have to be governed (Cavallo et al., 2021).

Table 1 Literature panorama in the field of open innovation in governance during the 2000s' decade

References	Geographical and/or thematic field
Feller et al. (2009)	Utility of hierarchical relationships and the market system to supply and acquire intellectual property (IP) and/or innovation capabilities from sources external to the firm Inter-organizational relationships that facilitate open innovation they can be categorized in order to exchange intellectual property or innovation capability. This categorization revealed four governance structures along ten dimensions which influence knowledge dispersion, uncertainty and transaction costs on the emergence of governance structures for open innovation. It was proven the prominence of information asymmetry is a key issue in choosing and designing appropriate governance structures for open innovation
Scarbrough et al. (2009)	Europe/-Relevance of knowledge governance and processes with issues associated with large-scale R&D programs and inter-organizational associations of open innovation; that of a major inter-firm research program sponsored by the European Union (EU) in the aerospace sector The dominant role of adapting the dynamics of the innovation process, and particularly to shifts between the open and closed networks, it can offer very different routes to appropriating value from that process
Cassell (2008)	Europe/Decisions of governments' migration to an alternative operating system that uses free/open source Software (FOSS), they are taken by a range of factors, but are predominately driven by democratic values such as independence and self-determination than by a desire to cut costs or save money. Such an implementation is affected by a variety factors but of particular interest is the pursue of information technology's place within a city's organizational structure
Gonçalves (2004)	Europe/Among the wider social issues that are complementary to the economically oriented theories of innovation, they are including that of risk society and new modes of governance. In particular, approaches that govern industrial and technological innovation in the EU they are impacting on the performance and the patterns of the innovation system, revealing those ways in which institutions and procedures are responsive and manage emerging technological risk perceptions and participatory claims

- Governance refers to the rights available to members of an entity, the practices and decision-making processes that conduct power and resources, and coordinating stakeholders and help them to achieve their goals (Cavallo et al., 2021). Governance assumes managers assess the problem, potential knowledge sets, technologies, and parties able to address the problem, and then set the governance that can maximize the potential for high-value solutions (Nickerson & Zenger, 2004).
- Open innovation governance has typically been addressed as higher-level governance modes or lower-level governance mechanisms within a specific mode.

Table 2 Literature panorama in the field of open innovation in governance during the 2010s' decade

References	Geographical and/or thematic field
Mu and Wang (2022)	Investigation of how barriers and governance strategies are different between digital and non-digital open innovation (OI), arguing that relational barriers are more influential for non-digital OI, while capacity- and technical-related barriers are certainly challenging digital OI Political commitment and employment of intermediaries are universal strategies for OI. It is coercive and mandate strategies are effective only for inter-governmental OI. Offline participation among citizens and private actors fosters persuasive-oriented strategies and stress relational governance. Contrarily, online participation among citizens and private actors strategies focus on technical capacity building
Cavallo et al. (2021)	By applying an in-depth, longitudinal case study of a commercial software firm and a big science center co-developing a digital platform it was identified five processes through which the open innovation governance and its platform-generated outcome they are influenced to each other: setting the open innovation collaboration's governance, resolving the core's design issues, opening the open innovation collaboration's governance, shaping the periphery, and changing to platform governance Governance of the collaboration played a major role in converging tensions between the two partners, thus, positively impact on the designing of the digital platform. In turn of developing a digital platform in alignment with a big science center, the decisions surrounding the platform they are able to change the open innovation governance. Open innovation collaboration's governance sustains a direct access and knowledge about market needs and represents an important tool of collecting feedback from the users of the platform and suggesting improvements
Criado and Guevara-Gómez (2021b)	Spain/-The determination of those key features of collaborative governance processes guide open innovation initiatives, especially among the public sectors, during the COVID-19 crises Investigation of how open public innovation cases can generate public value to the society during the COVID-19 crises in national level of analysis Collaboration among governments can advance their innovative capabilities, especially at a digitalized context. In this respect, the improvement of citizen's involvement and the deliberation practices or network building are determining specifications of open innovation towards collaborative governance processes in terms of accountability and legitimacy of these initiatives
Liu and Zhang (2021)	China/-A successful implementation of open innovation necessitates firms to build close relationships with external innovators. Relational governance, also characterized as social control, can effectively manage inter-organizational relationships, though, the role of relational governance on firms' open innovation remains equivocal Utility of conditional process model analyzed the interplay of relational governance, open innovation, and firms' innovation performance and examine the influence of environmental dynamism. It was proven that relational governance has a positive impact on (inbound and outbound) firms' open innovation and innovation performance Open innovation mediates the association between relational governance and firms' innovation performance. Highly environmental dynamics can enhance the indirect effect of relational governance on firms' innovation performance through open innovation

(continued)

Table 2 (continued)

References	Geographical and/or thematic field
Pedersen (2020)	Investigation of the purposes for which public sector organizations use open innovation, and how it creates value The public sector organizations primarily use open innovation to pursue one specific purpose, which is the innovation in society while creating value through improving citizens' quality of life and the quality of neighborhoods The co-specialization of IT and other resources in society (e.g. the transportation system) and the process to change citizen behavior, capabilities and experiences (like use of the transportation system more efficiently or nurturing the feel of safety when using the transportation system) A framework can be developed towards value creation from open innovation initiatives that pursues innovation in society. Such a framework supports public sector organizations to increase value creation and to solve wicked problems using open innovation, enabling researchers to focus future open innovation research on essential knowledge gaps
Pellegrini and Lazzarotti (2019)	Italy/Family firms are seen as a heterogeneous breed, whose differences can be determined by different levels of participation of non-family members in the governance mechanisms. Non-family members can act in favor of open innovation (OI). It was also stressed out the necessity to adequately operationalize the heterogeneity concept by means of fuzzy logic, under almost two hundred of Italian family firms surveyed. The involvement of non-family members can affect the extent to which firms draw on knowledge from external partners. It can be noted that the higher possible involvement of non-family members, results in higher collaboration with vertical partners along the supply chain
Remneland Wikhamn and Styhre (2019)	Investigating how the open innovation concept can be applied in large corporations aiming to work with small innovative firms. It was proposed a distinct governance structure that can be labeled as a corporate hub, distinguishing it from other "open governance forms", like market, network and bazaar governance, explaining the potential value that brings for coupled open innovation between large and small firms
Berthinier-Poncet et al. (2018)	France/Open innovation (OI) of small and medium-sized enterprises (SMEs) can be co-structured in clusters, while these specific agglomerations seem to offer SMEs some fruitful opportunities for networking and open innovation. Therefore, the intermediate role of cluster governance in supporting open innovation practices of clustered SMEs can be studied, highlighting direct and indirect support for OI projects of the technopolitan SMEs. It is noteworthy that cluster governance has to pay more attention to the support of collaborative projects and to allocate additional resources for developing an organizational climate for OI
Jugend et al. (2018)	Brazil/The operational linkages among open innovation, innovative performance and government support for innovation were studied within Brazilian firms. Data were obtained from two different firm samples, being related to incremental innovation, and radical innovation, respectively. Considering government support for innovation, sampling based on radical innovation sustained higher impact comparing to that of sampling based on incremental innovation. Moreover, the cooperation of external firms has positively impacting on firms' innovative performance, which was positively controlled by the size of the firms. It can be also denoted that radical innovation requires synergy and an intensifying focus regarding the constructs considered therein

(continued)

Table 2 (continued)

References	Geographical and/or thematic field
Li et al. (2018)	Open innovation activities can effectively deal with the externalities of resources and environment, while balancing the economic value and green value of organizations, being an effective green governance mode that reflects the characteristics of the main subject composition and mechanism operation of green governance Development of a green governance framework for the cooperation based on sustainable development among enterprises, governments, social organizations, the public and the nature. In this respect the synergies between human and nature are structuring this framework, including related theories of green governance, innovation subjects, innovation mechanisms and innovation mode The utility of such a framework can be applied to each country and region in order to develop green governance guidelines that are suitable for the environmental carrying capacity of their own countries or regions. Such a framework can be deployed by enterprises, enabling the drawing of green development strategies to coordinate economic values with green values
Clauss and Spieth (2017)	Utilization of governance mechanisms can be combined with joint processes, like that of knowledge sharing, in order to eliminate undesired behaviors, like the opportunism. Therefore, it is interesting to investigate the complex effects of multiple governance approaches on outcomes of open innovation networks in national and international contexts. It can be better understood that governance of open innovation networks plays a crucial role for their innovation performance, thereby providing sound explanations for the performance differences between certain networks. It was also indicated that the effects of governance mechanisms are bounded on the scope of the network
Guo et al. (2017)	China/Considering the crowdsourcing intermediary in China this study has focused on the impact of inter-organizational governance on trilateral trust-building. It was shown that formal control and relational governance mechanisms are proven vital for swift and knowledge-based trust in R&D crowdsourcing. While Chinese businesses continue to use guanxi, which are informal personal connections, as a relational and contingent mechanism to maintain affect-based trust, guanxi is susceptible to inhibit the growth of Internet-based crowdsourcing for open innovation in the Chinese entrepreneurship
Biswas and Akroyd (2016)	By deploying a qualitative case-study approach it was found that in an open innovation setting—where the producing partner relies on a research partner for all product development activities—a stage-gate product development process can act as a governance mechanism, enabling the development of trust and cooperation which nurtures a co-developmental relationship. Such a stage-gate process can be a flexible governance mechanism, which can adapt over time in alignment with the needs of the co-development partners in an open innovation setting, or other settings, such as the outsourcing arrangements that guide the design and implementation of future governance mechanisms. Accounting research practitioners and academics can better understand how a stage-gate process can be used as a governance mechanism to manage co-development projects in an open innovation setting

(continued)

Table 2 (continued)

References	Geographical and/or thematic field
Felin and Zenger (2014)	Different forms and manifestations of open innovation, as well as the internal or the closed types of innovation, they are valued as unique governance forms with different benefits and costs. The functionality of open or closed form of governance it is composed of a set of instruments that access different types of communication channels for knowledge sharing, different types of incentives, as well as different types of property rights for appropriating value from innovation. Matching between problem types and governance forms they are varied from open to closed and which support alternative forms of solution seeking. The delineation and discussion of four categories of open innovation governance forms, which are that of markets, partnerships, contests and tournaments, as well as user or community innovation, they can be compared to each other and with the two internal or closed forms of innovation governance: that of authority and consensus-based hierarchy. It is also noteworthy that the combination of diverse knowledge and incentives and an approach to property rights that encourages knowledge sharing allows this form of governance to support problem solving for relatively complex problems, with significant levels of hidden knowledge

Higher-level governance modes for open innovation include licensing, acquisitions, R&D contracts, spin-outs and corporate venture capital (Cavallo et al., 2021). Recent attributes of open innovation governance have been extended to more open modes such as hackathons, innovation contests, crowdsourcing, and platforms (Cavallo et al., 2021). Regardless open innovation governance is often portrayed as a discrete choice between alternative governance modes and mechanisms, in reality it is characterized more as a hybrid of various governance modes and related mechanisms, stressing out that both modes and mechanisms are essential to advance our understanding of governance (Cavallo et al., 2021). Actually, open innovation governance can be valued as the higher-level governance modes and lower-level governance mechanisms that enable organizations to lead and to control open innovation processes. In such a framework governance matches the complexity of the problem setting and the available solutions, admitting the uncertainty and the unknown ex-ante know-how involved in such problem resolving (Cavallo et al., 2021). As a result, governance-related literature has been increased mainly relying on informal governance mechanisms that offer flexibility in highly dynamic contexts, where contingencies and evolutions of complex project development are difficult to be pre-determined (Cavallo et al., 2021).

In a relevant managerial and strategic level, the nature of innovation activities changes from more exploratory to exploitative over time, which requires changes in how these activities are best managed and organized (Cavallo et al., 2021). Subsequently, the nature of the problems are also necessitating the governance requirements change during the evolution of an interorganizational alliance, thus, while the strategic focus was based on the entire process of an open innovation collaboration to observe the alignment of governance with the evolution of the open innovation over time, researches to date provide little insight as to how governance mechanisms and open innovation co-evolve, such as in cases when two organizations engaging in open innovation have different objectives (Cavallo et al., 2021). It is indicatively noted that companies' objectives are mainly commercial whereas research organizations such as higher education institutions also have the philosophy and the public mission of scientific knowledge development and diffusion (Cavallo et al., 2021). Such differences induce tensions in industry-research collaborations, making governance particularly attractive especially in the cases that enable organizations to lead and to control open innovation processes (Cavallo et al., 2021).

In the relevant literature it was argued that the development of digital platforms is the outcome of the innovation collaboration that makes current research settings even more promising in light of challenges induced by open innovation governance research. Such platforms are commonly involving a high degree of technological complexity as well as behavioral complexity, making it likely that tensions are further exacerbated (Cavallo et al., 2021). Such a platform core technological architecture consists of three cloud-based layers. The first "data" layer processes the data for cloud-based storage and preparation for further use. The second is the "authentication" layer that manages secure access to the data. The third is the "interfaces" layer connecting the data with applications. Overall, these three layers connect data and offer interoperability between different applications for users, i.e. the public administration agencies. The applications constitute the second part of the platform, the periphery. The platform periphery consists of core applications developed by the co-innovation lab and complementary applications developed by third party companies as well as by VertiSol. Core applications on the platform include accounting, human resources and various public services to citizens such as social security. These core applications play a central role in collecting data, which third parties could build on to develop new solutions to complex societal issues. For instance, third-party companies specialized in smart city services used the data from core applications to develop AI-based applications to solve pollution and mobility problems. In other words, the platform core and data offer value to the applications in the platform periphery, and the complementary applications increase the value of the platform core architecture (Cavallo et al., 2021).

Therefore, platforms are proven as particularly interesting tools to study the evolution of open innovation governance, as platform should be considered both the solution being developed in the open innovation collaboration as well as an open innovation governance mode (Cavallo et al., 2021). Subsequently, it can be argued that the governance of the open innovation collaboration and the development of the digital platform mutually influenced each other. In analyzing the evolution of the partnership and the digital platform together, we not only generated insights into "how" the open innovation collaboration and the platform were governed, but also "why" such governance decisions were made (Cavallo et al., 2021).

Prevailing Mechanisms and Collaboration Types Developed at Open Innovation in Governance

Focusing on collaborations developed at open innovation in governance it is apparent that while the governance modes offer a high-level framework to guide the overall collaboration, the mechanisms are those that govern the day-to-day behavior in such a collaboration. These governance mechanisms are instrumental to allocate decision and property rights (Cavallo et al., 2021), offer incentives to engage in the innovation process, and establish communication channels (Cavallo et al., 2021). Such governance mechanisms may range from contractual to more relational, such as trust and inter-firm socialization (Cavallo et al., 2021). It is interesting to denote that open innovation governance is increasingly becoming a socio-technical phenomenon where tacit coordination and inter-organizational processes can be enabled through digital technologies. Simulation software, databases and web repositories can act as governance mechanisms to further align interests through generating a common ground by making knowledge transparent and available to all parties (Cavallo et al., 2021).

At the development of open innovation projects in governance, open innovation networks are grown considering the efficient utilization of governance mechanisms, which coordinate joint processes—like knowledge sharing and eliminate undesired behaviors, like opportunism (Clauss & Spieth, 2017). In approaching what should be the structure and the affection of multiple governance approaches on outcomes of open innovation networks with a national and an international scope, three governance mechanisms have been proposed in the relevant literature (Clauss & Spieth, 2017): transactional governance, relational governance and institutionalized governance, which all significantly foster innovation outcomes of open innovation networks. In national open innovation networks, only relational governance exerts positive effects, internationally transactional and institutionalized governance is necessary (Clauss & Spieth, 2017).

A plausible explanation of why open-oriented policies and co-ordinations have not yet fully associated with innovation policies it is grounded on the multi-level character of innovation policies and the diversity of national innovation systems. Therefore, major stumbling blocks are impeding the open innovation policies in real world, public and private, entrepreneurship. Among the most notable peculiarities of retarding innovation policies they are that of "vertical policy co-ordination" and "horizontal policy learning". In the relevant literature both these policies have been characterized as the main goals of applying the open innovation policies (Kaiser & Prange, 2017).

Acknowledging these organizational features it should be denoted that open innovation policies are only likely to constitute a valuable mode of governance if national and regional specifications are carefully taken into account, under the preconditions that actors at each territorial level are considered during the entire policy process, and qualitative benchmark indicators are developed considering the diversification of national innovation systems and the concurring regional idiosyncrasies (Kaiser & Prange, 2017).

In spatial and municipalities contexts a high level of innovativeness has been anticipated whenever cities are in collaboration with public and private organizations that allow municipalities to tap into networks of executing projections by companies and clusters (Bakici et al., 2013). In this context firms can utilize public open innovation (POI) intermediaries that operate in the public sector. In specifying the spatial context in terms of developed and developing countries it can be argued that:

- At a modeled multi-case study the participation of POI intermediaries and local governments in developed and highly industrialized European countries revealed that certain public or private companies act as bridges—POI intermediary—across the large cognitive distances between municipalities and a network of organizations, while undertaking the collaboration of actors and executing innovation projects. Therefore, policy makers can be motivated to enhance the innovativeness and the competitiveness of cities, being proven useful tools for municipality spaces and authorities to improve their innovation process and overcoming possible obstacles (Bakici et al., 2013).

- Research can be focused on the ways under which the institutional pillars underpinning national innovation ecosystems can be applied to an industry cluster level, particularly in emerging countries. Organizational challenges and implications for theory and practice are still to be explored in the application of a systems perspective as a way to foster industry cluster innovation and promote a more effective national innovation ecosystem (Klarin et al., 2021).
- Research advancements of open innovation initiatives towards consolidating collaborative governance processes they need further exploration. Therefore, avoidance of social biases might reflect very positive outcomes from the inteviewees' side (Criado & Guevara-Gómez, 2021b). Despite of researches conducted during the COVID-19 crisis, post-crisis analyses are needed to assess the impact of these open innovation cases in collaborative governance structures (Criado & Guevara-Gómez, 2021b).
- In depth clarification of the interactions developed between relational governance and open innovation, deepening our understanding of the value co-creation principle of open innovation (Liu & Zhang, 2021).
- Open innovation cannot generally be used to open up public sector organizations or to give citizens more influence in public sector or democratic processes. It has been signified that open innovation, until now, has primarily affected solving minor problems, not large-scale wicked problems in society (Pedersen, 2020).

From the relevant literature it is noteworthy the case of open innovation initiative that was based on the idea of creating a "hub" inside the corporate walls, where small external innovative firms SMEs are invited to locate their development work, with the possibility to interact also with the large firm. In defining and identifying governance structures, there are several important parameters, including the forms of selection in which external actors are allowed to participate; the forms of interactions that the initiative is designed for; the control mechanisms established to avoid opportunism and unethical behavior, and the forms of value generated and shared among the participants. In Table 3, the compositional structure and the determining parameters for three governance structures that are related to open innovation—market, network, and bazaar governance—they have been depicted. Moreover, in this Table 1 there are chronological timeframes in which the two views of governance: traditional-open innovative have been evolved within the last four decades of referencing, while the evolutionary type of "corporate hub" it is also outlined.

Based on Table 3 it can be denoted that networks are not directly oriented to formal structure of authority but they are based on mutual interests and markets reputation. Network relationships are characterized as indefinite, sequential, long-term and complex, having normative sanctions, rather than purely legal. Subsequently networks support non-market and non-hierarchical modes of exchange, having also a distinct governance structure of collective action. Similarly, bazaar governance has been emerged as a separate governance structure, based on the open source phenomenon in software development. Bazaar governance sustains open access, open license legal contract, short-term and anonymity relations, not prerequisite long-term relations, comparing to network governance types. Bazaar can also utilize

Table 3 The evolutionary characteristics from traditional governance towards open innovative governance

Form types	Market		Network		Bazaar	Corporate Hub
	Traditional governance	Open innovative governance	Traditional governance	Open innovative governance	Traditional governance	Open innovative governance
Selection	Participation has focused on supply and demand	Participation has focused on supply and demand	Access and participation through relationships	Access and participation through relationships	No barriers on access and participation	Selecting participants by the host
Mechanisms of control	Law rules	Law rules	Sanctions by exclusion, isolation	Sanctions by exclusion, isolation	Free-riding, non-controlled	Control by trust and contracts, while each actor owns their IP
Interactive	One-time transactions are commonly occurred	One-time transactions are commonly occurred	Evolutionary trends over time	Evolutionary trends over time	No long-term interactions needed	Ongoing, informal, formal
Valuation	IP is a tradable asset of valuation	IP is a tradable asset of valuation	Sharing and co-constructive valuation among stakeholders	Sharing and co-constructive valuation among stakeholders	Free for all value	Valuation is attributed on steady exchanges towards synergies' development
Decade	1980s', 1990s'	2010s'-present	1990s	2010s'-present	2000s'	2010s'-present

Source Modification by the source citation of Remneland Wikhamn and Styhre (2019, p. 453)

the open license legal contract which However bazaar governance (a) prevents users from appropriating the end-result for their own profit maximization, and (b) facilitates strong network externalities and generative knowledge transactions (Remneland Wikhamn & Styhre, 2019).

In this context the governance type of corporate hub differs from the traditional modes of hierarchy, market, network or bazaar since it is a blending of all four (Table 1). The corporate hub supports the benefits of hierarchical governance including building a shared infrastructure with processes and routines, setting up formal and informal roles and responsibilities, as well as enforcing control through policies, cultures/norms, and direct supervision. Furthermore, corporate hub is proven as firm-centric with carefully selected and limited number of geographically co-located on the same site actors. Actors can freely trade or exchange their intellectual property with whomever they want on the open market fostering long-term relational and trust-based view. Hence, contrarily to the bazaar governance, at the corporate hub the intellectual property and pecuniary motives are primarily offered for the majority of the stakeholders. In this context, free-riding is characterized by high anonymity and low access restrictions (Remneland Wikhamn & Styhre, 2019).

The dynamic and the evolutionary characteristics of governance are especially fitting to the technological and the digitalized applications/projects. In such an approach it was conducted a research to better understand what community-based free software projects are and what governance characteristics (structure and control) differentiate them from traditional organizations, thus reflecting on this business model (Ferraz & Dos Santos, 2021). Among the reported reflections it was determined that even though it is possible to distinguish community-based free software projects from traditional organizations, a (not always considered) crucial factor refers to the transformations resulting from the development of these projects. Therefore, relevant studies can consider the context of functioning, as well as those changes and interorganizational relationships established by the projects over time. In such a way approximations between projects and traditional organizations can occur, even if community characteristics are maintained (Ferraz & Dos Santos, 2021).

Literature and exploratory researches allowed researchers to determine that the governance of free software communities has not proved to be something rigid and definitive, but it constituted a dynamic framework of flexible contours and strong adaptability to the environment and the evolution of the relevant projects (Ferraz & Dos Santos, 2021). Although the developmental aspect is crucial for governance recognized by some studies, it is not always discussed in detail in empirical researches (Ferraz & Dos Santos, 2021). In this respect, free software projects can be considered as arrangements that follow the community logic, in contrast to traditional organizations, without (as in a significant part of the cases) being concerned with debating the temporal and maturing circumstances in which they meet. Projects that emerged at the organizational level and established interorganizational relationships, present formalizations of the structure and the control processes in alignment with the informality typical of community initiatives. This fact demonstrates the complexity of governance since the community is an integral part of an environment that has mutually influenced it over time (Ferraz & Dos Santos, 2021).

Although it is theoretically possible to trace the governance characteristics that differentiate community free software ventures from traditional organizations, the reality may not happen that way. Bringing approaches that involve the transformations experienced by the projects, considering the context in which the community is nurtured and the organizational interfaces developed, it allows the presentation of more realistic viewpoints. Fundamental contributions can be directed to the careful positioning of community arrangements in organizational research, especially with regard to the dichotomy between communities versus traditional organizations. Although governance in communities is still considered controversial and there is no consensus among different literature approaches, the results achieved regarding free software projects they can operate in a manner close to that of traditional organizations, even if they maintain community traits (Ferraz & Dos Santos, 2021).

Another important research objective refers to the necessity researchers to interpret how interdependencies emerge between the outcomes and the governance choices (Cavallo et al., 2021). Such changes to the open innovation problem and solution can be dealt with through including upfront flexibility in the chosen governance mechanisms such as incomplete contracts or more relational governance mechanisms (Cavallo et al., 2021). Since open innovation governance is dynamic in nature it co-evolves with the related innovation outcome towards more open forms of governance. Future research challenges are to study open innovation governance and its outcome longitudinally, in order those dynamics to be fully captured. Besides, understanding of governing open innovation with big science (educational) centers, where such collaborations of open innovation practices between big science centers and companies are increasingly common in cases that the company is the supplier of innovations (Cavallo et al., 2021). The critical point here is how big science centers can co-develop innovations with companies as peers, thus, co-developing as peers is a careful co-evolutionary process in which the organizations are prone to learn how to collaborate and address emerging tensions through: (a) the governance, (b) adjusting the governance based on evolving insights, and (c) justifying and gathering evidence for competing views to conclude to the best solution (Cavallo et al., 2021).

In recent years governance mechanisms evolved to higher levels of openness in response to new problems, as opposed to repeating the same cycle. The increased openness of the governance is key aspect to benefiting more from the open innovation. While traditional approaches have shown how R&D scientists in and with big science (educational) centers have to permeate boundaries to benefit from outside knowledge, there are contemporary approaches suggesting the key role of the evolving governance to allow others to permeate boundaries and become part of the open innovation (Cavallo et al., 2021). It is also noticeable how the innovation outcome and governance become increasingly open through managerial tools adopted, as that of (literature reported) co-innovation lab, as a boundary organization to effectively manage diverging interests between companies and their collaborative partners/parties (Cavallo et al., 2021).

A realistic governing of open innovation collaboration can be evolved towards a more external and open organization that includes other organizations and actively governs interactions on structured digital platforms, as opposed to staying an intermediary between the two originally involved organizations. Boundary resources and boundary organizations play similar roles in governing the access of parties to the open innovation process; however, boundary resources have typically been associated with governing platforms and boundary organizations with governing collaborations (Cavallo et al., 2021). Therefore, future researches can certainly include boundary organizations as a mode of open innovation governance in existing typologies, while focusing on how modes and mechanisms of open innovation governance shape each other, and on how the stability-variety tension occurred between collaborators developing the platform core technological infrastructure. Subsequently, detailed evidence should be provided on how specifically some inter-organizational governance mechanisms worked so as to ensure resourcing and securing to face the paradox of change at the core level for technology ecosystems (Cavallo et al., 2021).

Moreover, it cannot be undermined the importance of the "historical context" of prior collaboration with the third parties in successfully governing open innovation collaborations, suggesting that such a history of collaboration and alliance literature should enable a better understanding of prior experience with the same partner, being an important driver in such a collaboration success (Cavallo et al., 2021). Future research should also take boundary conditions into account to further improve our understanding of governing open innovation collaborations. It is critical to uncover some of the dynamics in open innovation governance and how these change over time, acknowledging that open innovation governance is a complex phenomenon where different permeable boundaries and analytical techniques need to be managed, especially in terms of selecting and collaborating with a broader category of research institutions such as universities, funding and technology providers (Cavallo et al., 2021).

4 Discussion

Open innovation literature is differentiating transactional governance from and relational governance. The transactional governance emphasizes at IP as the building block for knowledge exchange and collaboration. Relational governance stresses out legitimacy, interactions, norms and trust as means for the building up of successful long-term shared value (Remneland Wikhamn & Styhre, 2019). Therefore, corporate hub is productively bridging transactional with relational governance, being benefited from the relational characteristics (mainly generativity, serendipity, exploration), but still maintaining corporate control over intellectual property for the individual firms. The innovation process can be defined as a "selective revealing" tool in open source projects, where actors freely reveal some information to the community in order to signify "sharing and protection" and "value creation and value capture" balancing out (Remneland Wikhamn & Styhre, 2019).

Besides to defining and framing the operation of open innovation in governance at the previous sections, it is also vital to determine how governance is adaptable or achieves sustainability while running open innovation contexts. Indeed, sustainable governance looks at wealth beyond the singular province of profit. "*Learning Sustainability*" teaches us that wealth comes from the environment and people as well as the profit sector. Governance must find ways to deliver equitable services and wealth to those that are governed (Hawken, 2022). Governments are predominately concern the protection and the promotion of the best interests of the people governed through delivering equitable chances, services, wealth, thus envisaging strategies that in every possible way promote sustainable development (Hawken, 2022). Economic politics advance the governments running like a business. Certainly, it remains challenging to find ways to be more efficient economically, either at businesses and at governmental sides. However, businesses' objectives are (or should be) significantly different than that of governmental objectives, since business aims at creating profit, whereas government aims at creating and protecting wealth. Thus, sustainable governance looks at wealth beyond the singular province of profit. Subsequently, learning sustainability "guides" wealth to come from the environment and people as well as the profit sector. Business is by its nature a private enterprise, thus, being accountable only to shareholders and those shareholders demand profit (Hawken, 2022).

Governments have to consider the responsibility of a variety of factors, such as society, culture, humanity, political realities of economic policy, religious and other organized beliefs, that all shape a sustainable future. While it is a fact that governments play an important and even critical role if we are to have a sustainable future, good governments can provide vehicles for informed decision-making and invest to maintain the integrity and the health of a democratic system, through developing and maintaining strategies, policies, and programs to foster a future that works (Hawken, 2022). Moreover, one of the prime challenges of good government is to find the political and bureaucratic flexibility to create and to maintain accountable policies and programs. Therefore, it is also fundamental the constant adaptation abilities to new circumstances. From a leadership point of view good leaders sustain the responsibility to find ways through the checks and the balances that good governance requires. Therefore, the promotion of sustainability through government means continuously and proactively investing in democratic principles, since good government can (a) promote sustainable economic strategies and (b) provide for safety and security, well-being, education, and supporting that the bottom line is a healthy environment (Hawken, 2022).

Based on Fig. 1 it is noteworthy that at pursuing external collaboration the shared work in the end may result in valuing needs to be protected by IP and divided among the participants, especially through formalizing and locking relationships in contracts. Besides, formal collaboration partnerships and a break down negotiation of everything, they are encouraged to explore interesting things without knowing where it will lead. Such a formalized way of knowledge and ideas flow is established between the large corporation and the small innovative firms, where synergies could be developed and taken advantage of as emerging mutually trusting relationships. In this respect there are carefully selected participants, while opportunities can emerge for the hosting corporation to provide challenging work tasks for its best employees. Subsequently the internal employees are being called for meetings with the hub SMEs offering them a glimpse of entrepreneurial environment of new challenges and problems to look into, while sparing them any obligation of enacting the advice in practice (Remneland Wikhamn & Styhre, 2019). Nurturing the open innovation initiative can be a good source for corporate branding while fostering creativity, openness and proactiveness to existing and potential key stakeholders: employees, partners, shareholders. However, it is a reality that while SMEs still have the responsibility for their development processes and are exposed to the risk of failure, larger corporations are feasible without the need for overly bureaucratic arrangements, project staffing or new venture investments (Remneland Wikhamn & Styhre, 2019).

Another crucial aspect of governmental sustainability towards value creation is the privatization. However, privatization and similar service-oriented delivery tools, it does not replace the role of government, and it is the government or state that must always shoulder the responsibility of what happens in society, economy, administration, and politics. In the current globalization age of corporate capitalism, many governments renounce the responsibilities they traditionally have performed and by privatization have transferred the burden of social and economic tasks on citizens who lack the ability or capability to function in society. This is a commonly occurred problem among developing countries, being primarily reported among the advanced nations of the West and is forced upon the governments in developing nations so subject to the influence of the former ones the global sweeping privatization and structural adjustment programs recommended on developing nations by the International Monetary Fund and the World Bank. They are examples of externally imposed pressure that have served as powerful strategic instruments of implementing globalization of corporate capitalism worldwide (Farazmand, 2004). Rapid privatization necessitates governments to promote self-governing organizations in all sectors. Unless governments retake their role in society and citizens reclaim their rights and roles in economy, society, and governance systems, then, public administration and human resource management cannot succeed and their capacity could diminish rather than enhance, especially in the age of rapid globalization and global integration (Farazmand, 2004).

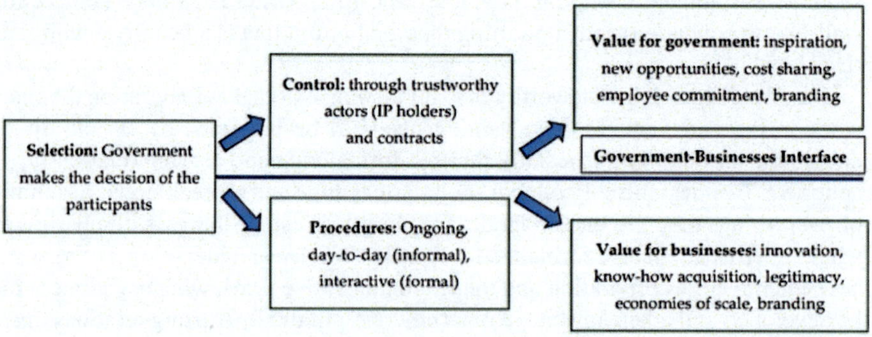

Fig. 1 Governmental sustainability in alignment of value creation. *Source* Modification of source citation by Remneland Wikhamn and Styhre (2019, p. 456)

5 Conclusion

Public sector organizations have increasingly focused on citizen contribution by adopting instruments known from open innovation. While collaborating with the periphery and leveraging external knowledge, government institutions can initiate social innovation and stimulate a positive change for society. The involvement of citizens in an ideation platform can by initiated by local governments, in better understanding the motivations that affect participation intensity (Schmidthuber et al., 2019).

Another critical constraint is the power imbalance, where expertise of public sector leaders in designing and launching initiatives are undoubtedly proving their importance during crisis periods. However, this serves to limit input from other actors into decision-making. In such a framework of collaborations, future researches can be directed to find ways of exploiting such individual expertise while also redistributing authority to some extent (Criado & Guevara-Gómez, 2021a). Finally, future researches can be directed in deeper investigating:

- A range of data from across public and private sectors, in order to illustrate the arguments and to identify key policy and implementation recommendations of generalized applicability (Fishenden & Thompson, 2013).
- Research constraints that can be overcome regarding the existing research gap on linking between governance and performance in open innovation networks and delineating challenging areas or governmental operations worthy further researches, nationally or globally. By considering that the effect of governance mechanisms varies under different contextual conditions, future researches can be also directed to the ongoing debate on combined effects of governance mechanisms (Clauss & Spieth, 2017).
- The structural causality between internal and external resources, focusing on the role of open innovation to green innovation, dividing it into green process and green product innovation (Roha et al., 2021).
- Research considerations should emphasize on the mediating role of open innovation in enhancing green process innovation along with the direct and indirect effect of intellectual property rights and government support on green innovation (Roha et al., 2021).
- Potential benefits of open government data initiatives, though significant, there are vulnerable and balanced out from lack of participation by public agencies in such efforts (Zhenbin et al., 2020). Therefore, concurring implications have been fully investigated regarding the role of open government data policy entrepreneurs in openly sharing government-owned datasets with the public (Chatfield & Reddick, 2018).

Another critical orientation of future studies is how the concept of open innovation will adapt to the expected changes in the global (both natural- and built-)environment. It is a reality that human interference with nature has not only damaged ecosystems and the environment but has also affected the scope for livelihood security of current and future generations. Therefore, attempts have been made by the scientific community to understand the root cause of global environmental change (GEC) at various research pathways for the coming decades. Besides, several research innovations are especially running within the last two decades to address environmental issues, protection of ecosystems, as well as human impacts through multi-disciplinary approaches (Anon, 2011). Recovery of degraded ecosystems and restoration of environment are now responsibilities of civil society organizations and other end-users of the field-based activities, while protected areas and co-management approaches have been commonly practiced in different parts of the world toward assigning property rights to open access environmental goods. Severe research attempts have also oriented to bridge the gap between the scientific findings and implementation towards achieving tangible results that enhance environmental quality. Several propositions should enable a meeting of scientists and experts of national and international repute to discuss and debate research outcomes to face the new challenges in the wake of disaster induced environmental changes (Anon., 2011). It is expected that such open science international forums can increase on disaster induced environmental issues pertaining to coastal areas of various parts of the world. Human induced impacts and open innovation perspectives, especially linking rapid urbanization and global population growth, are some of the contributing factors for GEC, the severity of regional or global natural disasters and their impacts on environment, economy, and community is yet to be studied and fully understood, including (Anon, 2011): Property rights associated measures for ecosystem conservation; Urbanization and societal transformations for a sustainable development; Land uses change, soil degradation, and environmental impact assessment; Water cycle, carbon and air quality changes; Climate change mitigation issues and adaptation methods; Clean energy technologies/Renewable energy technologies; Economics, policies, and governance; Bioclimatic architecture and disaster resilience at the built environment.

Conflicts of Interest The author declares no conflict of interest.

Funding This research received no external funding.

References

Anon. (2011). Call for conference sessions—International open science conference: Global environmental change challenges and innovations. *International Journal of Disaster Resilience in the Built Environment, 2*(2). https://doi.org/10.1108/ijdrbe.2011.43502baa.004

Bakici, T., Almirall, E., & Wareham, J. (2013). The role of public open innovation intermediaries in local government and the public sector. *Technology Analysis and Strategic Management, 25*(3), 311–327. https://doi.org/10.1080/09537325.2013.764983

Berthinier-Poncet, A., Grama-Vigouroux, S., & Saidi, S. (2018). Open innovation practices of clustered SMEs: The intermediate role of cluster governance. In *Chapter 9: Researching open innovation in SMEs* (pp. 275–306). World Scientific eds. https://doi.org/10.1142/9789813230972_0009

Biswas, S., & Akroyd, C. (2016). The governance of inter-firm co-development projects in an open innovation setting. *Pacific Accounting Review, 28*(4), 446–457. https://doi.org/10.1108/PAR-03-2016-0030

Cassell, M. (2008). Why governments innovate: Adoption and implementation of open source software by Four European Cities. *International Public Management Journal, 11*(2), 193–213. https://doi.org/10.1080/10967490802095680

Cavallo, A., Burgers, H., Ghezzi, A., & Van de Vrande, V. (2021).The evolving nature of open innovation governance: A study of a digital platform development in collaboration with a big science centre.*Technovation, 102370*https://doi.org/10.1016/j.technovation

Chatfield, A.-T., & Reddick, C.-G. (2018). The role of policy entrepreneurs in open government data policy innovation diffusion: An analysis of Australian Federal and State Governments. *Government Information Quarterly, 35*(1), 123–134. https://doi.org/10.1016/j.giq.2017.10.004

Čirjevskis, A. (2021). Exploring the link of real options theory with dynamic capabilities framework in open innovation-type merger and acquisition deals. *Journal of Risk and Financial Management, 14*(4), 168. https://doi.org/10.3390/jrfm14040168

Clauss, T., & Spieth, P. (2017). Governance of open innovation networks with national vs international scope. *Journal of Strategy and Management, 10*(1), 66–85. https://doi.org/10.1108/JSMA-07-2015-0057

Criado, J. I., & Guevara-Gómez, A. (2021a). Collaborating in response to crisis: Effective governance of open innovation initiatives. *Annals in Social Responsibility, 7*(2), 49–51. https://doi.org/10.1108/ASR-06-2021-0024

Criado, J. I., & Guevara-Gómez, A. (2021b). Public sector, open innovation, and collaborative governance in lockdown times. A research of Spanish cases during the COVID-19 crisis. *Transforming Government: People, Process and Policy, 15*(4), 612–626. https://doi.org/10.1108/TG-08-2020-0242

Farazmand, A. (2004). Innovation in strategic human resource management: Building capacity in the age of globalization. *Public Organization Review, 4*(1), 3–24.

Farazmand, A. (2014). *Crisis and emergency management: Theory and practice* (2nd ed.). Routledge imprint, Taylor & Francis eds.

Felin, T., & Zenger, T. R. (2014). Closed or open innovation? Problem solving and the governance choice. *Research Policy, 43*(5), 914–925. https://doi.org/10.1016/j.respol.2013.09.006

Feller, J., Hayes, J., O'Reilly, P., & Finnegan, P. (2009). Institutionalising information asymmetry: Governance structures for open innovation. *Information Technology and People, 22*(4), 297–316. https://doi.org/10.1108/09593840911002423

Ferraz, I. N., & Dos Santos, C. D. (2021). Organization of free and opensource software projects: In-between the community and traditional governance. *Brazilian Business Review, 18*(3), 334–342.

Fishenden, J., & Thompson, M. (2013). Digital government, open architecture, and innovation: Why public sector IT will never be the same again. *Journal of Public Administration Research and Theory, 23*(4), 977–1004. https://doi.org/10.1093/jopart/mus022

Gonçalves, M.-E. (2004). Risk society and the governance of innovation in Europe: Opening the black box? *Science and Public Policy, 31*(6), 457–464. https://doi.org/10.3152/147154304781779796

Guo, W., Feng, J. B., McKenna, B., & Zhang, P. (2017). Inter-organizational governance and trilateral trust building: A case study of crowdsourcing-based open innovation in China. *Asian Business and Management, 16*(3), 187–207. https://doi.org/10.1057/s41291-017-0019-1

Hawken. (2022). *Learning sustainability—Sustainable solutions: Government*. Retrieved June 17, 2022, from http://www.learningsustainability.com/government.html

Hurst. (2022). *What is the role of the CTO?* Retrieved June 17, 2022, from https://www.information-age.com/what-is-the-role-of-the-cto-123498412/

Jugend, D., Jabbour, C. J. C., & Janaina, A. (2018). Alves Scaliza; Robson Sø Rocha; José Alcides GobboJunior; Hengky Latan; Manoel Henrique Salgado. Relationships among open innovation, innovative performance, government support and firm size: Comparing Brazilian firms embracing different levels of radicalism in innovation. *Technovation, 74–75*, 54–65. https://doi.org/10.1016/j.technovation.2018.02.004

Kaiser, R., & Prange, H. (2017). Managing diversity in a system of multi-level governance: The open method of co-ordination in innovation policy. *Journal of European Public Policy, 11*(2), 249–266. https://doi.org/10.1080/1350176042000194421

Klarin, A., Sharmelly, R., & Suseno, Y. (2021). A systems perspective in examining industry clusters: Case studies of clusters in Russia and India. *Journal of Risk and Financial Management, 14*(8), 367. https://doi.org/10.3390/jrfm14080367

Li, W., Xu, J., & Zheng, M. (2018). Green governance: New perspective from open innovation. *Sustainability, 10*(11), 3845. https://doi.org/10.3390/su10113845

Liedong, T.-A. (2020). Augustine Awuah Peprah, Joseph Ebot Eyong. Institutional voids and innovation governance: A conceptual exposition of the open versus closed architecture choice. *Strategic Change, 29*, 57–66. https://doi.org/10.1002/jsc.2310

Liu, L., & Zhang, H. (2021). How does inter-organizational relational governance propel firms' open innovation? A conditional process analysis. *Sustainability, 13*(18), 10209. https://doi.org/10.3390/su131810209

Mu, R., & Wang, H. (2022). A systematic literature review of open innovation in the public sector: Comparing barriers and governance strategies of digital and non-digital open innovation. *Public Management Review, 24*(4), 489–511. https://doi.org/10.1080/14719037.2020.1838787

Nickerson, J. A., & Zenger, T. R. (2004). A knowledge-based theory of the firm: The problem-solving perspective. *Organization Science, 15*(6), 617–632. http://www.jstor.org/stable/30034765

Omar, A. A., Mohan, A. V., & Zhao, X. (2017). Can government policies drive open innovation type platforms? Ideas from the MSC Malaysia flagship applications. *Science, Technology and Society, 22*(3), 490–505. https://doi.org/10.1177/0971721817724315

Pedersen, K. (2020). What can open innovation be used for and how does it create value? *Government Information Quarterly, 37*(2), 101459. https://doi.org/10.1016/j.giq.2020.101459

Pellegrini, L., & Lazzarotti, V. (2019). How governance mechanisms in family firms impact open innovation choices: A fuzzy logic approach. *Creativity and Innovation Management, 28*(4), 486–500. https://doi.org/10.1111/caim.12331

Remneland Wikhamn, B., & Styhre, A. (2019). Corporate hub as a governance structure for coupled open innovation in large firms. *Creativity and Innovation Management, 28*(4), 450–463. https://doi.org/10.1111/caim.12338

Roha, T., Lee, K., & YeonYang, J. (2021). How do intellectual property rights and government support drive a firm's green innovation? The mediating role of open innovation. *Journal of Cleaner Production, 317*, 128422. https://doi.org/10.1016/j.jclepro.2021.128422

Scarbrough, H., & Amaeshi, K. (2009). Knowledge governance for open innovation: Evidence from an EU R&D collaboration. In *Chapter 9: Knowledge governance: Processes and perspectives.* (Oxford Scholarship Online eds). https://doi.org/10.1093/acprof:oso/9780199235926.003.0009

Schmidthuber, L., Piller, F., Bogers, M., & Hilgers, D. (2019). Citizen participation in public administration: Investigating open government for social innovation. *R&D Management, 49*(3), 343–355.

Tucci, L. (2014). *Information age—Definition.* Retrieved June 17, 2022, from https://www.techtarget.com/searchcio/definition/Information-Age

Yu, Z. (2022). Development of public administration research with a bibliometric analysis. *Scientific Programming, 4959930.*

Zhenbin, Y., Kankanhalli, A., Ha, S., & Tayi, G.-K. (2020). What drives public agencies to participate in open government data initiatives? An innovation resource perspective. *Information and Management, 57*(3), 103179. https://doi.org/10.1016/j.im.2019.103179